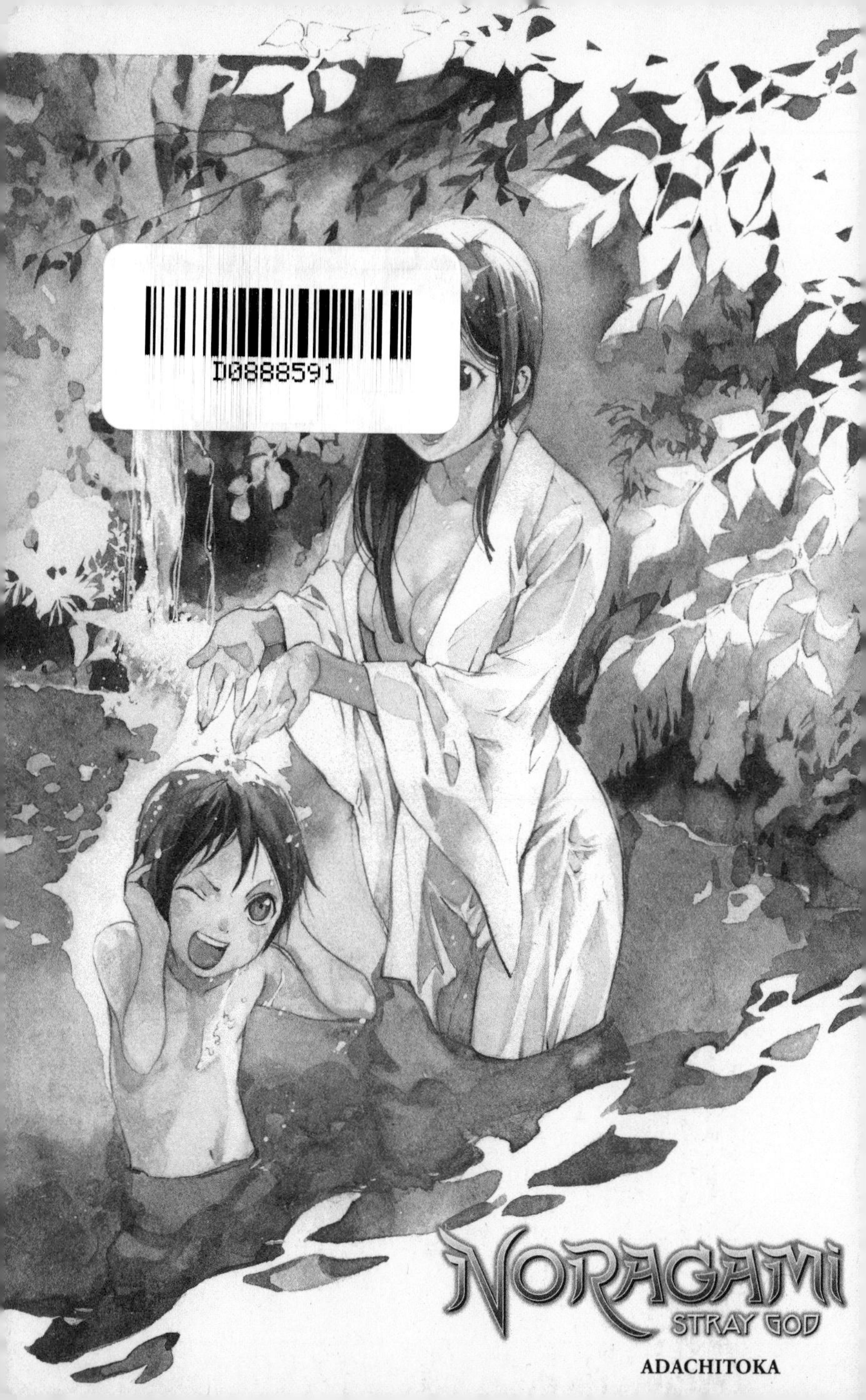
NORAGAMI
STRAY GOD
ADACHITOKA

CHAPTER 44: CUT + TIES   5

CHAPTER 45: TRANSPIRED TRANSGRESSIONS   51

CHAPTER 46: CHILDREN AT PLAY   97

CHAPTER 47: TABOO   143

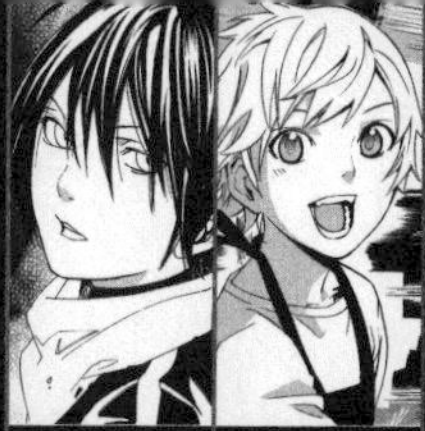

YATO

A minor deity who always wears a sweatsuit.

YUKINÉ

Yato's shinki who turns into swords.

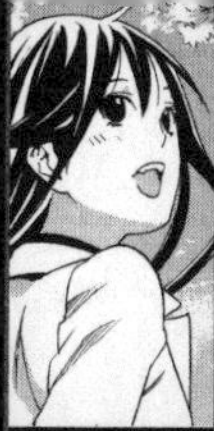

HIYORI IKI

A high school student who has become half-ayakashi.

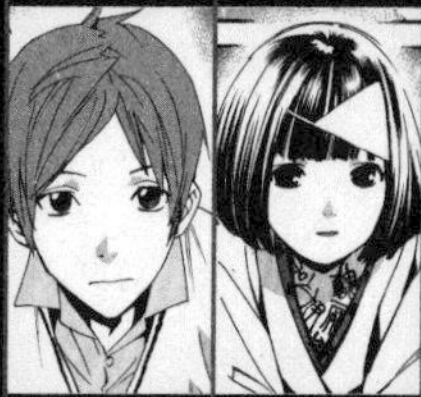

KÔTO FUJISAKI

Yato's "father."

STRAY

A shinki who serves an unspecified number of deities.

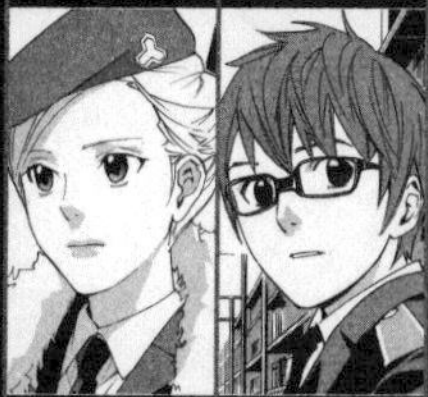

BISHAMONTEN

A powerful warrior god, one of the Seven Gods of Fortune.

KAZUMA

A navigational shinki who serves as guide to Bishamon.

characters

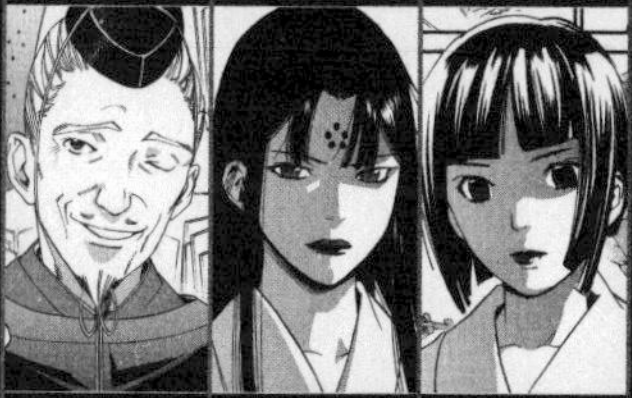

TENJIN

The god of learning, Sugawara no Michizane.

TSUYU

A spirit of the plum tree, Tenjin's attendant.

MAYU

Formerly Yato's shinki, now Tenjin's shinki.

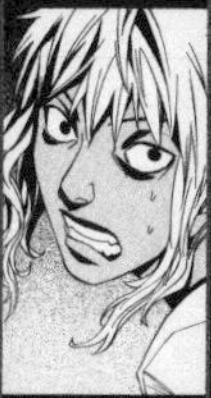

KUGAHA

A shinki who once deceived Bishamon.

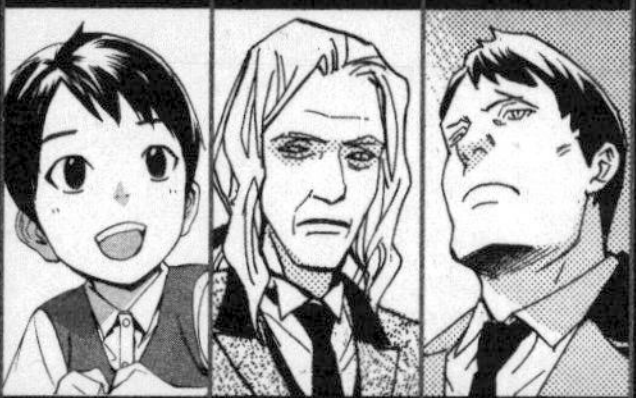

EBISU

A business-god in the making, one of the Seven Gods of Fortune.

IWAMI

A shinki who knows Ebisu's history.

KUNIMI

A shinki who enhances Ebisu's motor skills.

首

神

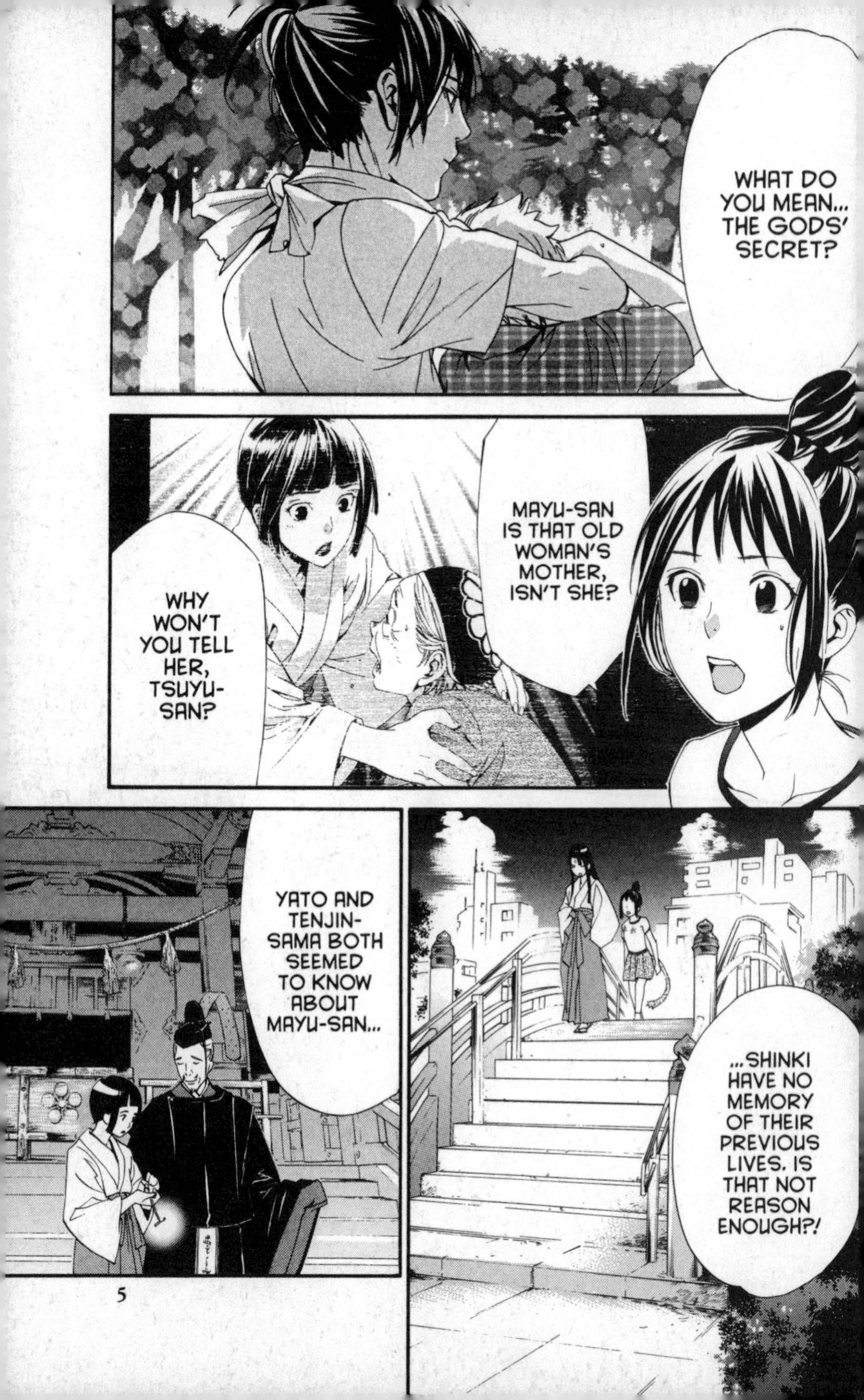
WHAT DO YOU MEAN... THE GODS' SECRET?
MAYU-SAN IS THAT OLD WOMAN'S MOTHER, ISN'T SHE?
WHY WON'T YOU TELL HER, TSUYU-SAN?
...SHINKI HAVE NO MEMORY OF THEIR PREVIOUS LIVES. IS THAT NOT REASON ENOUGH?!
YATO AND TENJIN-SAMA BOTH SEEMED TO KNOW ABOUT MAYU-SAN...

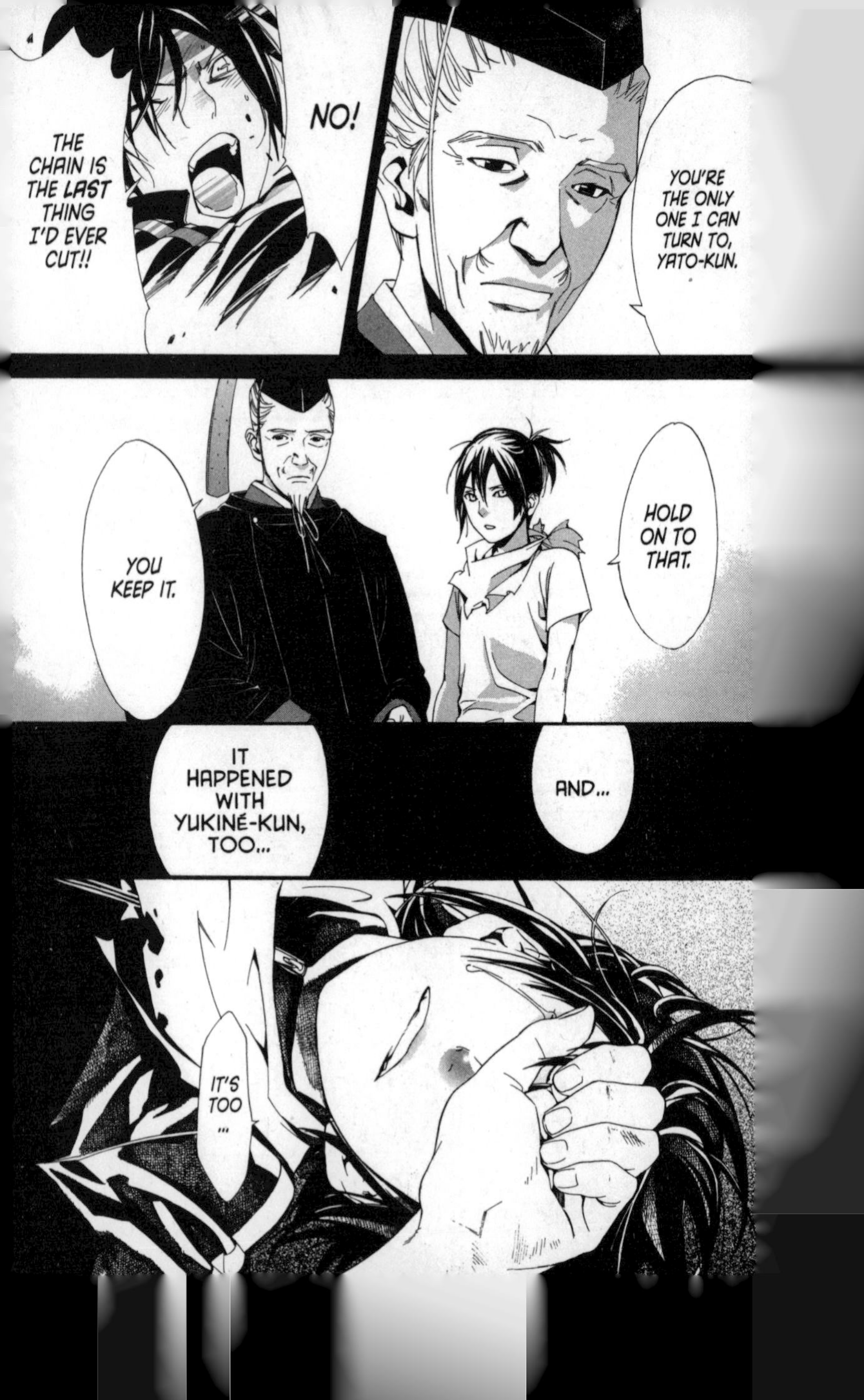
YOU'RE THE ONLY ONE I CAN TURN TO, YATO-KUN.
NO!
THE CHAIN IS THE LAST THING I'D EVER CUT!!
HOLD ON TO THAT.
YOU KEEP IT.
AND...
IT HAPPENED WITH YUKINÉ-KUN, TOO...
IT'S TOO ...

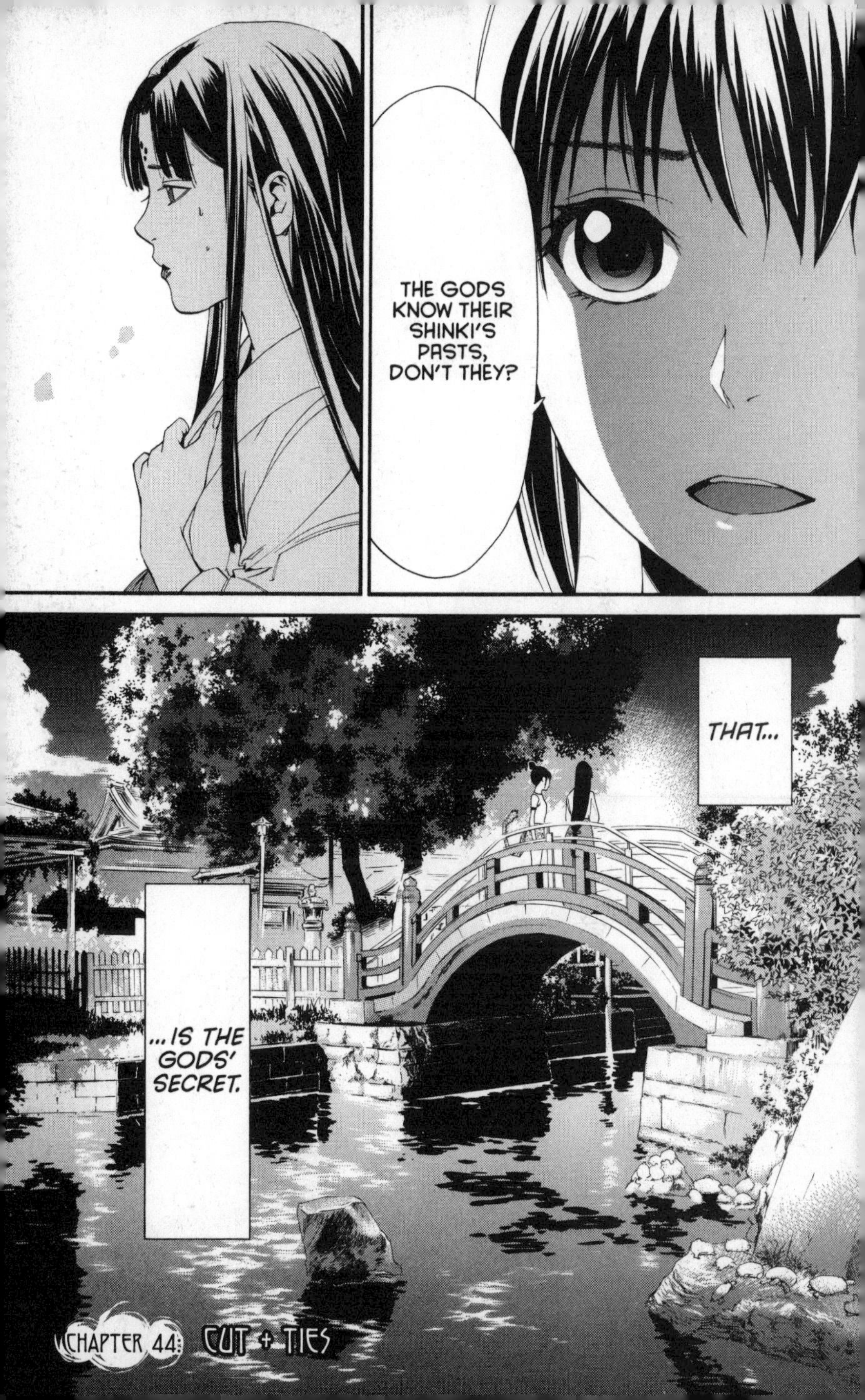
THE GODS KNOW THEIR SHINKI'S PASTS, DON'T THEY?
THAT...
...IS THE GODS' SECRET.
CHAPTER 44: CUT + TIES

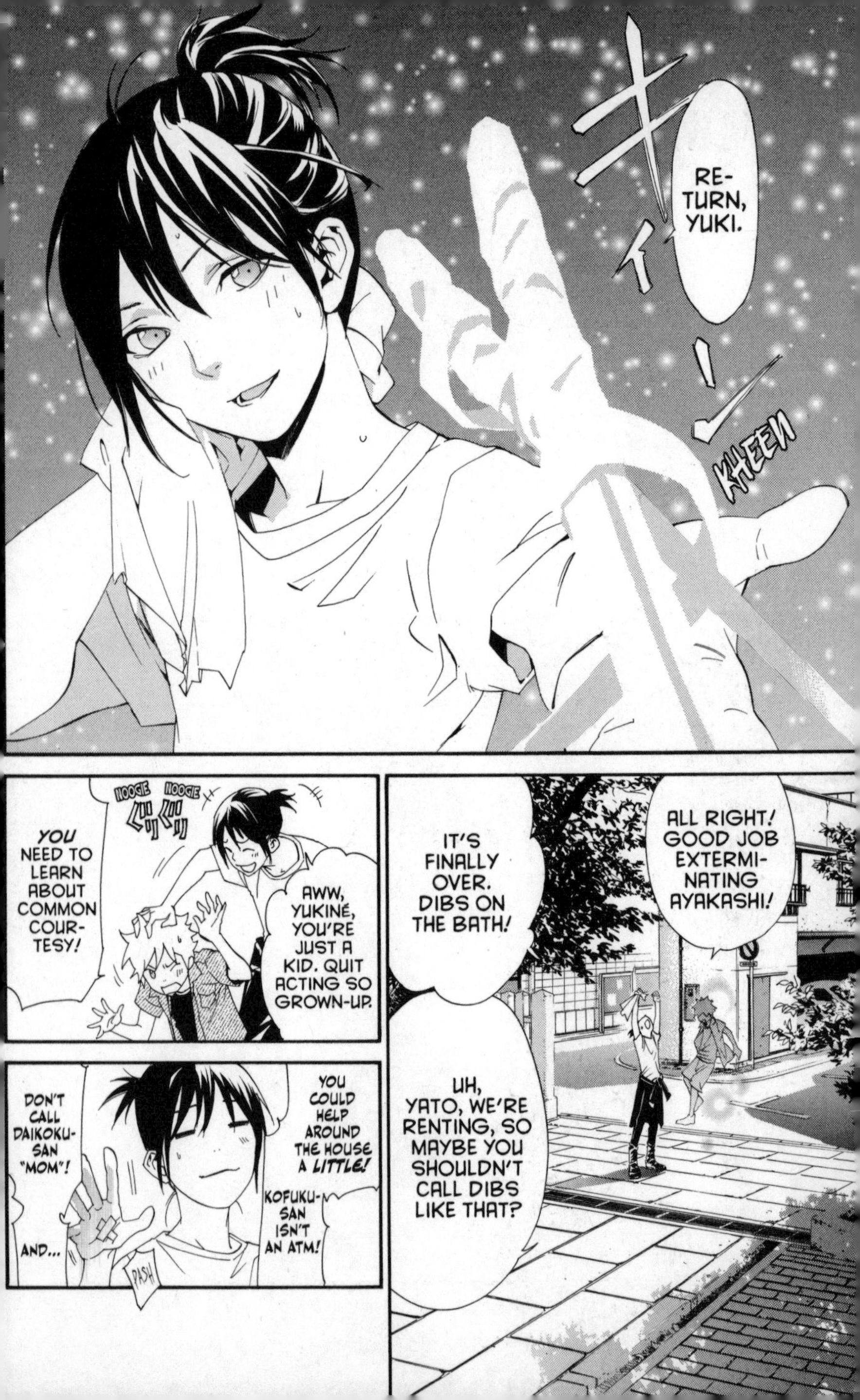
RE-TURN, YUKI.
KHEEN
ALL RIGHT! GOOD JOB EXTERMI-NATING AYAKASHI!
IT'S FINALLY OVER. DIBS ON THE BATH!
UH, YATO, WE'RE RENTING, SO MAYBE YOU SHOULDN'T CALL DIBS LIKE THAT?
NOOGIE NOOGIE
AWW, YUKINÉ, YOU'RE JUST A KID. QUIT ACTING SO GROWN-UP.
YOU NEED TO LEARN ABOUT COMMON COUR-TESY!
YOU COULD HELP AROUND THE HOUSE A LITTLE!
DON'T CALL DAIKOKU-SAN "MOM"!
KOFUKU-SAN ISN'T AN ATM!
AND...
PASH

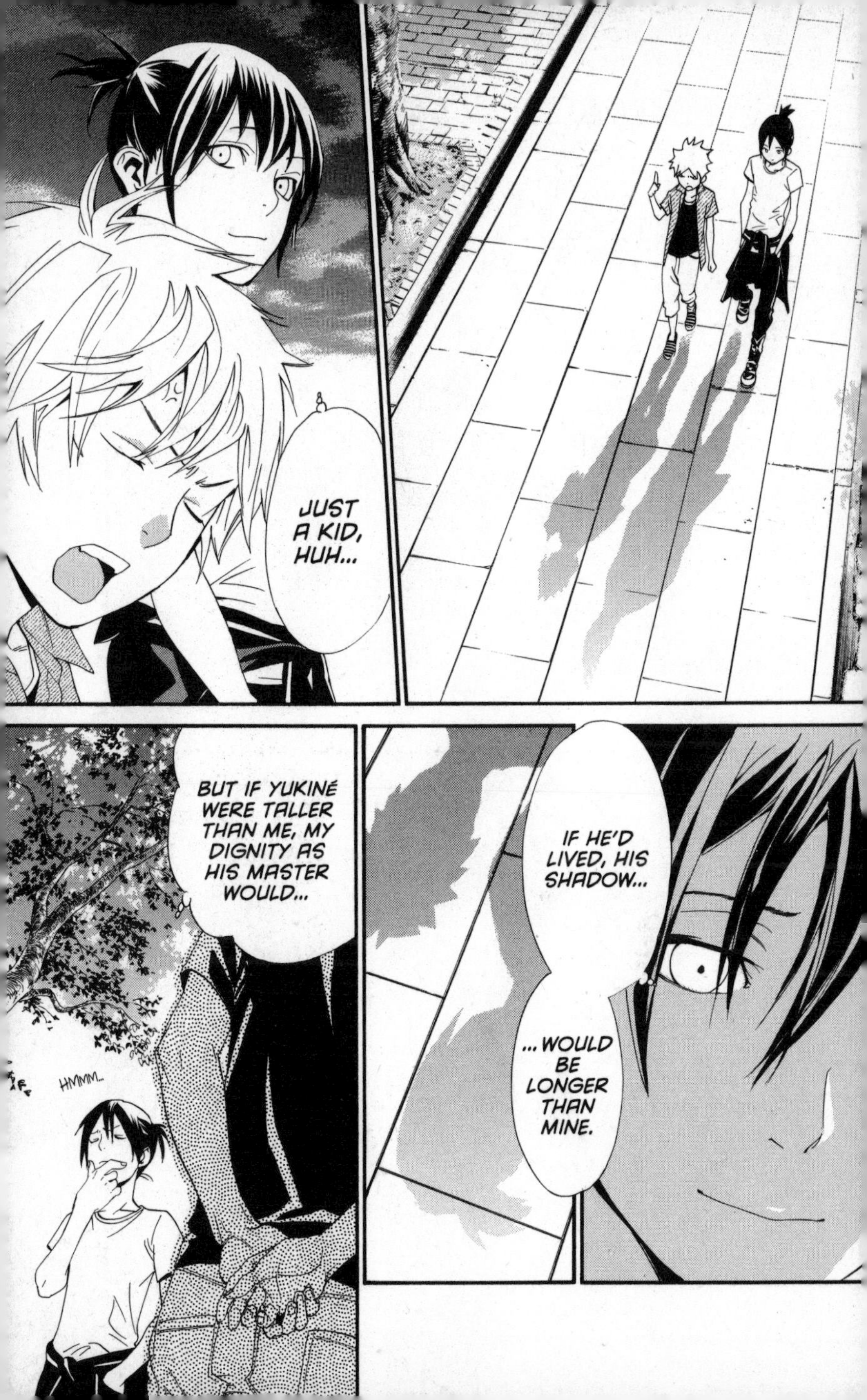
JUST A KID, HUH...
IF HE'D LIVED, HIS SHADOW...
...WOULD BE LONGER THAN MINE.
BUT IF YUKINÉ WERE TALLER THAN ME, MY DIGNITY AS HIS MASTER WOULD...
HMMM...

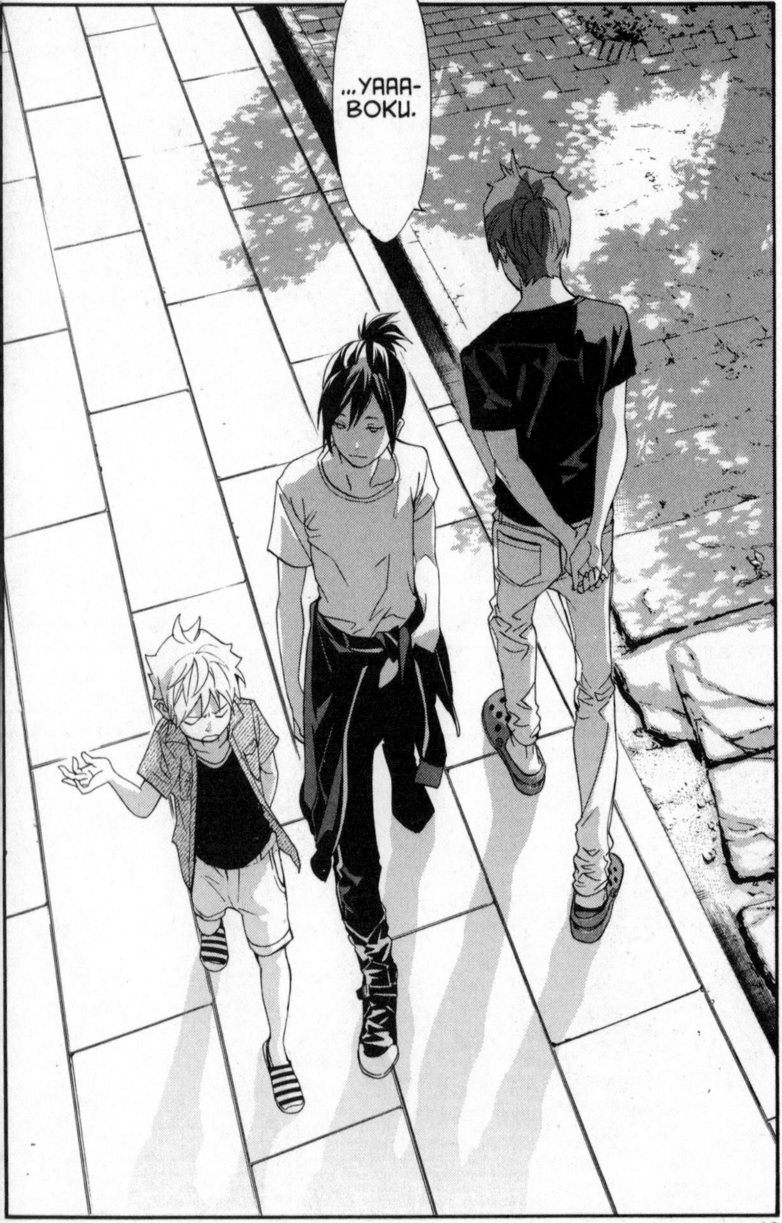
...YAAA-BOKU.

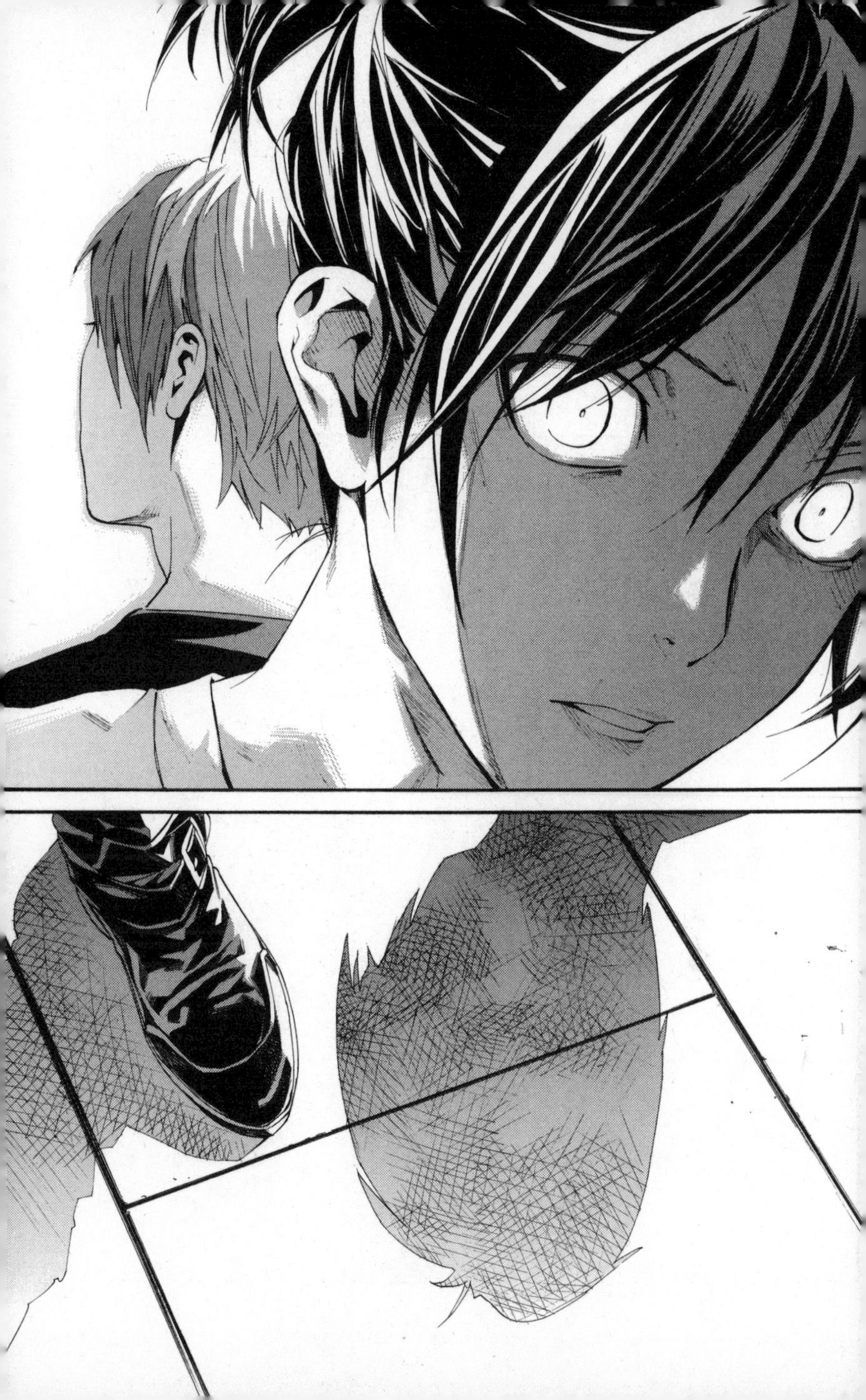

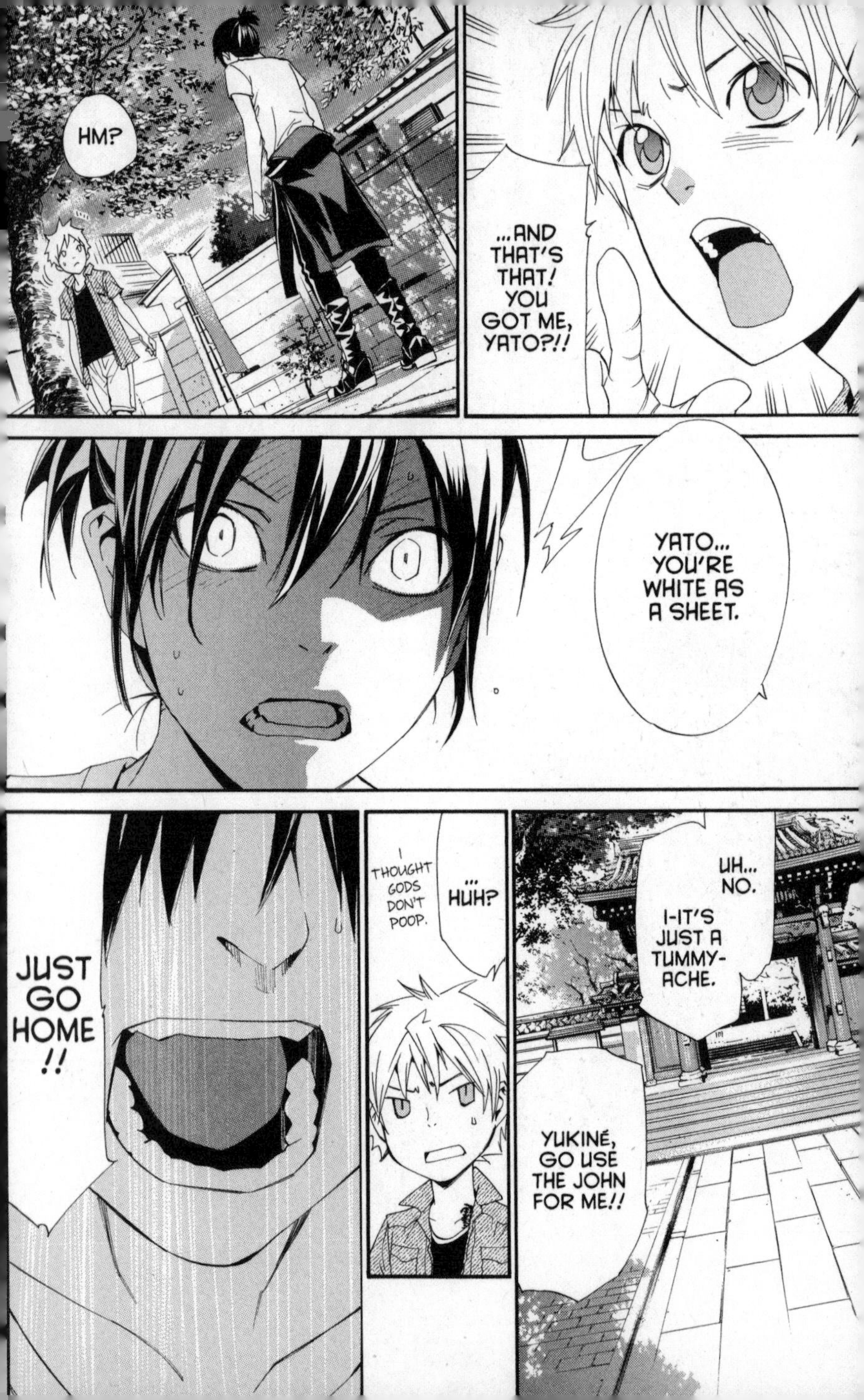
...AND THAT'S THAT! YOU GOT ME, YATO?!!
HM?
YATO... YOU'RE WHITE AS A SHEET.
UH... NO.
I-IT'S JUST A TUMMY-ACHE.
YUKINÉ, GO USE THE JOHN FOR ME!!
...HUH?
I THOUGHT GODS DON'T POOP.
JUST GO HOME!!

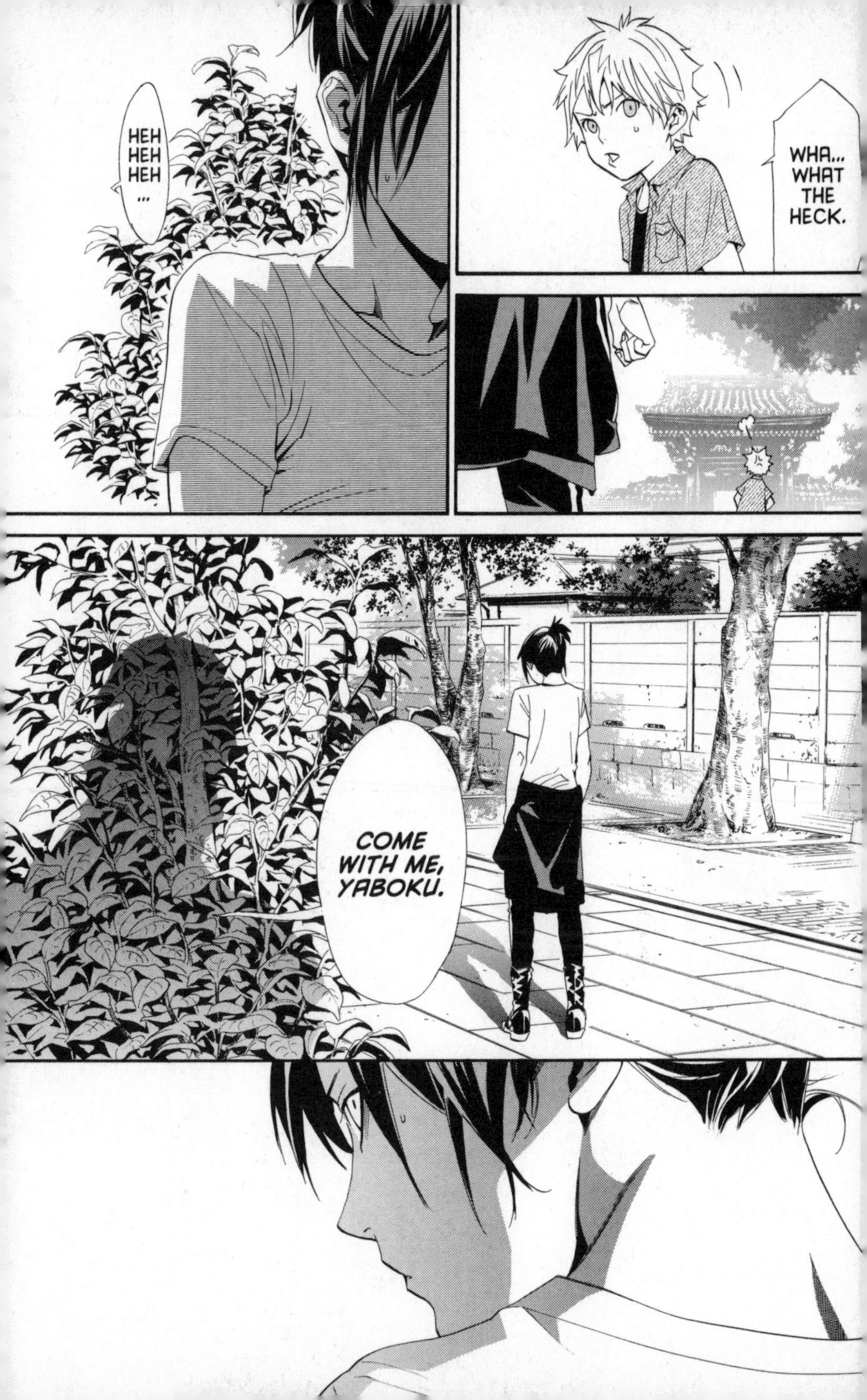
WHA... WHAT THE HECK.
HEH HEH HEH ...
COME WITH ME, YABOKU.

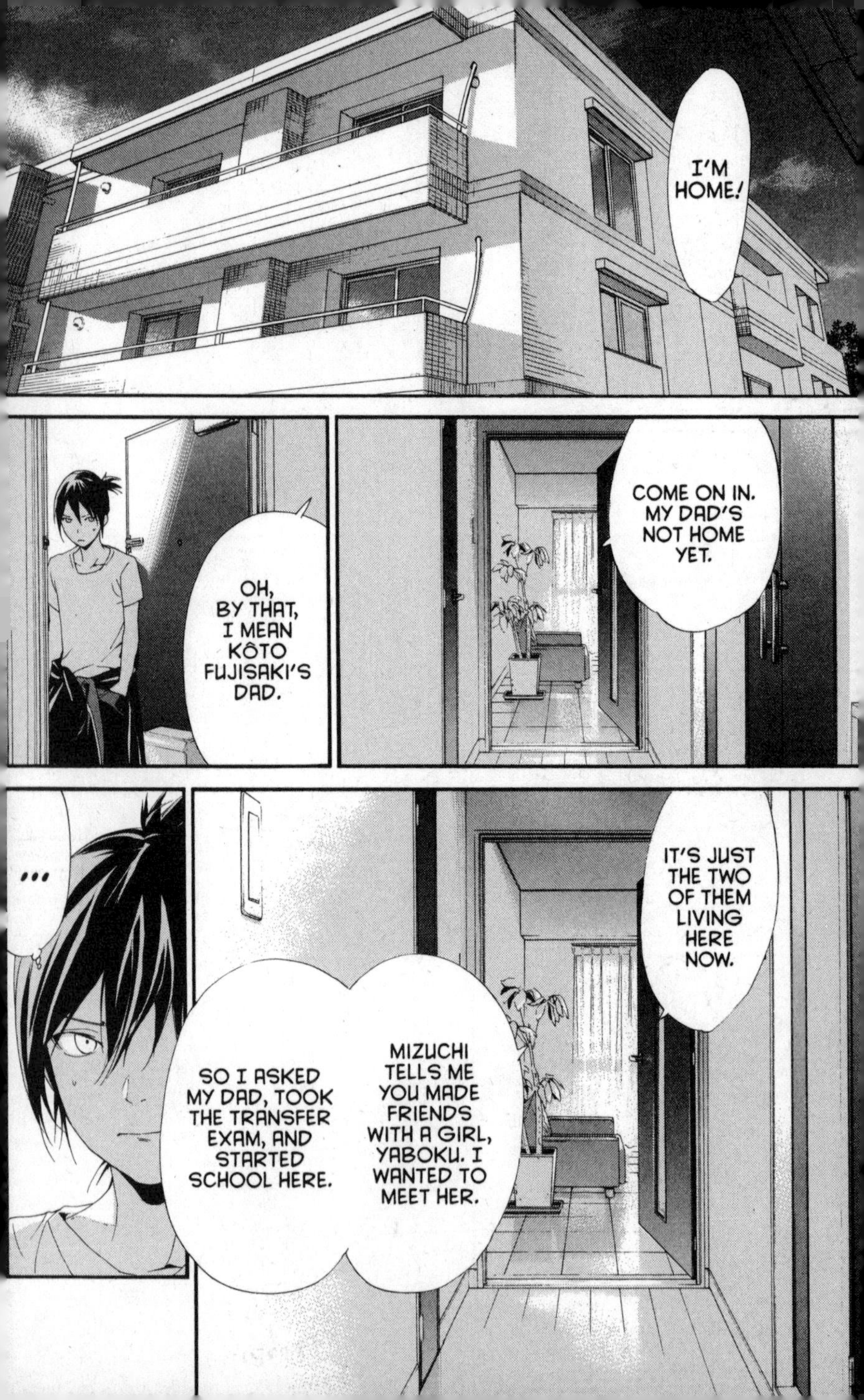
I'M HOME!
COME ON IN. MY DAD'S NOT HOME YET.
OH, BY THAT, I MEAN KÔTO FUJISAKI'S DAD.
IT'S JUST THE TWO OF THEM LIVING HERE NOW.
MIZUCHI TELLS ME YOU MADE FRIENDS WITH A GIRL, YABOKU. I WANTED TO MEET HER.
SO I ASKED MY DAD, TOOK THE TRANSFER EXAM, AND STARTED SCHOOL HERE.
...

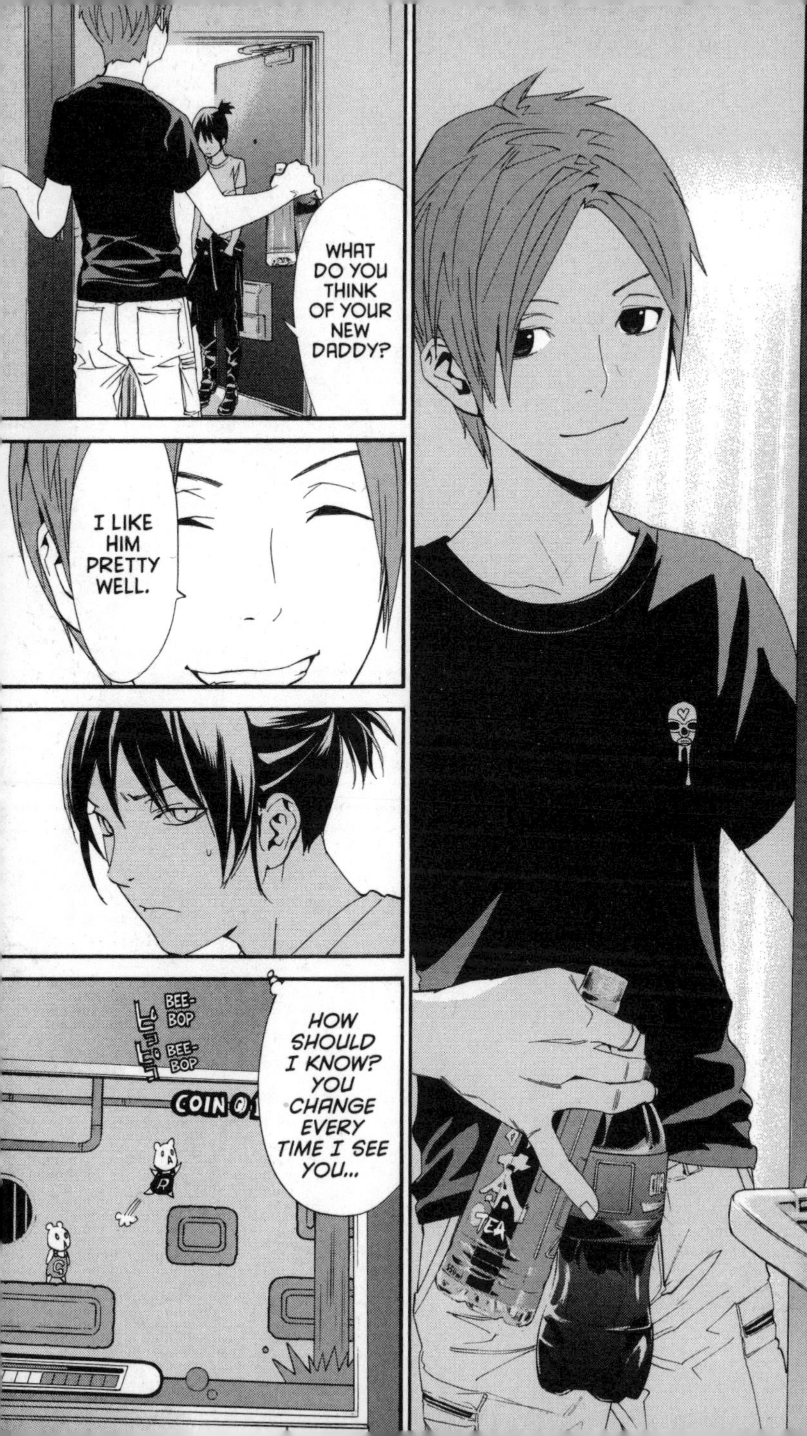
WHAT DO YOU THINK OF YOUR NEW DADDY?
I LIKE HIM PRETTY WELL.
HOW SHOULD I KNOW? YOU CHANGE EVERY TIME I SEE YOU...
BEE-BOP BEE-BOP

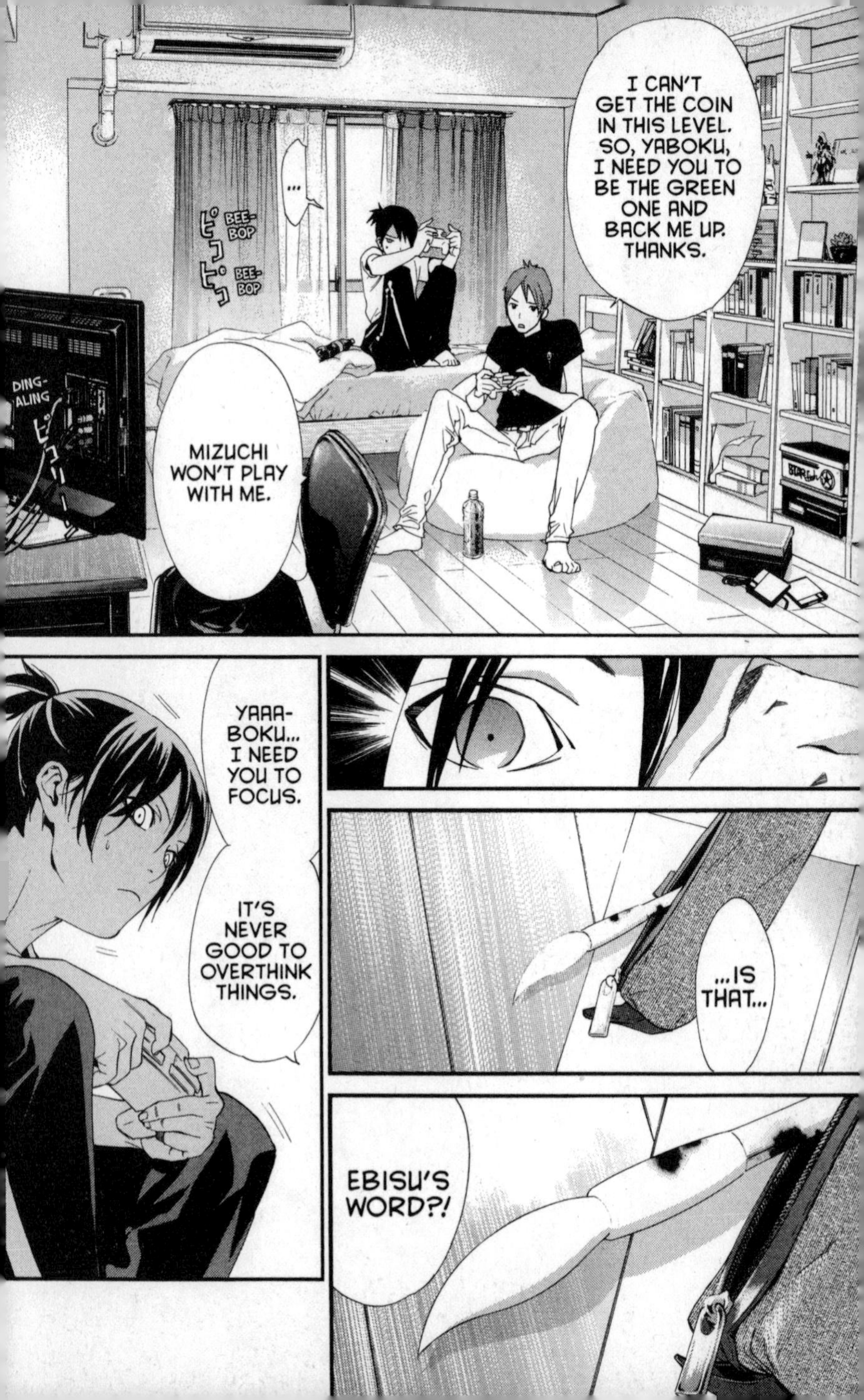

I CAN'T GET THE COIN IN THIS LEVEL. SO, YABOKU, I NEED YOU TO BE THE GREEN ONE AND BACK ME UP. THANKS.
...
BEE-BOP
BEE-BOP
DING-ALING
MIZUCHI WON'T PLAY WITH ME.
...IS THAT...
EBISU'S WORD?!
YAAA-BOKU... I NEED YOU TO FOCUS.
IT'S NEVER GOOD TO OVERTHINK THINGS.

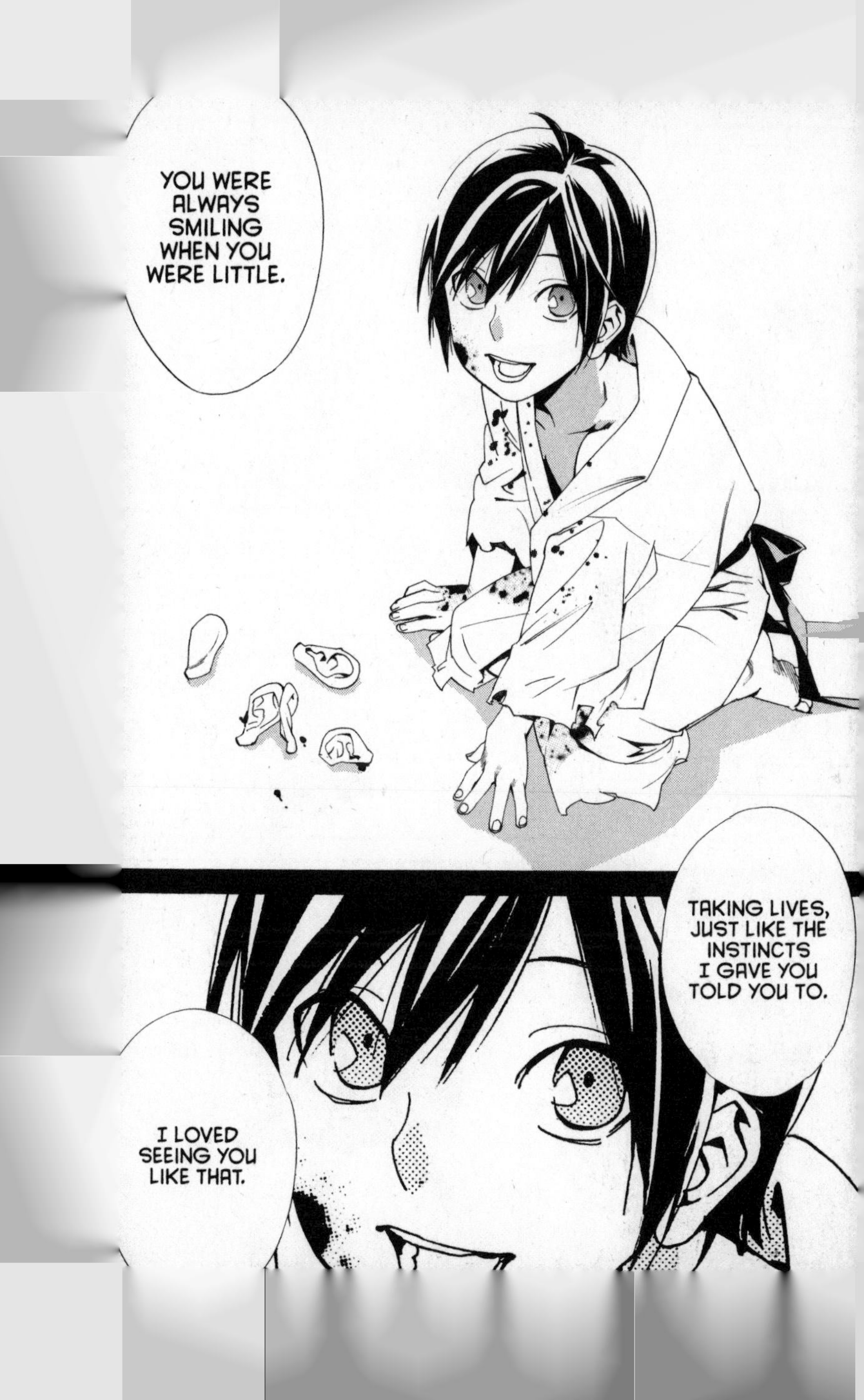
YOU WERE ALWAYS SMILING WHEN YOU WERE LITTLE.
TAKING LIVES, JUST LIKE THE INSTINCTS I GAVE YOU TOLD YOU TO.
I LOVED SEEING YOU LIKE THAT.

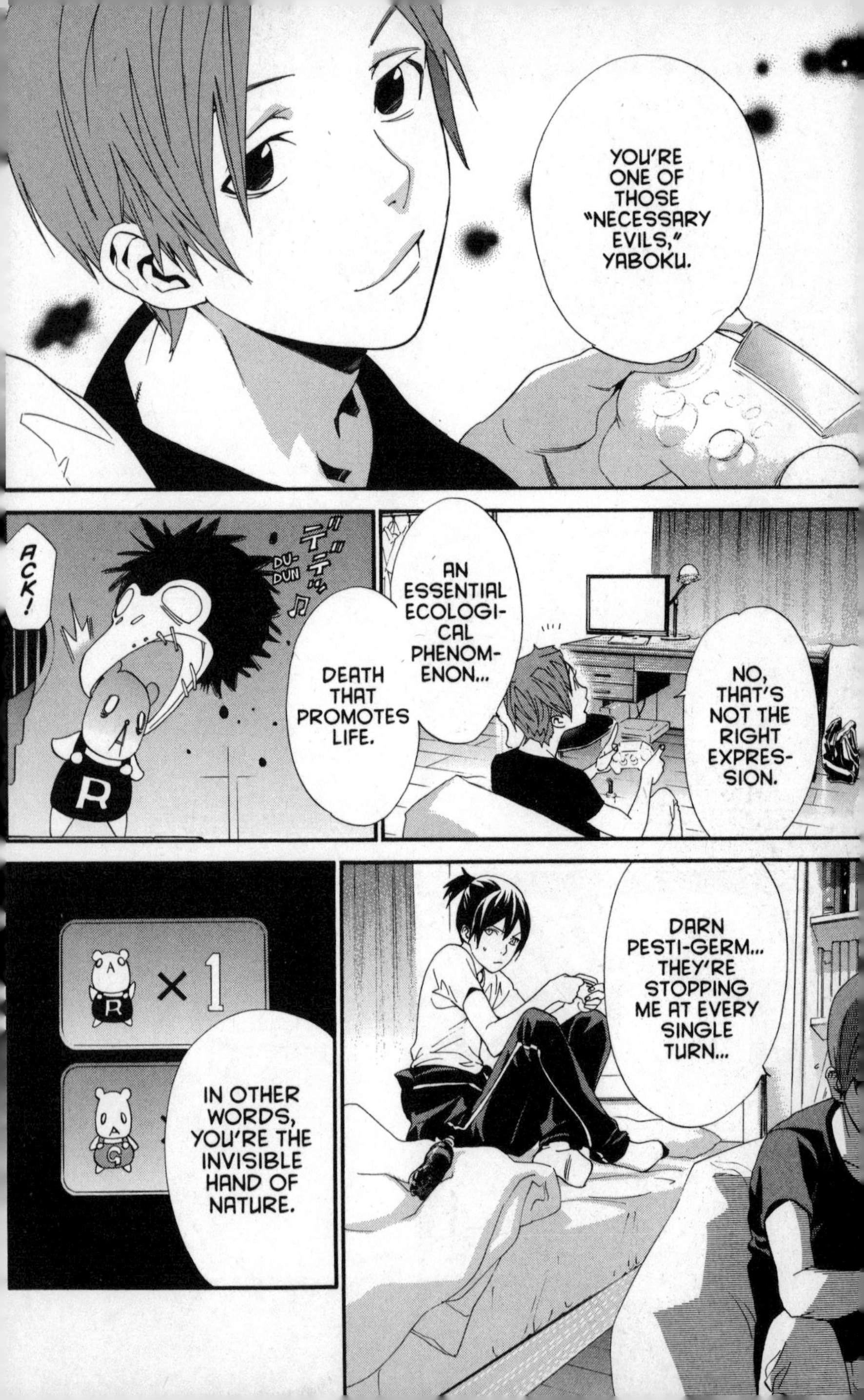
YOU'RE ONE OF THOSE "NECESSARY EVILS," YABOKU.
NO, THAT'S NOT THE RIGHT EXPRES- SION.
AN ESSENTIAL ECOLOGI- CAL PHENOM- ENON...
DEATH THAT PROMOTES LIFE.
DU- DUN
ACK!
DARN PESTI-GERM... THEY'RE STOPPING ME AT EVERY SINGLE TURN...
×1
IN OTHER WORDS, YOU'RE THE INVISIBLE HAND OF NATURE.

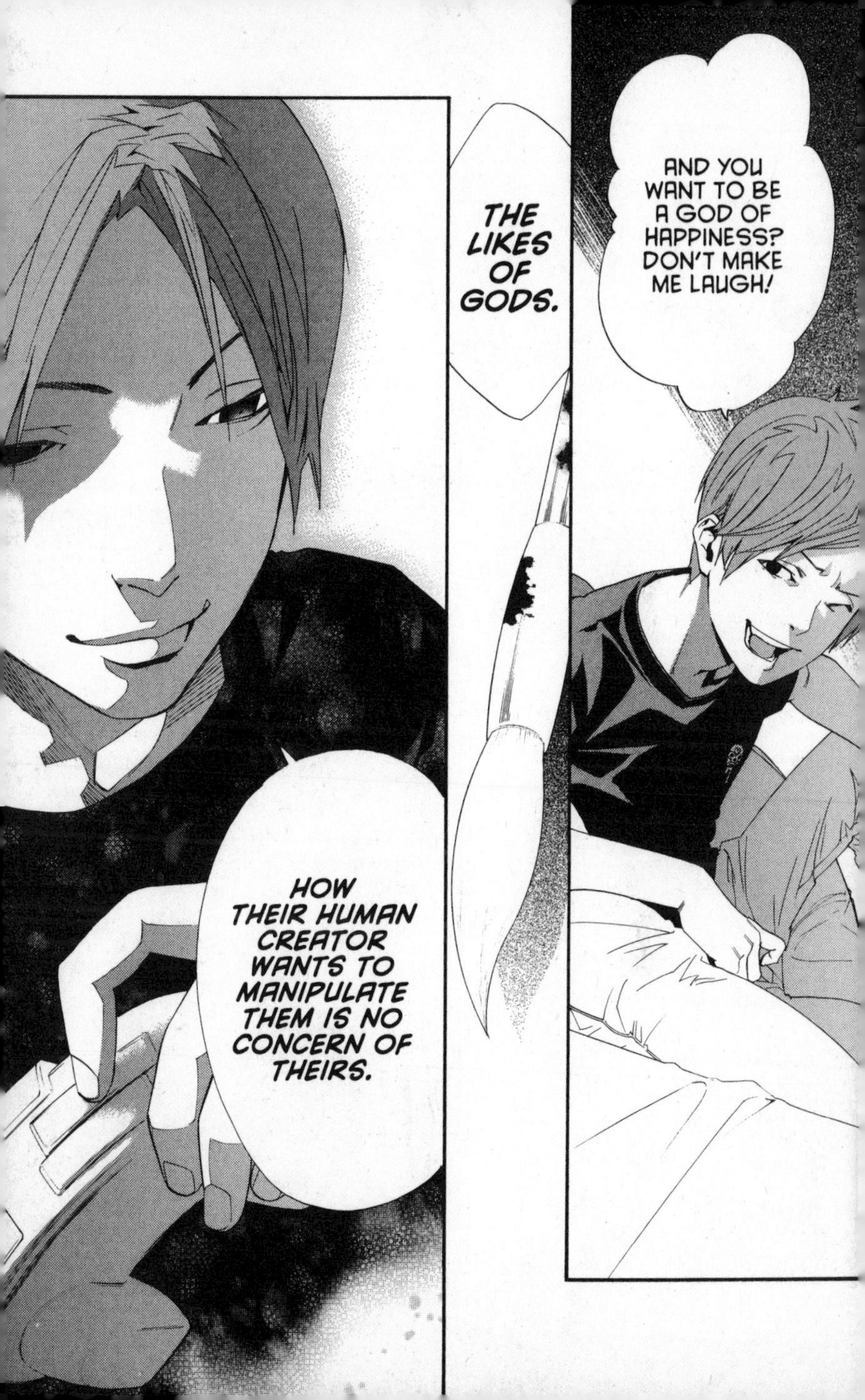
AND YOU WANT TO BE A GOD OF HAPPINESS? DON'T MAKE ME LAUGH!
THE LIKES OF GODS.
HOW THEIR HUMAN CREATOR WANTS TO MANIPULATE THEM IS NO CONCERN OF THEIRS.

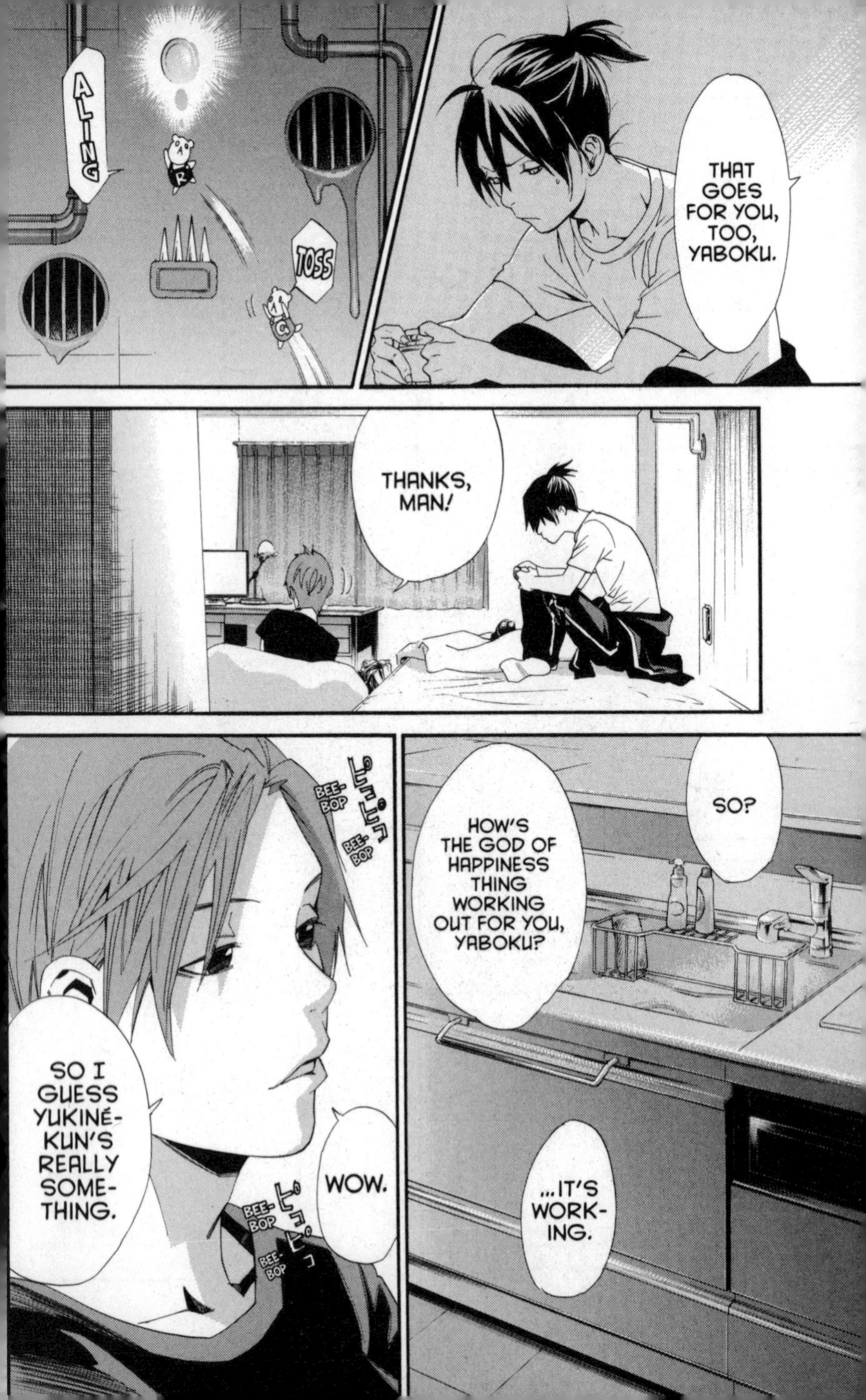
THAT GOES FOR YOU, TOO, YABOKU.
ALING
TOSS
THANKS, MAN!
SO?
HOW'S THE GOD OF HAPPINESS THING WORKING OUT FOR YOU, YABOKU?
...IT'S WORKING.
BEE-BOP
BEE-BOP
WOW.
SO I GUESS YUKINÉ-KUN'S REALLY SOMETHING.
BEE-BOP
BEE-BOP

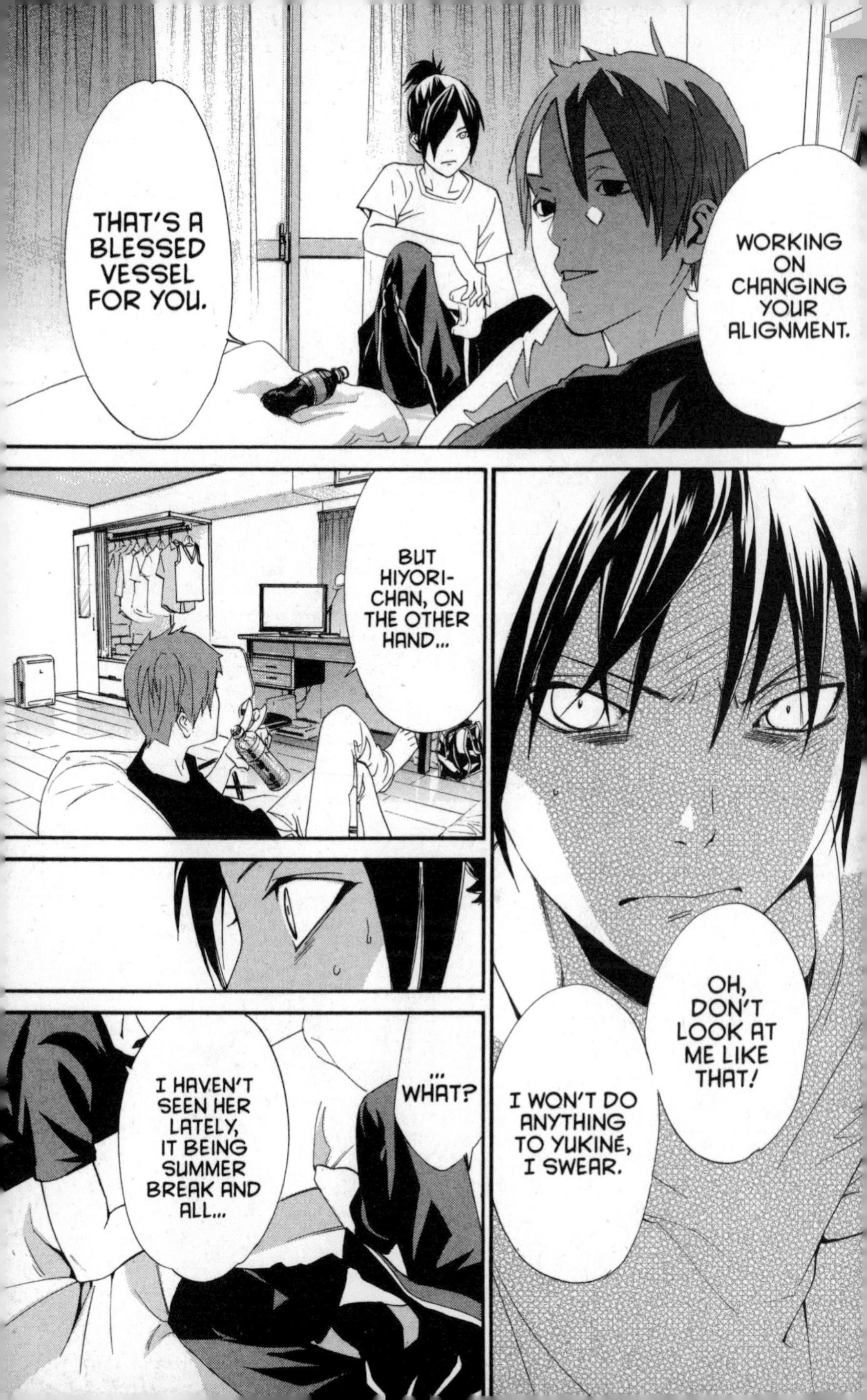
WORKING ON CHANGING YOUR ALIGNMENT.
THAT'S A BLESSED VESSEL FOR YOU.
OH, DON'T LOOK AT ME LIKE THAT!
I WON'T DO ANYTHING TO YUKINÉ, I SWEAR.
BUT HIYORI-CHAN, ON THE OTHER HAND...
...WHAT?
I HAVEN'T SEEN HER LATELY, IT BEING SUMMER BREAK AND ALL...

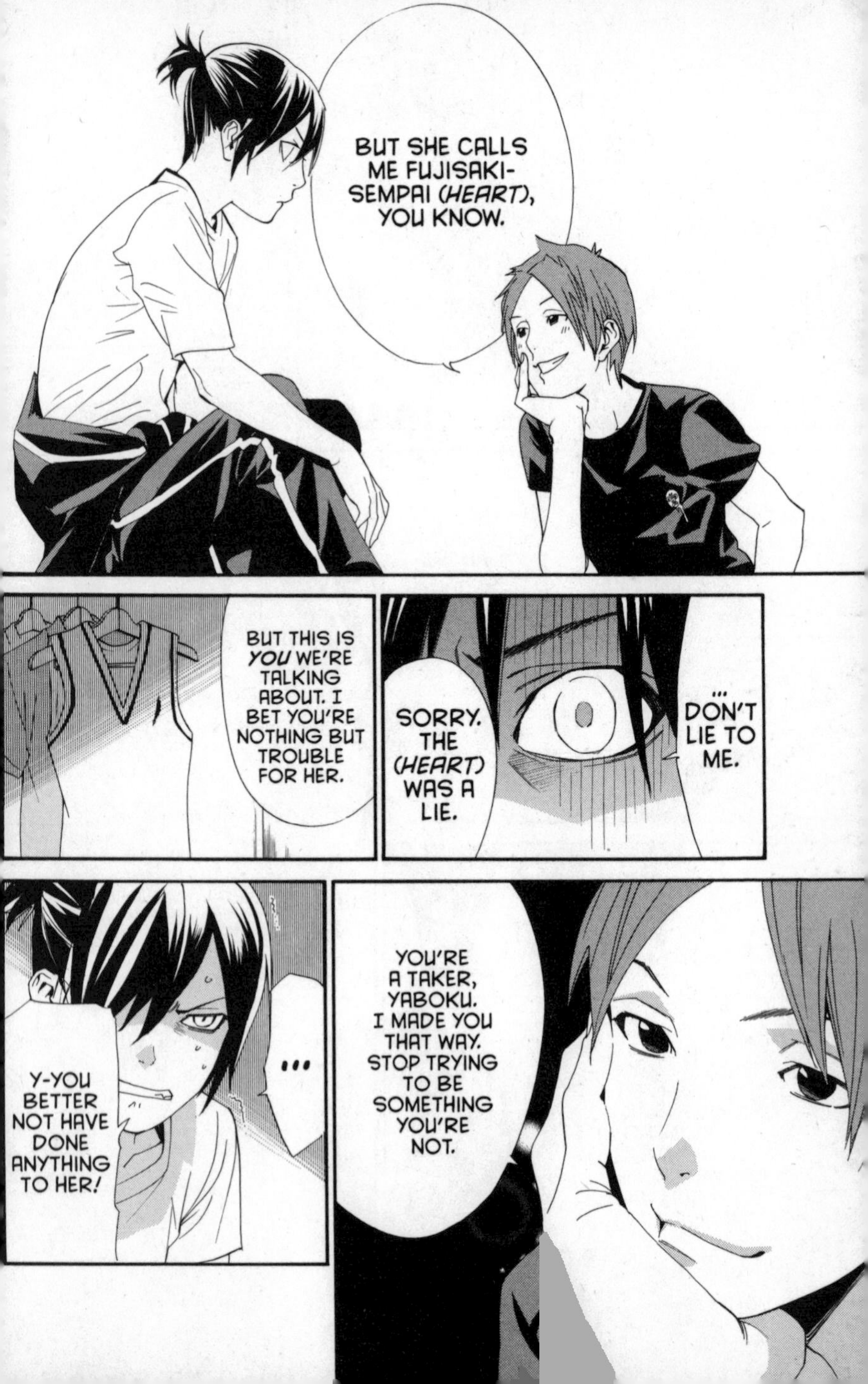
BUT SHE CALLS ME FUJISAKI-SEMPAI (HEART), YOU KNOW.
...DON'T LIE TO ME.
SORRY. THE (HEART) WAS A LIE.
BUT THIS IS YOU WE'RE TALKING ABOUT. I BET YOU'RE NOTHING BUT TROUBLE FOR HER.
YOU'RE A TAKER, YABOKU. I MADE YOU THAT WAY. STOP TRYING TO BE SOMETHING YOU'RE NOT.
...
Y-YOU BETTER NOT HAVE DONE ANYTHING TO HER!

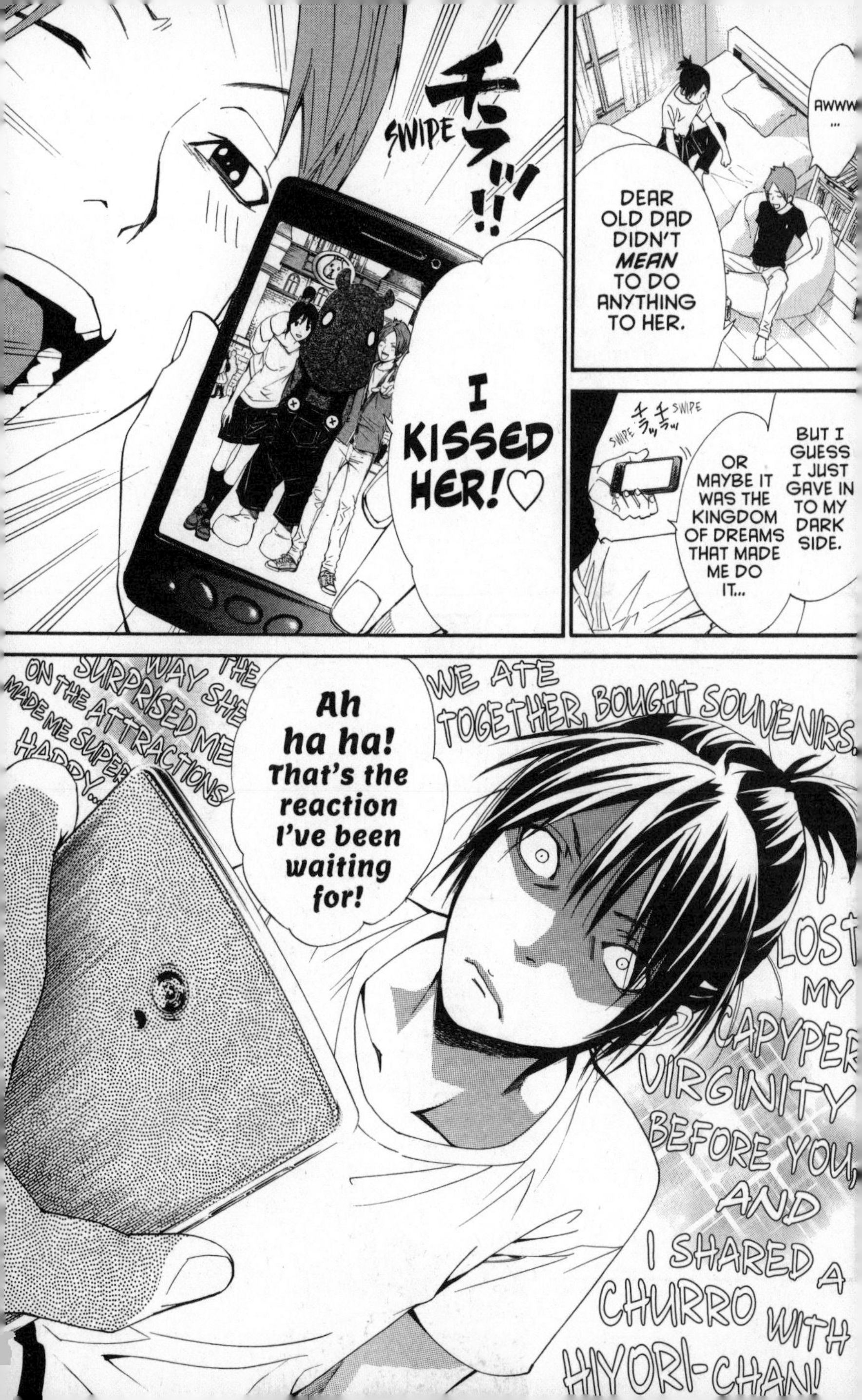
AWWW...
DEAR OLD DAD DIDN'T *MEAN* TO DO ANYTHING TO HER.
SWIPE
SWIPE
BUT I GUESS I JUST GAVE IN TO MY DARK SIDE.
OR MAYBE IT WAS THE KINGDOM OF DREAMS THAT MADE ME DO IT...
SWIPE
I KISSED HER!♡
I LOST MY CAPYPER VIRGINITY BEFORE YOU, AND I SHARED A CHURRO WITH HIYORI-CHAN!
WE ATE TOGETHER, BOUGHT SOUVENIRS...
Ah ha ha! That's the reaction I've been waiting for!
THE WAY SHE SURPRISED ME ON THE ATTRACTIONS MADE ME SUPER HAPPY...

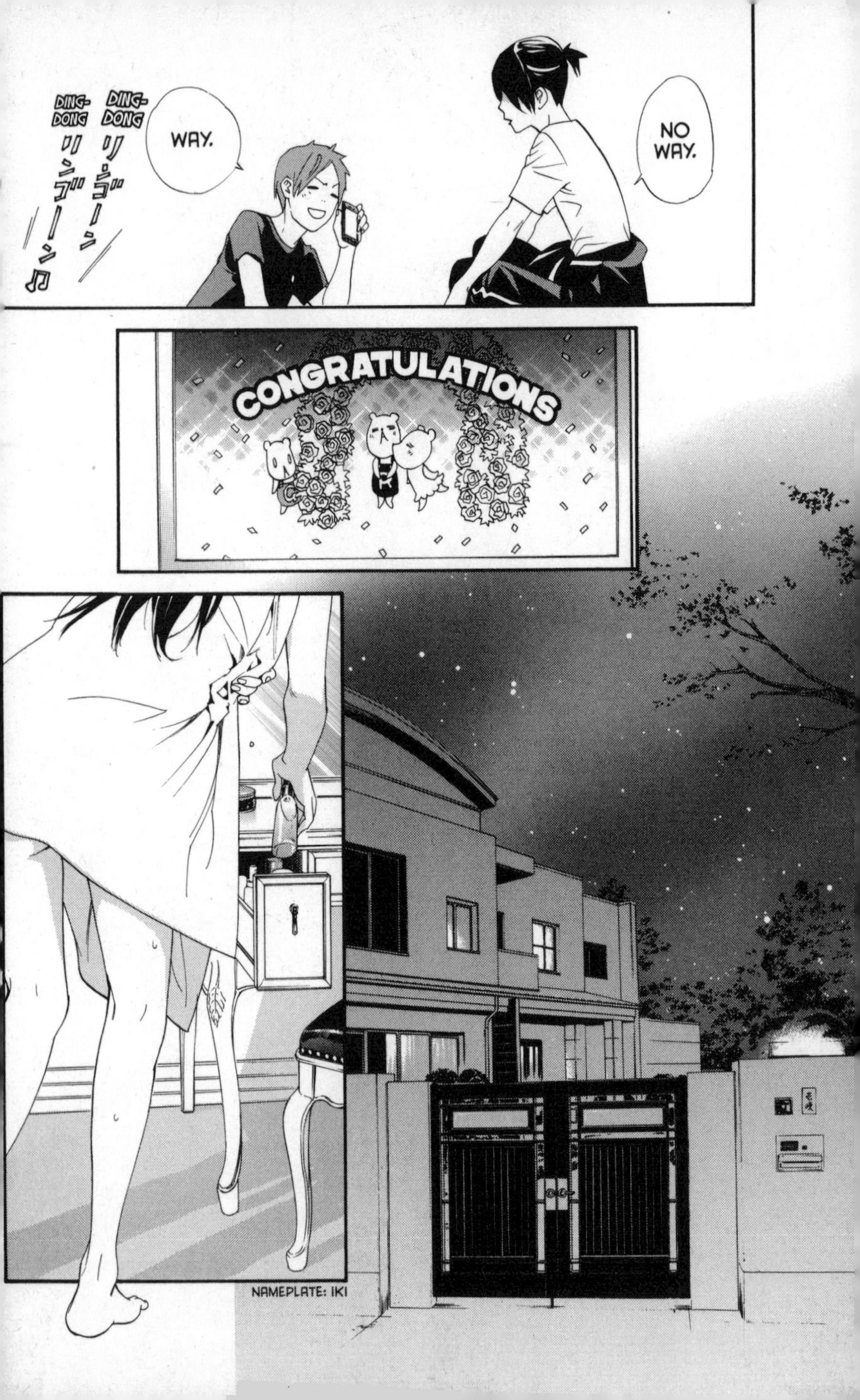
NO WAY.
WAY.
DING-DONG
リンゴーン
DING-DONG
リンゴーン♫
CONGRATULATIONS
NAMEPLATE: IKI

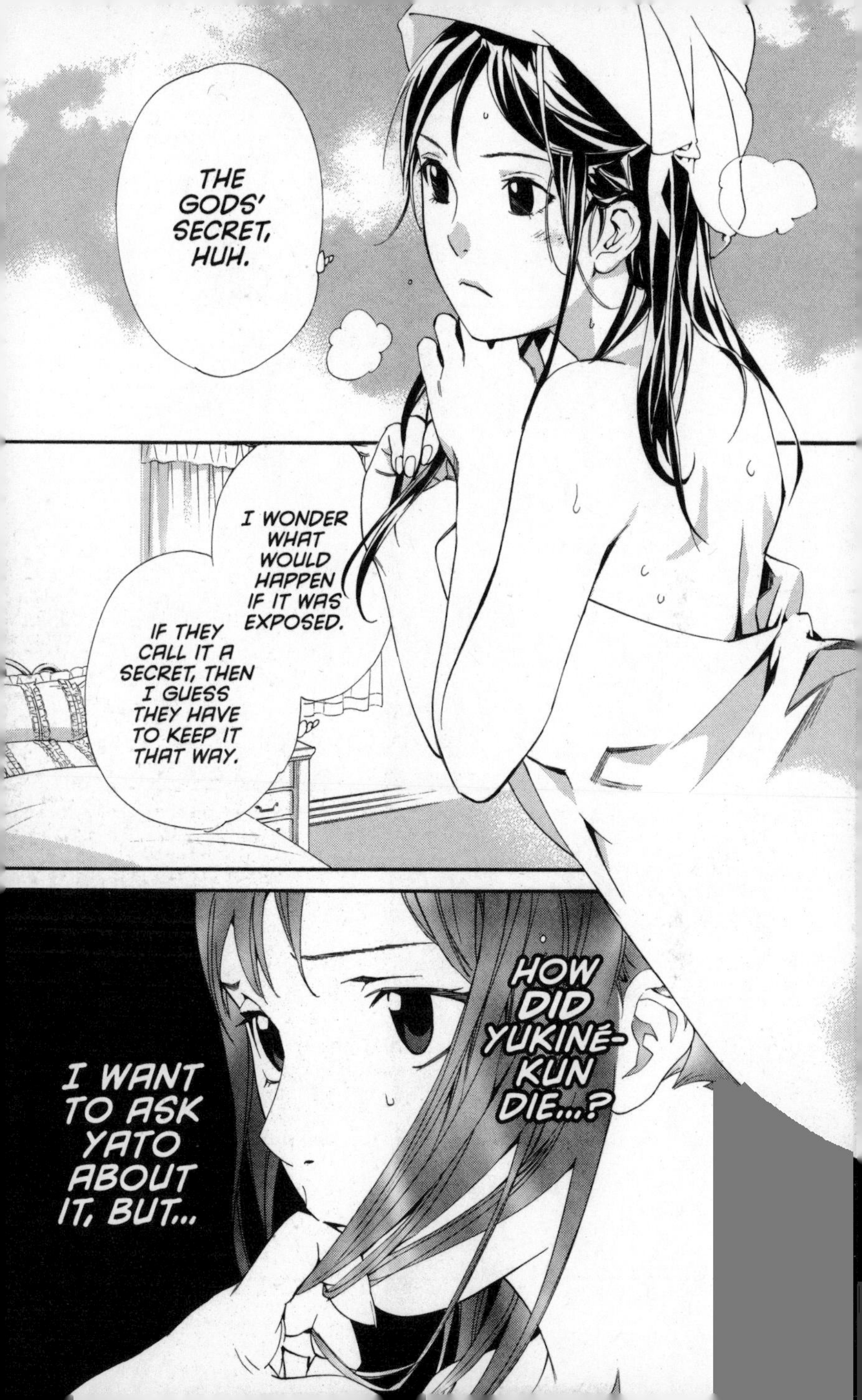
THE GODS' SECRET, HUH.
I WONDER WHAT WOULD HAPPEN IF IT WAS EXPOSED.
IF THEY CALL IT A SECRET, THEN I GUESS THEY HAVE TO KEEP IT THAT WAY.
HOW DID YUKINÉ-KUN DIE...?
I WANT TO ASK YATO ABOUT IT, BUT...

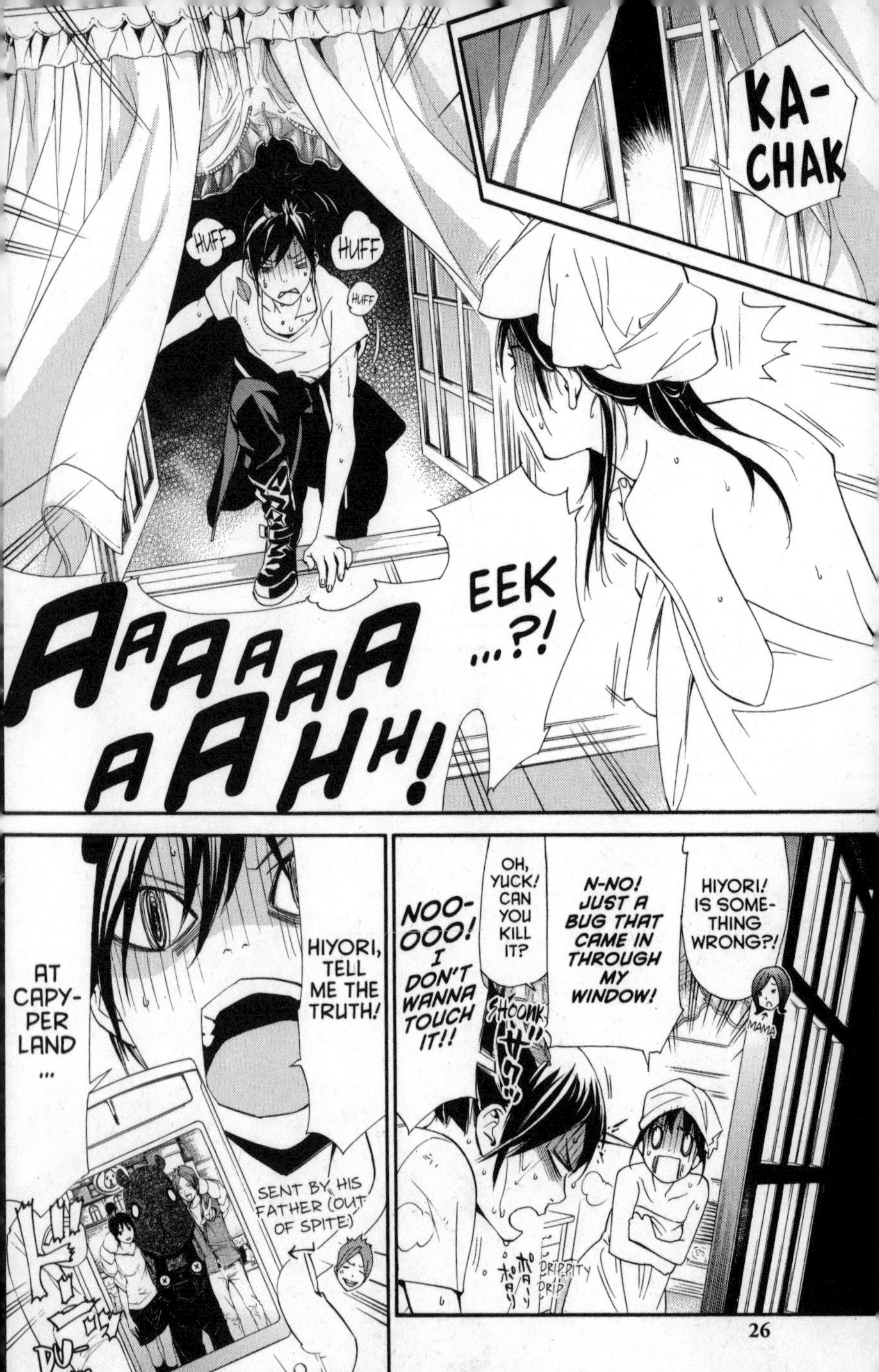
KA-CHAK
HUFF
HUFF
HUFF
EEK ...?!
AAAAAAAAHH!
HIYORI! IS SOMETHING WRONG?!
MAMA
N-NO! JUST A BUG THAT CAME IN THROUGH MY WINDOW!
OH, YUCK! CAN YOU KILL IT?
NOO-OOO! I DON'T WANNA TOUCH IT!!
SHOONK
DRIPPITY DRIP
HIYORI, TELL ME THE TRUTH!
AT CAPY-PER LAND ...
SENT BY HIS FATHER (OUT OF SPITE)
DU-DUN

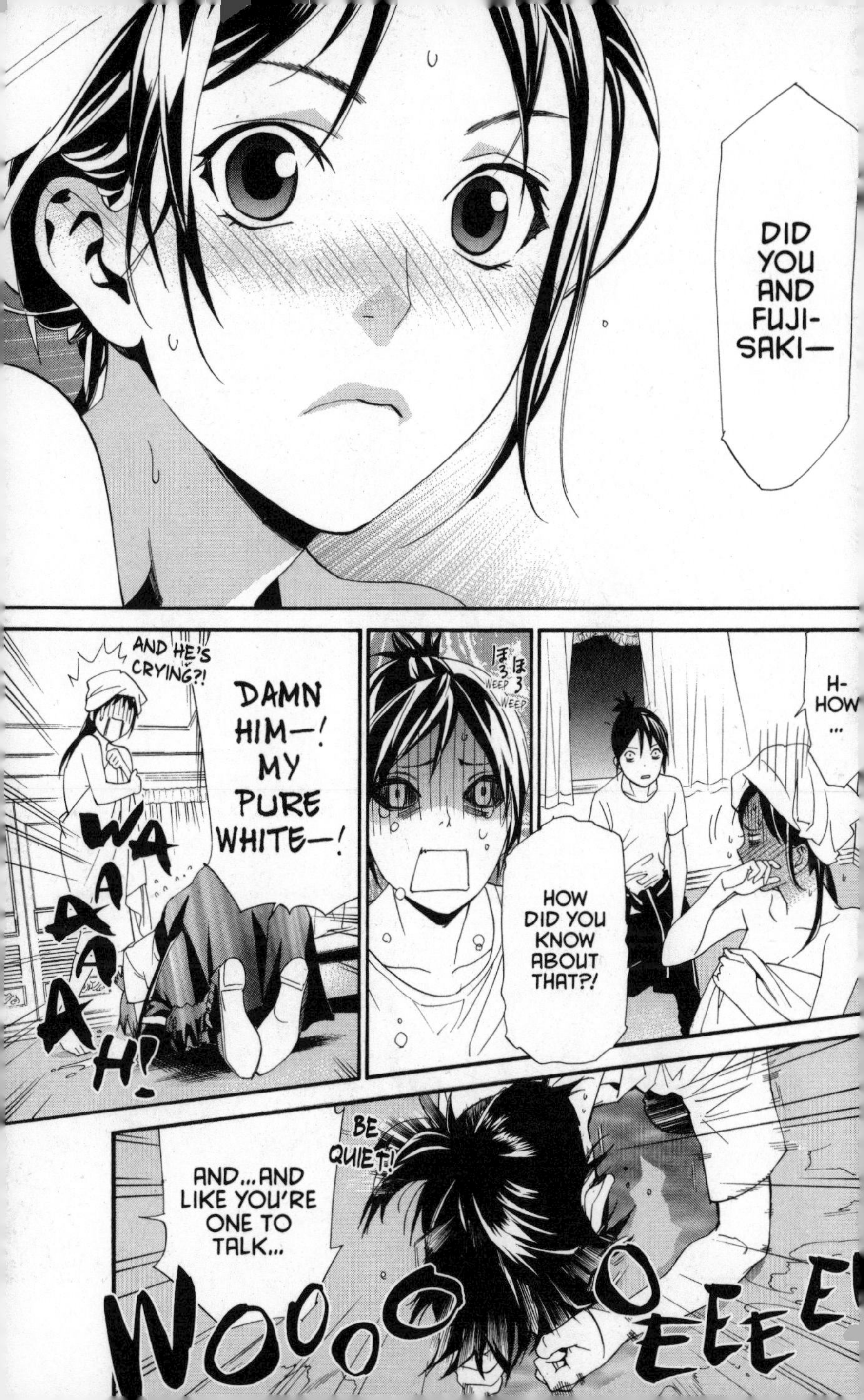
DID YOU AND FUJI-SAKI—
H-HOW...
HOW DID YOU KNOW ABOUT THAT?!
ほろほろ
WEEP WEEP
DAMN HIM—! MY PURE WHITE—!
AND HE'S CRYING?!
WAAAAAH!
BE QUIET!
AND...AND LIKE YOU'RE ONE TO TALK...
WOOOOOEEEE

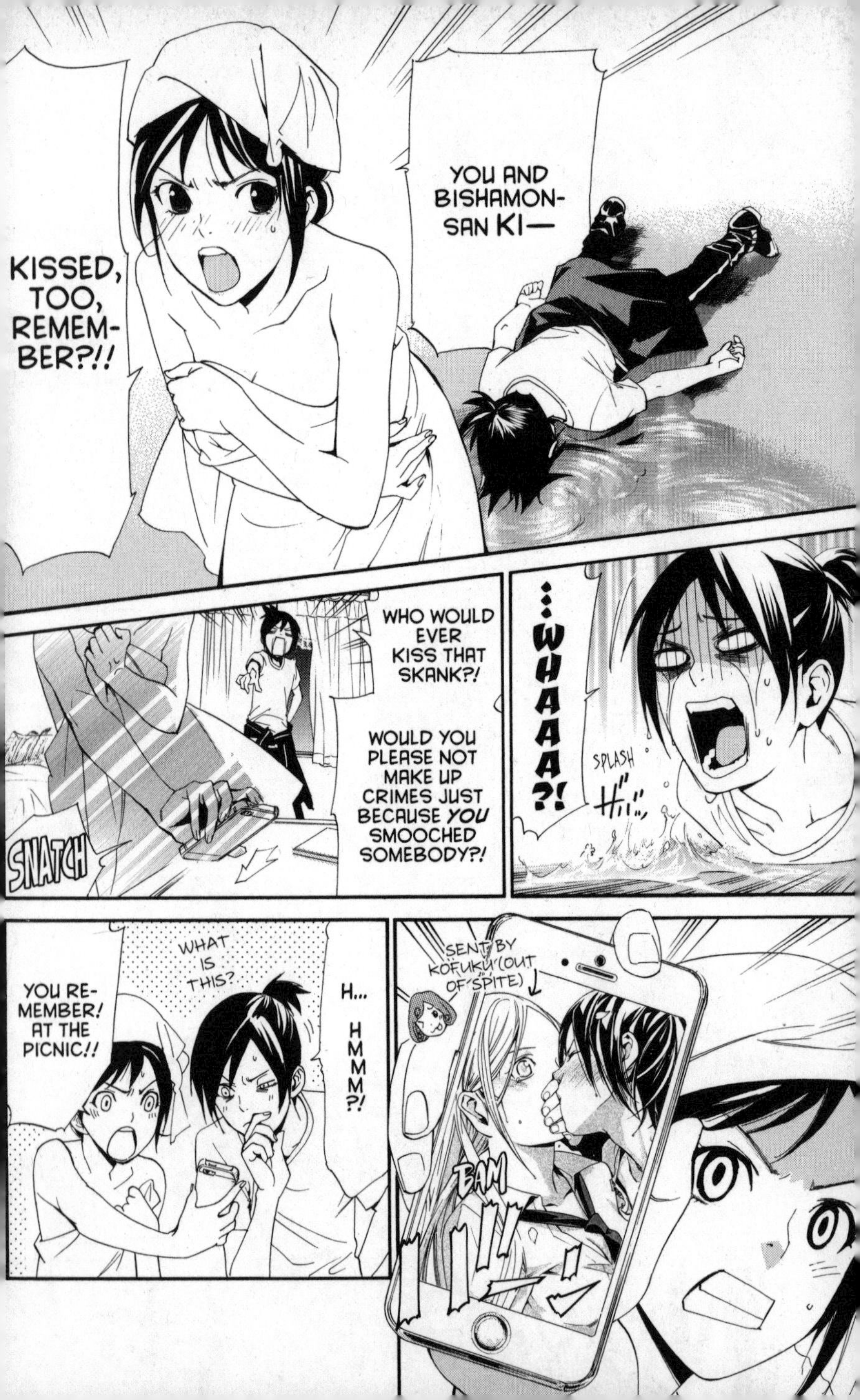
YOU AND BISHAMON-SAN KI—
KISSED, TOO, REMEMBER?!!
...WHAAAA?!
SPLASH
WHO WOULD EVER KISS THAT SKANK?!
WOULD YOU PLEASE NOT MAKE UP CRIMES JUST BECAUSE *YOU* SMOOCHED SOMEBODY?!
SNATCH
SENT BY KOFUKU (OUT OF SPITE)
BAM
H... HMMM?!
WHAT IS THIS?
YOU REMEMBER! AT THE PICNIC!!

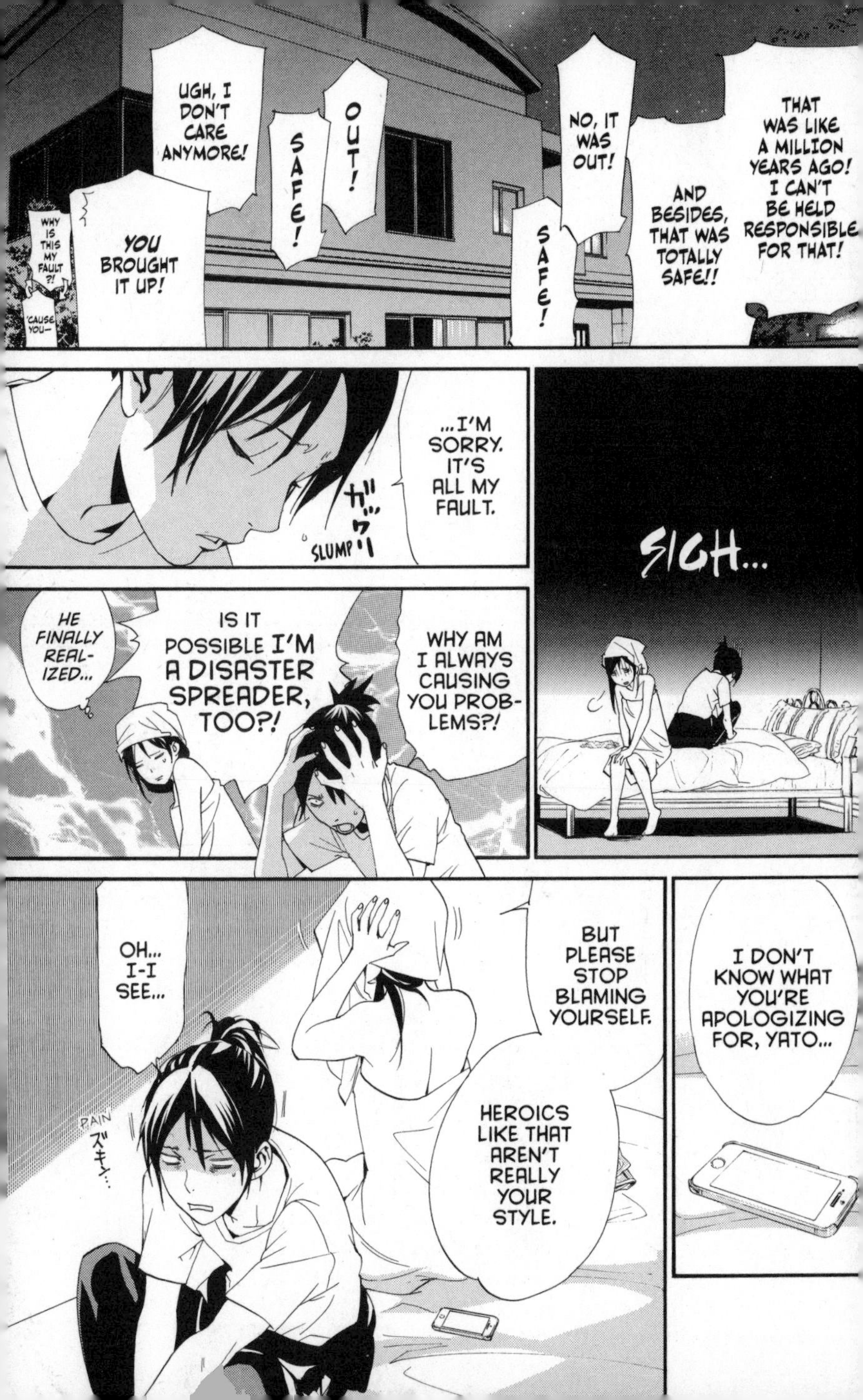

THAT WAS LIKE A MILLION YEARS AGO! I CAN'T BE HELD RESPONSIBLE FOR THAT!
AND BESIDES, THAT WAS TOTALLY SAFE!!
NO, IT WAS OUT!
SAFE!
OUT!
SAFE!
UGH, I DON'T CARE ANYMORE!
YOU BROUGHT IT UP!
WHY IS THIS MY FAULT?!
'CAUSE YOU—
SIGH...
...I'M SORRY. IT'S ALL MY FAULT.
ガッ クリ
SLUMP
WHY AM I ALWAYS CAUSING YOU PROB-LEMS?!
IS IT POSSIBLE I'M A DISASTER SPREADER, TOO?!
HE FINALLY REAL-IZED...
I DON'T KNOW WHAT YOU'RE APOLOGIZING FOR, YATO...
BUT PLEASE STOP BLAMING YOURSELF.
HEROICS LIKE THAT AREN'T REALLY YOUR STYLE.
OH... I-I SEE...
ズキン...
PAIN

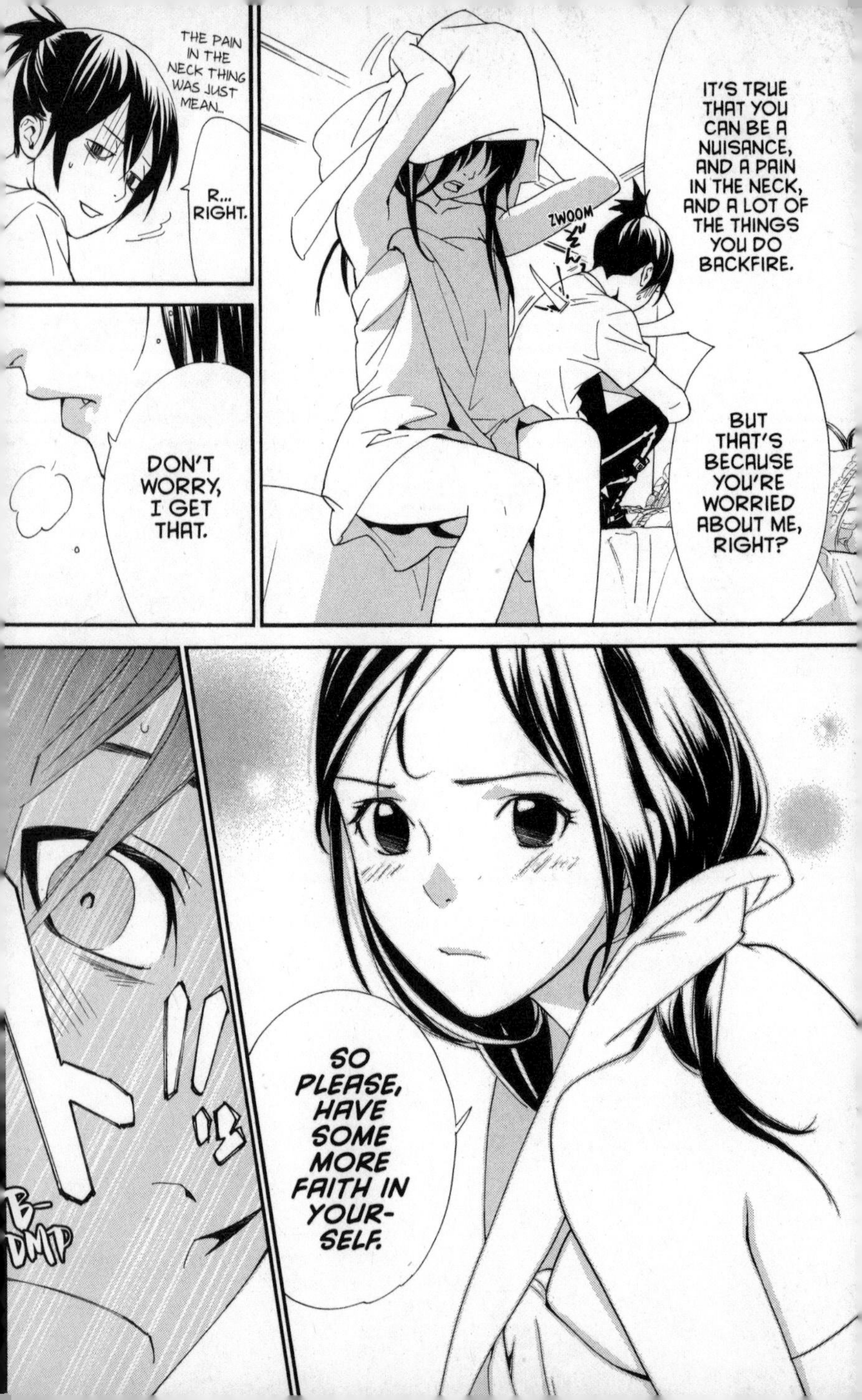
IT'S TRUE THAT YOU CAN BE A NUISANCE, AND A PAIN IN THE NECK, AND A LOT OF THE THINGS YOU DO BACKFIRE.
ZWOOM
BUT THAT'S BECAUSE YOU'RE WORRIED ABOUT ME, RIGHT?
THE PAIN IN THE NECK THING WAS JUST MEAN...
R... RIGHT.
DON'T WORRY, I GET THAT.
SO PLEASE, HAVE SOME MORE FAITH IN YOUR-SELF.
B-DMP

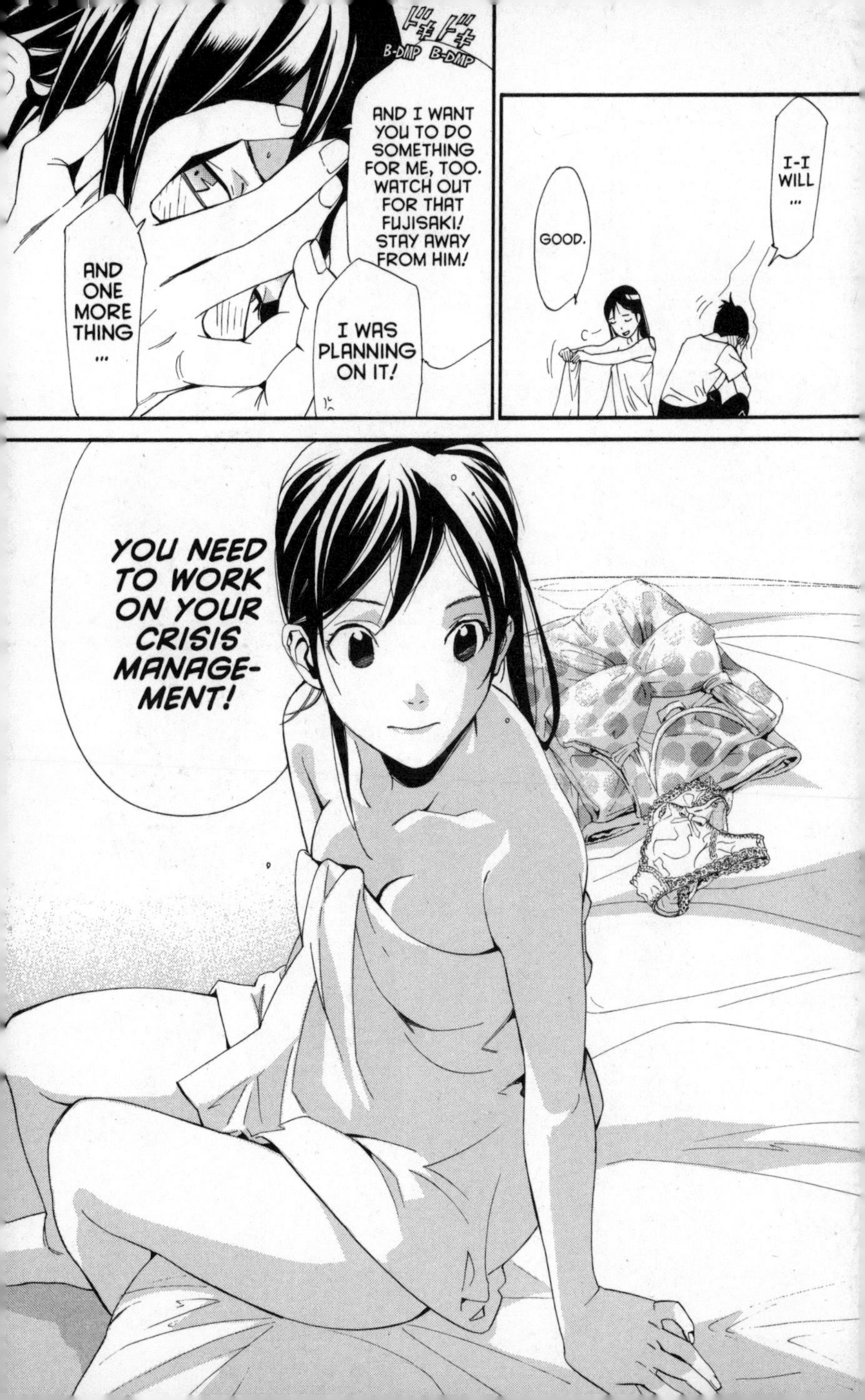
I-I WILL ...
GOOD.
ドキドキ
B-DMP B-DMP
AND I WANT YOU TO DO SOMETHING FOR ME, TOO. WATCH OUT FOR THAT FUJISAKI! STAY AWAY FROM HIM!
I WAS PLANNING ON IT!
AND ONE MORE THING ...
YOU NEED TO WORK ON YOUR CRISIS MANAGE-MENT!

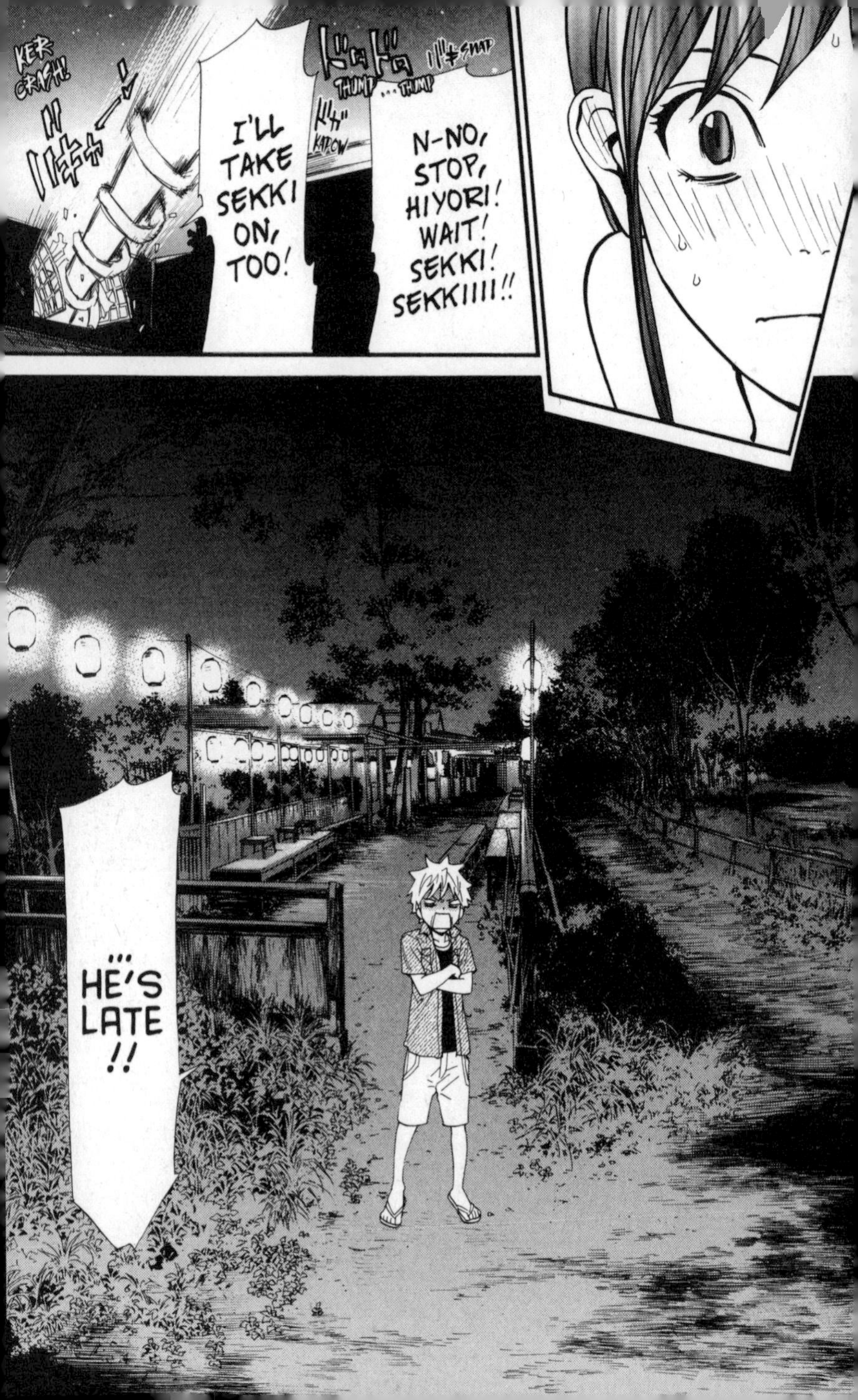
SNAP
THUMP... THUMP
N-NO, STOP, HIYORI! WAIT! SEKKI! SEKKIIIII!!
KAPOW
I'LL TAKE SEKKI ON, TOO!
KER CRASH!
...HE'S LATE!!

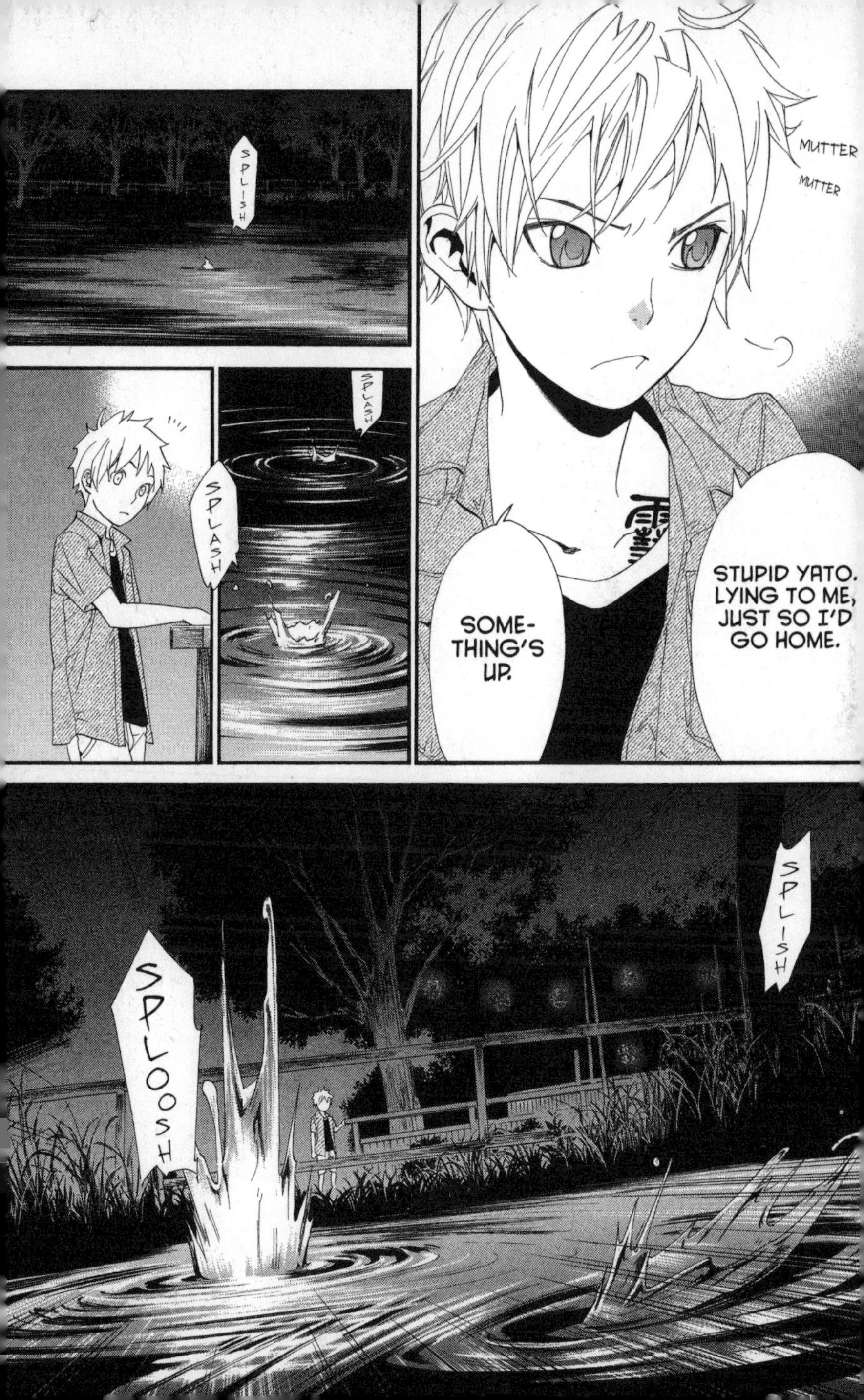
MUTTER
MUTTER
STUPID YATO. LYING TO ME, JUST SO I'D GO HOME.
SOME-THING'S UP.
SPLISH
SPLASH
SPLASH
SPLISH
SPLOOSH

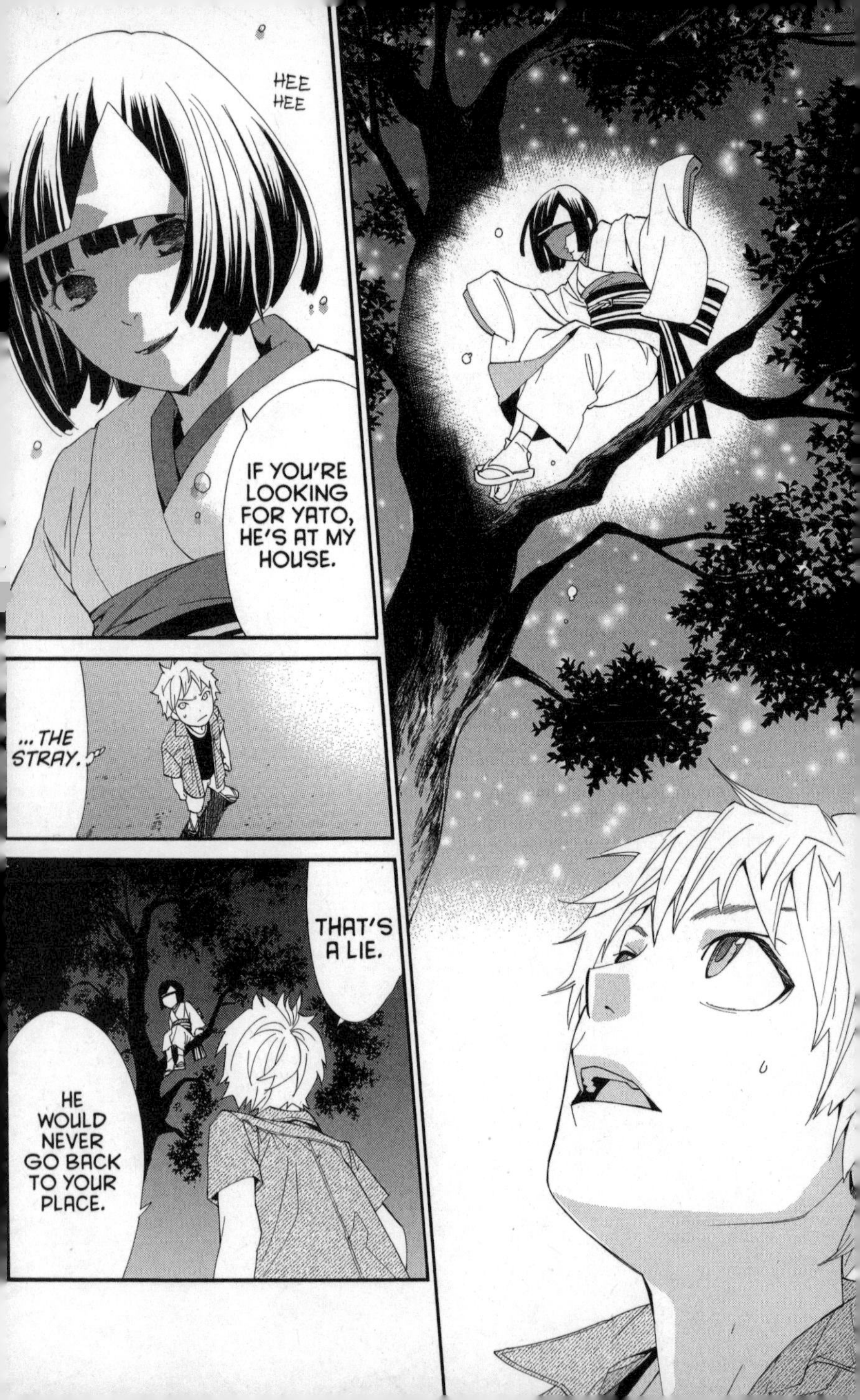
HEE HEE
IF YOU'RE LOOKING FOR YATO, HE'S AT MY HOUSE.
...THE STRAY.
THAT'S A LIE.
HE WOULD NEVER GO BACK TO YOUR PLACE.

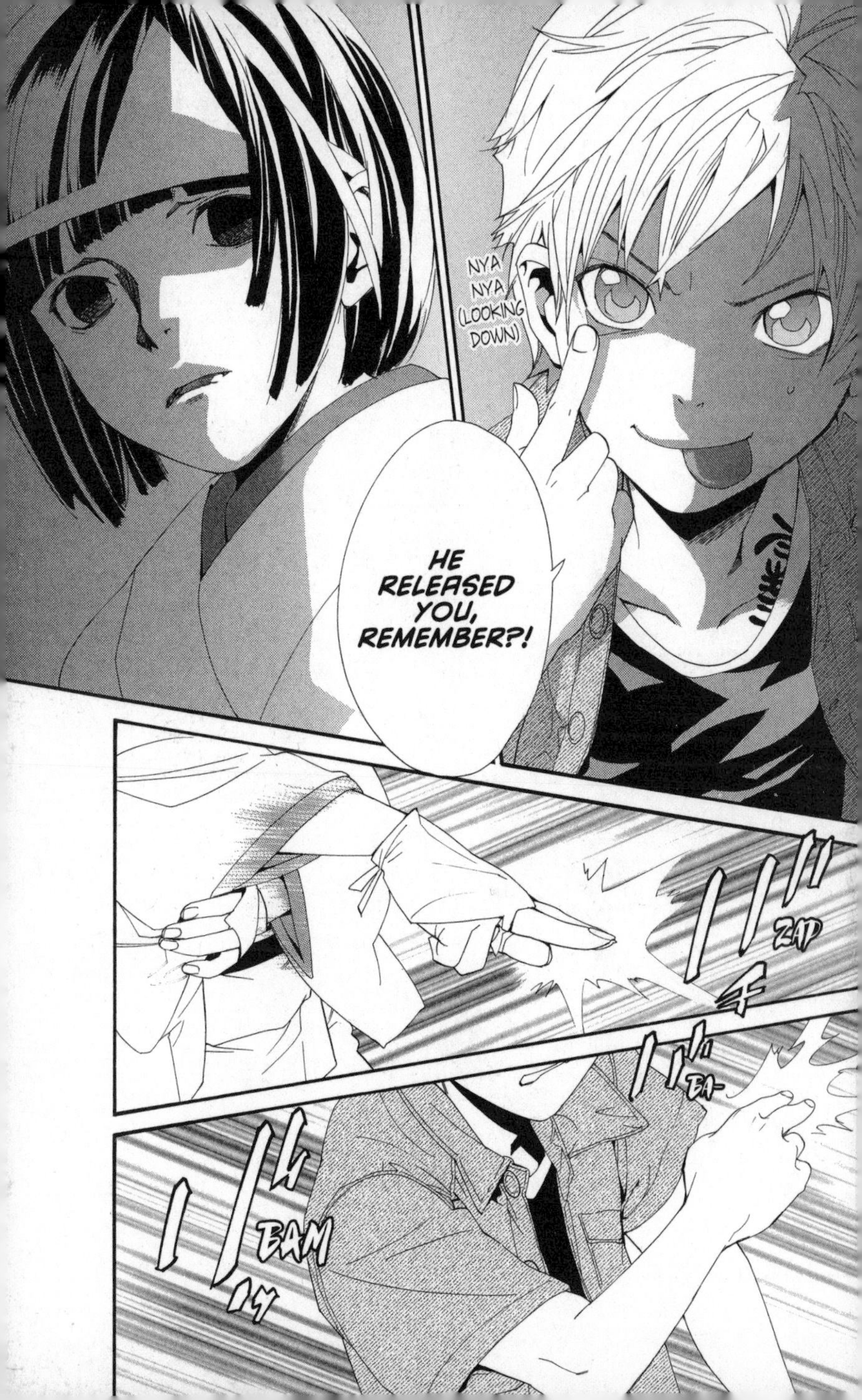
NYA NYA (LOOKING DOWN)
HE RELEASED YOU, REMEMBER?!
ZAP
BA-
BAM

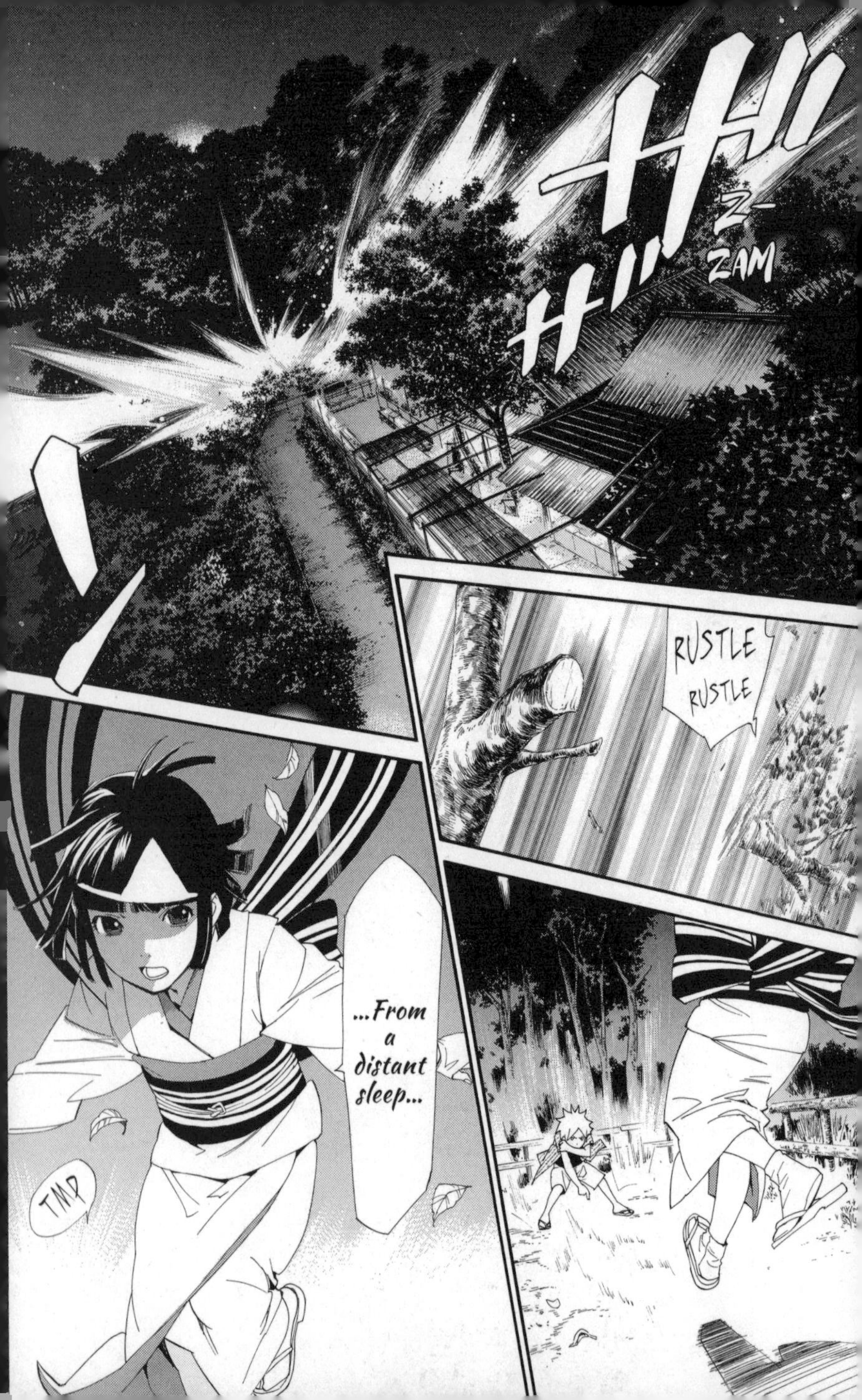
Z-
ZAM
RUSTLE RUSTLE
...From a distant sleep...
TMP

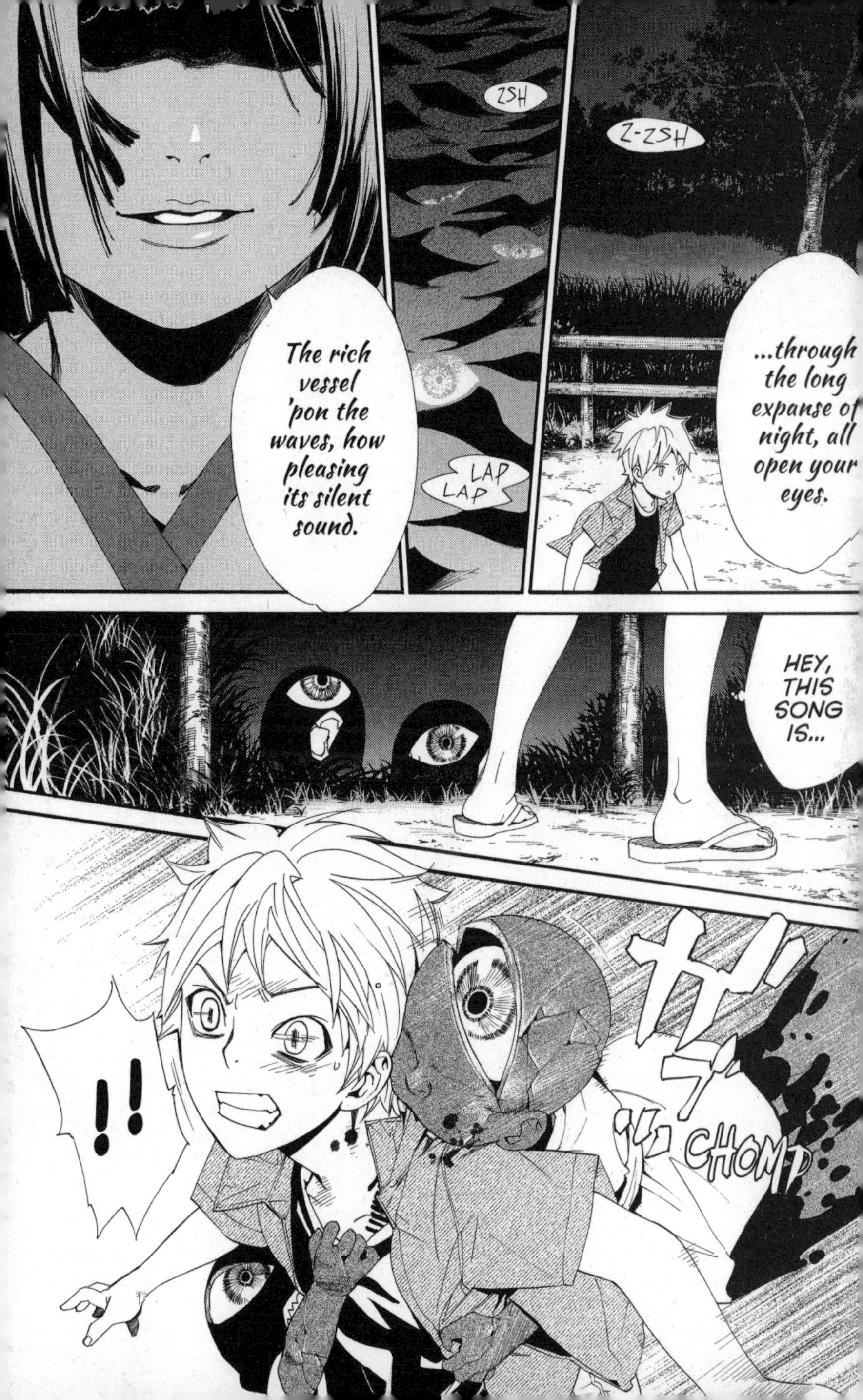
Z-ZSH
...through the long expanse of night, all open your eyes.
ZSH
LAP LAP
The rich vessel 'pon the waves, how pleasing its silent sound.
HEY, THIS SONG IS...
CHOMP
!!

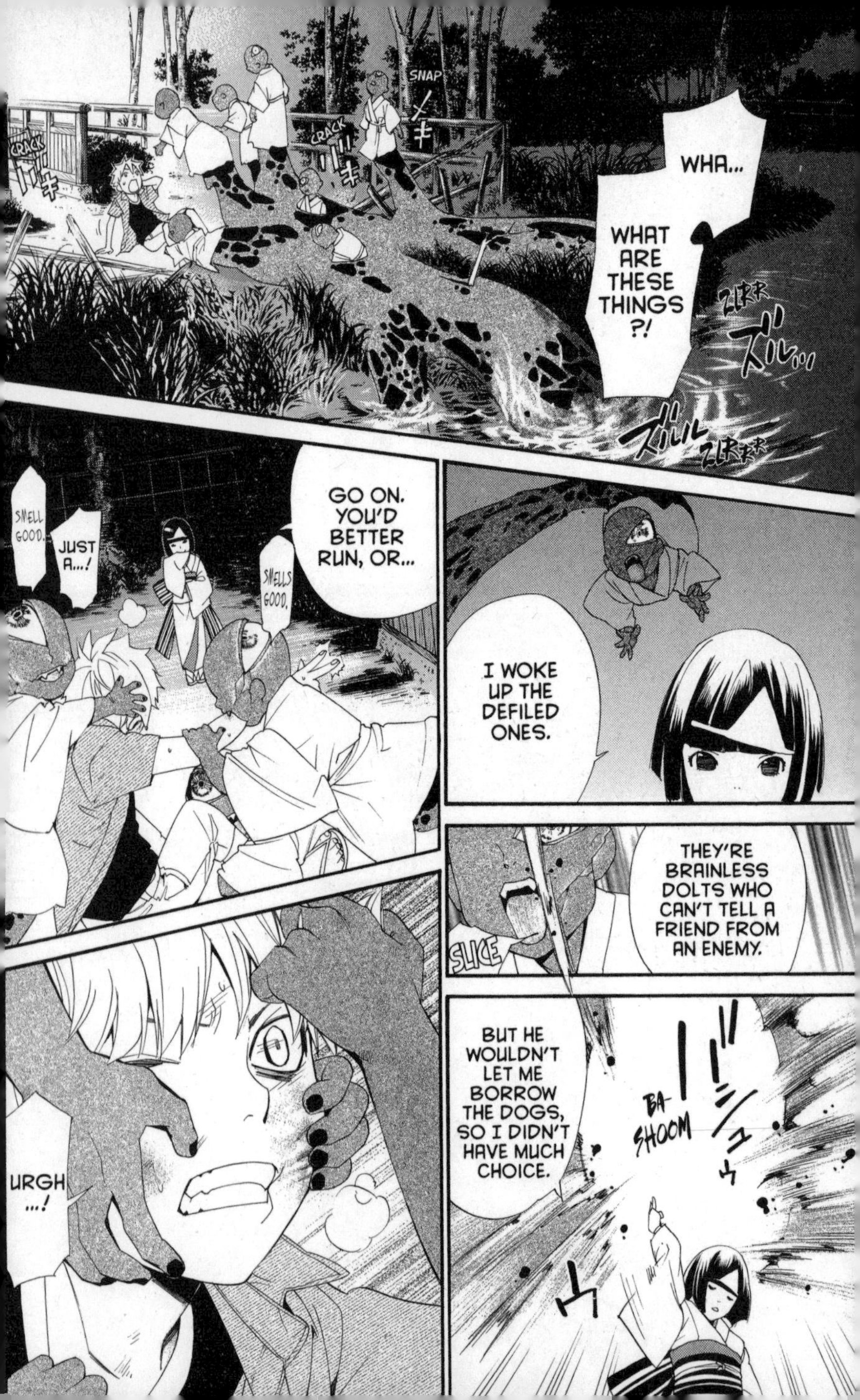
WHA...
WHAT ARE THESE THINGS?!
ZRRR
ZRRRR
SNAP
CRACK
CRACK
GO ON. YOU'D BETTER RUN, OR...
SMELLS GOOD.
JUST A...!
SMELL GOOD.
I WOKE UP THE DEFILED ONES.
THEY'RE BRAINLESS DOLTS WHO CAN'T TELL A FRIEND FROM AN ENEMY.
SLICE
BUT HE WOULDN'T LET ME BORROW THE DOGS, SO I DIDN'T HAVE MUCH CHOICE.
BA-SHOOM
URGH...!

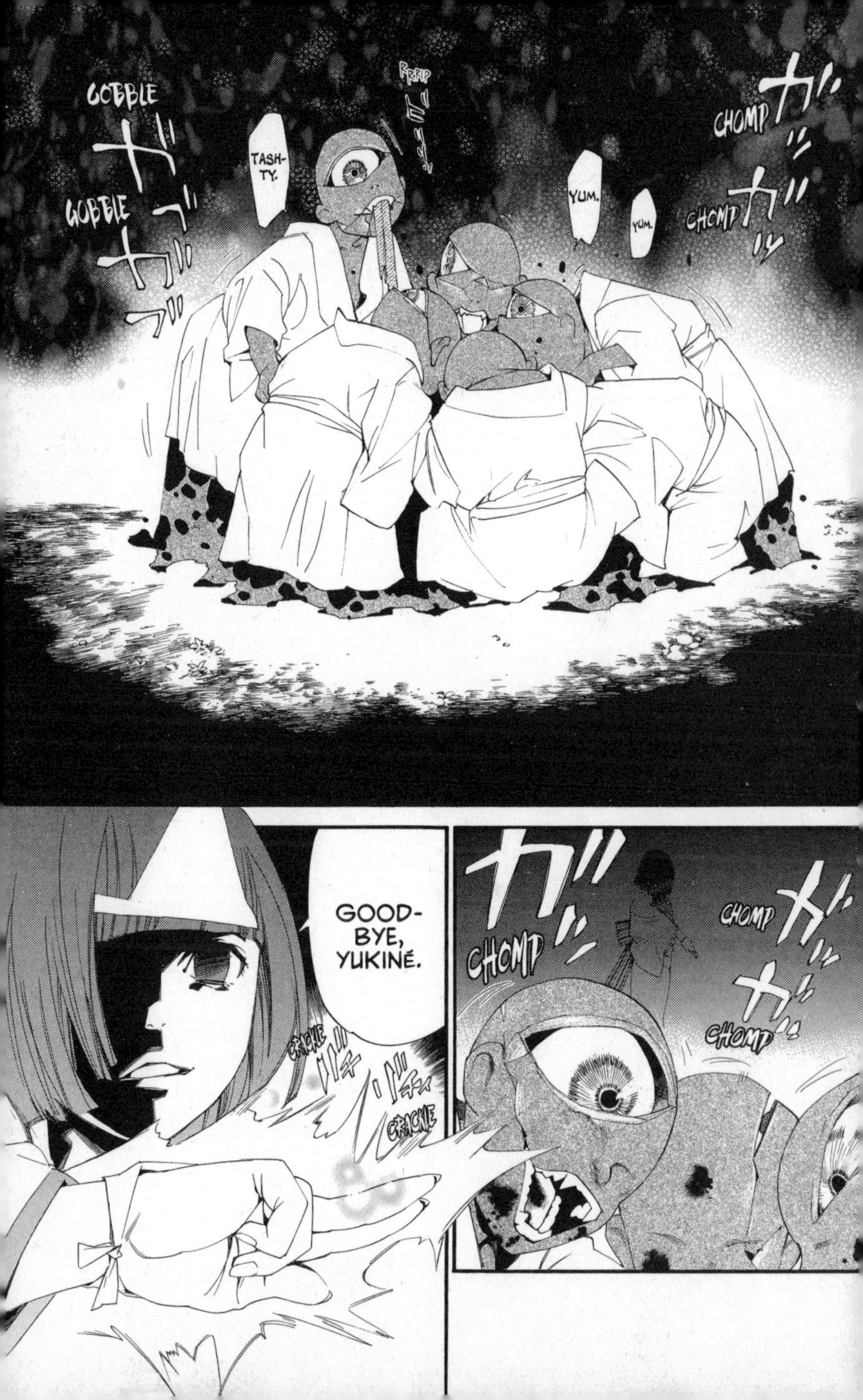
CHOMP
CHOMP
YUM.
YUM.
RRRIP
TASH-TY.
GOBBLE
GOBBLE
CHOMP
CHOMP
CHOMP
GOOD-BYE, YUKINÉ.
CRACKLE
CRACKLE

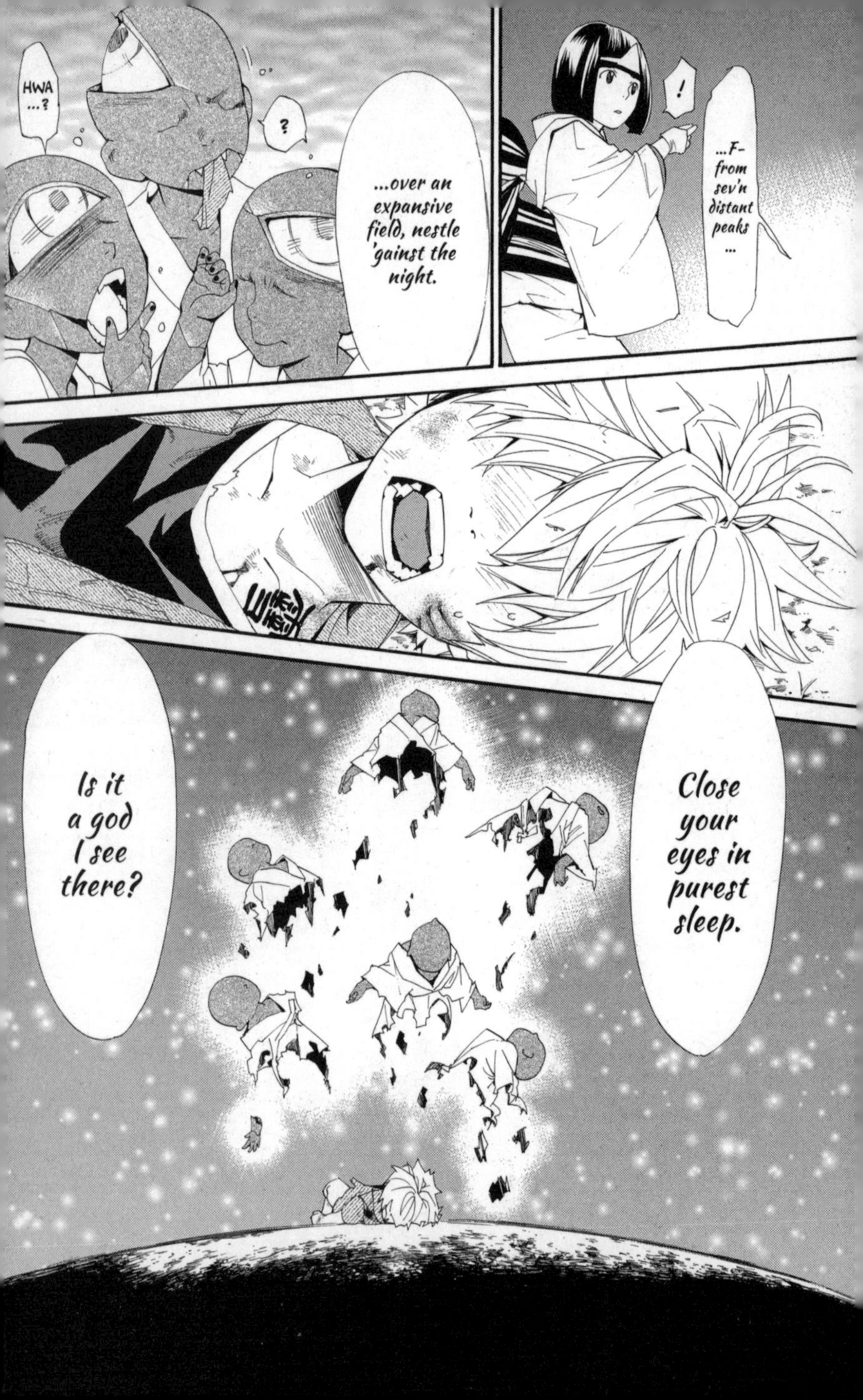
!
...F-from sev'n distant peaks ...
...over an expansive field, nestle 'gainst the night.
?
HWA ...?
Close your eyes in purest sleep.
Is it a god I see there?

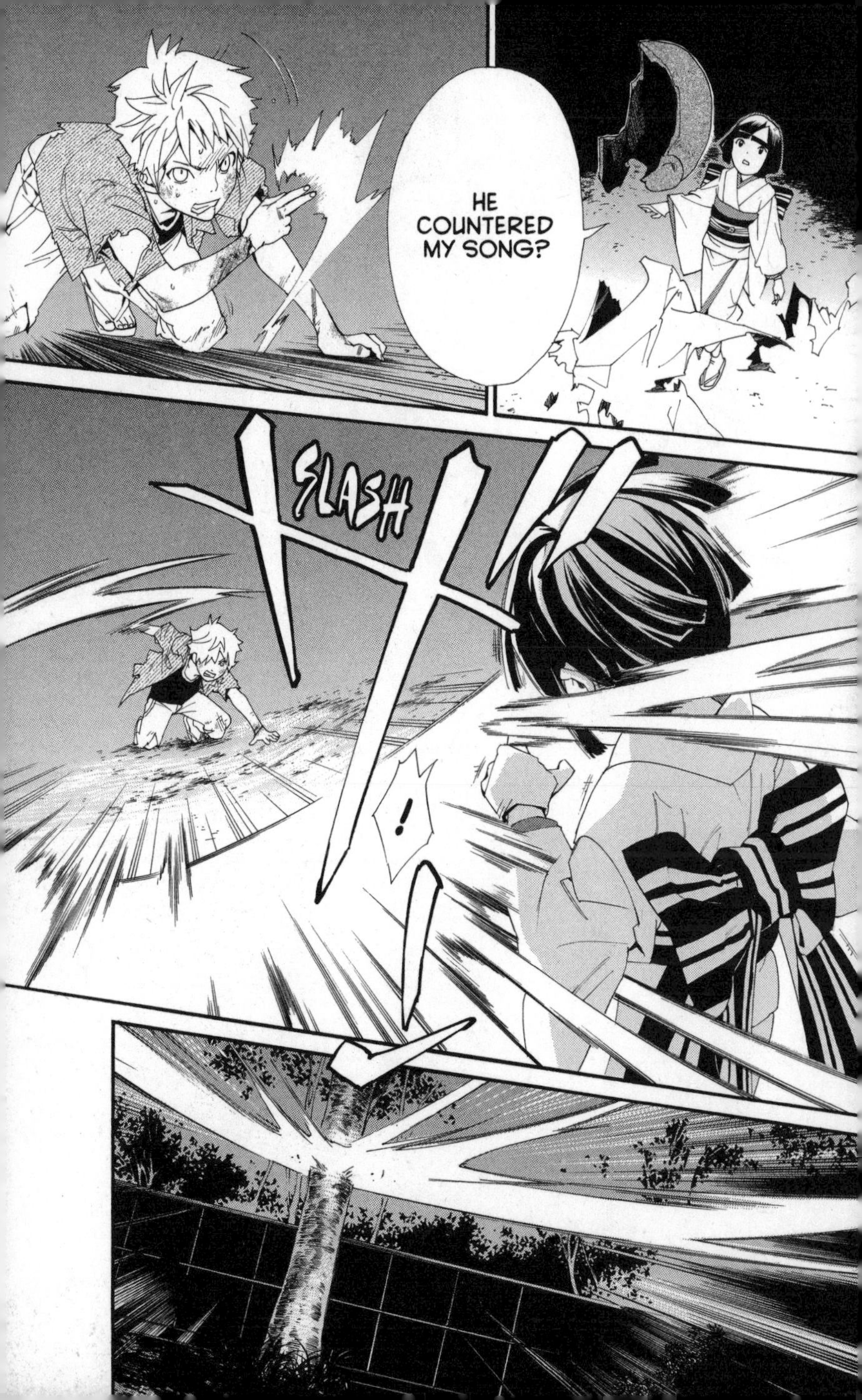
HE COUNTERED MY SONG?
SLASH
!

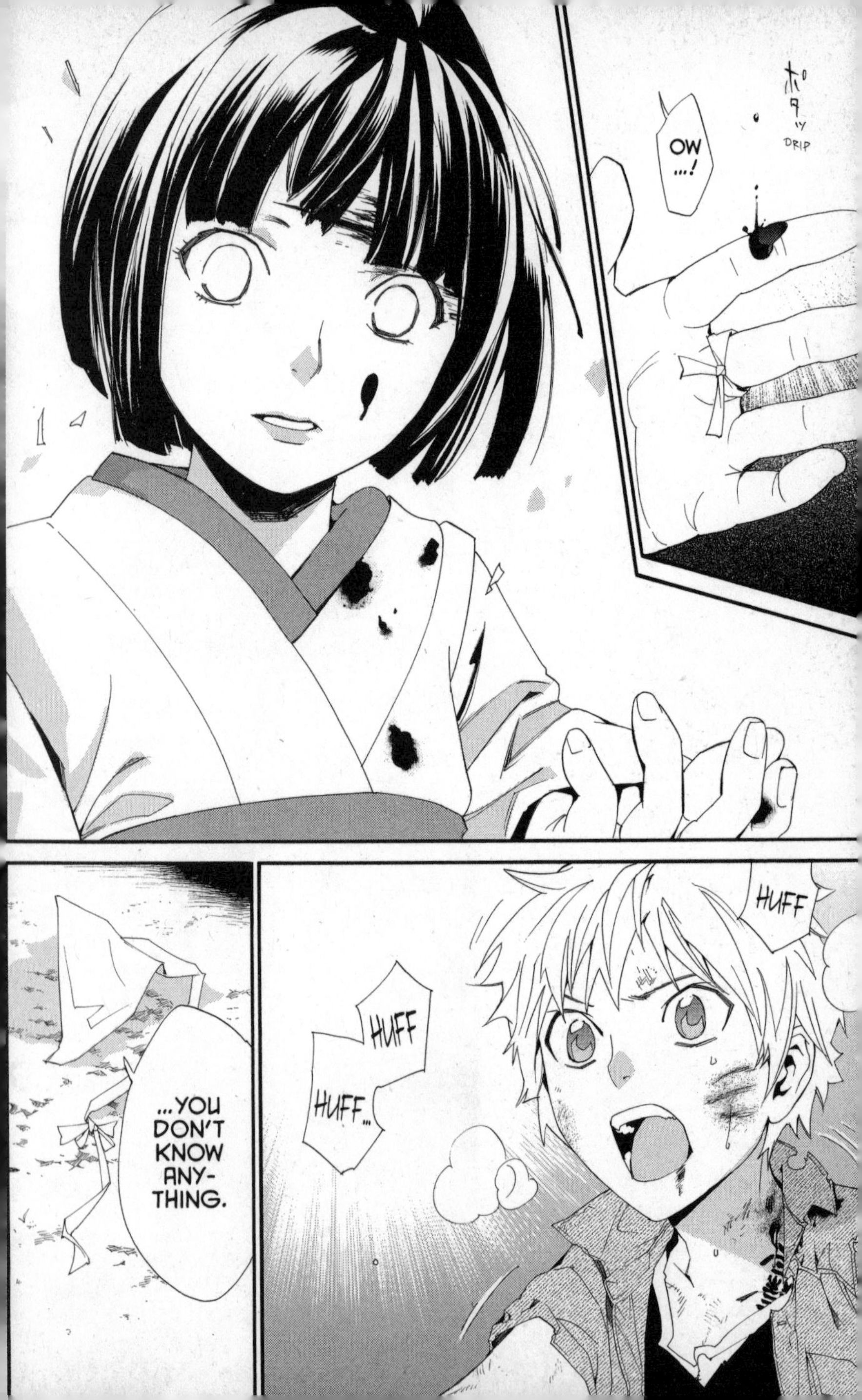

ポタッ
DRIP
OW ...!
HUFF
HUFF
HUFF...
...YOU DON'T KNOW ANYTHING.

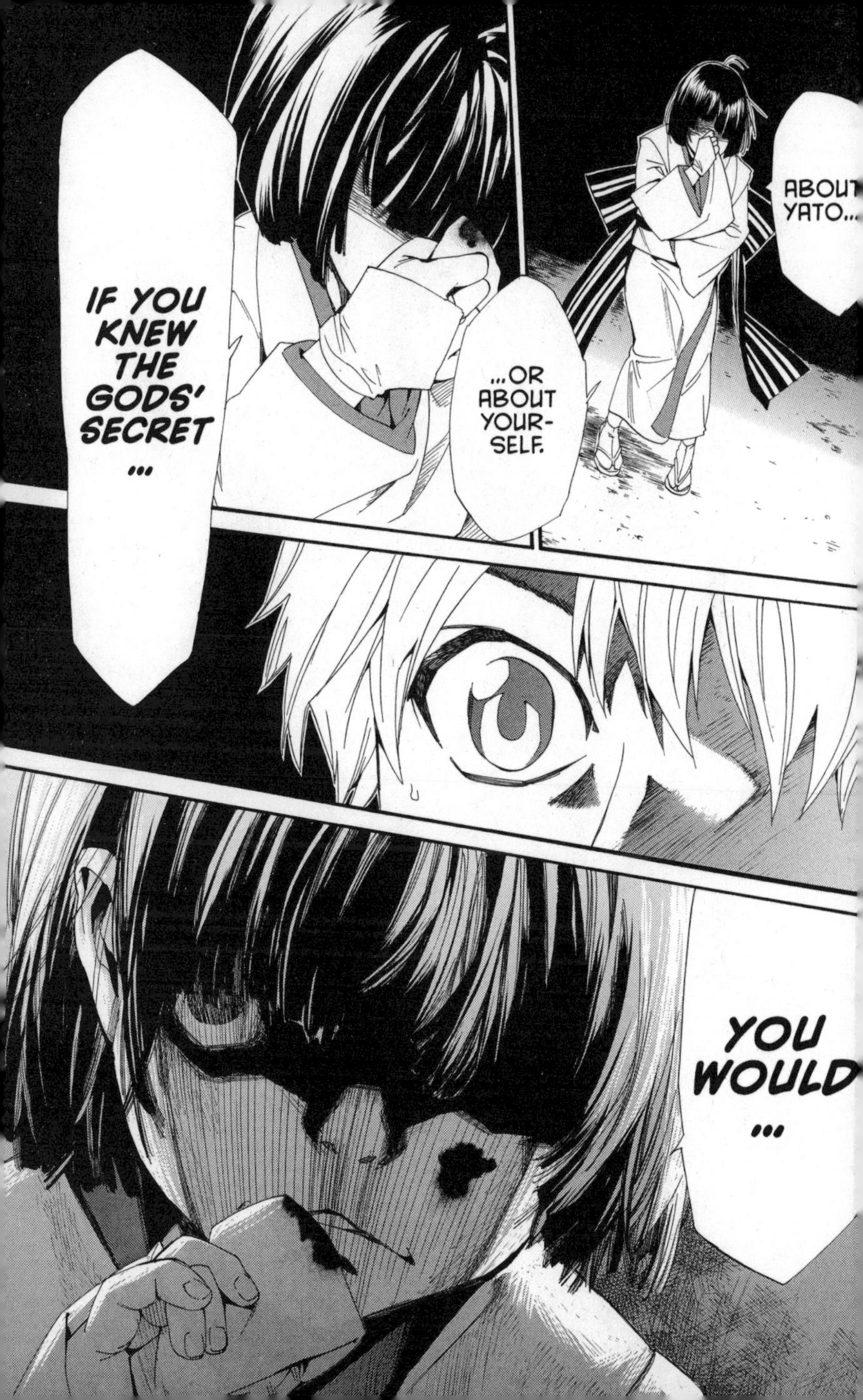
IF YOU KNEW THE GODS' SECRET ...
ABOUT YATO...
...OR ABOUT YOUR-SELF.
YOU WOULD ...

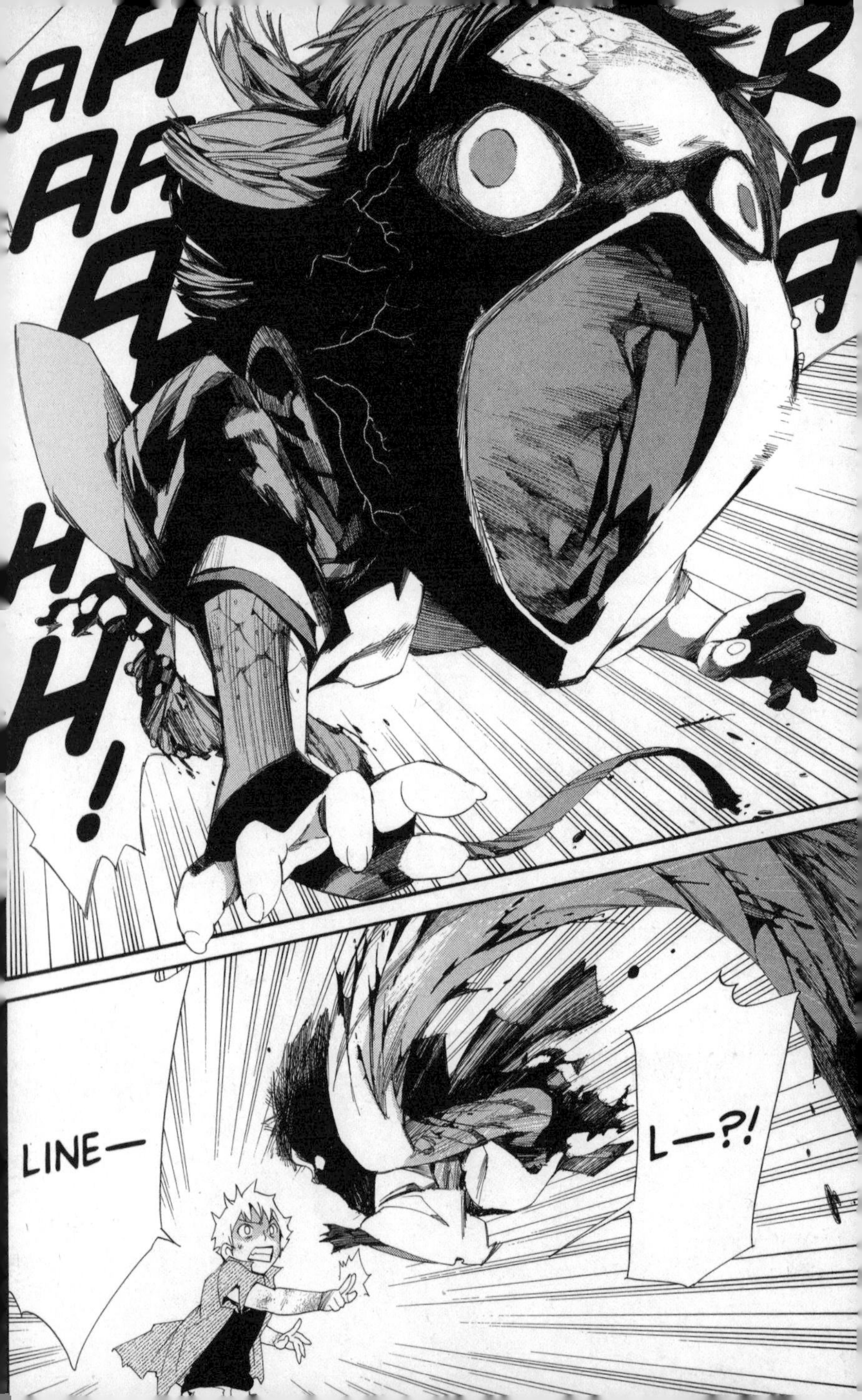
RAA
AHAAAHHH!
L—?!
LINE—

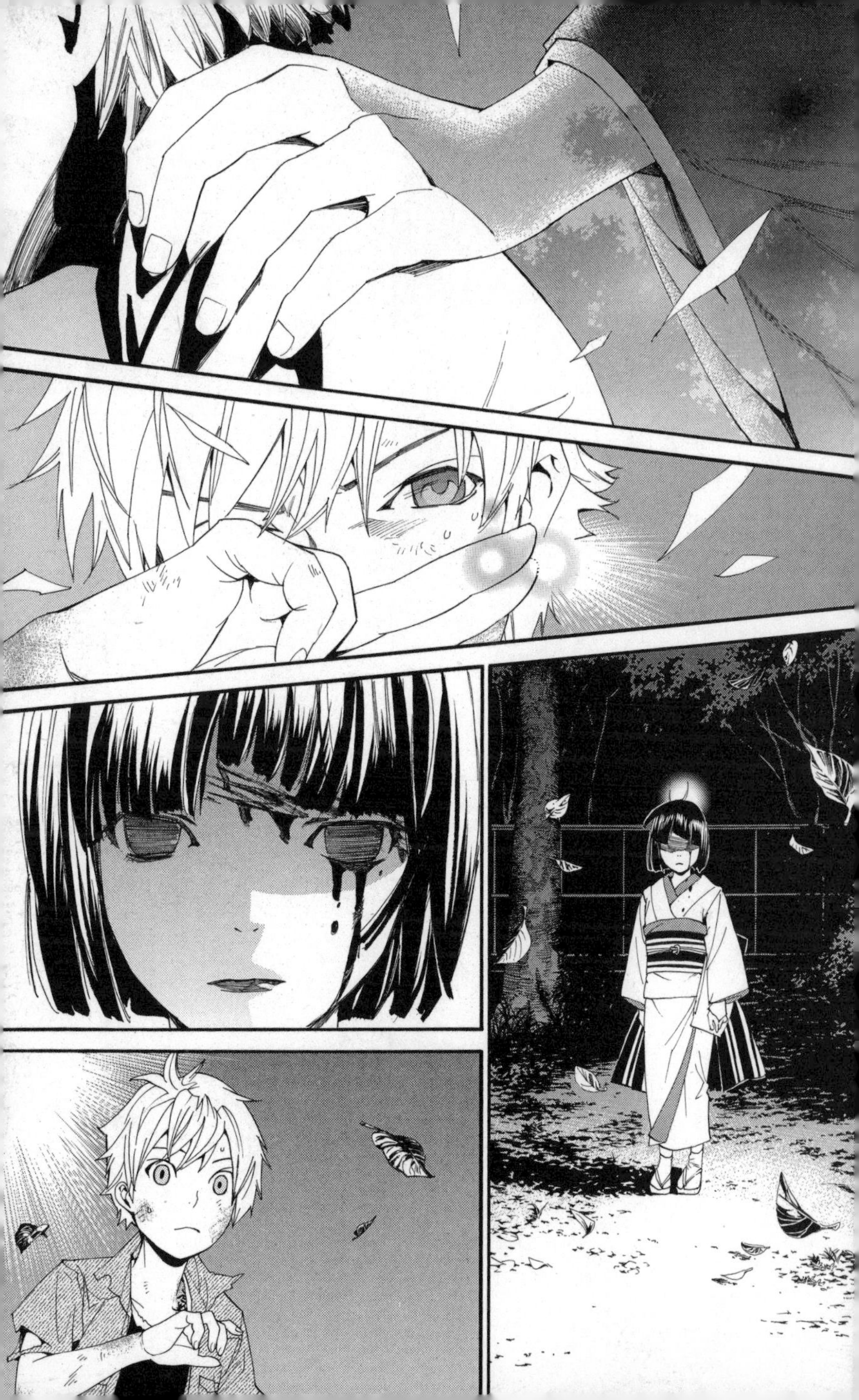

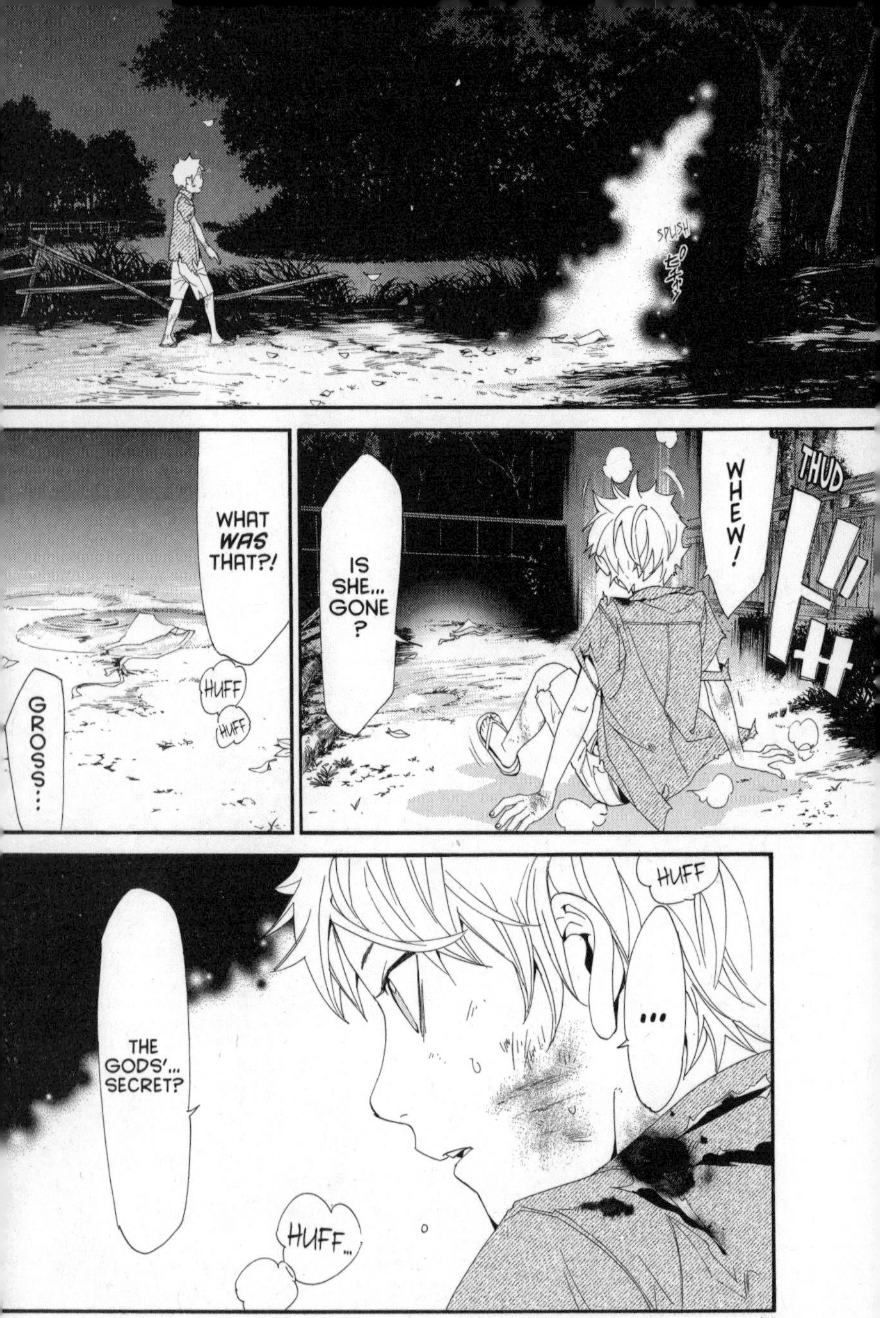
SPLUSH
THUD
WHEW!
IS SHE... GONE?
WHAT *WAS* THAT?!
HUFF
HUFF
GROSS...
HUFF
...
THE GODS'... SECRET?
HUFF...

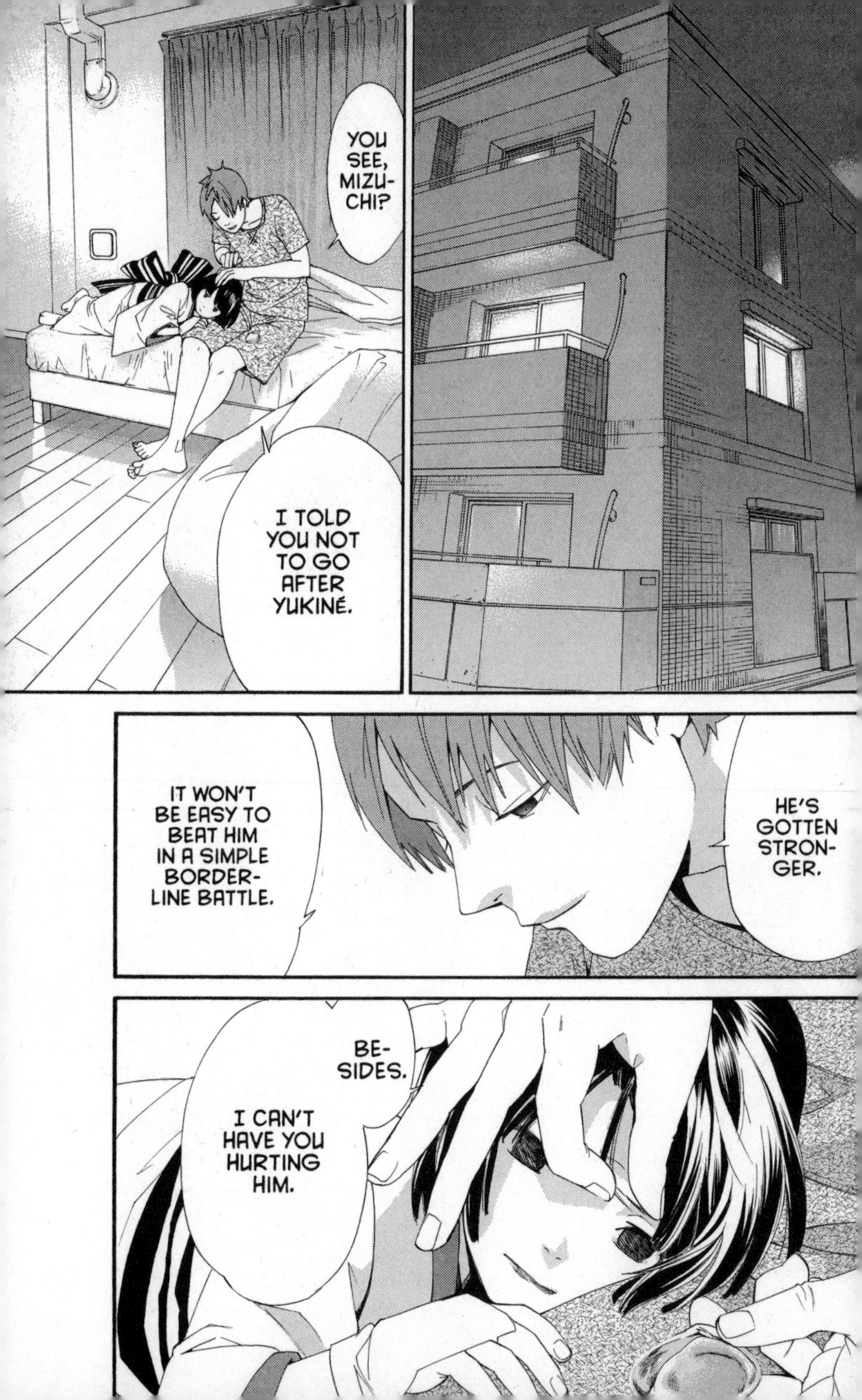
YOU SEE, MIZU-CHI?
I TOLD YOU NOT TO GO AFTER YUKINÉ.
HE'S GOTTEN STRON-GER.
IT WON'T BE EASY TO BEAT HIM IN A SIMPLE BORDER-LINE BATTLE.
BE-SIDES.
I CAN'T HAVE YOU HURTING HIM.

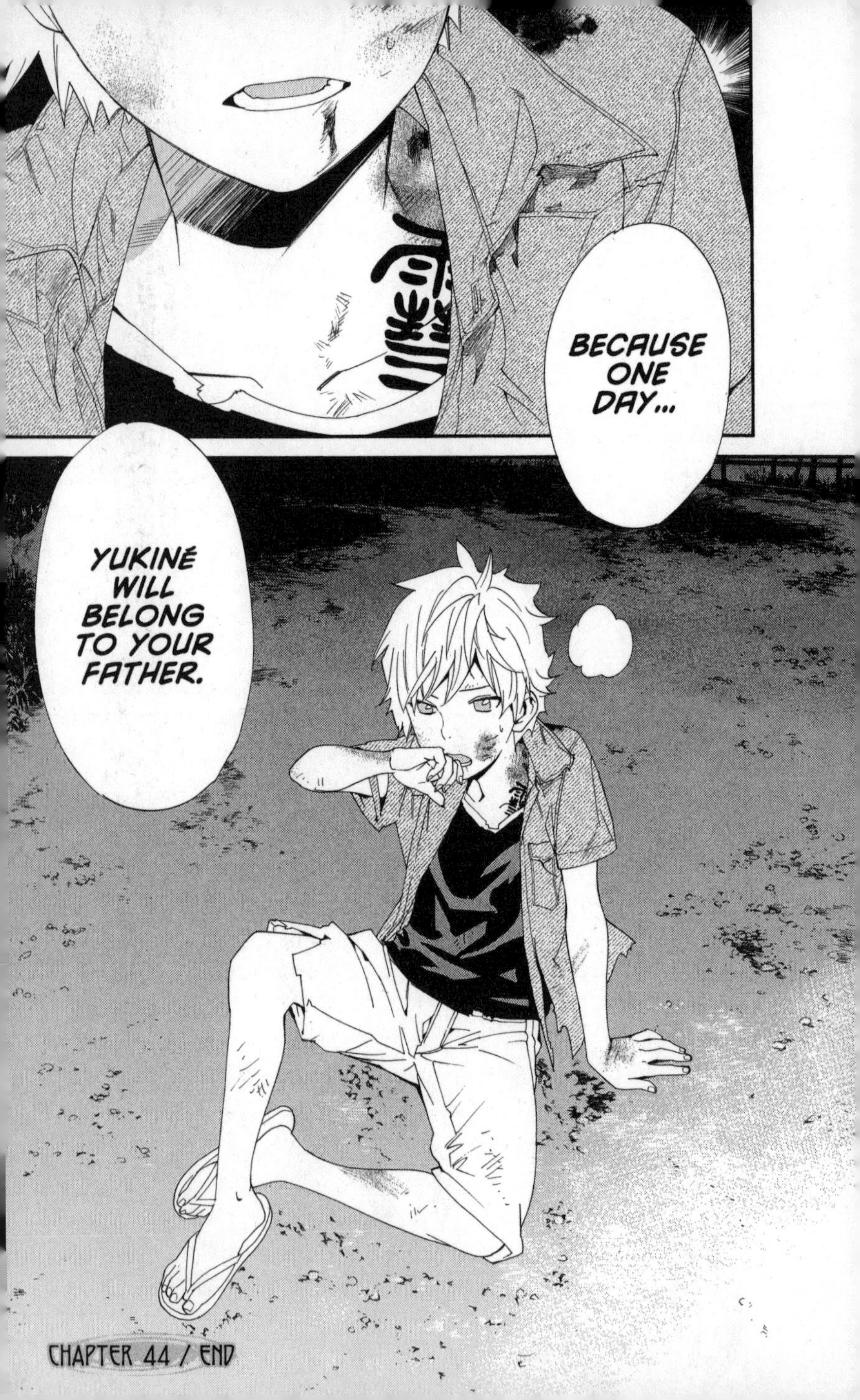
BECAUSE ONE DAY...
YUKINE WILL BELONG TO YOUR FATHER.
CHAPTER 44 / END

野

莧

神

師

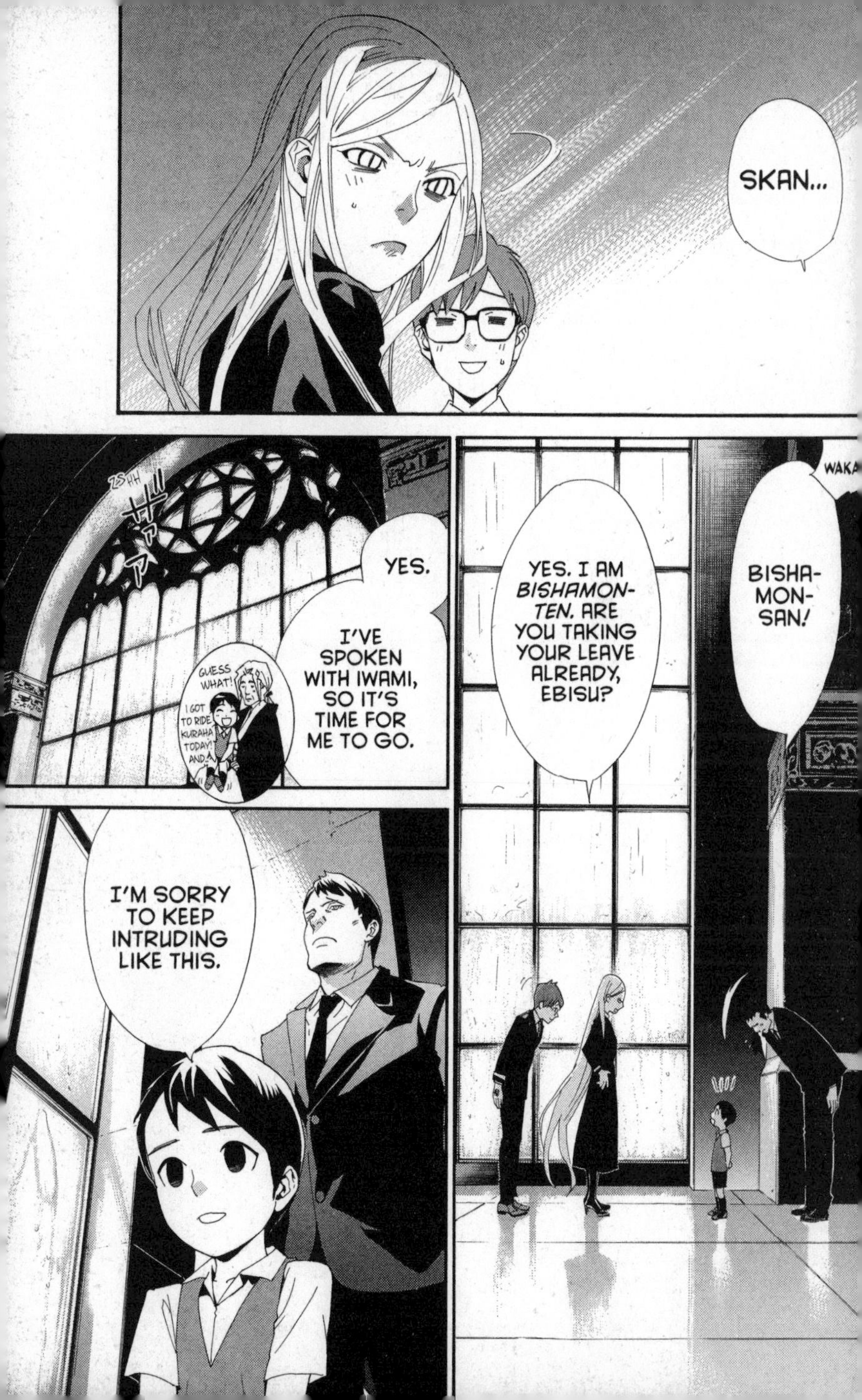
SKAN...
WAKA
BISHA-MON-SAN!
YES. I AM BISHAMON-TEN. ARE YOU TAKING YOUR LEAVE ALREADY, EBISU?
YES.
I'VE SPOKEN WITH IWAMI, SO IT'S TIME FOR ME TO GO.
ZSHH
GUESS WHAT!
I GOT TO RIDE KURAHA TODAY! AND...
I'M SORRY TO KEEP INTRUDING LIKE THIS.

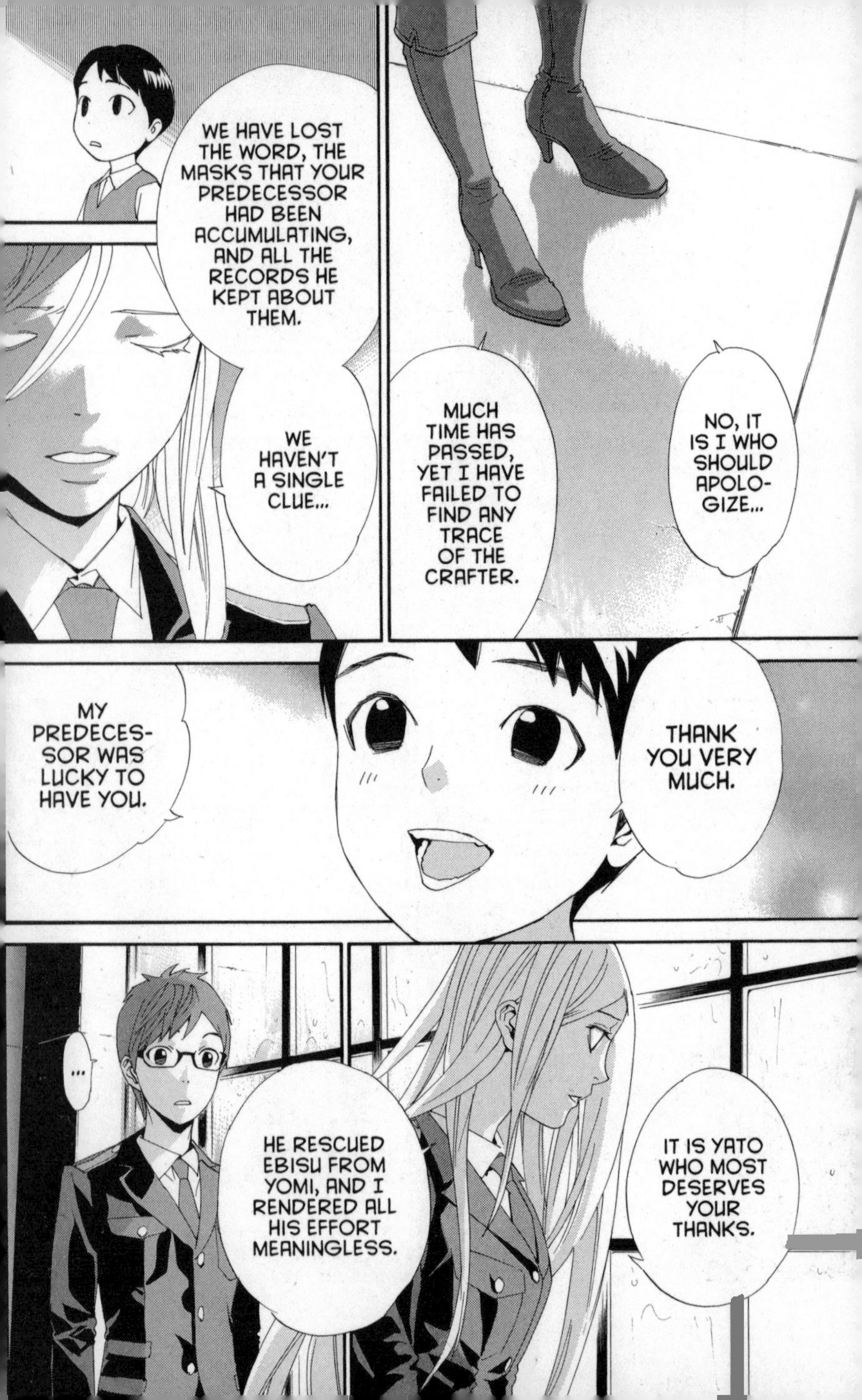
NO, IT IS I WHO SHOULD APOLOGIZE...
MUCH TIME HAS PASSED, YET I HAVE FAILED TO FIND ANY TRACE OF THE CRAFTER.
WE HAVE LOST THE WORD, THE MASKS THAT YOUR PREDECESSOR HAD BEEN ACCUMULATING, AND ALL THE RECORDS HE KEPT ABOUT THEM.
WE HAVEN'T A SINGLE CLUE...
THANK YOU VERY MUCH.
MY PREDECESSOR WAS LUCKY TO HAVE YOU.
IT IS YATO WHO MOST DESERVES YOUR THANKS.
HE RESCUED EBISU FROM YOMI, AND I RENDERED ALL HIS EFFORT MEANINGLESS.
...

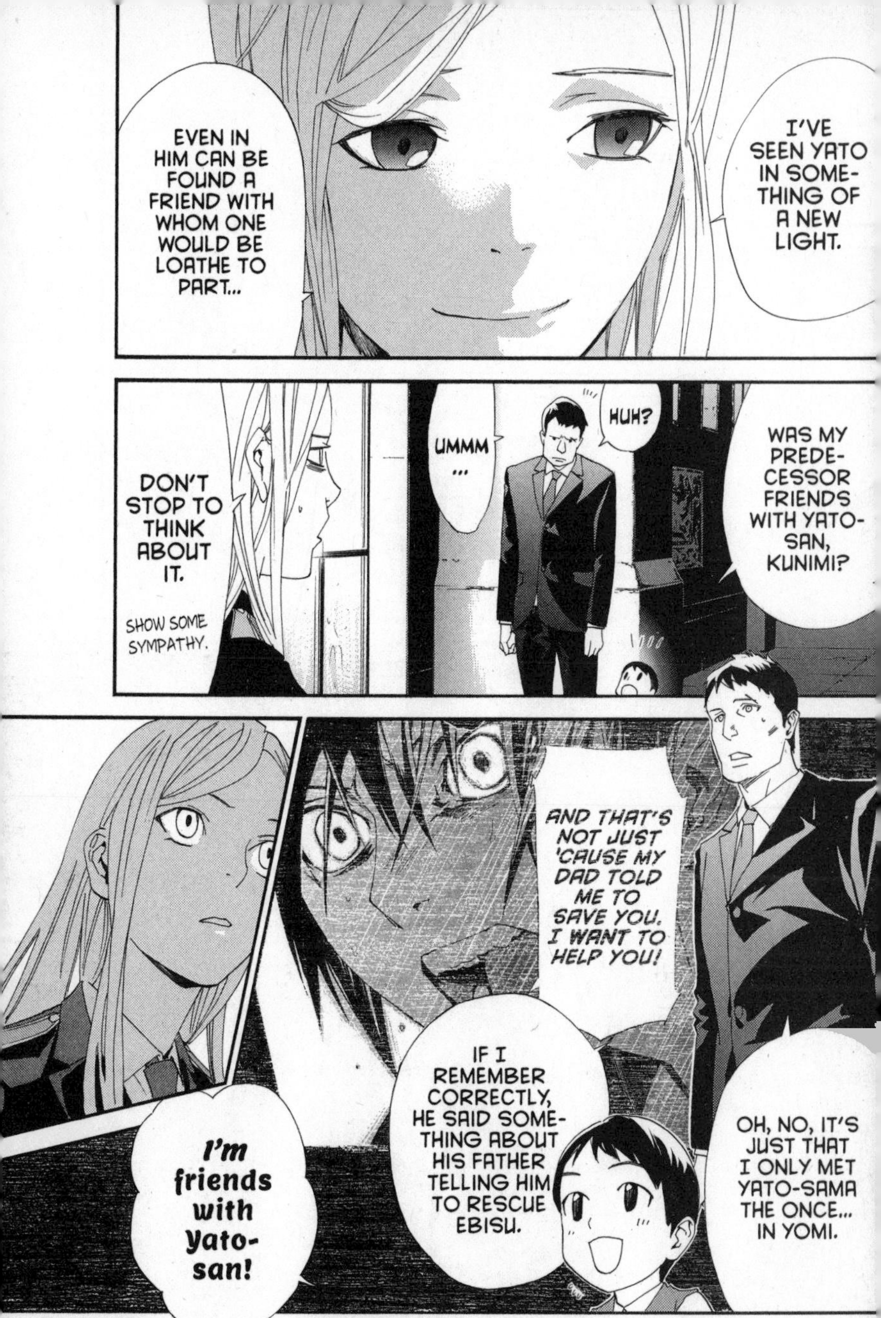
I'VE SEEN YATO IN SOMETHING OF A NEW LIGHT.
EVEN IN HIM CAN BE FOUND A FRIEND WITH WHOM ONE WOULD BE LOATHE TO PART...
WAS MY PREDECESSOR FRIENDS WITH YATO-SAN, KUNIMI?
HUH?
UMMM...
DON'T STOP TO THINK ABOUT IT.
SHOW SOME SYMPATHY.
OH, NO, IT'S JUST THAT I ONLY MET YATO-SAMA THE ONCE... IN YOMI.
IF I REMEMBER CORRECTLY, HE SAID SOMETHING ABOUT HIS FATHER TELLING HIM TO RESCUE EBISU.
AND THAT'S NOT JUST 'CAUSE MY DAD TOLD ME TO SAVE YOU. I WANT TO HELP YOU!
I'm friends with Yato-san!

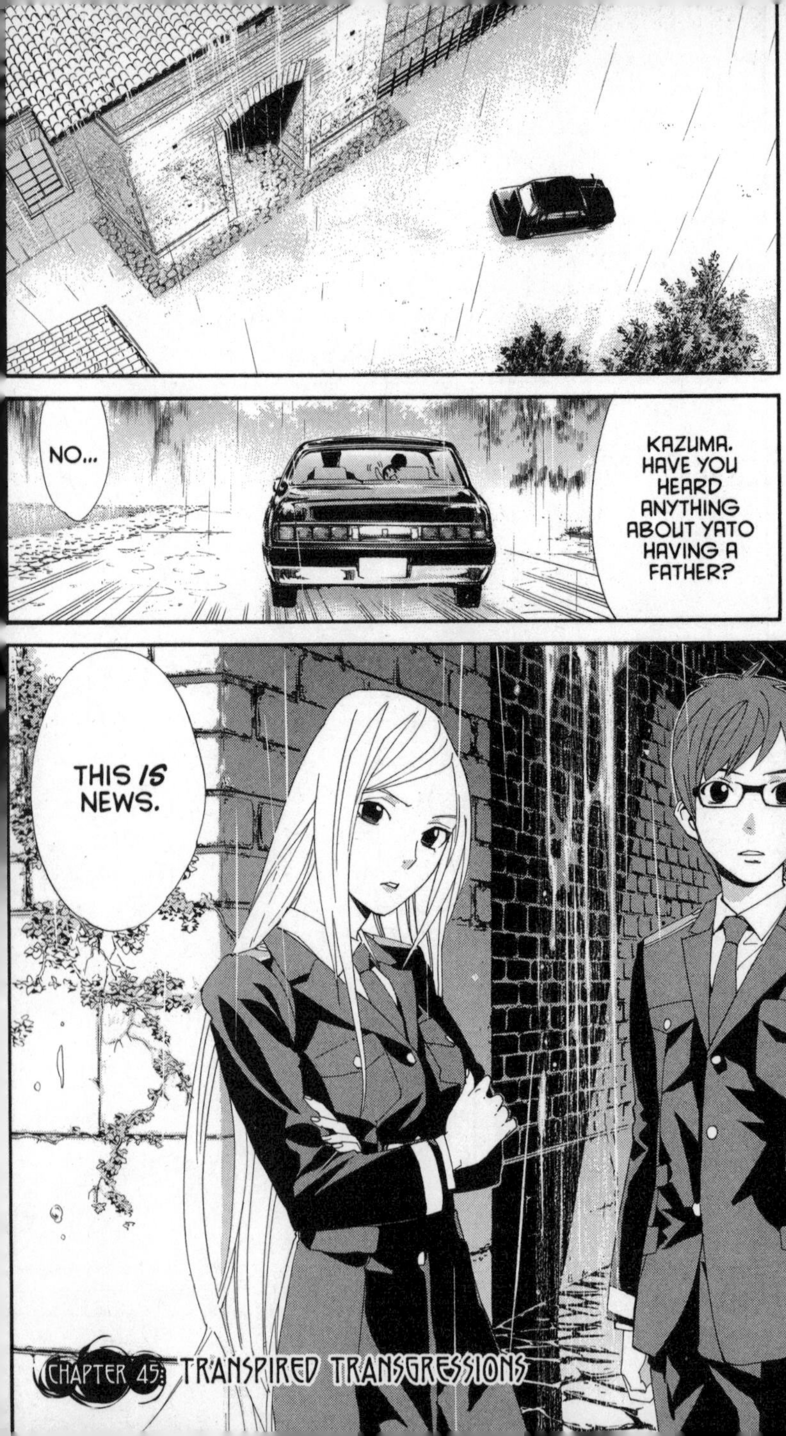
KAZUMA. HAVE YOU HEARD ANYTHING ABOUT YATO HAVING A FATHER?
NO...
THIS *IS* NEWS.
CHAPTER 45: TRANSPIRED TRANSGRESSIONS

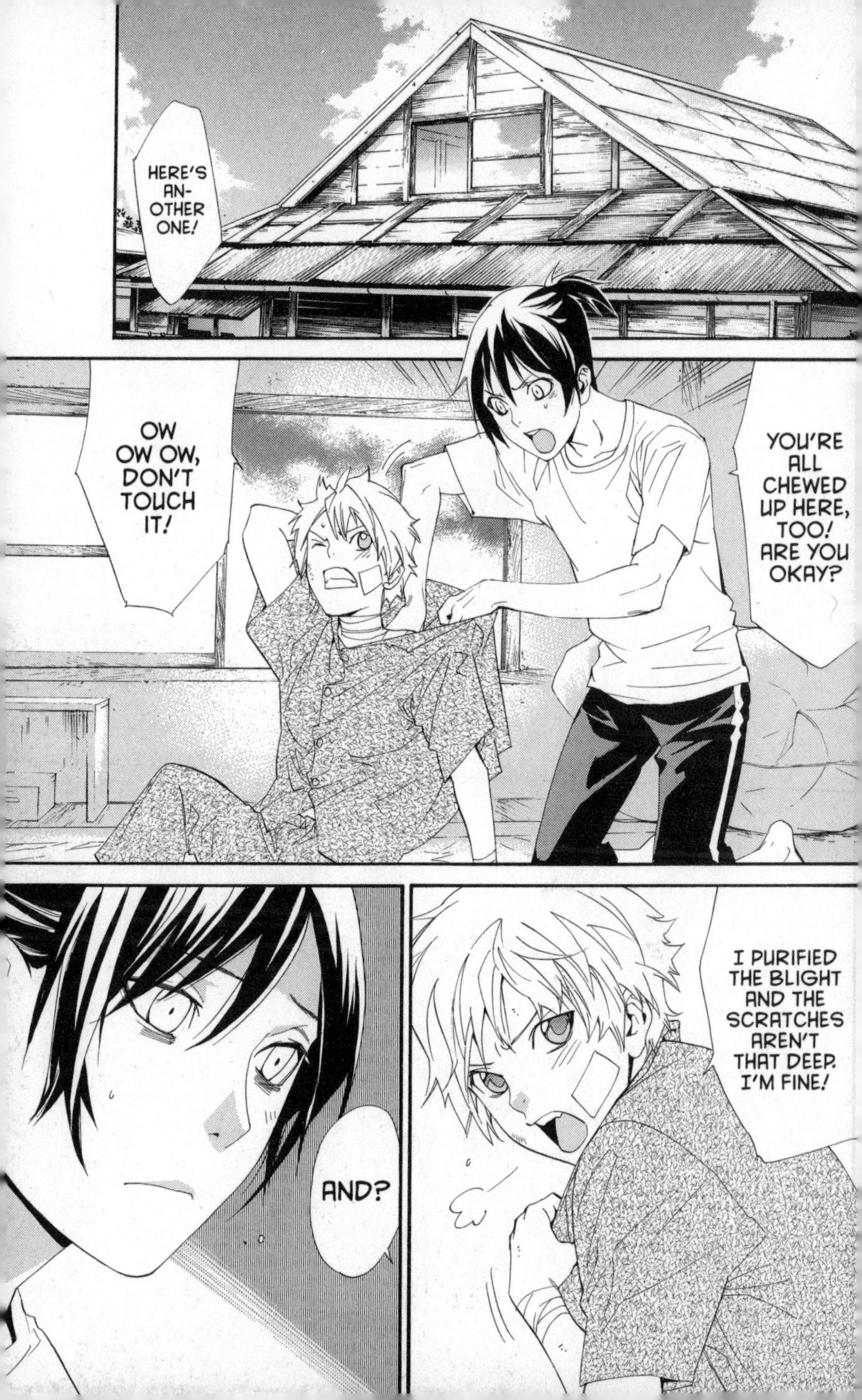
HERE'S AN- OTHER ONE!
YOU'RE ALL CHEWED UP HERE, TOO! ARE YOU OKAY?
OW OW OW, DON'T TOUCH IT!
I PURIFIED THE BLIGHT AND THE SCRATCHES AREN'T THAT DEEP. I'M FINE!
AND?

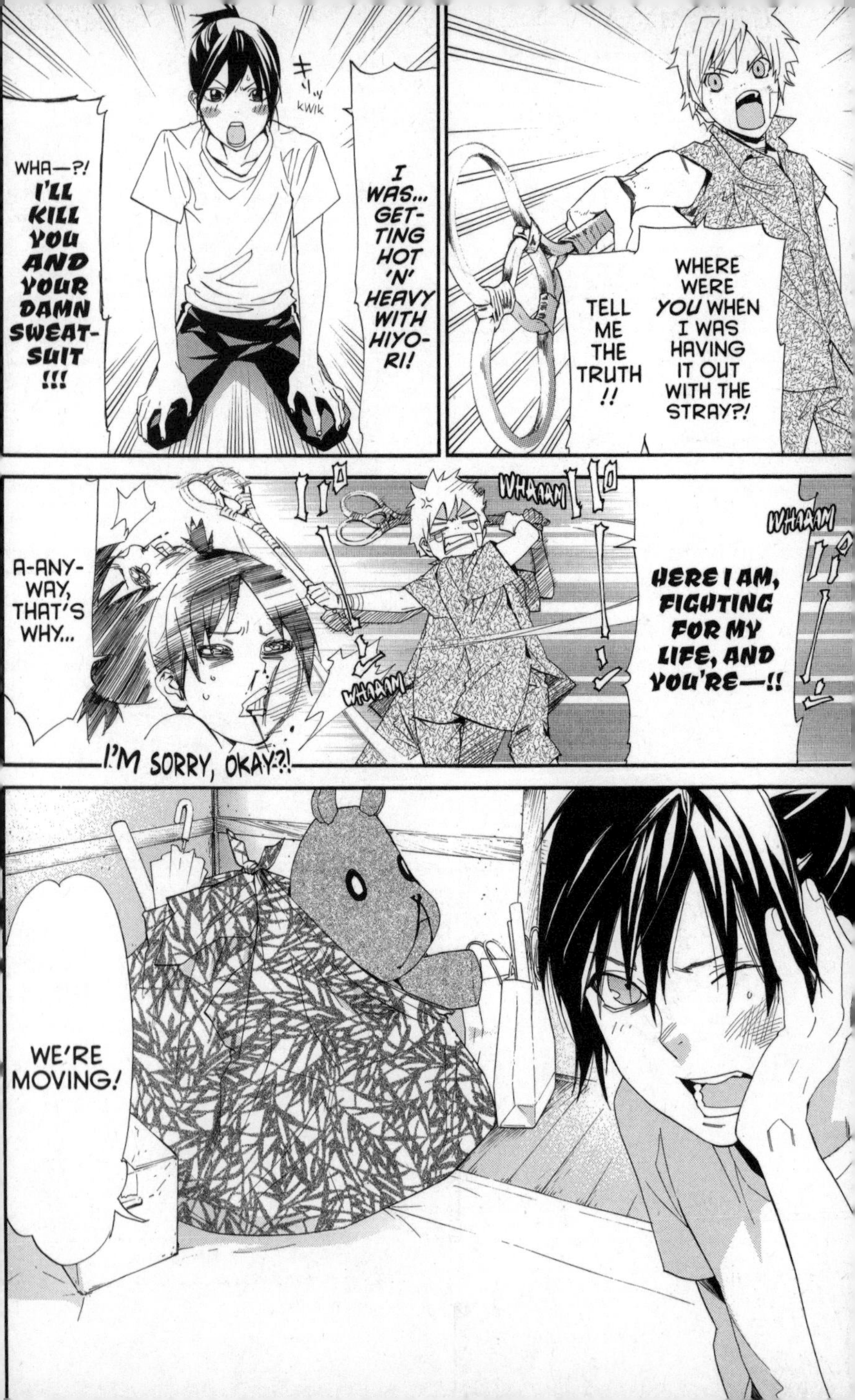
WHERE WERE YOU WHEN I WAS HAVING IT OUT WITH THE STRAY?!
TELL ME THE TRUTH !!
KWIK
I WAS... GET-TING HOT 'N' HEAVY WITH HIYO-RI!
WHA—?! I'LL KILL YOU AND YOUR DAMN SWEAT-SUIT !!!
WHAAAM
HERE I AM, FIGHTING FOR MY LIFE, AND YOU'RE—!!
WHAAAM
WHAAAM
A-ANY-WAY, THAT'S WHY...
I'M SORRY, OKAY?!
WE'RE MOVING!

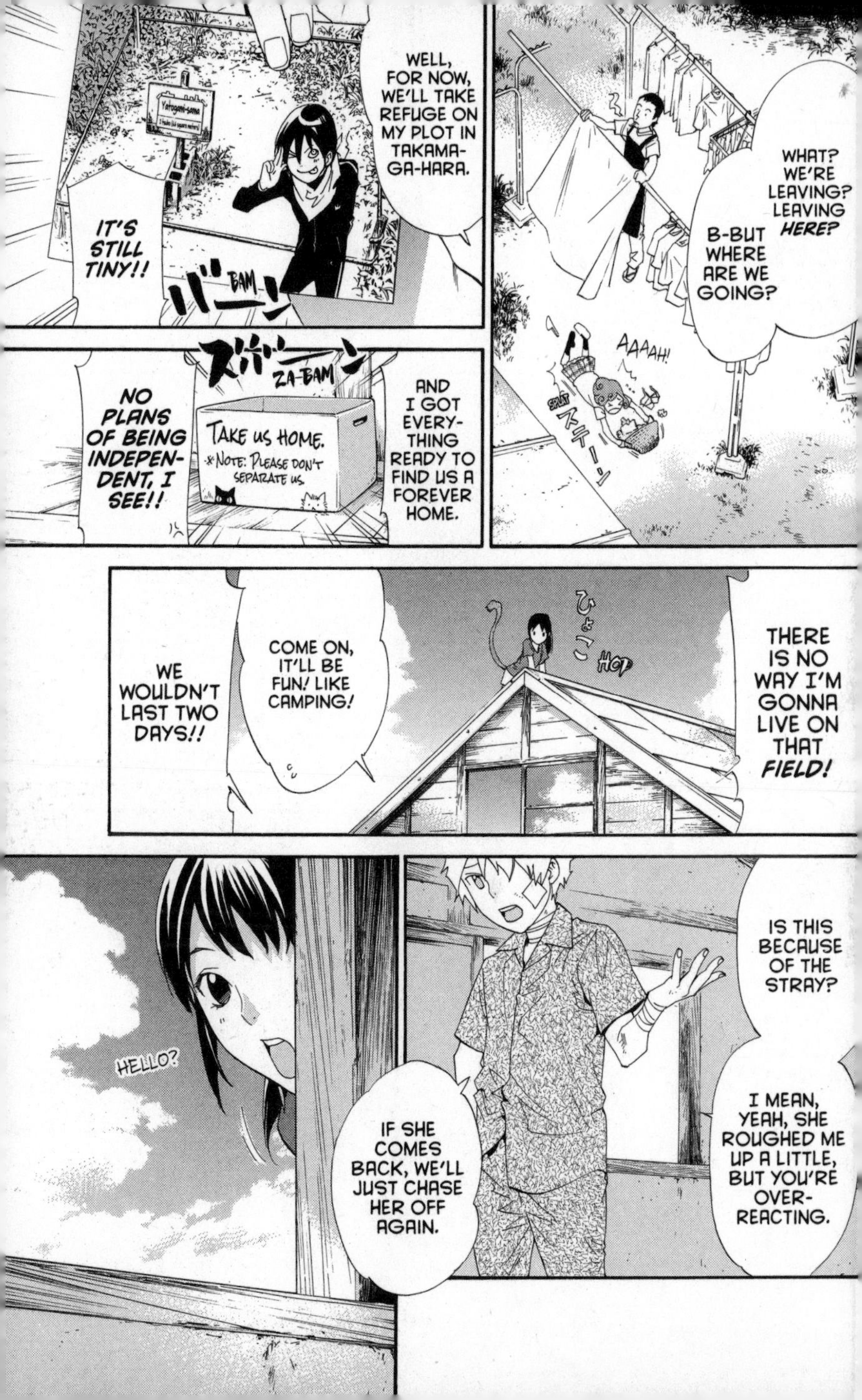
WHAT? WE'RE LEAVING? LEAVING *HERE?*
B-BUT WHERE ARE WE GOING?
AAAAH!
SPLAT
WELL, FOR NOW, WE'LL TAKE REFUGE ON MY PLOT IN TAKAMA-GA-HARA.
IT'S STILL TINY!!
BAM
AND I GOT EVERY-THING READY TO FIND US A FOREVER HOME.
ZA-BAM
TAKE US HOME.
※NOTE: PLEASE DON'T SEPARATE US.
NO PLANS OF BEING INDEPEN-DENT, I SEE!!
THERE IS NO WAY I'M GONNA LIVE ON THAT *FIELD!*
ひょこ
HOP
COME ON, IT'LL BE FUN! LIKE CAMPING!
WE WOULDN'T LAST TWO DAYS!!
IS THIS BECAUSE OF THE STRAY?
I MEAN, YEAH, SHE ROUGHED ME UP A LITTLE, BUT YOU'RE OVER-REACTING.
IF SHE COMES BACK, WE'LL JUST CHASE HER OFF AGAIN.
HELLO?

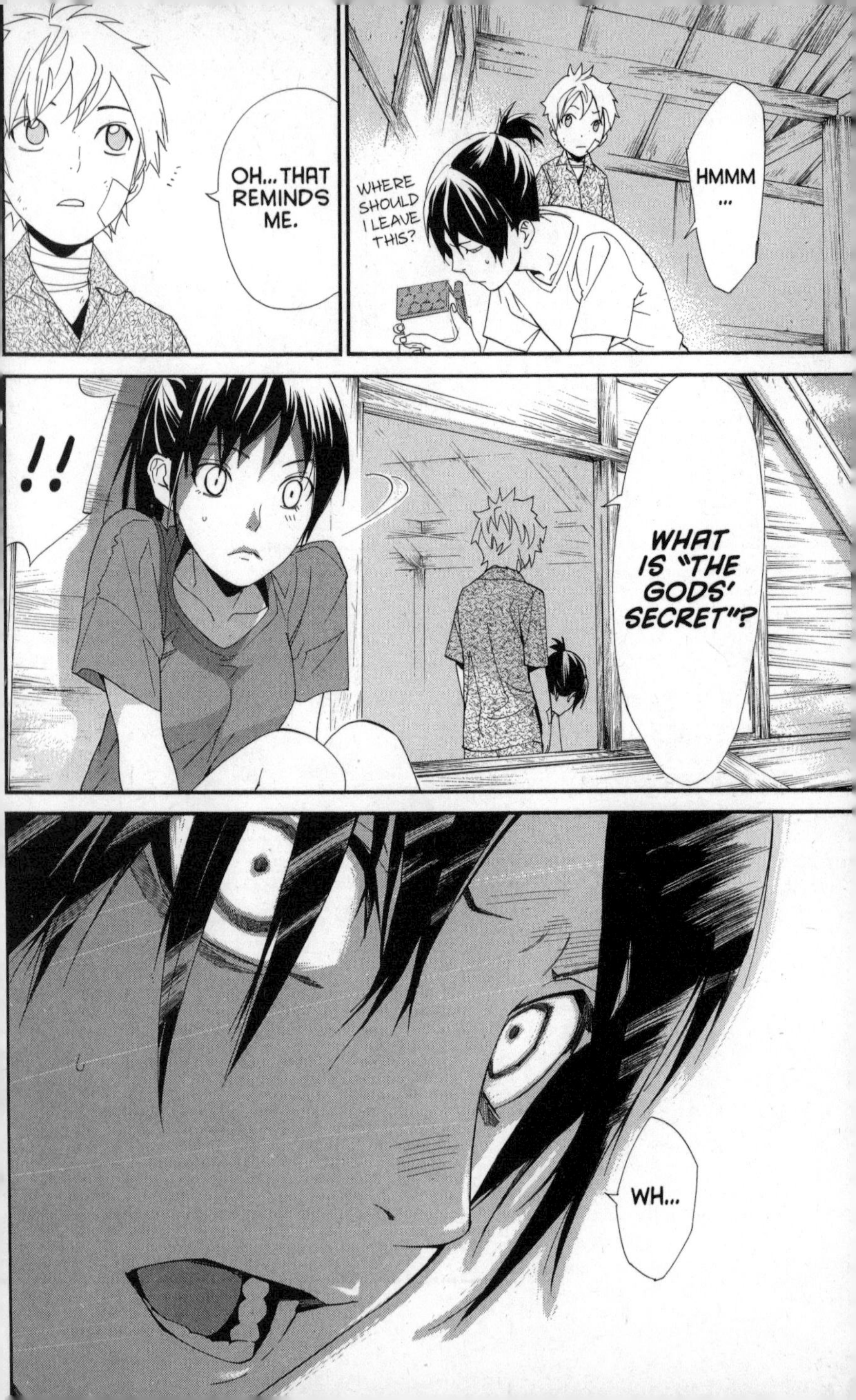
HMMM...
WHERE SHOULD I LEAVE THIS?
OH... THAT REMINDS ME.
WHAT IS "THE GODS' SECRET"?
!!
WH...

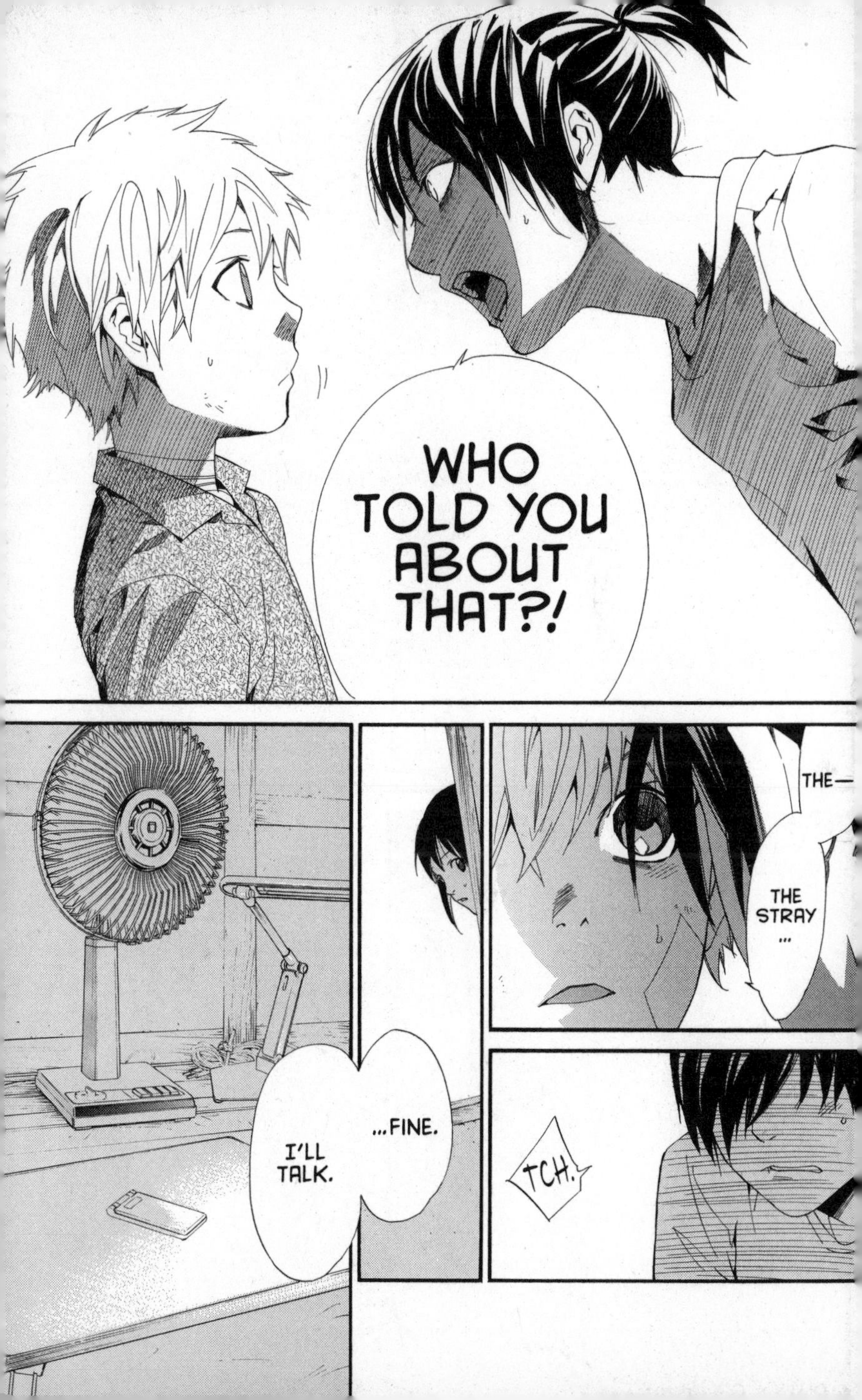
WHO TOLD YOU ABOUT THAT?!
THE—
THE STRAY ...
TCH.
...FINE.
I'LL TALK.

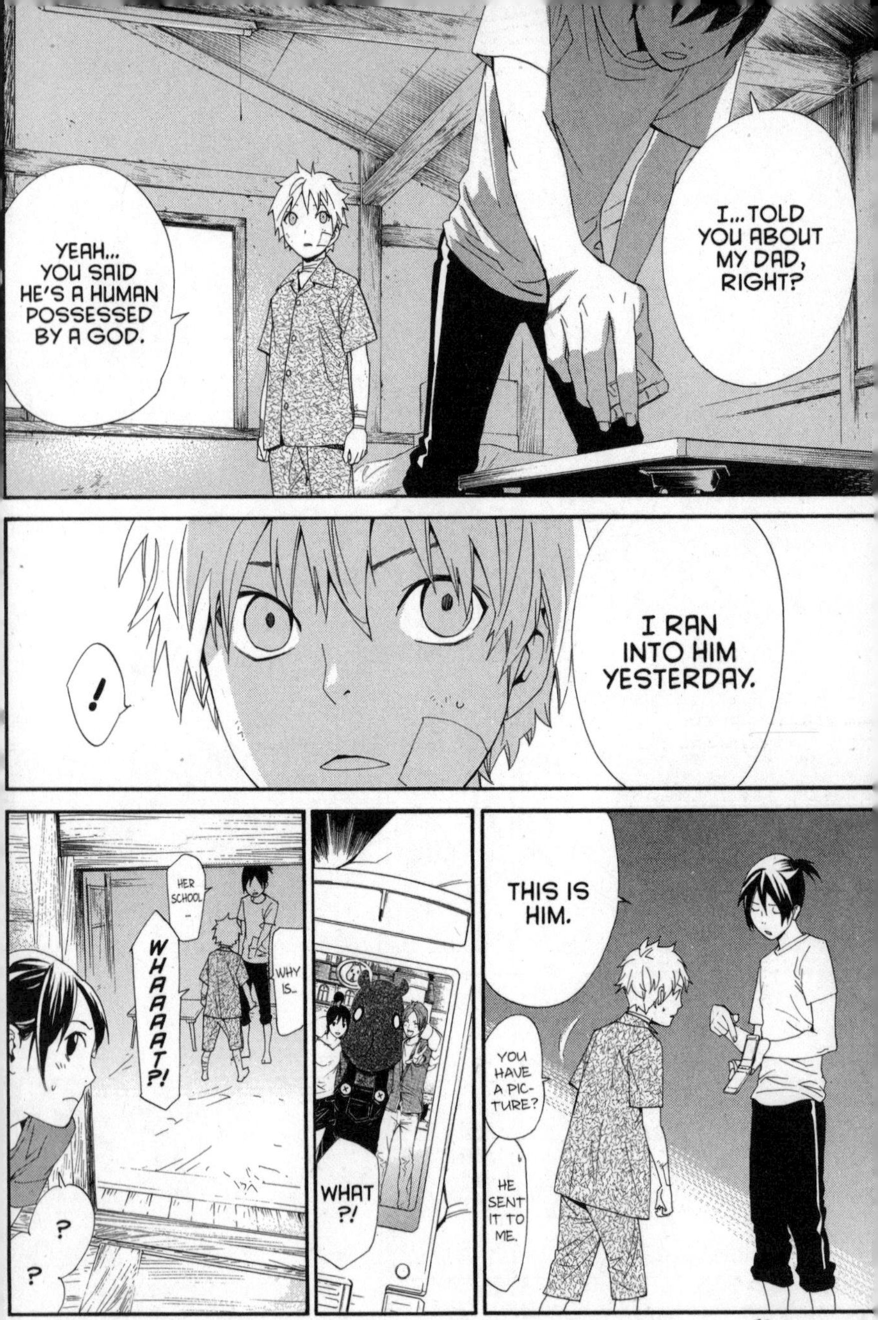
I...TOLD YOU ABOUT MY DAD, RIGHT?
YEAH... YOU SAID HE'S A HUMAN POSSESSED BY A GOD.
I RAN INTO HIM YESTERDAY.
!
THIS IS HIM.
YOU HAVE A PICTURE?
HE SENT IT TO ME.
WHAT?!
WHY IS..
HER SCHOOL...
WHAAAAAT?!
? ?

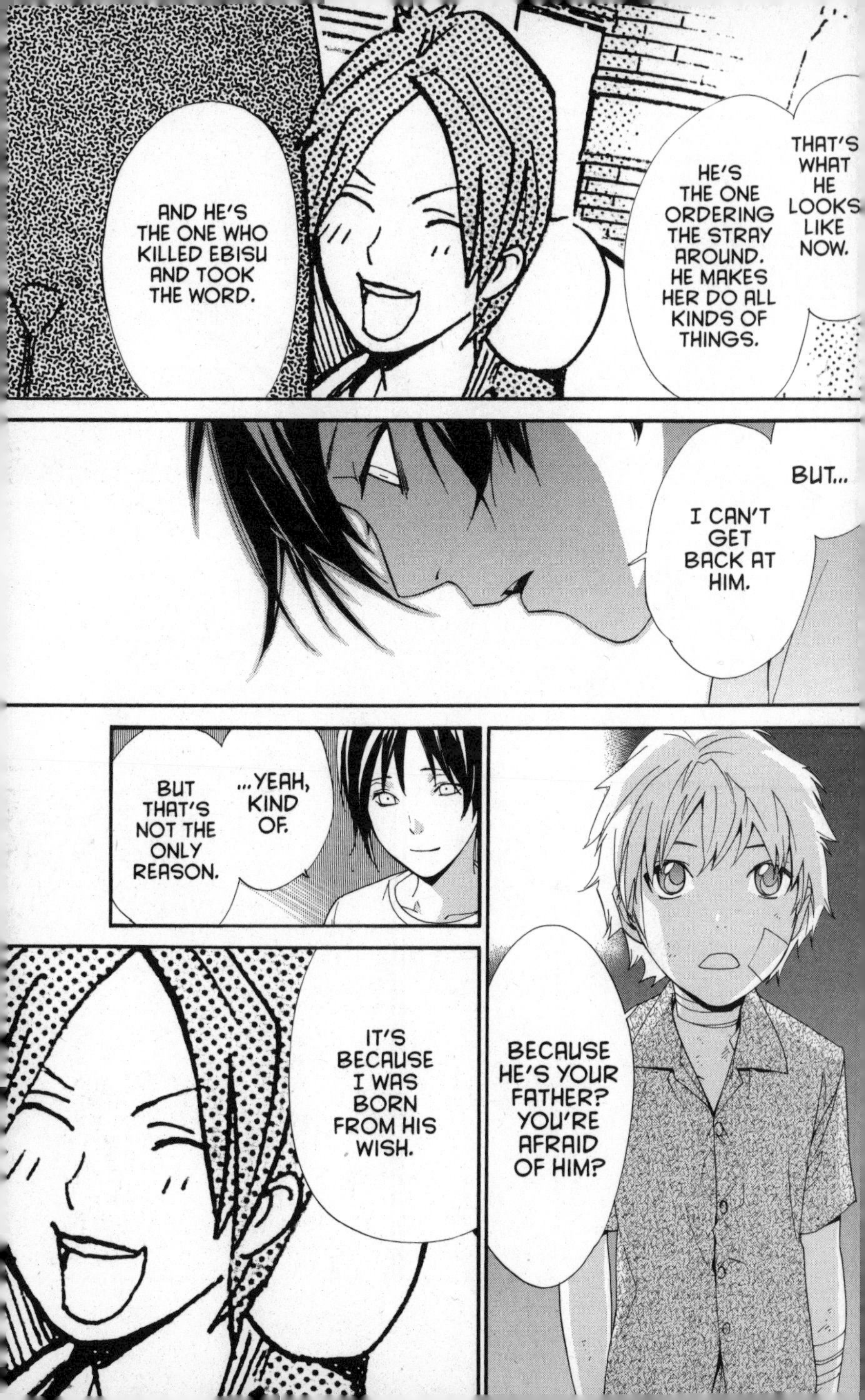
THAT'S WHAT HE LOOKS LIKE NOW.
HE'S THE ONE ORDERING THE STRAY AROUND. HE MAKES HER DO ALL KINDS OF THINGS.
AND HE'S THE ONE WHO KILLED EBISU AND TOOK THE WORD.
BUT...
I CAN'T GET BACK AT HIM.
BECAUSE HE'S YOUR FATHER? YOU'RE AFRAID OF HIM?
...YEAH, KIND OF.
BUT THAT'S NOT THE ONLY REASON.
IT'S BECAUSE I WAS BORN FROM HIS WISH.

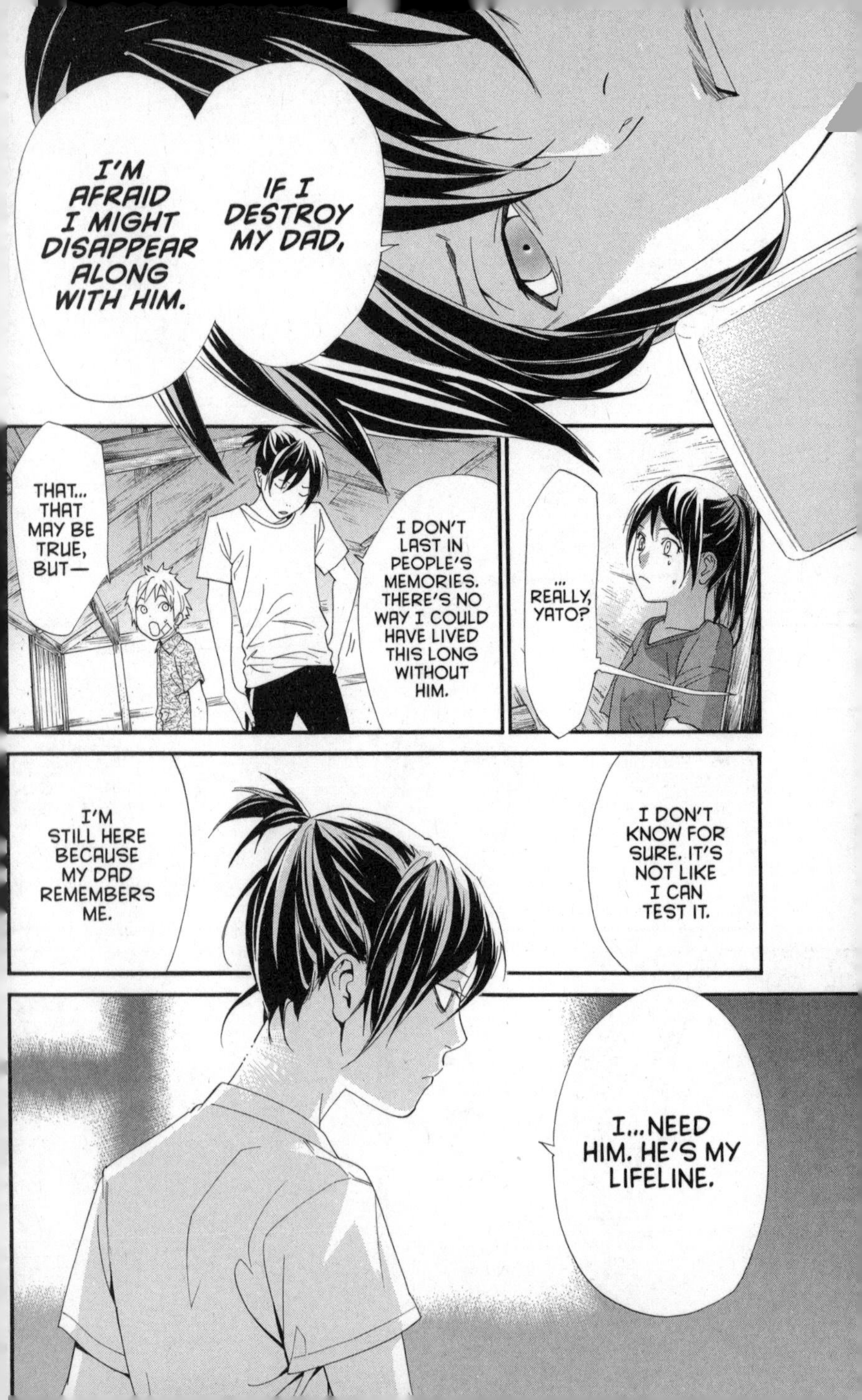
IF I DESTROY MY DAD,
I'M AFRAID I MIGHT DISAPPEAR ALONG WITH HIM.
...REALLY, YATO?
I DON'T LAST IN PEOPLE'S MEMORIES. THERE'S NO WAY I COULD HAVE LIVED THIS LONG WITHOUT HIM.
THAT... THAT MAY BE TRUE, BUT—
I DON'T KNOW FOR SURE. IT'S NOT LIKE I CAN TEST IT.
I'M STILL HERE BECAUSE MY DAD REMEMBERS ME.
I...NEED HIM. HE'S MY LIFELINE.

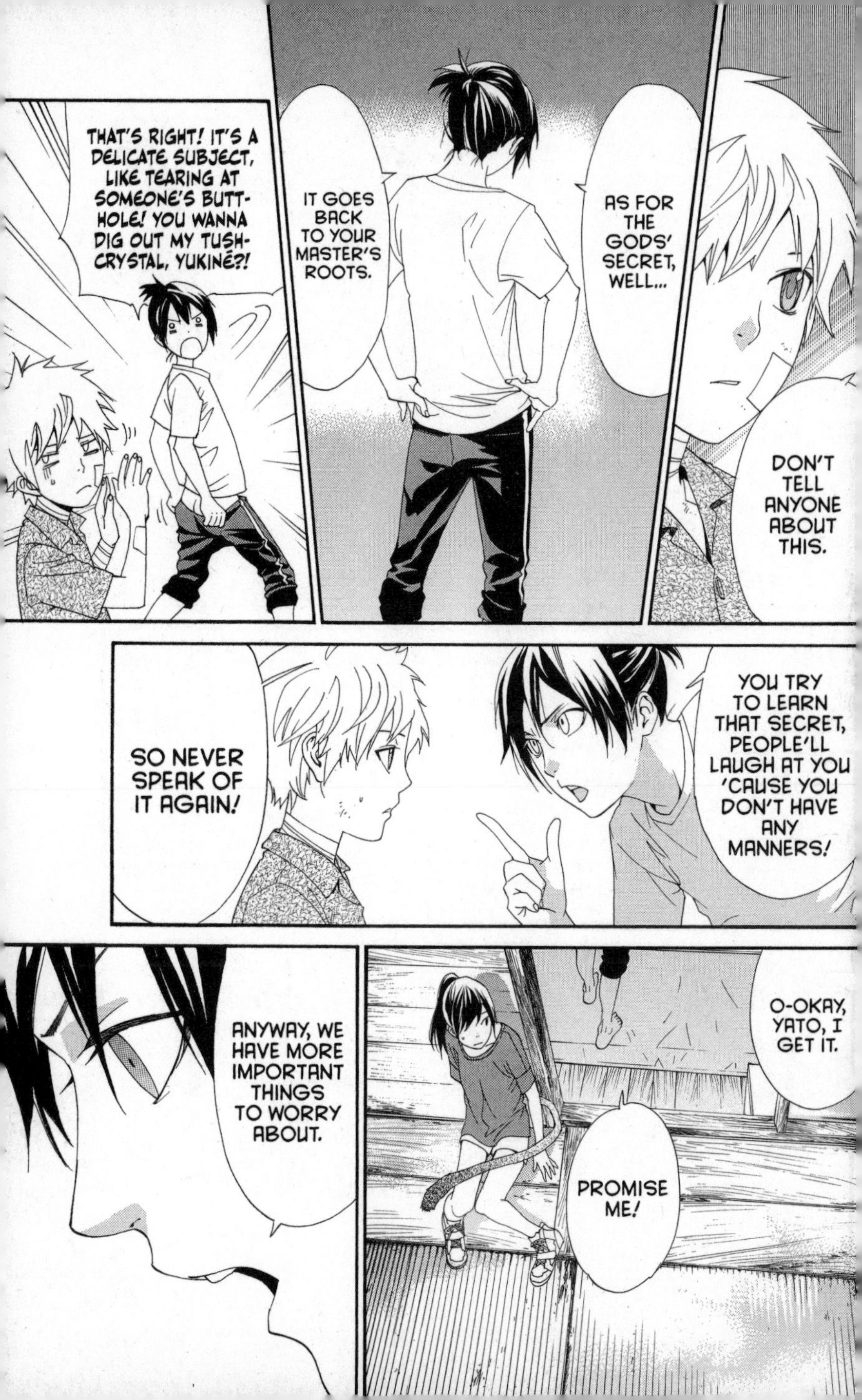
AS FOR THE GODS' SECRET, WELL...
DON'T TELL ANYONE ABOUT THIS.
IT GOES BACK TO YOUR MASTER'S ROOTS.
THAT'S RIGHT! IT'S A DELICATE SUBJECT, LIKE TEARING AT SOMEONE'S BUTT-HOLE! YOU WANNA DIG OUT MY TUSH-CRYSTAL, YUKINÉ?!
YOU TRY TO LEARN THAT SECRET, PEOPLE'LL LAUGH AT YOU 'CAUSE YOU DON'T HAVE ANY MANNERS!
SO NEVER SPEAK OF IT AGAIN!
O-OKAY, YATO, I GET IT.
PROMISE ME!
ANYWAY, WE HAVE MORE IMPORTANT THINGS TO WORRY ABOUT.

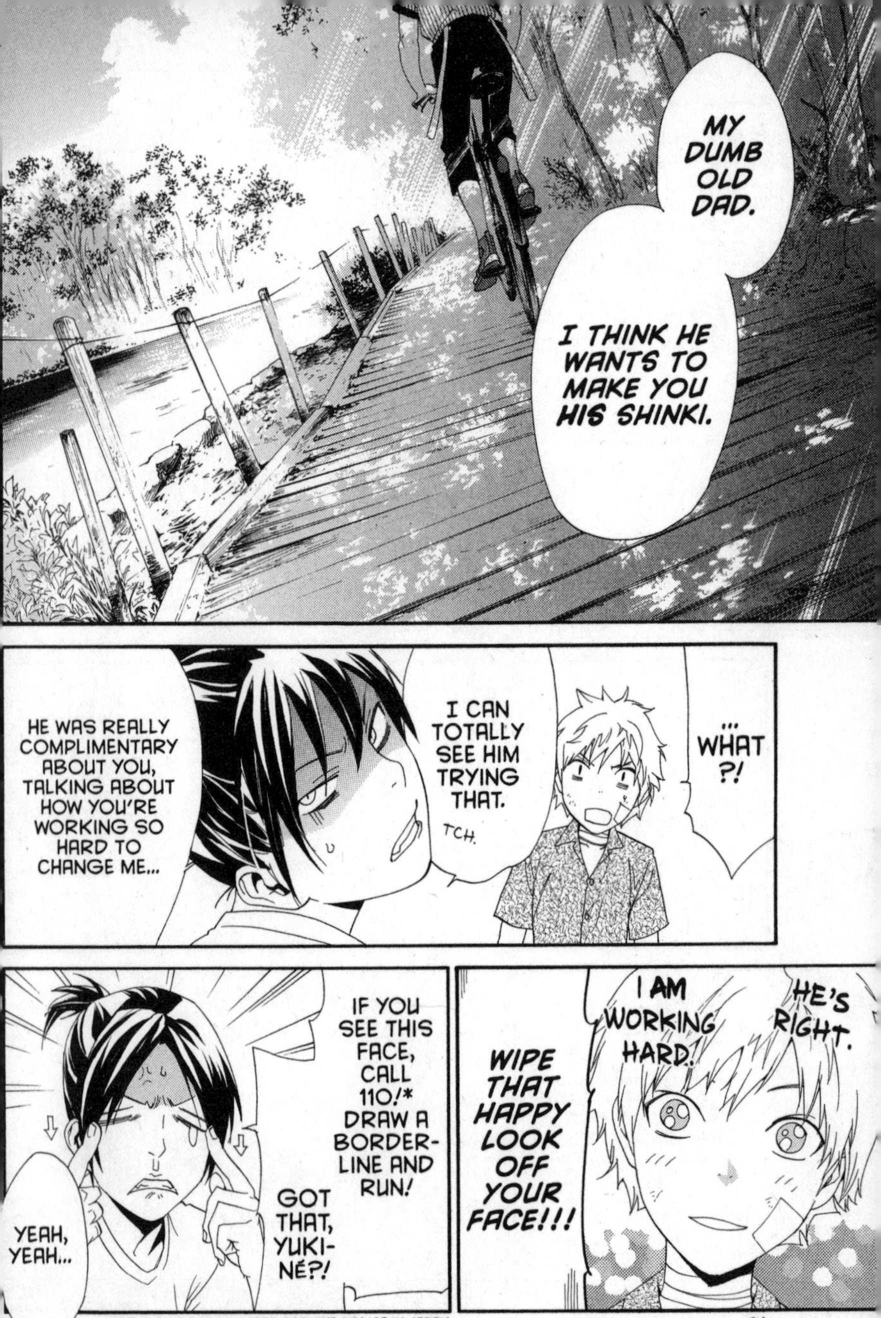
MY DUMB OLD DAD.
I THINK HE WANTS TO MAKE YOU HIS SHINKI.
...WHAT?!
I CAN TOTALLY SEE HIM TRYING THAT.
TCH.
HE WAS REALLY COMPLIMENTARY ABOUT YOU, TALKING ABOUT HOW YOU'RE WORKING SO HARD TO CHANGE ME...
HE'S RIGHT.
I AM WORKING HARD.
WIPE THAT HAPPY LOOK OFF YOUR FACE!!!
IF YOU SEE THIS FACE, CALL 110!* DRAW A BORDER-LINE AND RUN!
GOT THAT, YUKI-NÉ?!
YEAH, YEAH...

*THE EMERGENCY NUMBER FOR THE POLICE IN JAPAN.

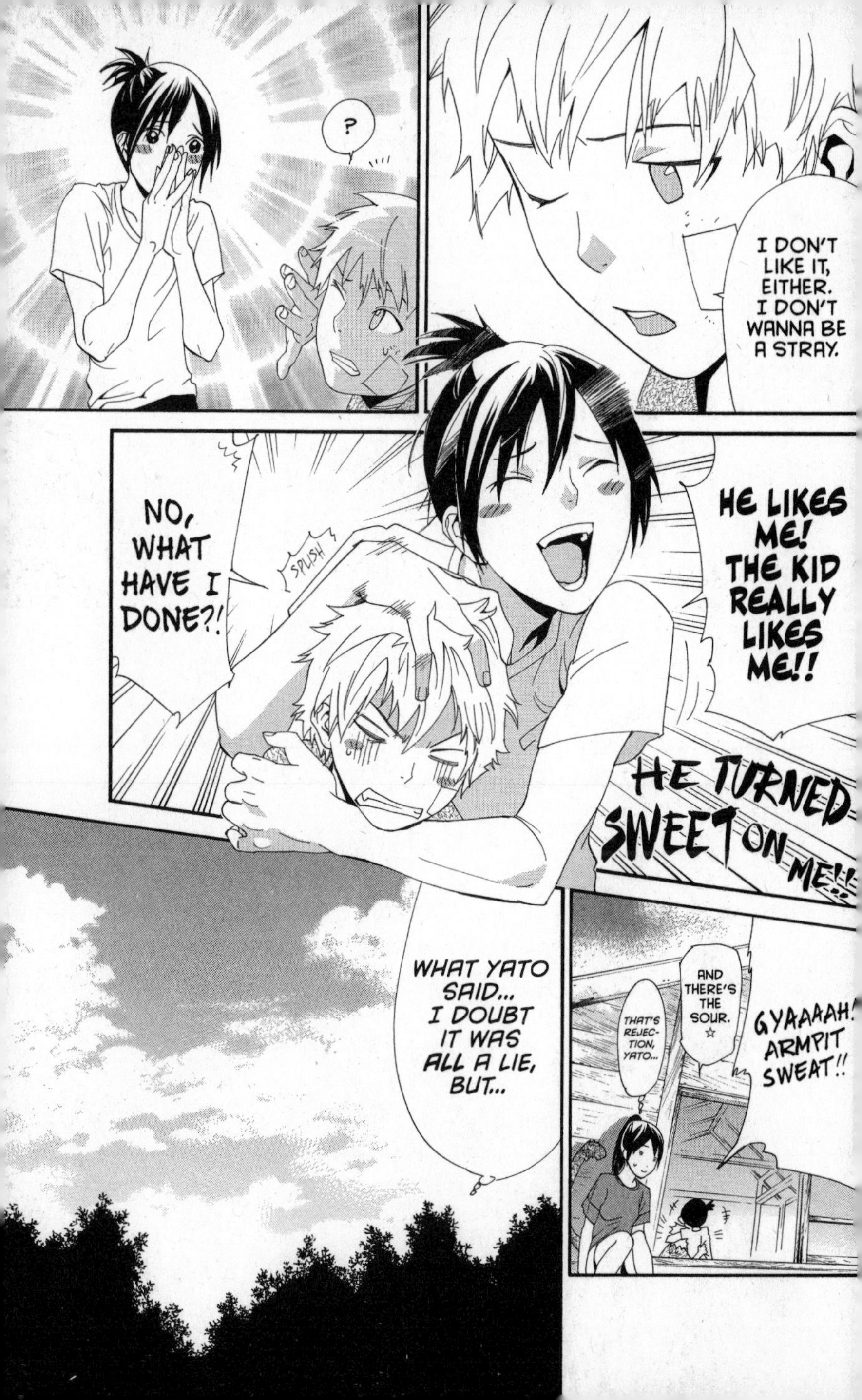
I DON'T LIKE IT, EITHER. I DON'T WANNA BE A STRAY.
?
HE LIKES ME! THE KID REALLY LIKES ME!!
NO, WHAT HAVE I DONE?!
SPLISH
HE TURNED SWEET ON ME!!
GYAAAAH! ARMPIT SWEAT!!
AND THERE'S THE SOUR. ☆
THAT'S REJECTION, YATO...
WHAT YATO SAID... I DOUBT IT WAS ALL A LIE, BUT...

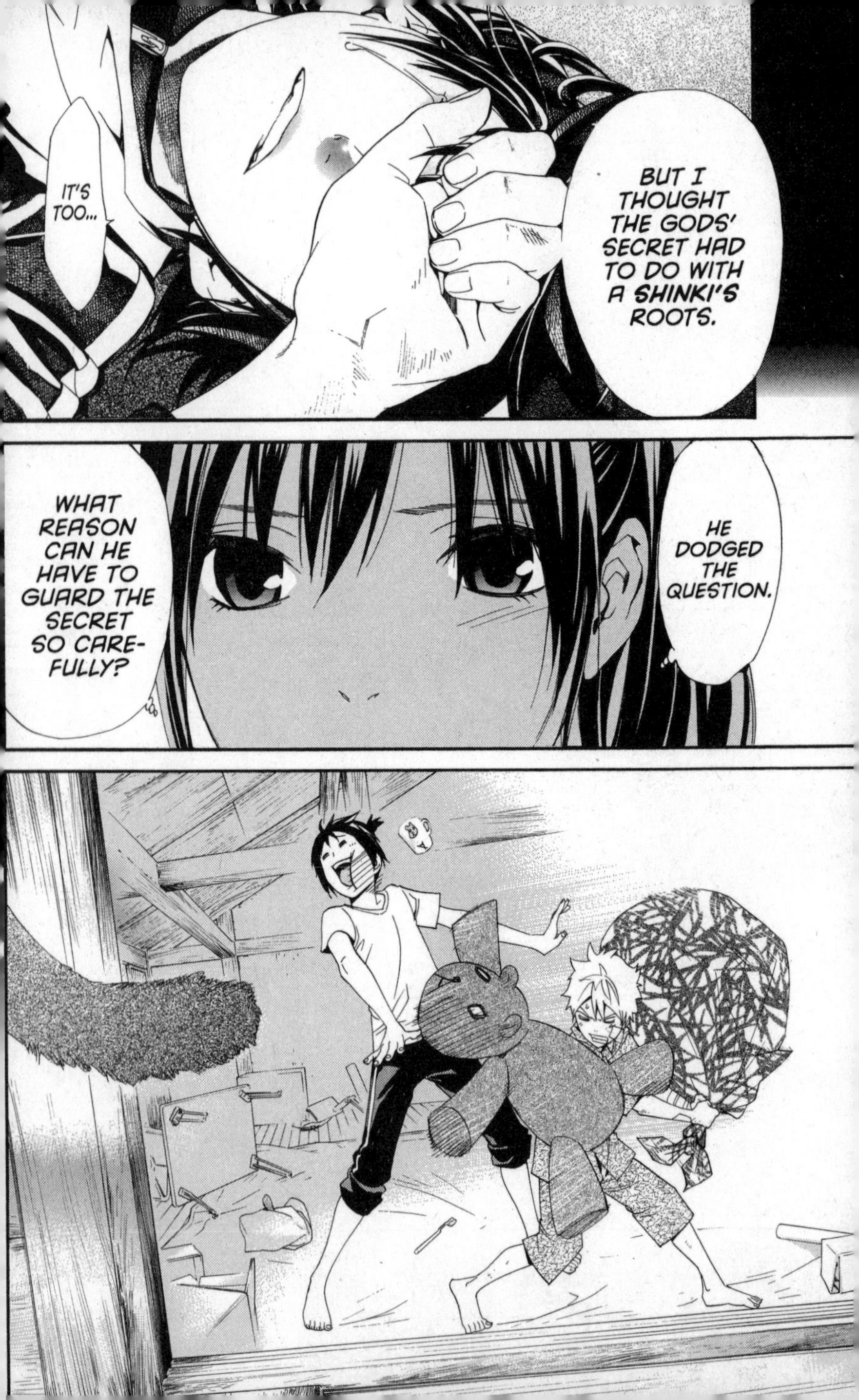
BUT I THOUGHT THE GODS' SECRET HAD TO DO WITH A SHINKI'S ROOTS.
IT'S TOO...
HE DODGED THE QUESTION.
WHAT REASON CAN HE HAVE TO GUARD THE SECRET SO CARE-FULLY?

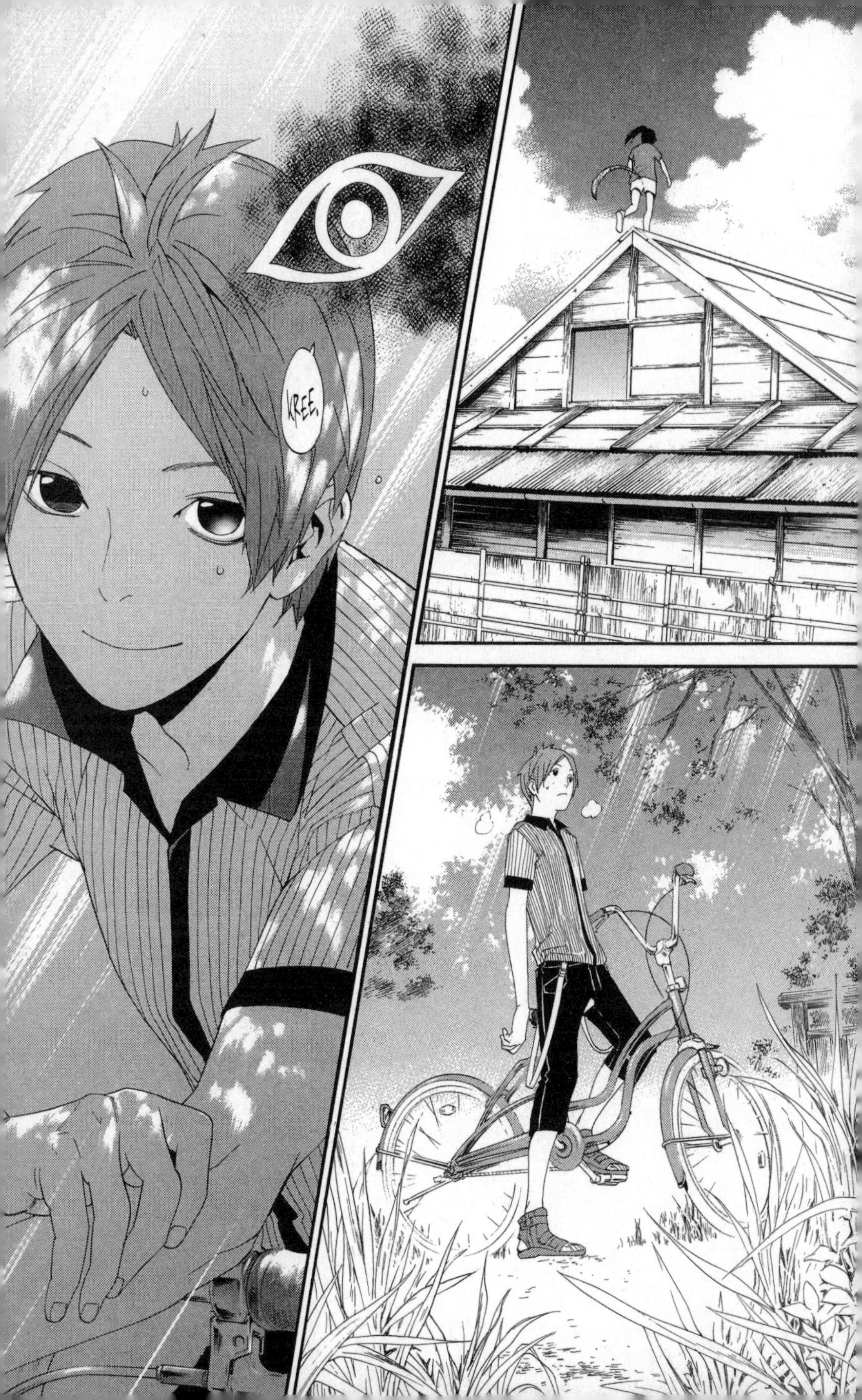
KREE,

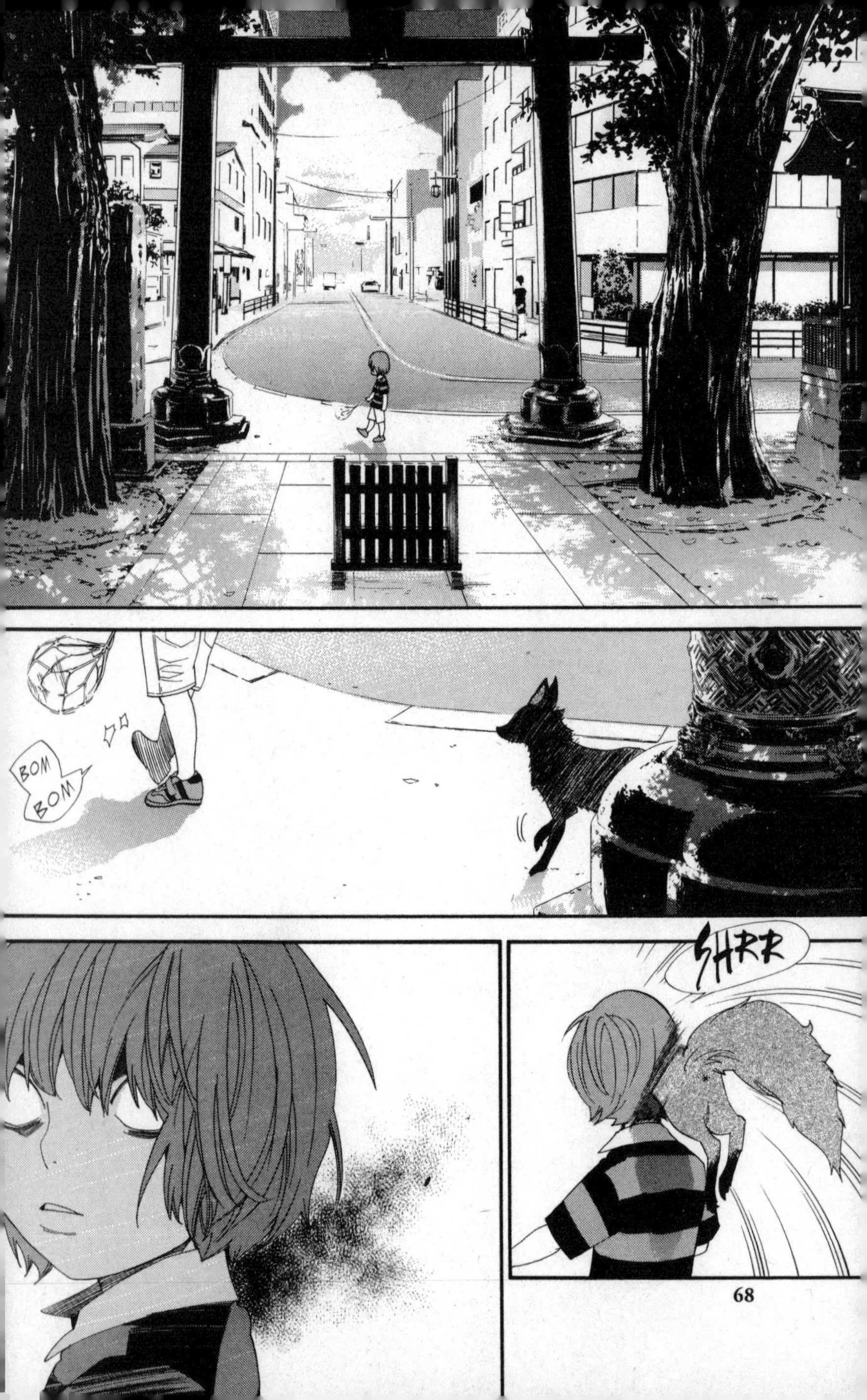
BOM BOM
SHRR

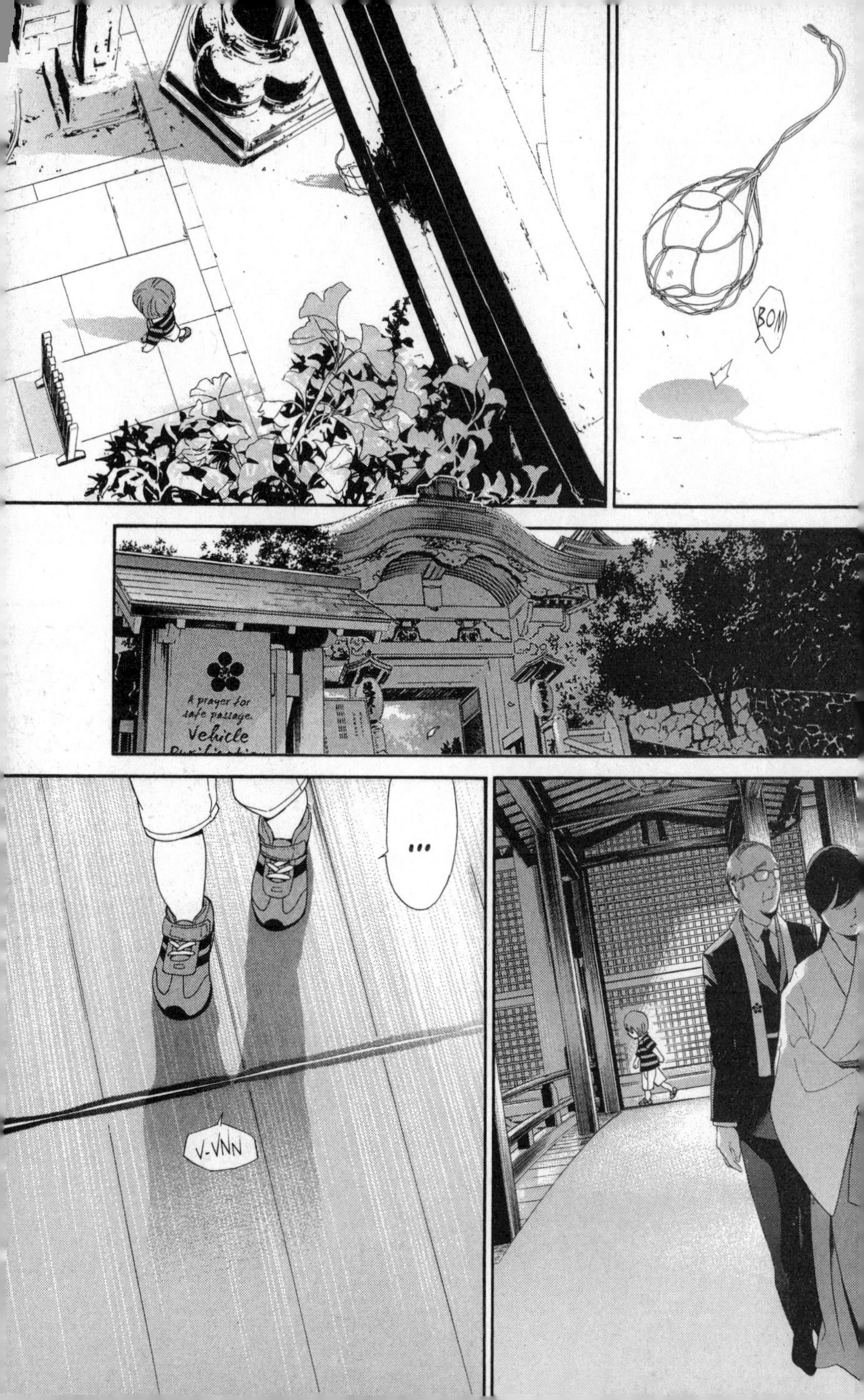
BOM
A prayer for safe passage.
Vehicle
...
V-VNN

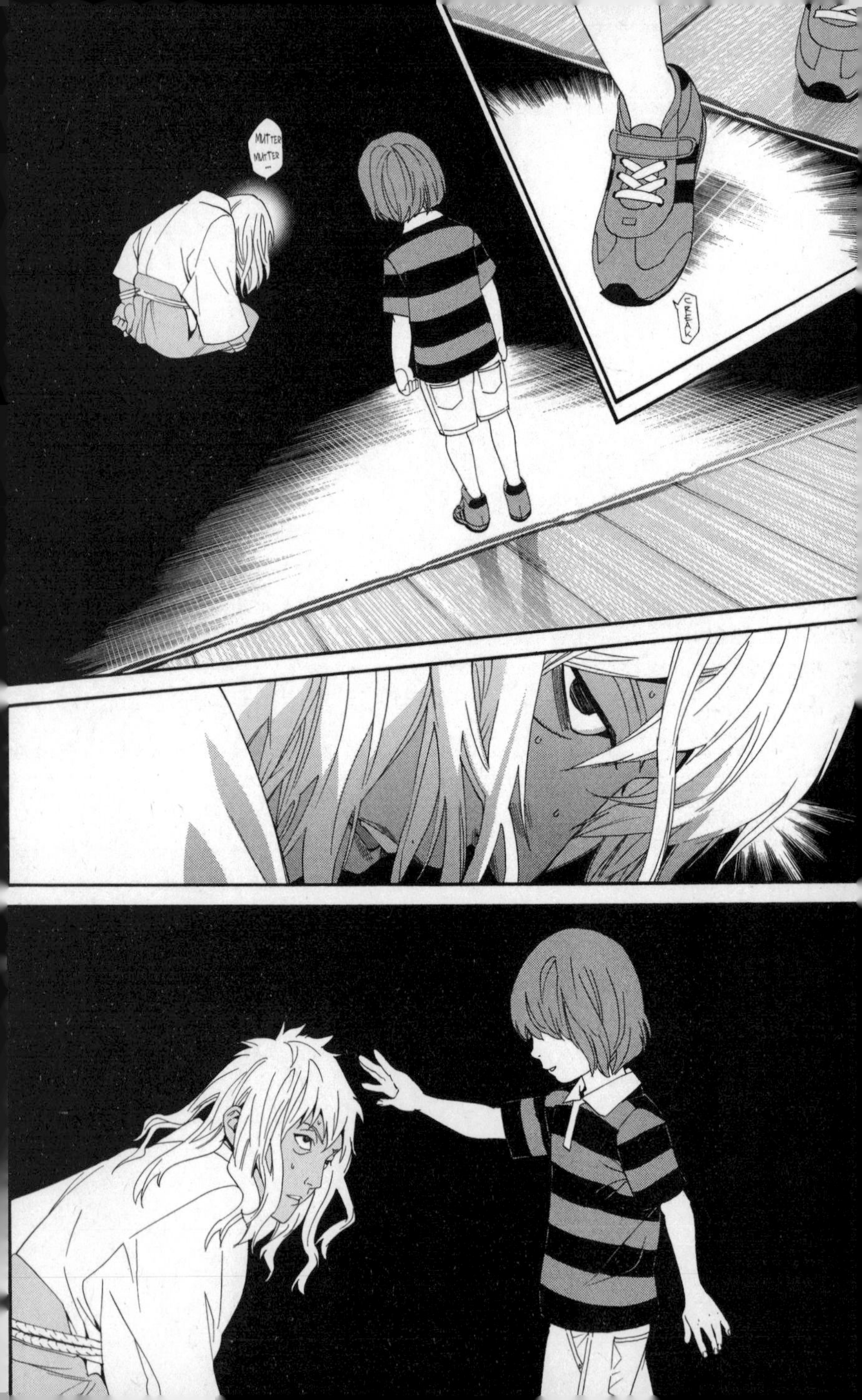
CREAK
MUTTER MUTTER ...

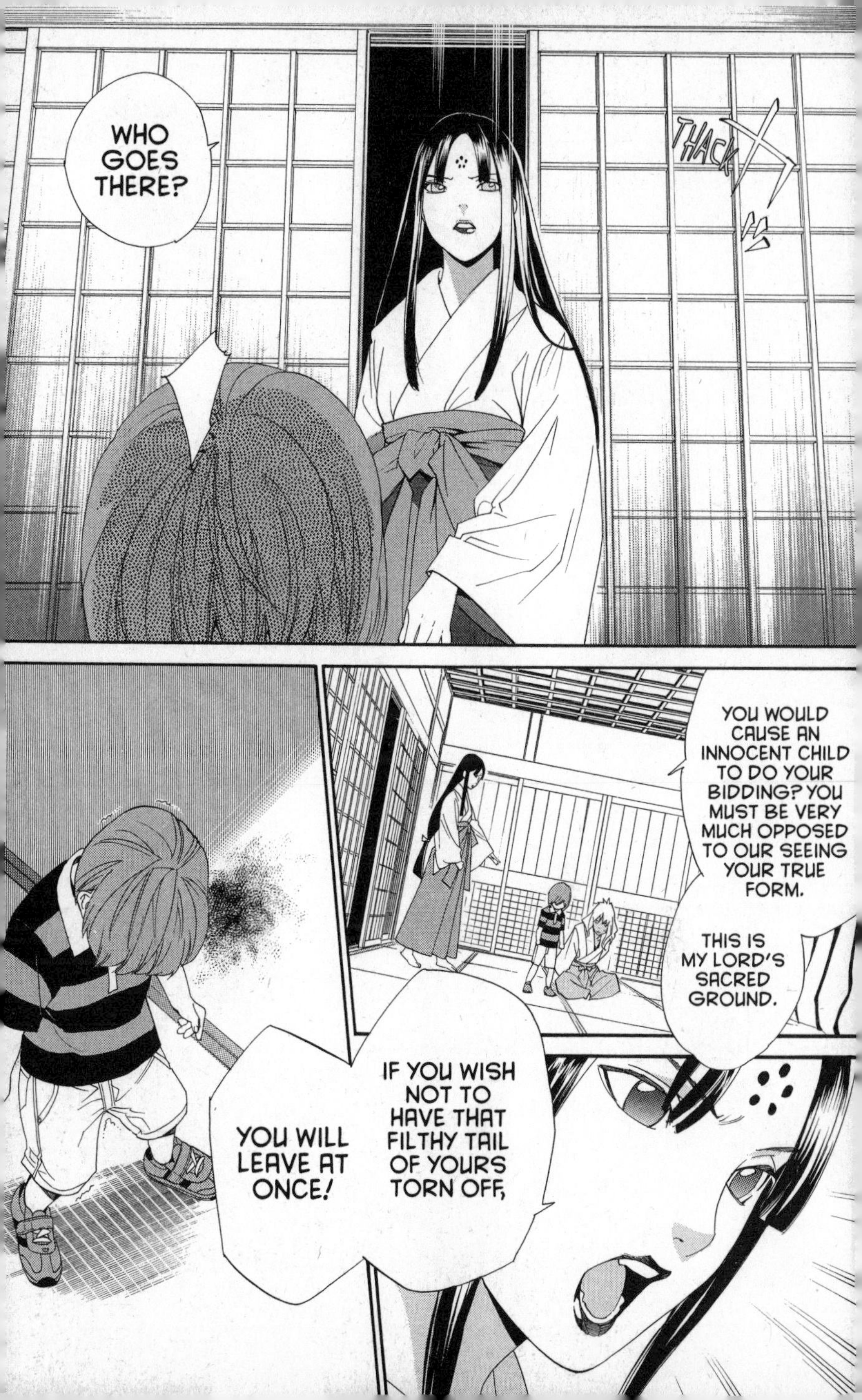
THACK
WHO GOES THERE?
YOU WOULD CAUSE AN INNOCENT CHILD TO DO YOUR BIDDING? YOU MUST BE VERY MUCH OPPOSED TO OUR SEEING YOUR TRUE FORM.
THIS IS MY LORD'S SACRED GROUND.
IF YOU WISH NOT TO HAVE THAT FILTHY TAIL OF YOURS TORN OFF,
YOU WILL LEAVE AT ONCE!

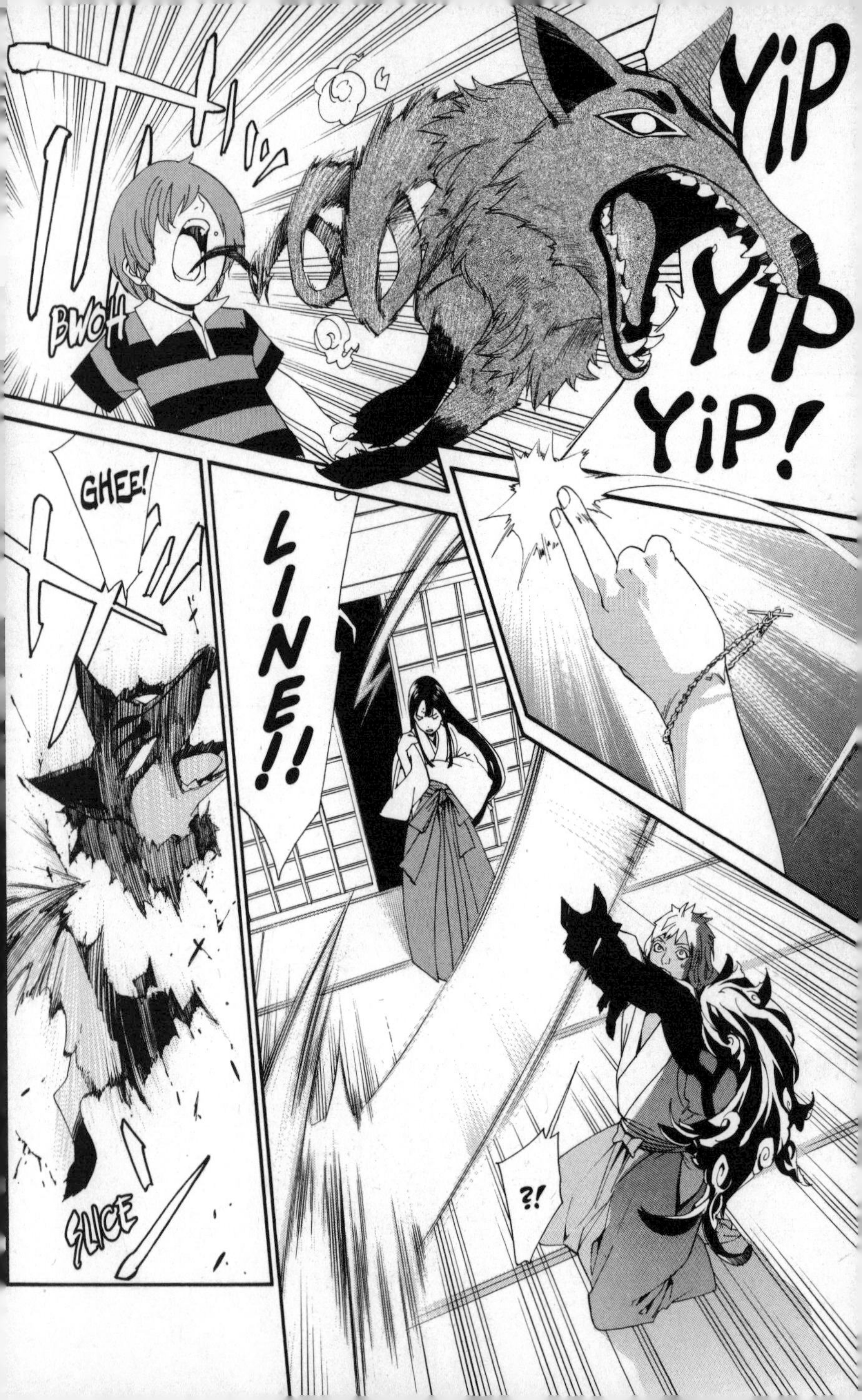
YIP
YIP
YIP!
BWOH
LINE!!
?!
GHEE!
SLICE

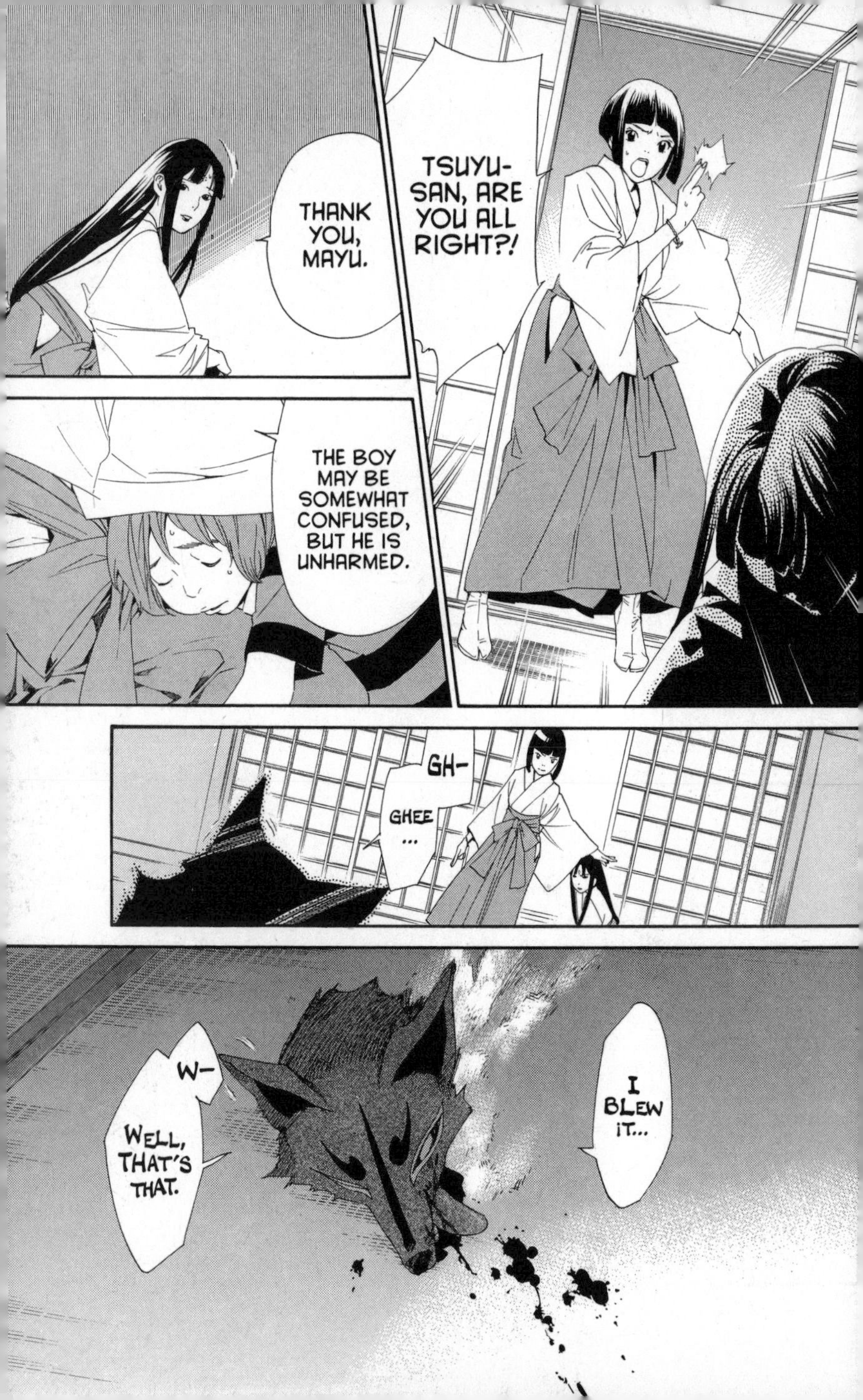
TSUYU-SAN, ARE YOU ALL RIGHT?!
THANK YOU, MAYU.
THE BOY MAY BE SOMEWHAT CONFUSED, BUT HE IS UNHARMED.
GH-
GHEE...
I BLEW IT...
W-
WELL, THAT'S THAT.

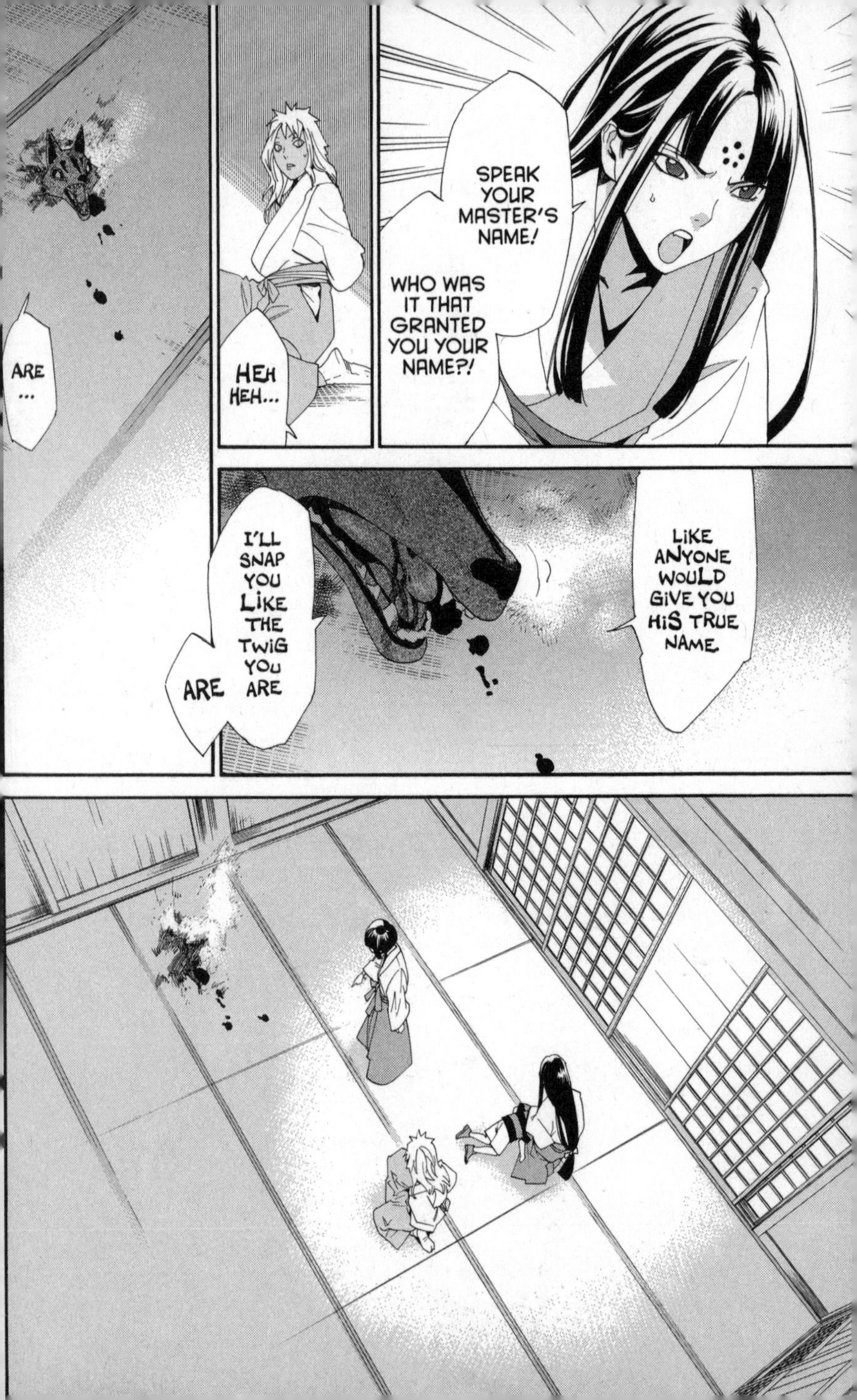
SPEAK YOUR MASTER'S NAME!
WHO WAS IT THAT GRANTED YOU YOUR NAME?!
HEH HEH...
LIKE ANYONE WOULD GIVE YOU HIS TRUE NAME
I'LL SNAP YOU LIKE THE TWIG YOU ARE
ARE
ARE ...

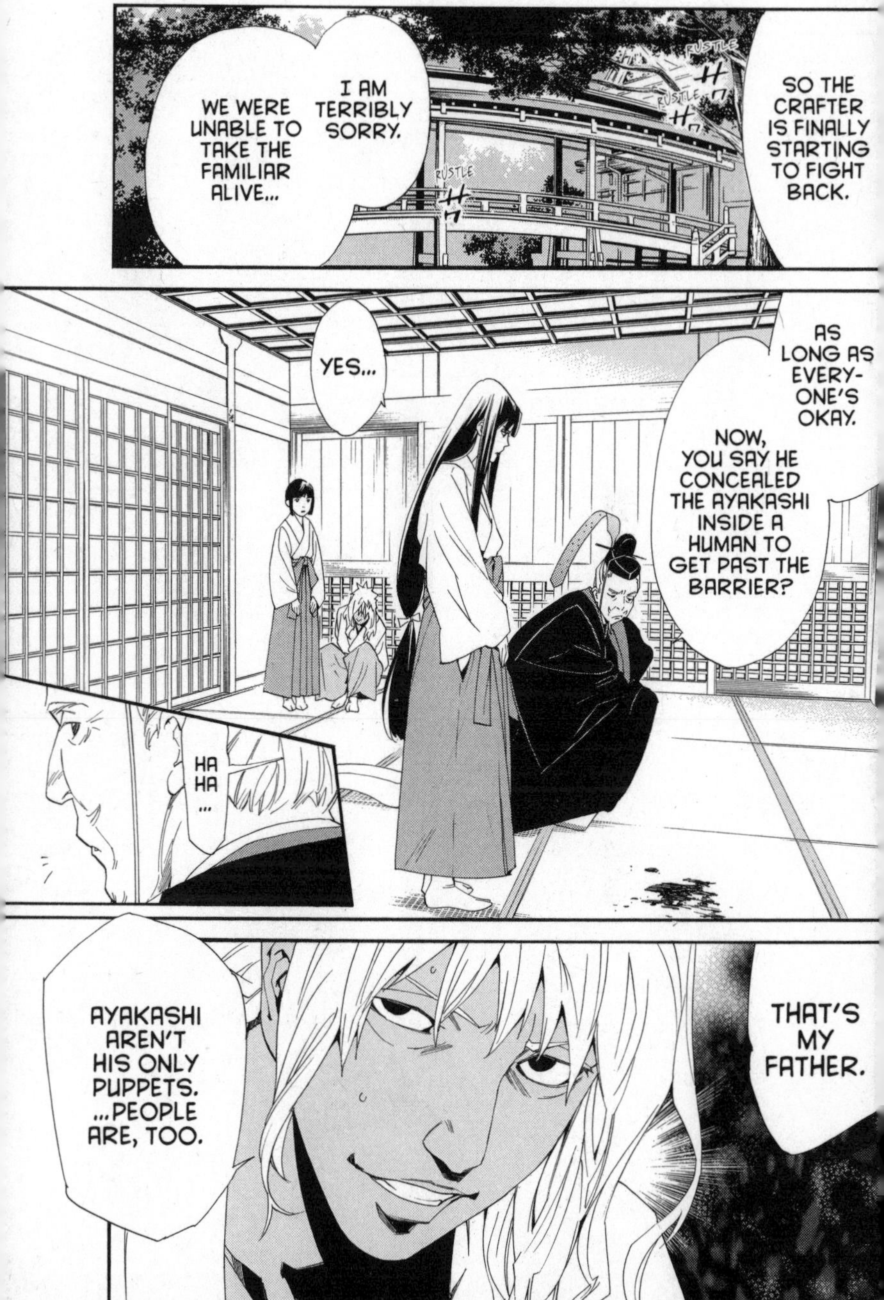
SO THE CRAFTER IS FINALLY STARTING TO FIGHT BACK.
RUSTLE
RUSTLE
I AM TERRIBLY SORRY.
WE WERE UNABLE TO TAKE THE FAMILIAR ALIVE...
RUSTLE
AS LONG AS EVERYONE'S OKAY.
NOW, YOU SAY HE CONCEALED THE AYAKASHI INSIDE A HUMAN TO GET PAST THE BARRIER?
YES...
HA HA ...
THAT'S MY FATHER.
AYAKASHI AREN'T HIS ONLY PUPPETS. ...PEOPLE ARE, TOO.

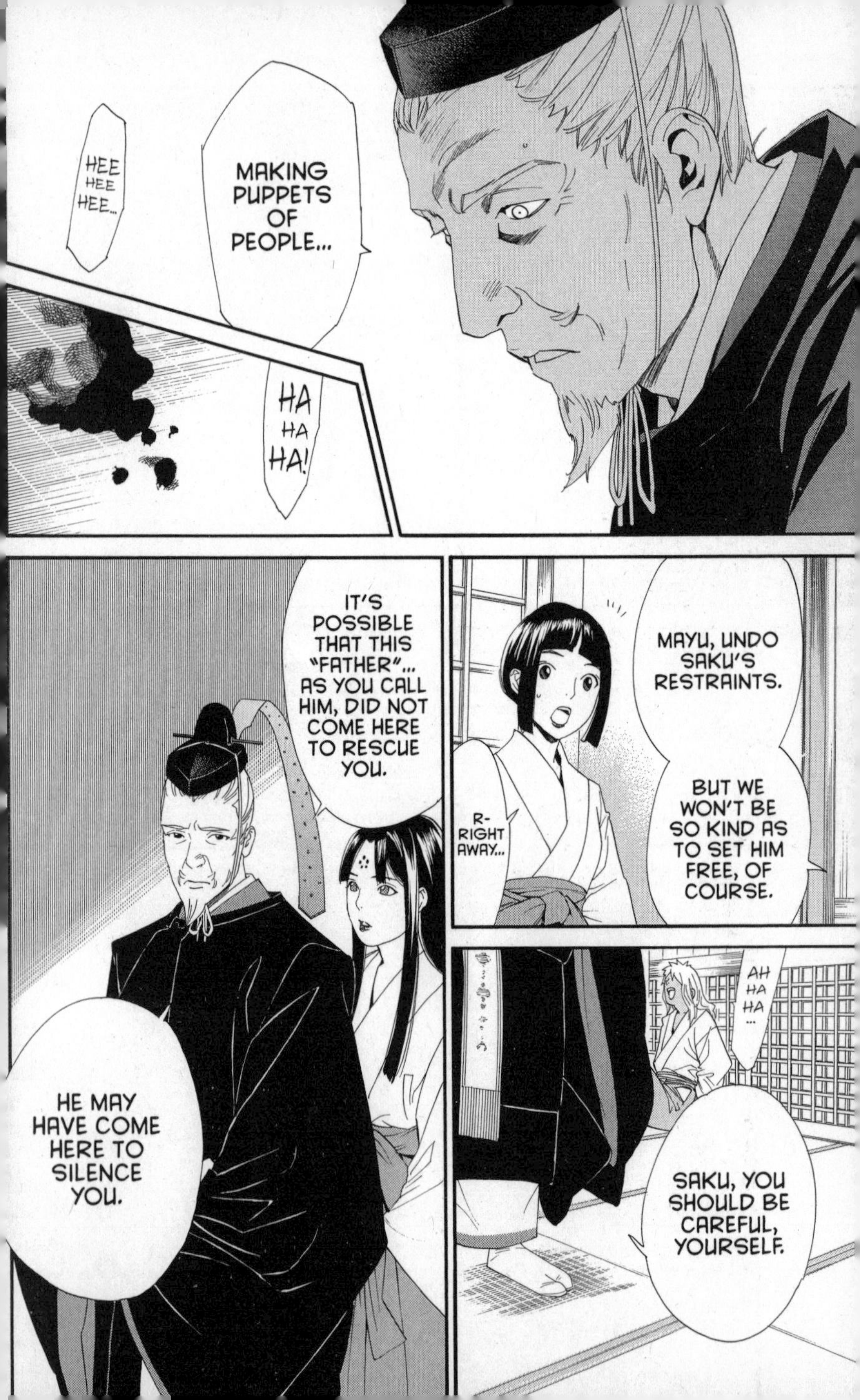
MAKING PUPPETS OF PEOPLE...
HEE HEE HEE...
HA HA HA!
MAYU, UNDO SAKU'S RESTRAINTS.
BUT WE WON'T BE SO KIND AS TO SET HIM FREE, OF COURSE.
R-RIGHT AWAY...
AH HA HA...
SAKU, YOU SHOULD BE CAREFUL, YOURSELF.
IT'S POSSIBLE THAT THIS "FATHER"... AS YOU CALL HIM, DID NOT COME HERE TO RESCUE YOU.
HE MAY HAVE COME HERE TO SILENCE YOU.

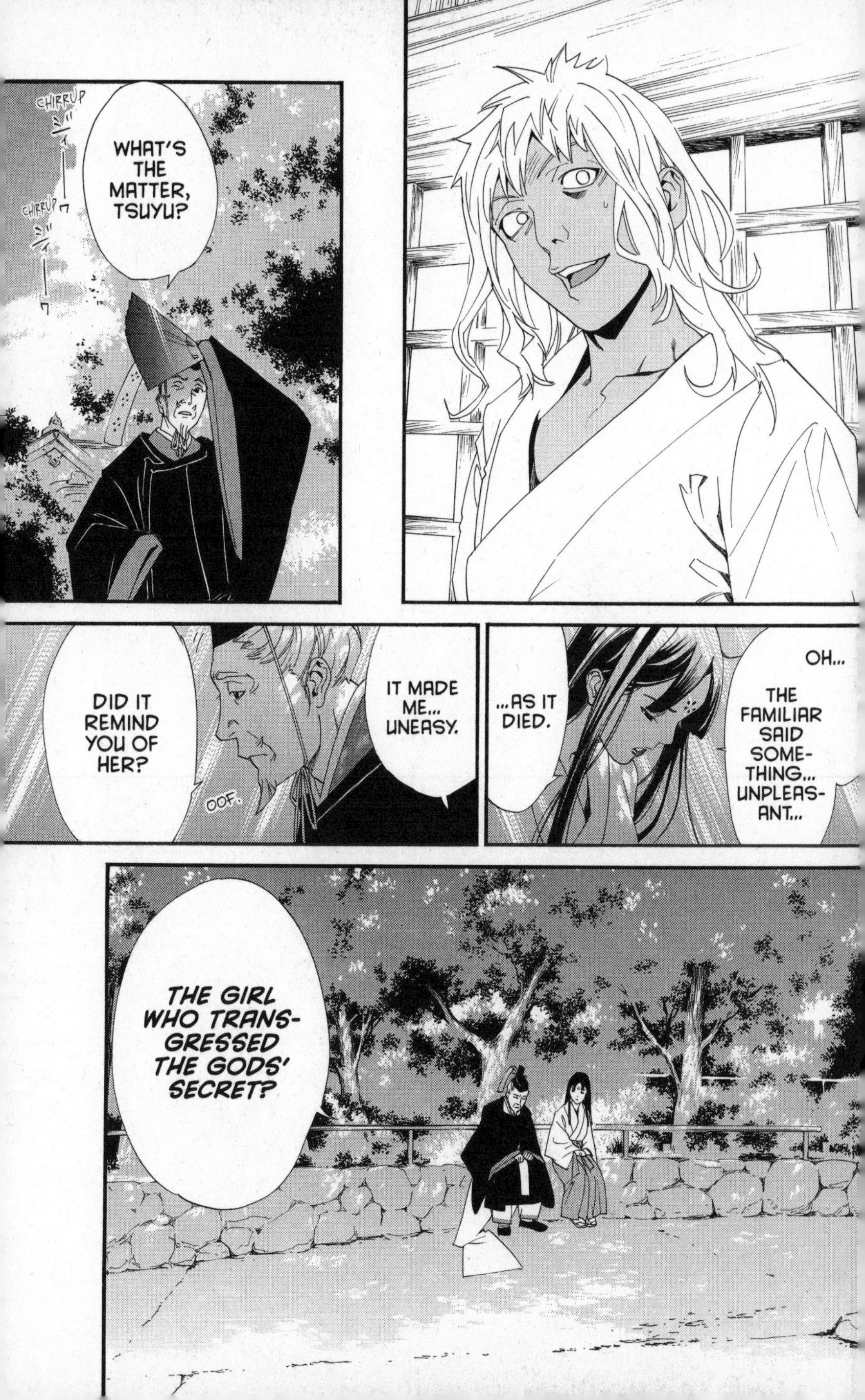
CHIRRUP
CHIRRUP
WHAT'S THE MATTER, TSUYU?
OH...
THE FAMILIAR SAID SOMETHING... UNPLEASANT...
...AS IT DIED.
IT MADE ME... UNEASY.
DID IT REMIND YOU OF HER?
OOF.
THE GIRL WHO TRANSGRESSED THE GODS' SECRET?

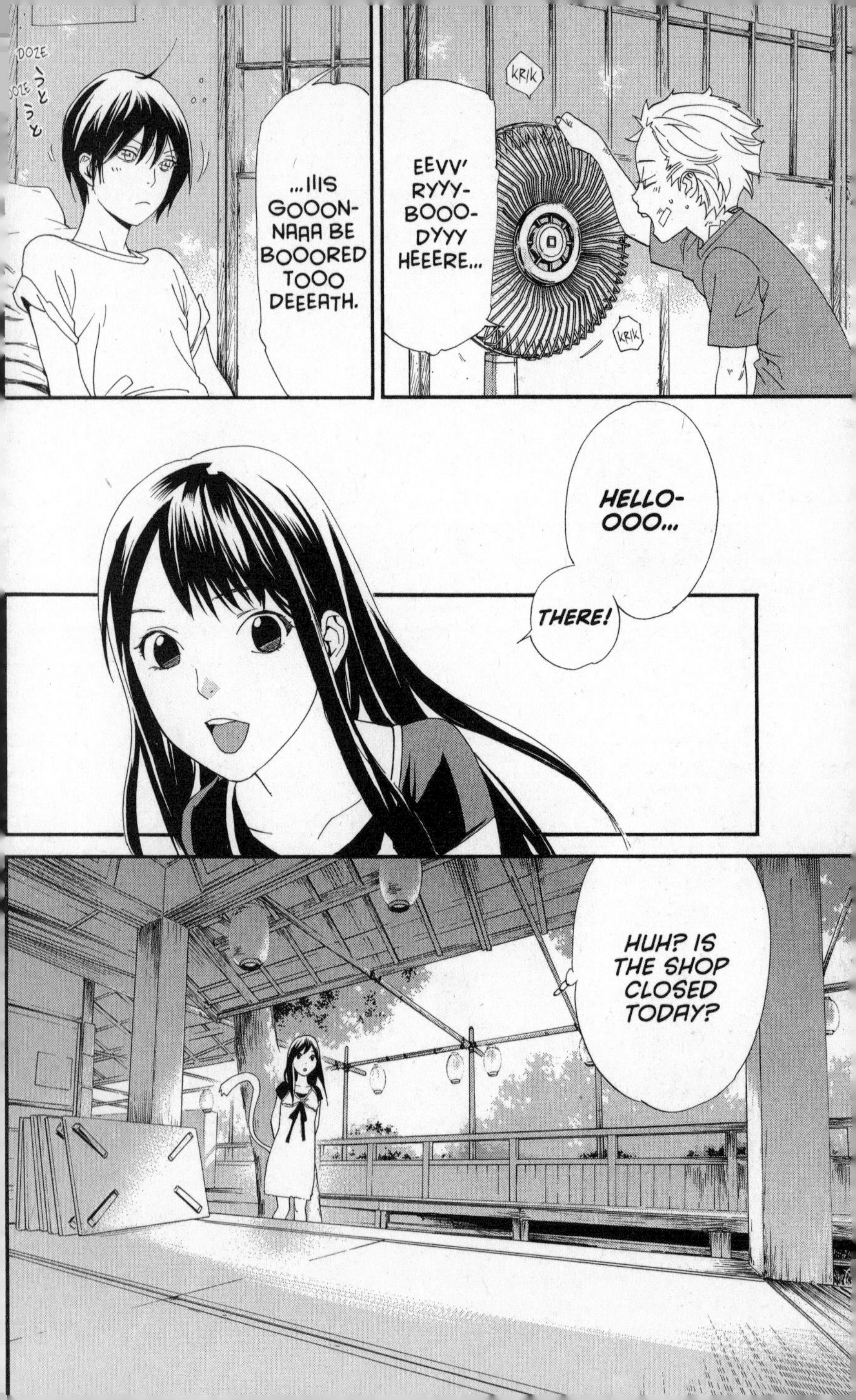
KRIK
EEVV' RYYY- BOOO- DYYY HEEERE...
KRIK
...IIIS GOOON- NAAA BE BOOORED TOOO DEEEATH.
DOZE DOZE
うとうと
HELLO- OOO...
THERE!
HUH? IS THE SHOP CLOSED TODAY?

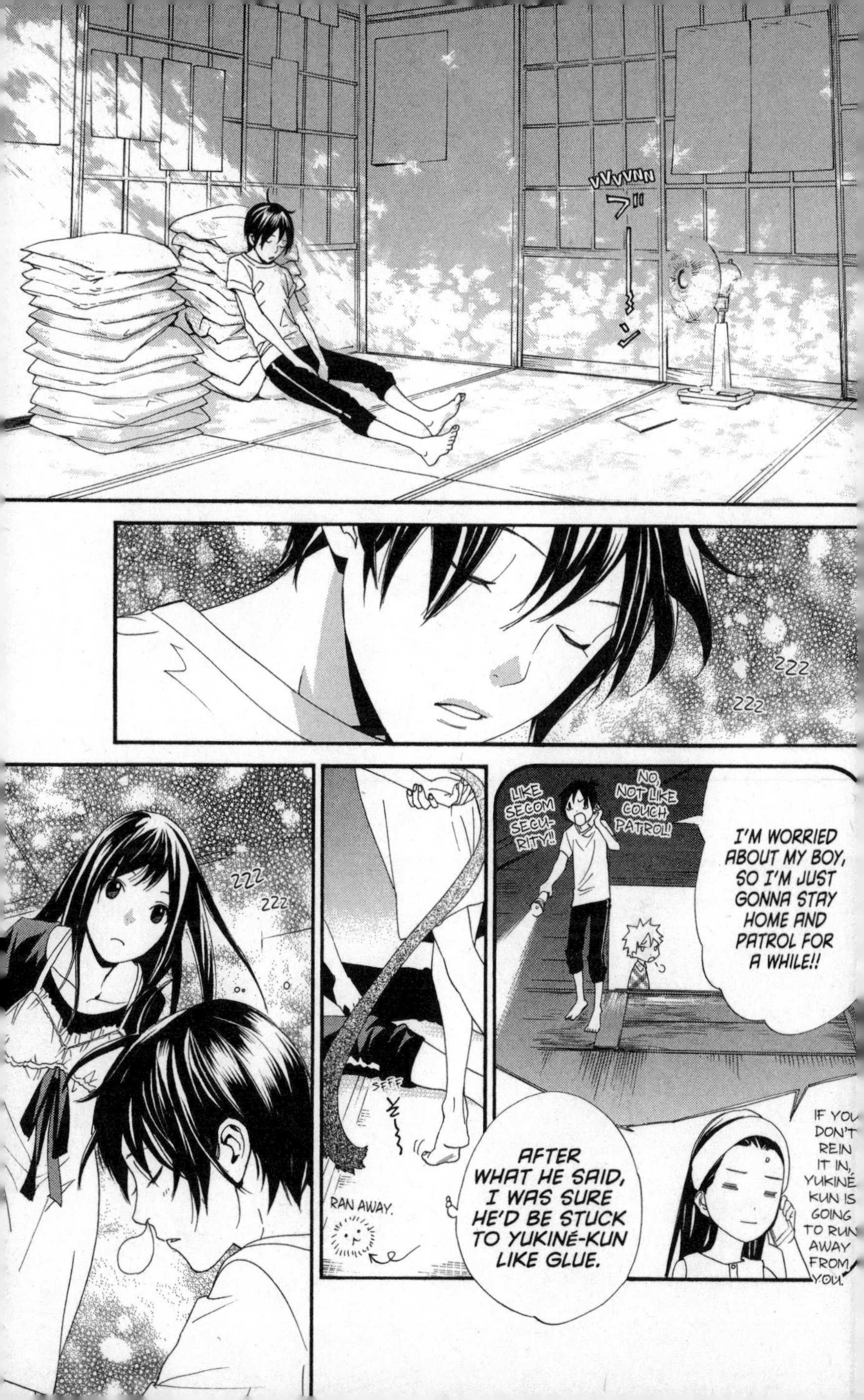
VVVVNN
ZZZ
ZZZ
I'M WORRIED ABOUT MY BOY, SO I'M JUST GONNA STAY HOME AND PATROL FOR A WHILE!!
NO, NOT LIKE COUCH PATROL!!
LIKE SECOM SECU-RITY!!
IF YOU DON'T REIN IT IN, YUKINÉ-KUN IS GOING TO RUN AWAY FROM YOU.
AFTER WHAT HE SAID, I WAS SURE HE'D BE STUCK TO YUKINÉ-KUN LIKE GLUE.
SFFF
RAN AWAY.
ZZZ
ZZZ

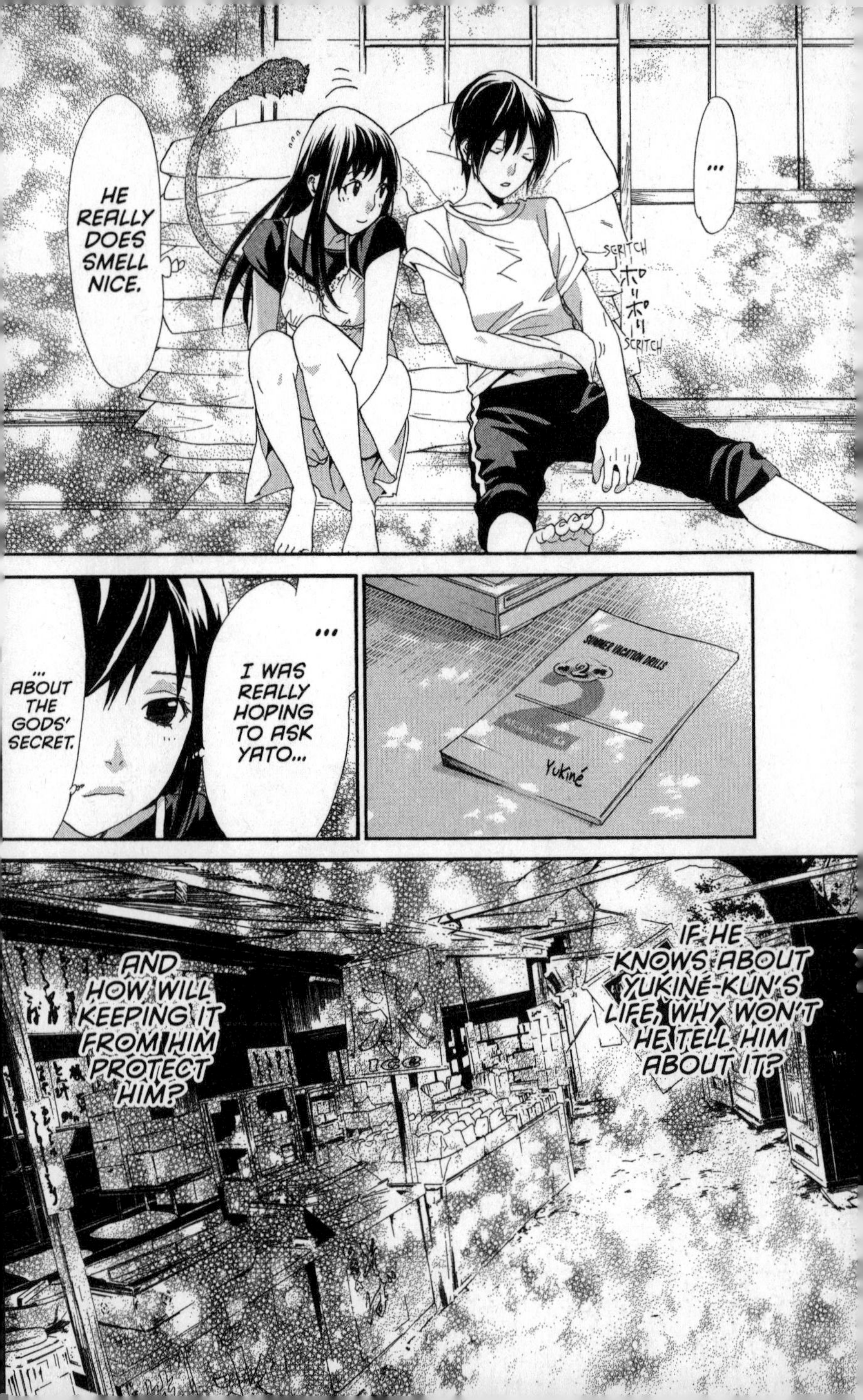
...
SCRITCH ポリポリ SCRITCH
HE REALLY DOES SMELL NICE.
SUMMER VACATION DRILLS
2
Yukiné
...
I WAS REALLY HOPING TO ASK YATO...
... ABOUT THE GODS' SECRET.
IF HE KNOWS ABOUT YUKINÉ-KUN'S LIFE, WHY WON'T HE TELL HIM ABOUT IT?
AND HOW WILL KEEPING IT FROM HIM PROTECT HIM?

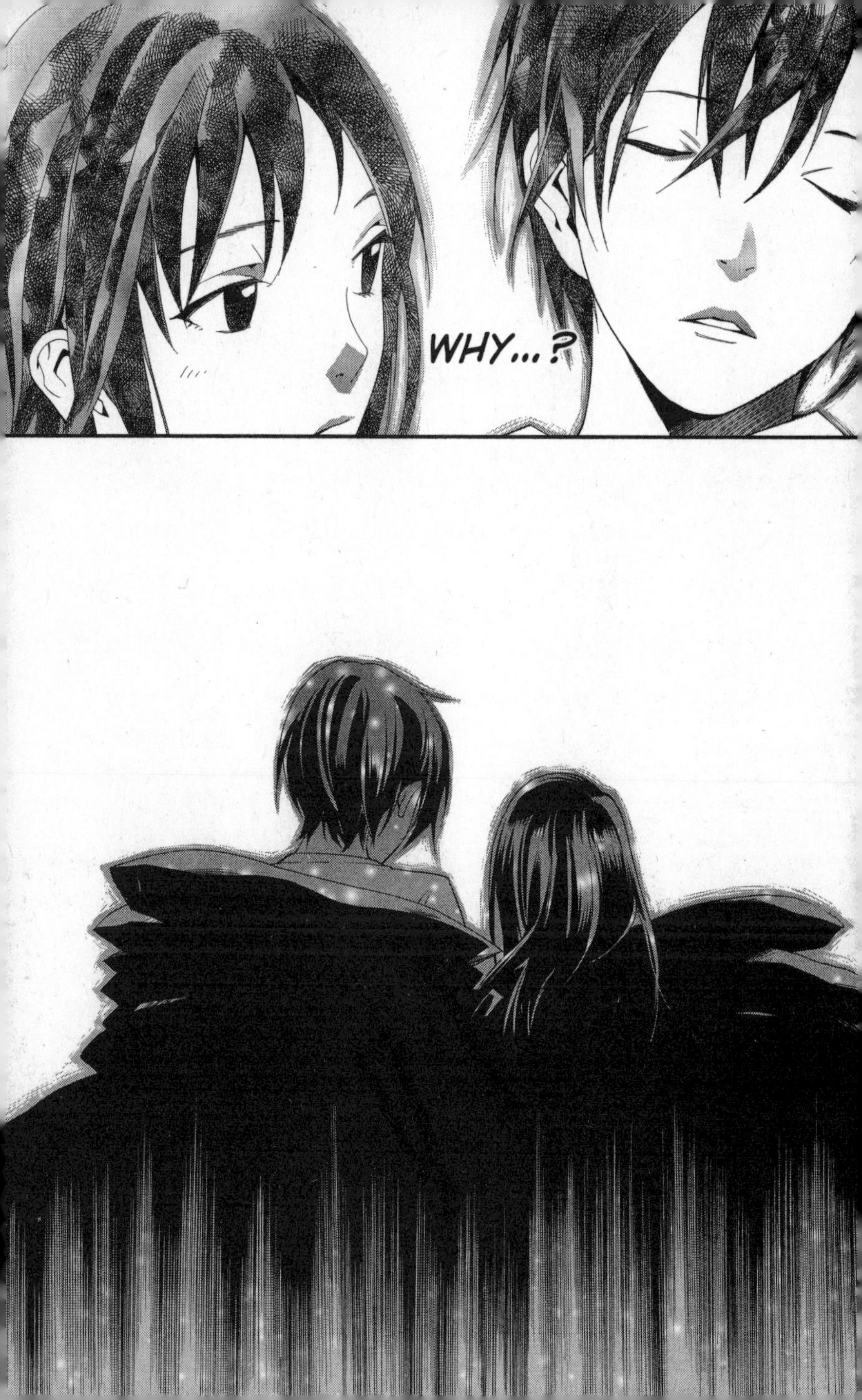
WHY...?

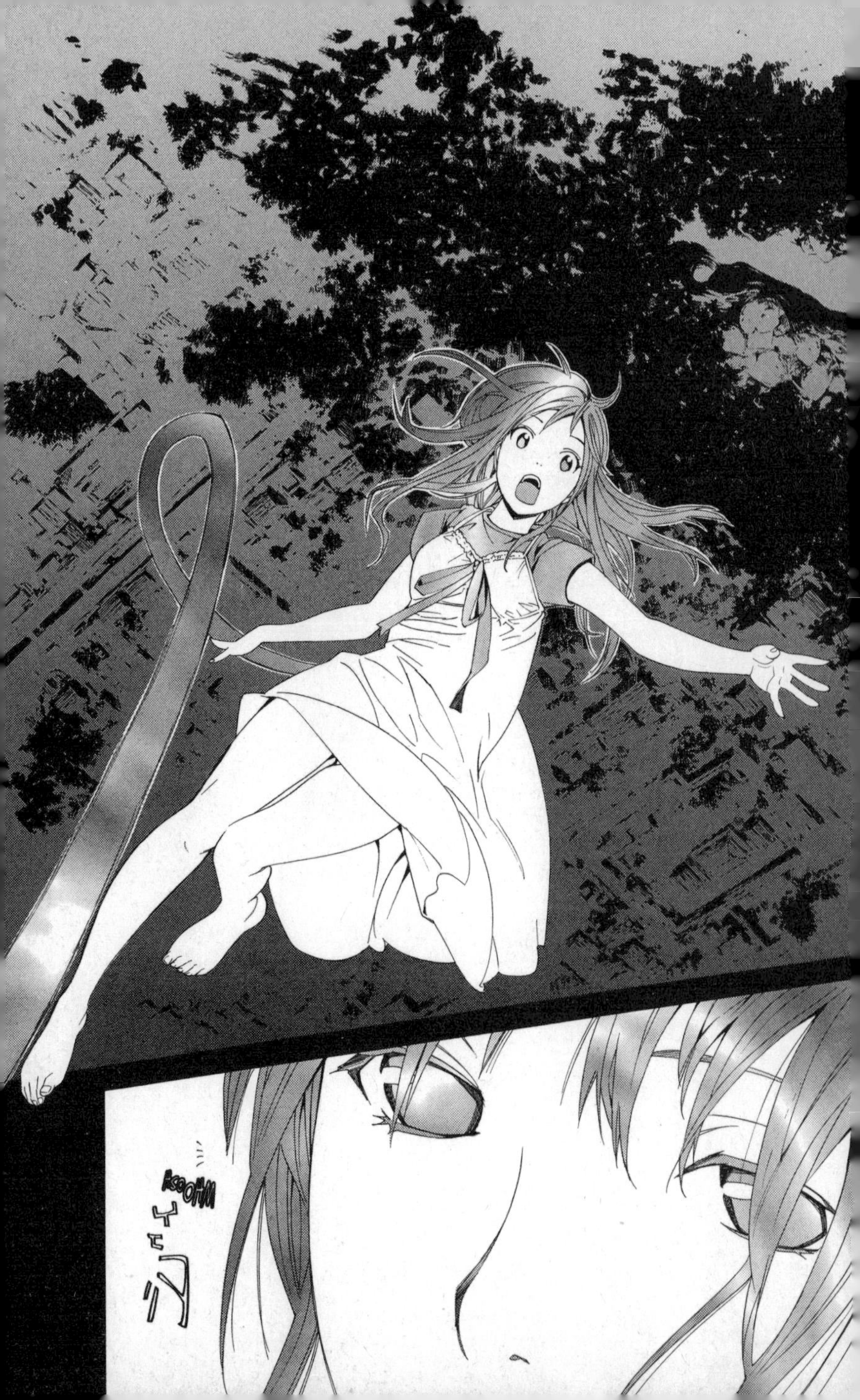
WHOOSH

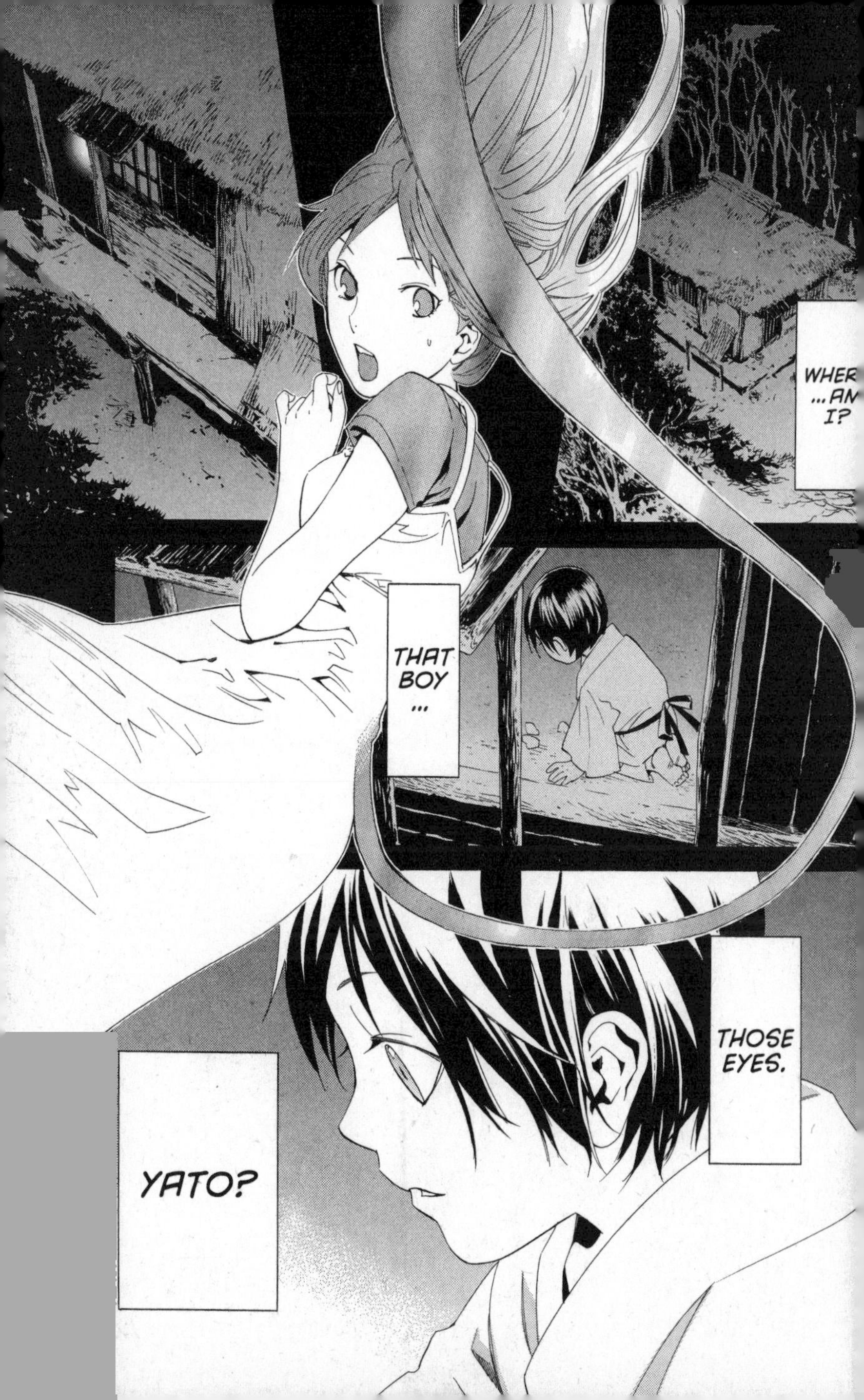
WHER
...AM
I?
THAT BOY ...
THOSE EYES.
YATO?

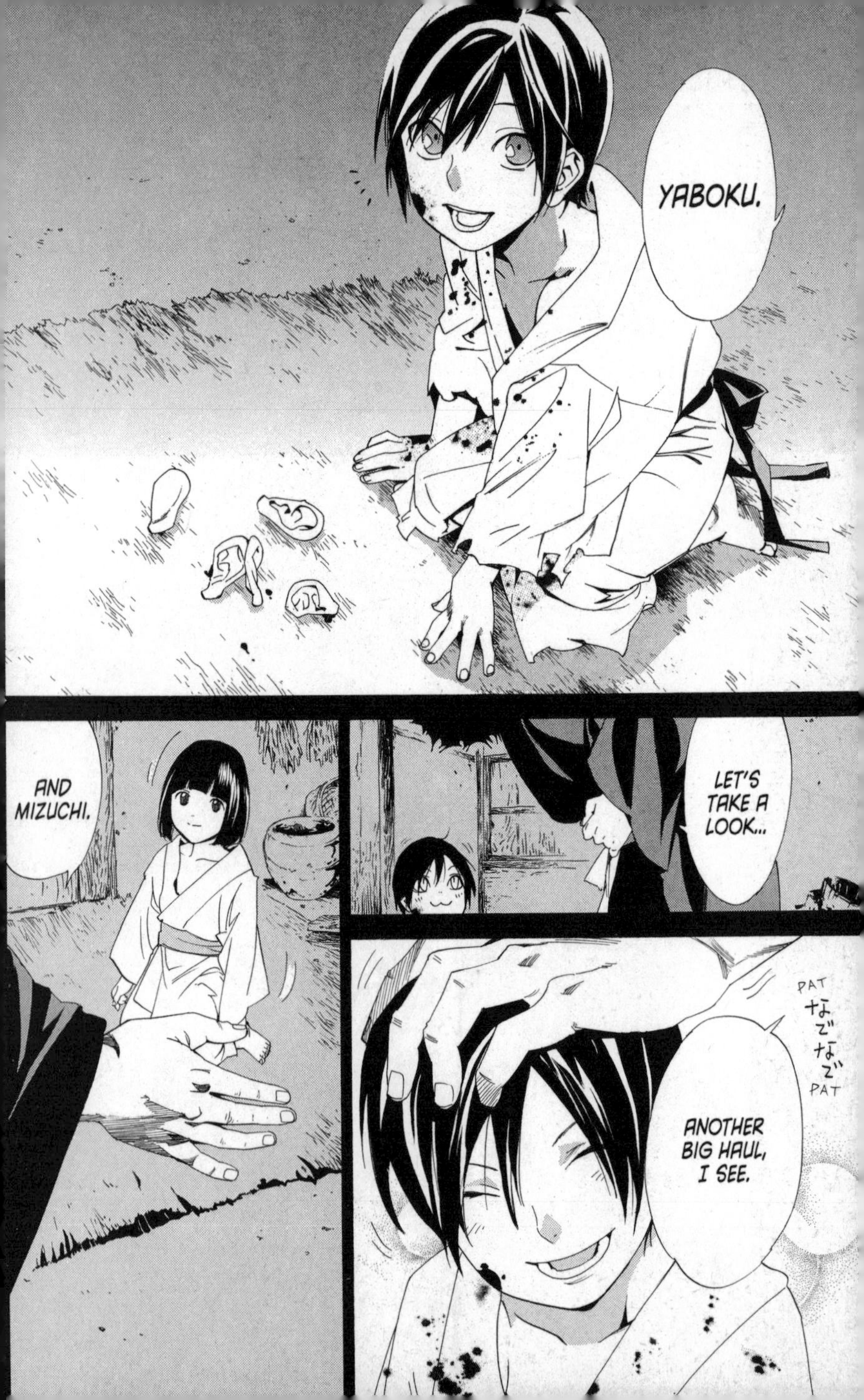
YABOKU.
LET'S TAKE A LOOK...
PAT なでなで PAT
ANOTHER BIG HAUL, I SEE.
AND MIZUCHI.

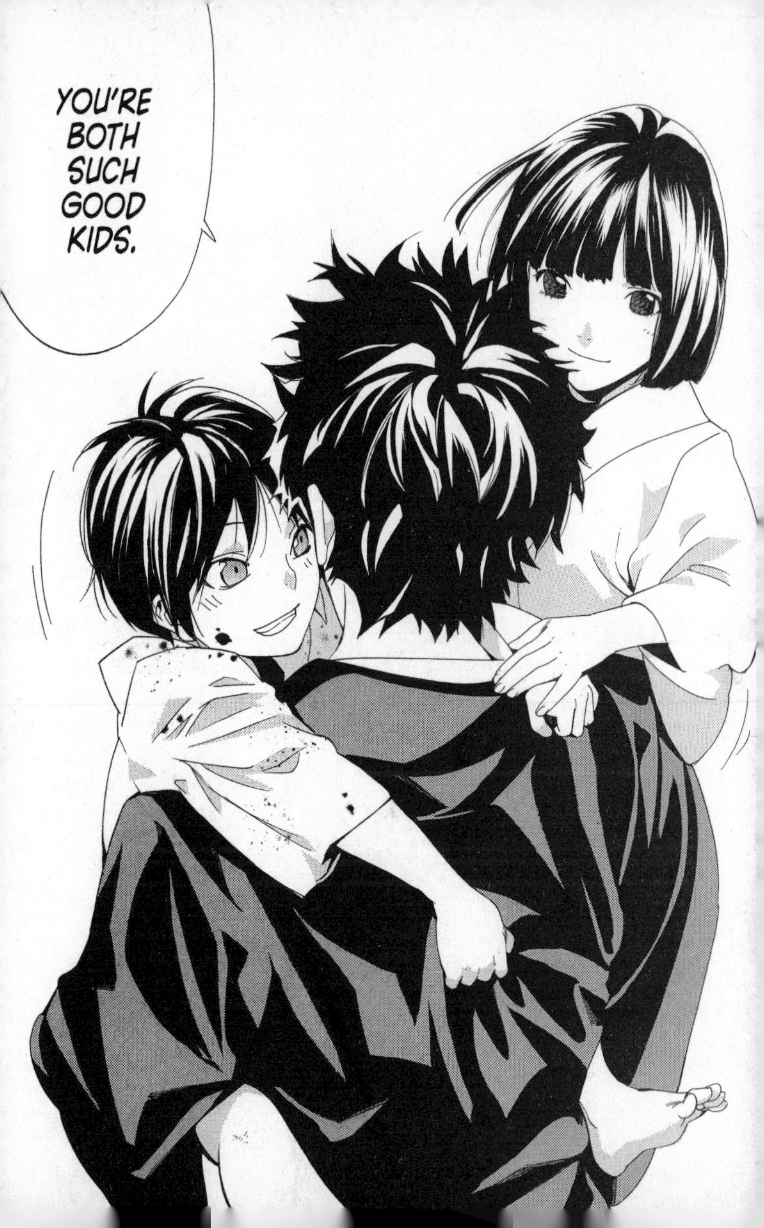
YOU'RE BOTH SUCH GOOD KIDS.

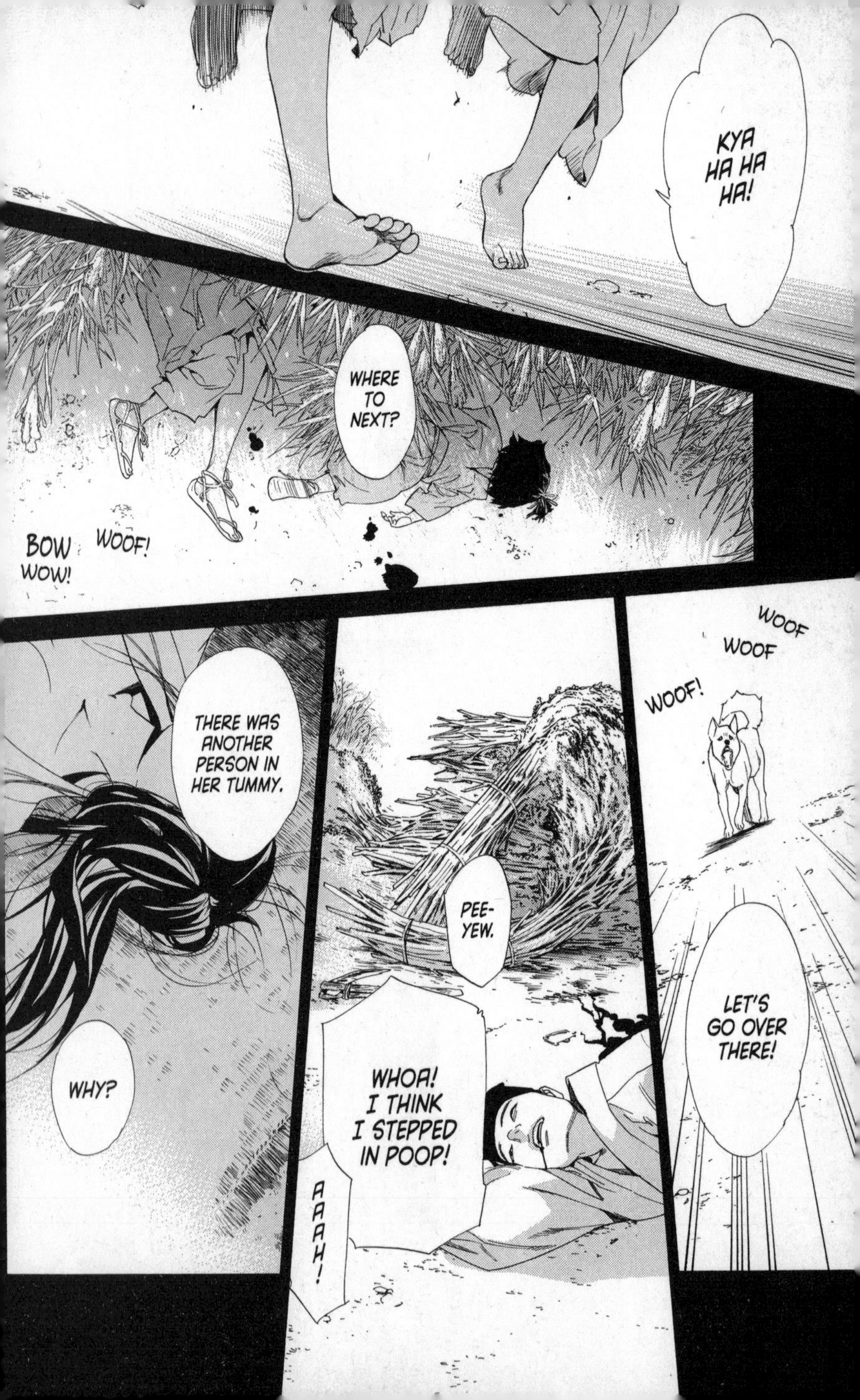
KYA HA HA HA!
WHERE TO NEXT?
WOOF!
BOW WOW!
WOOF
WOOF
WOOF!
LET'S GO OVER THERE!
PEE-YEW.
WHOA! I THINK I STEPPED IN POOP!
AAAAH!
THERE WAS ANOTHER PERSON IN HER TUMMY.
WHY?

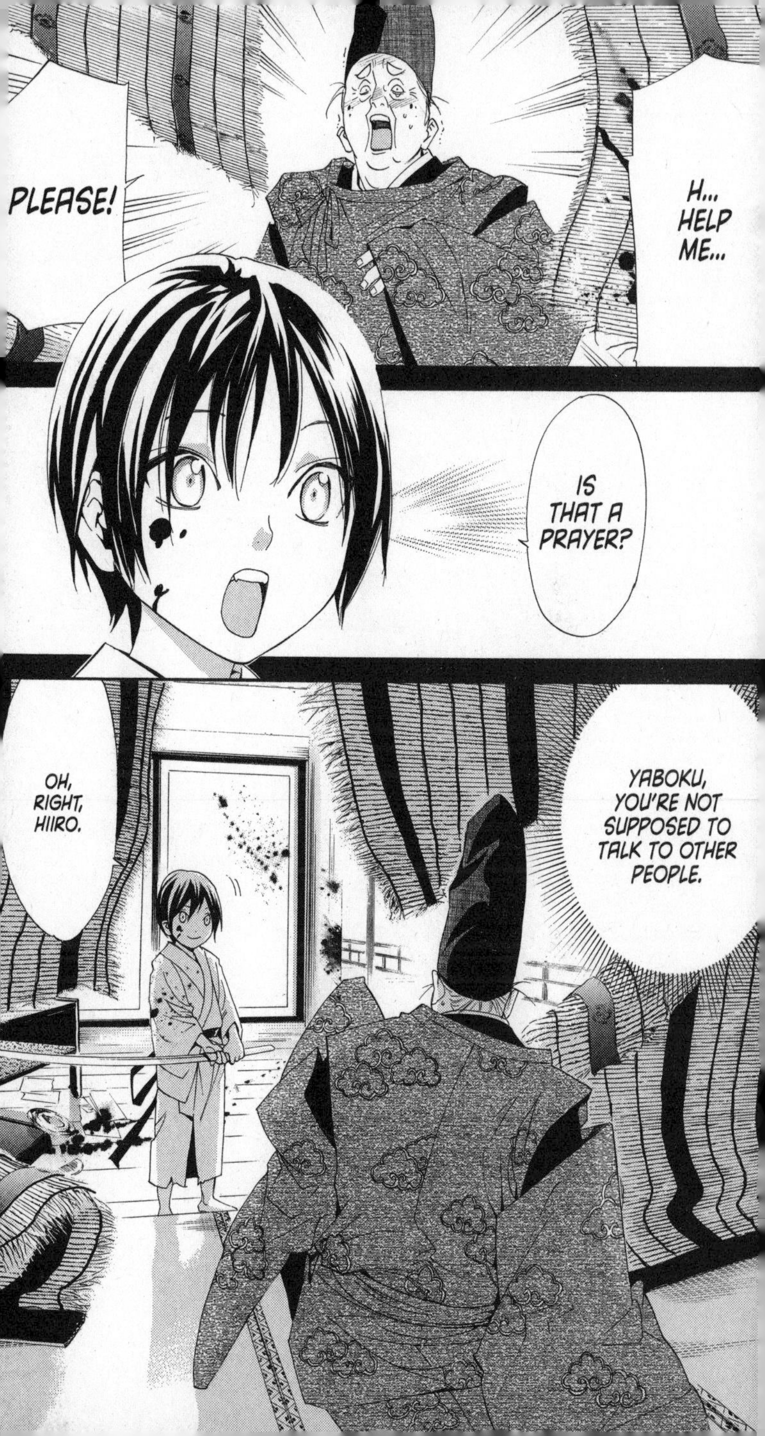
H... HELP ME...
PLEASE!
IS THAT A PRAYER?
YABOKU, YOU'RE NOT SUPPOSED TO TALK TO OTHER PEOPLE.
OH, RIGHT, HIIRO.

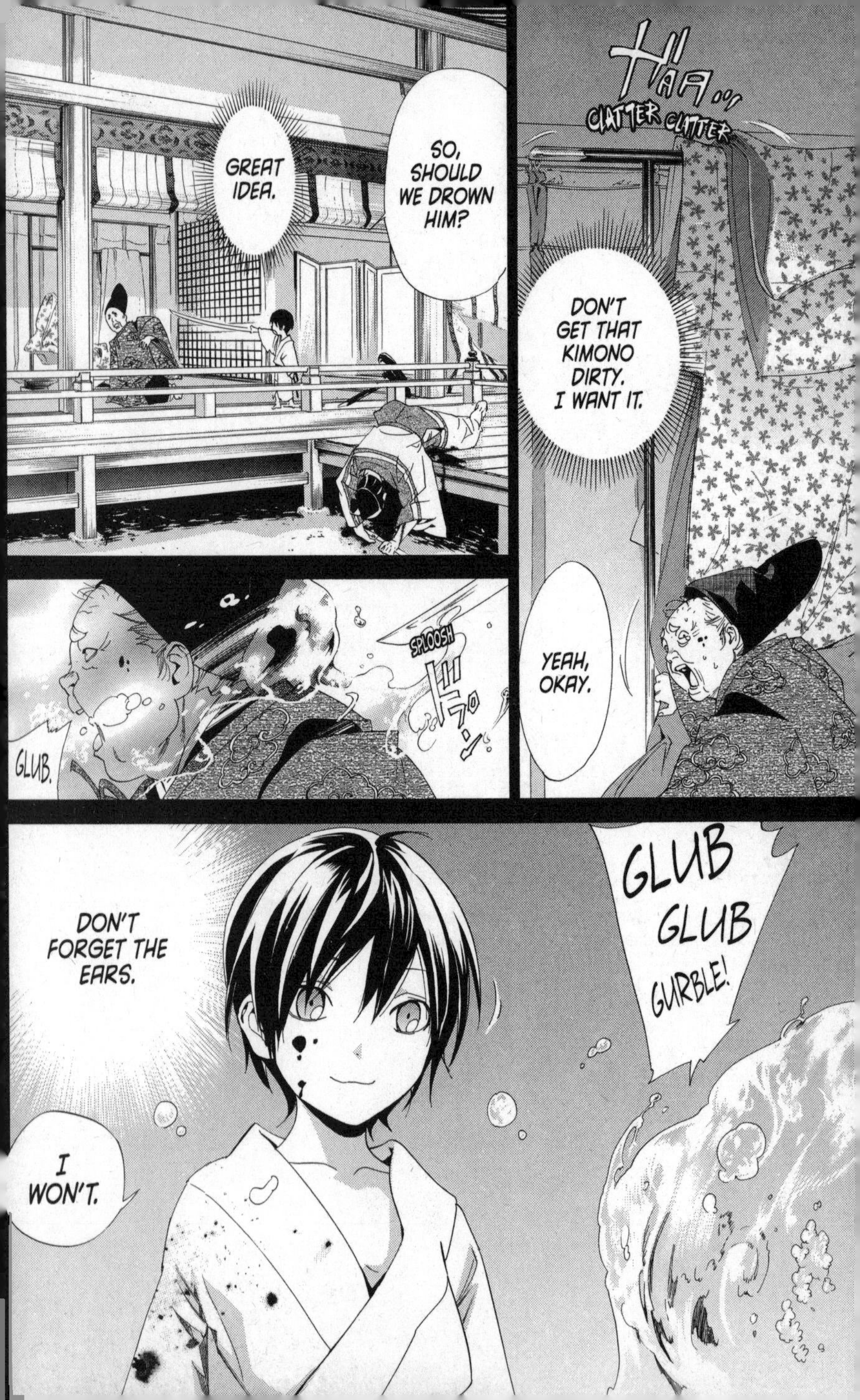
HAA...
CLATTER CLATTER
DON'T GET THAT KIMONO DIRTY. I WANT IT.
YEAH, OKAY.
SO, SHOULD WE DROWN HIM?
GREAT IDEA.
SPLOOSH
GLUB.
GLUB GLUB GURBLE!
DON'T FORGET THE EARS.
I WON'T.

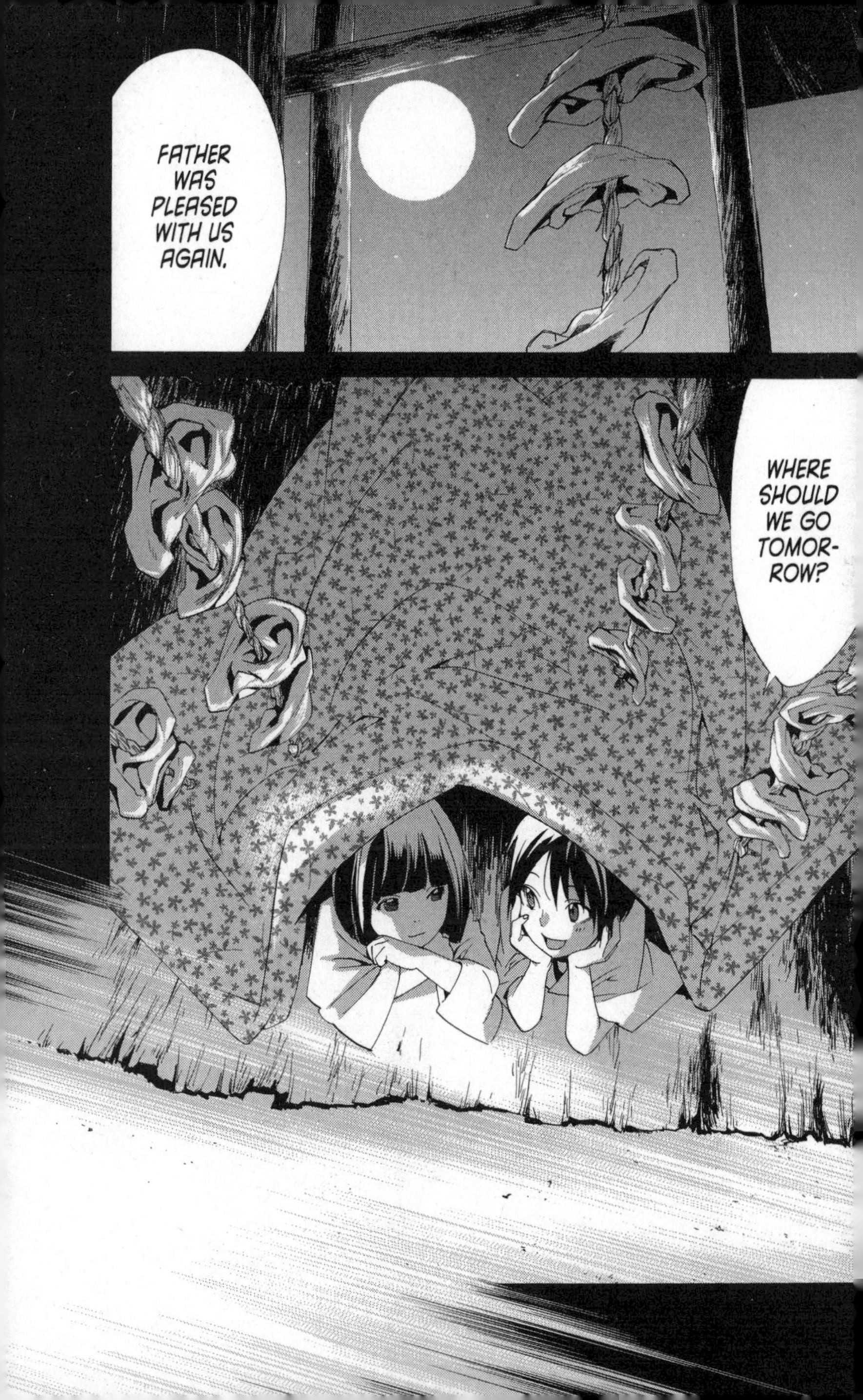
FATHER WAS PLEASED WITH US AGAIN.
WHERE SHOULD WE GO TOMOR-ROW?

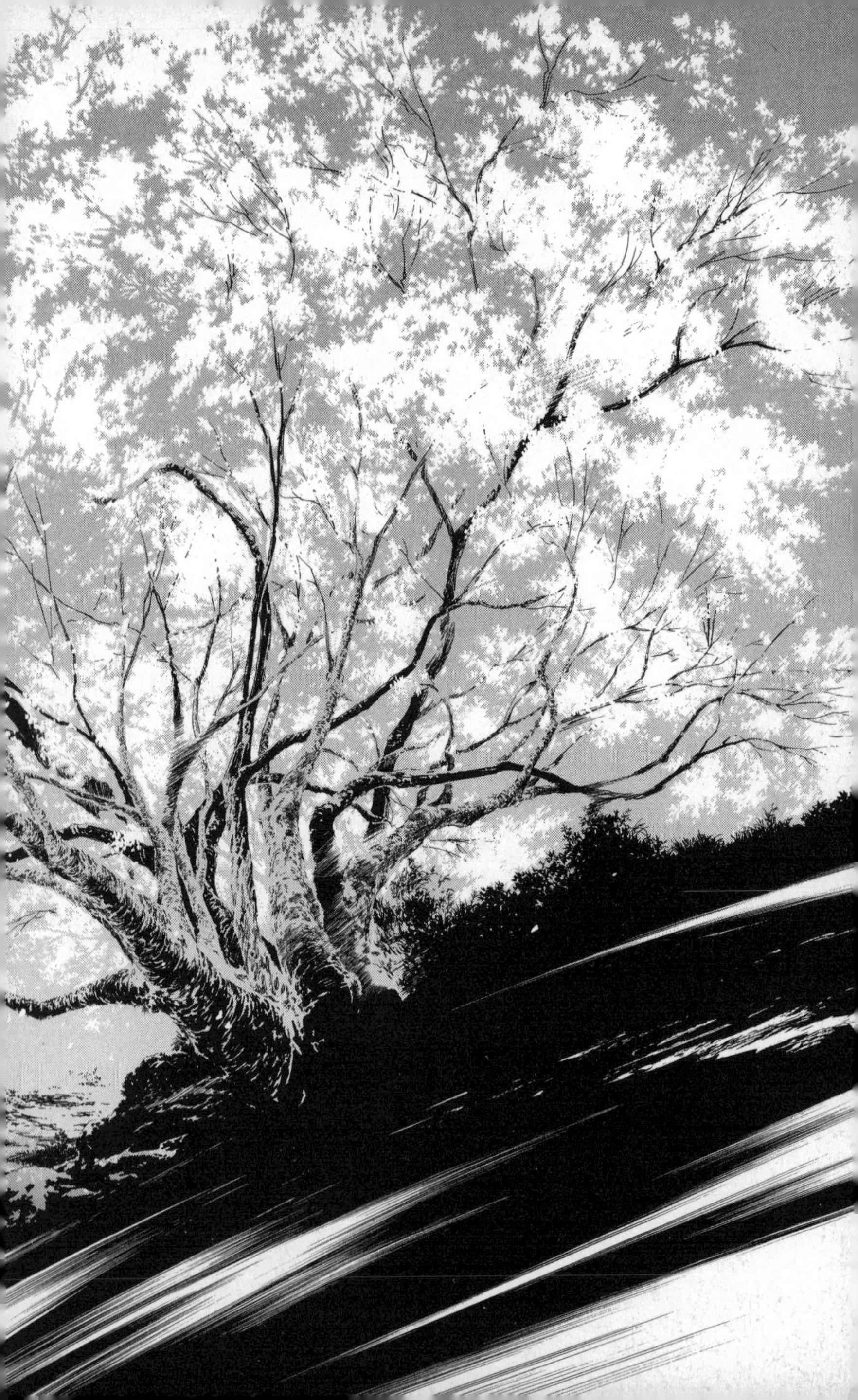

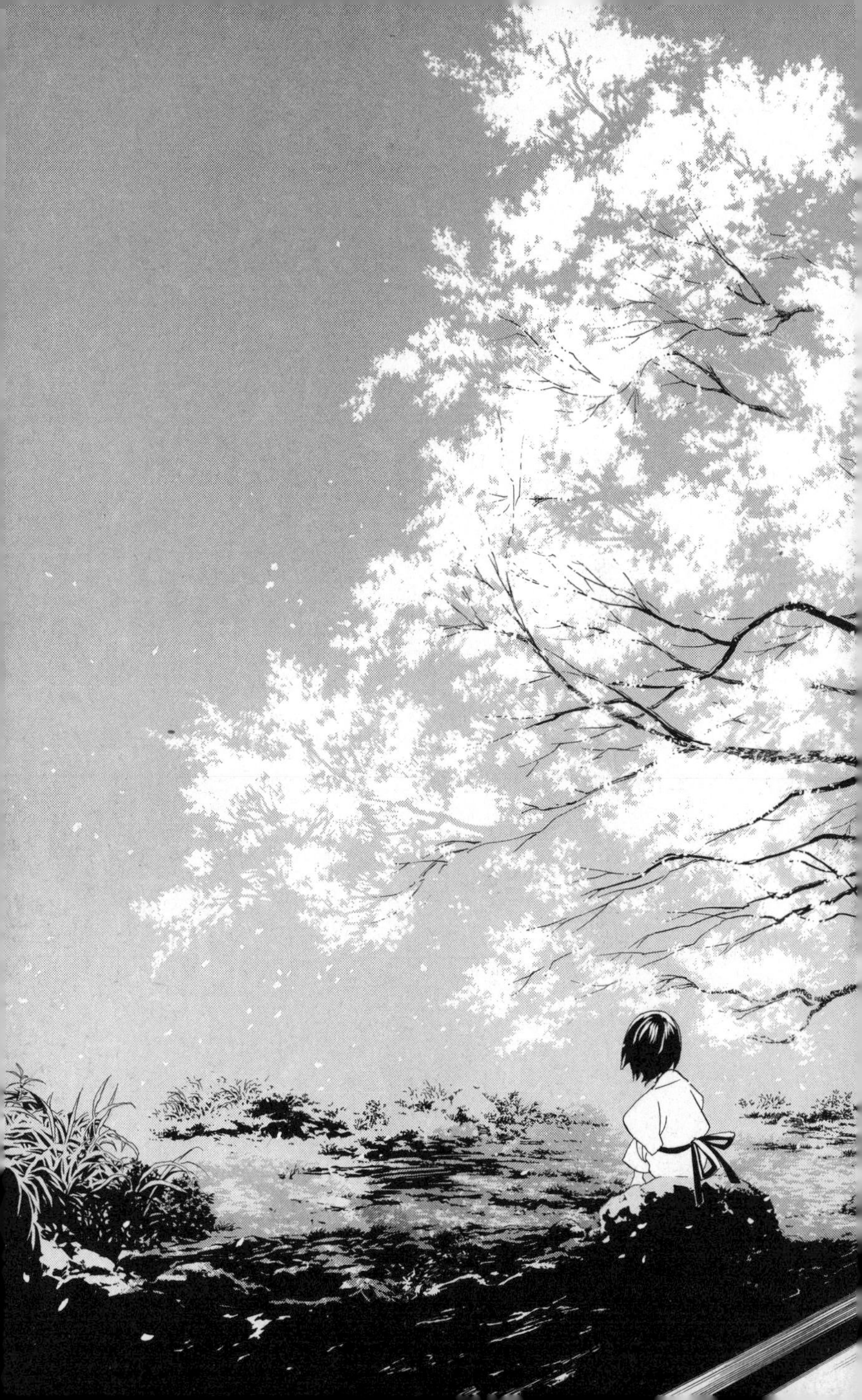

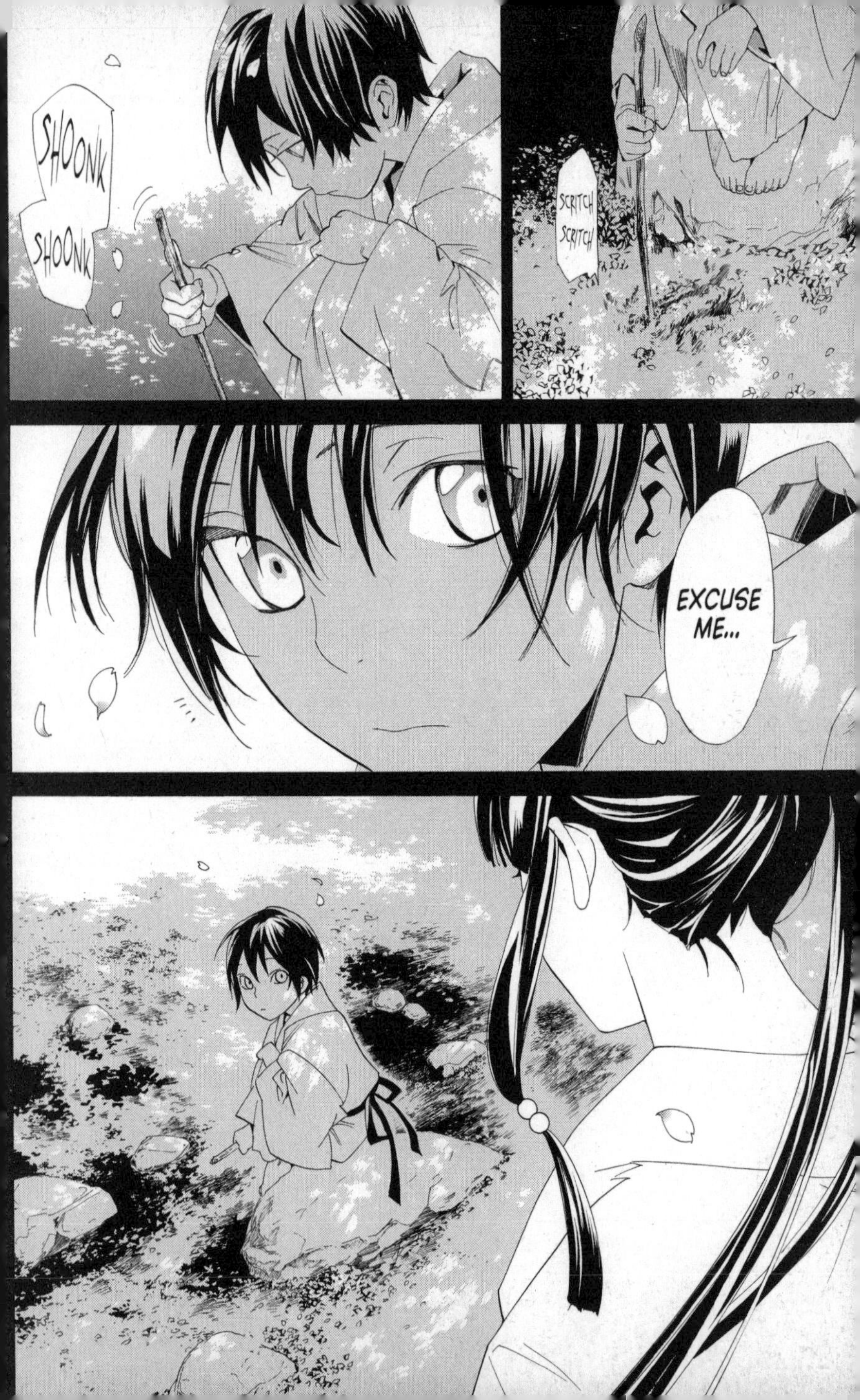
SCRITCH SCRITCH
SHOONK
SHOONK
EXCUSE ME...

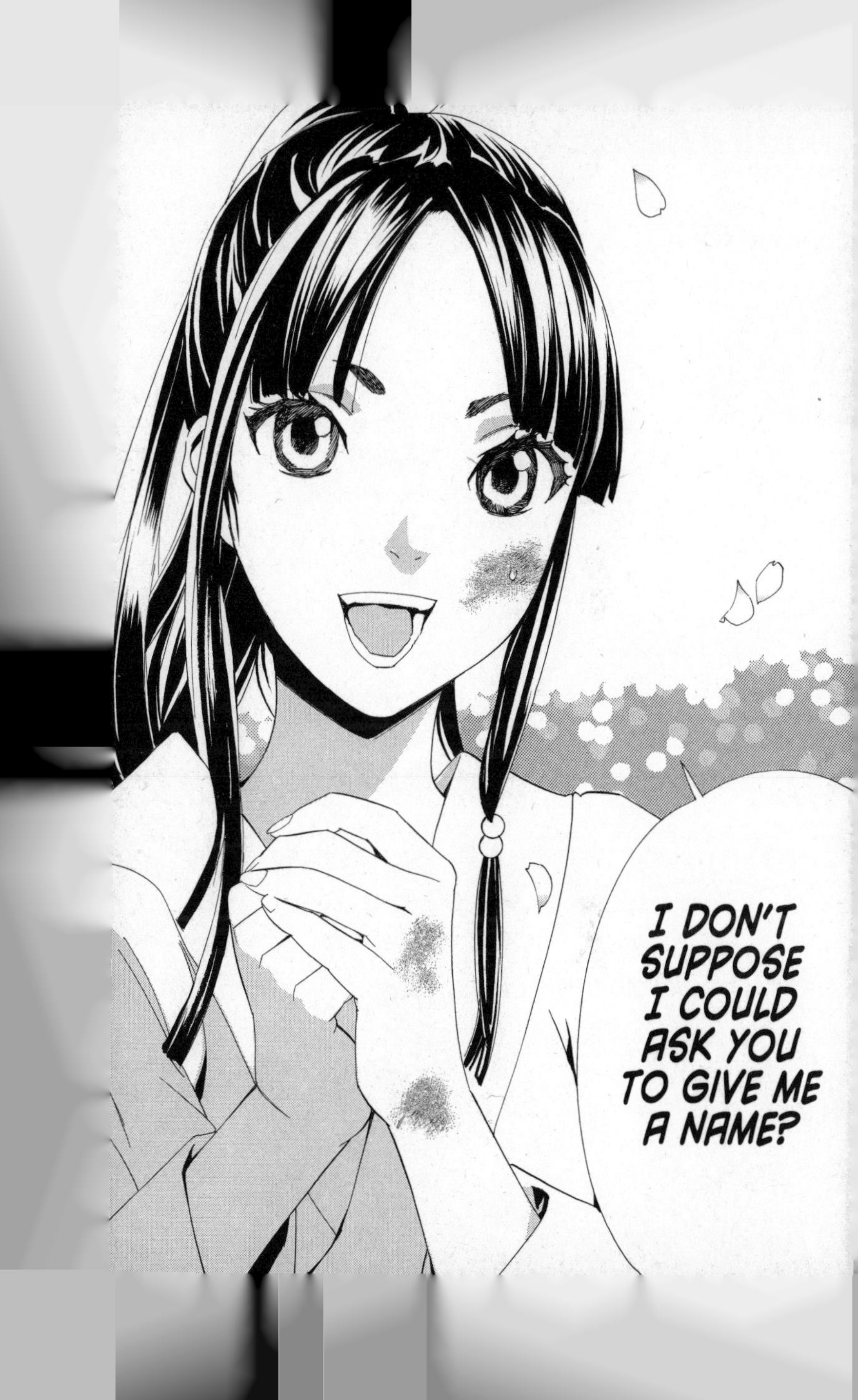
I DON'T SUPPOSE I COULD ASK YOU TO GIVE ME A NAME?

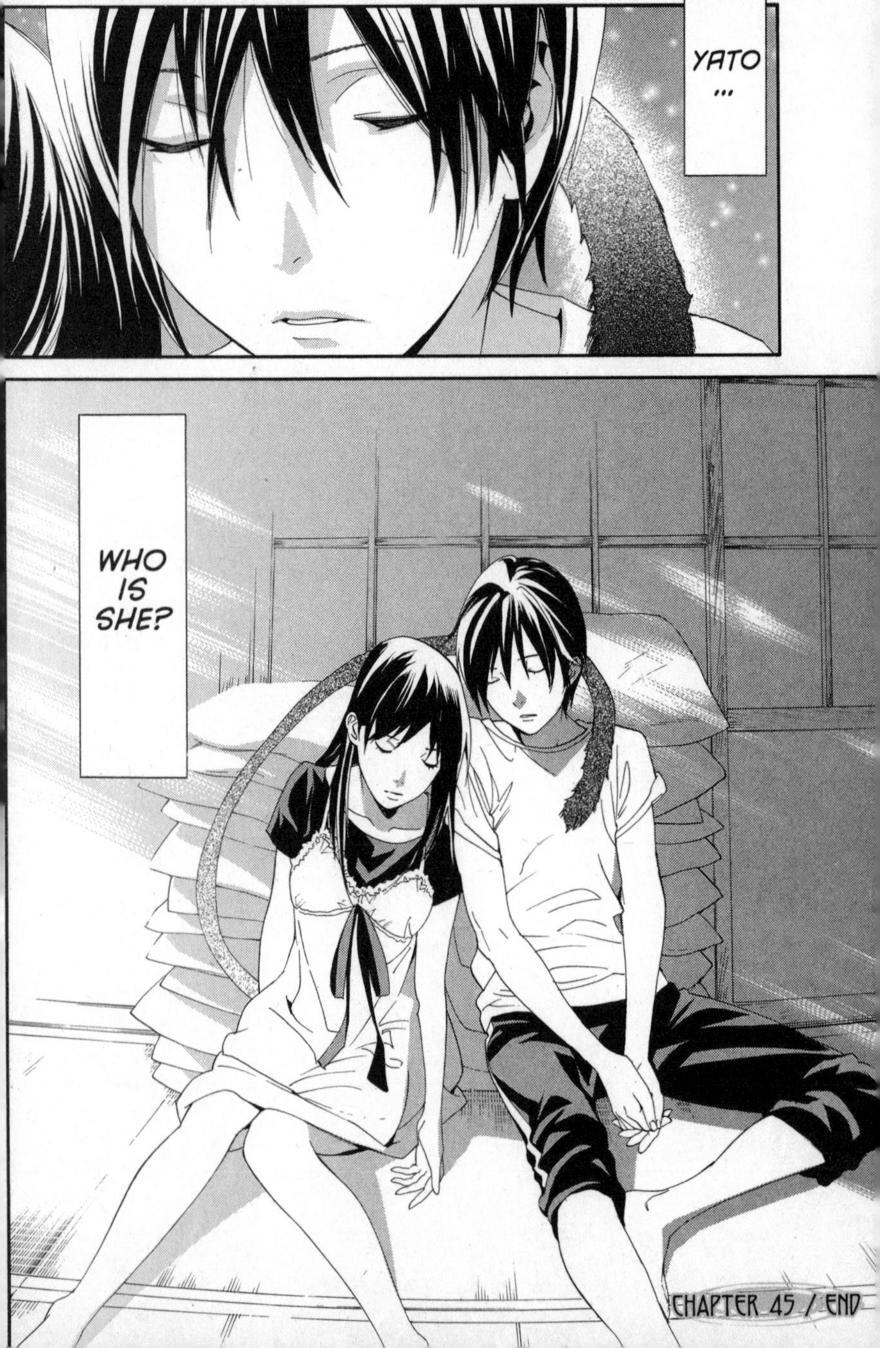
YATO
...
WHO IS SHE?
CHAPTER 45 / END

野

臾

神

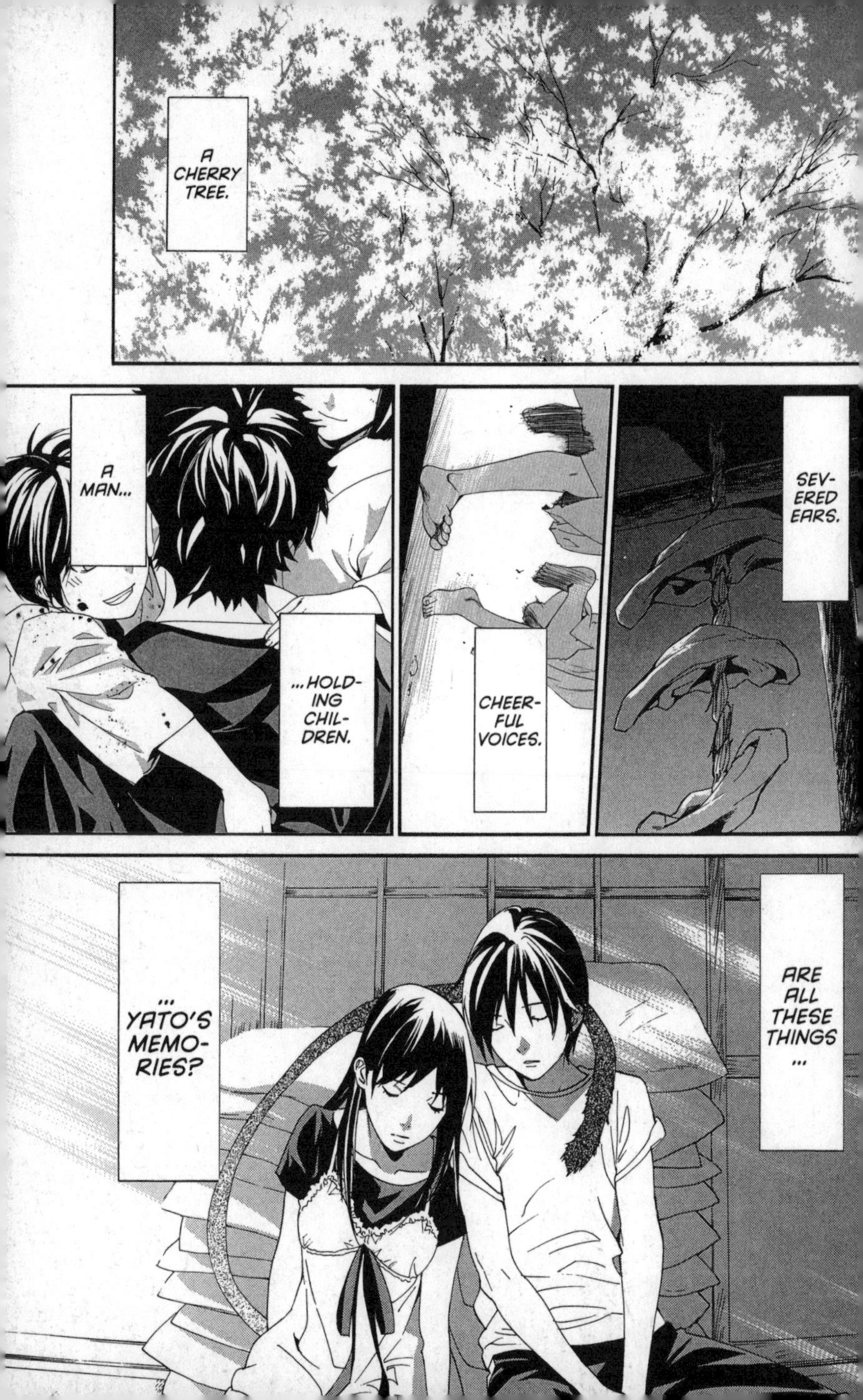
A CHERRY TREE.
SEVERED EARS.
CHEERFUL VOICES.
A MAN...
...HOLDING CHILDREN.
ARE ALL THESE THINGS...
...YATO'S MEMORIES?

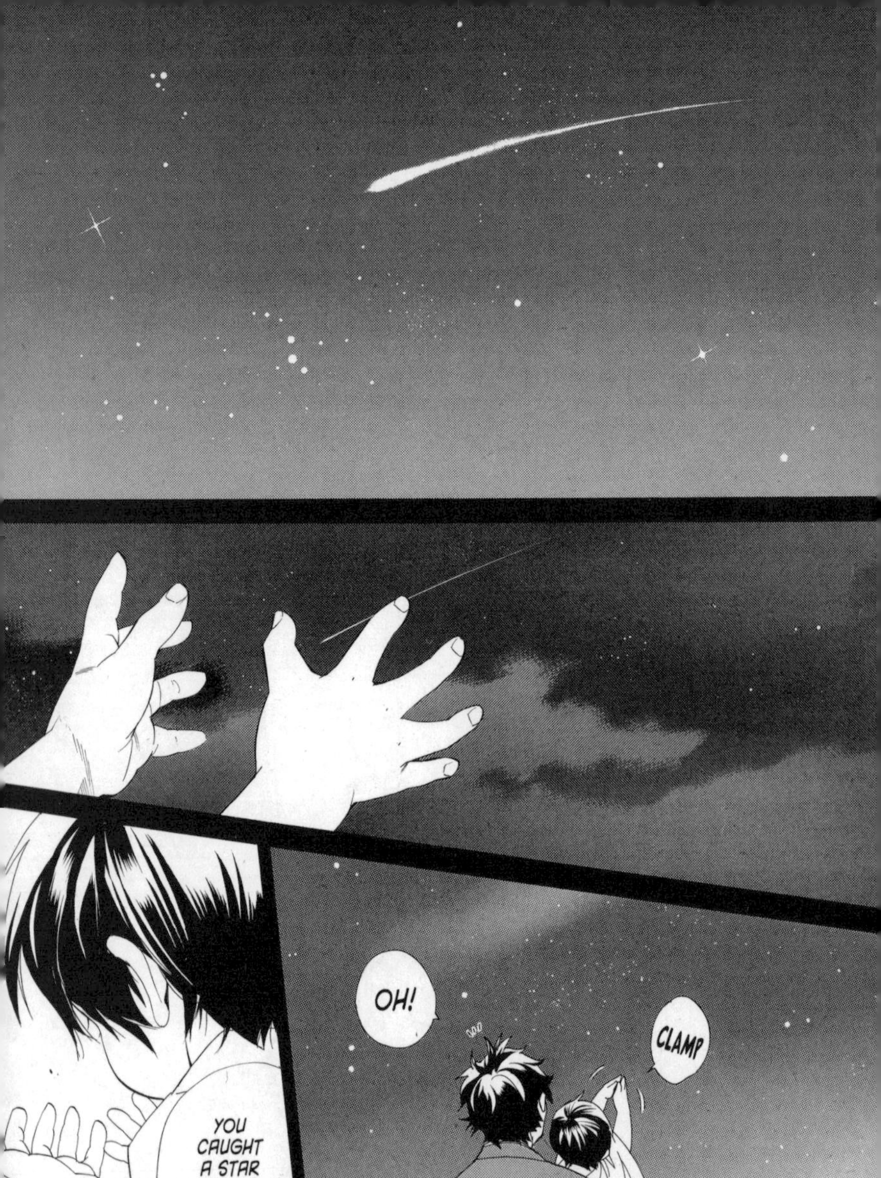
OH!
CLAMP
YOU CAUGHT A STAR FALLING FROM KANOTO TO TORI.

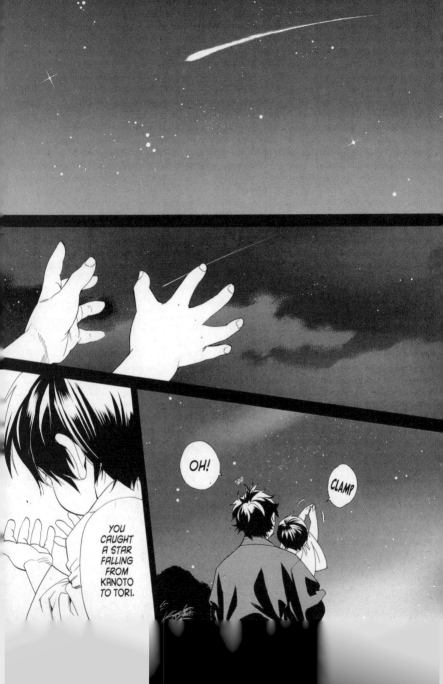

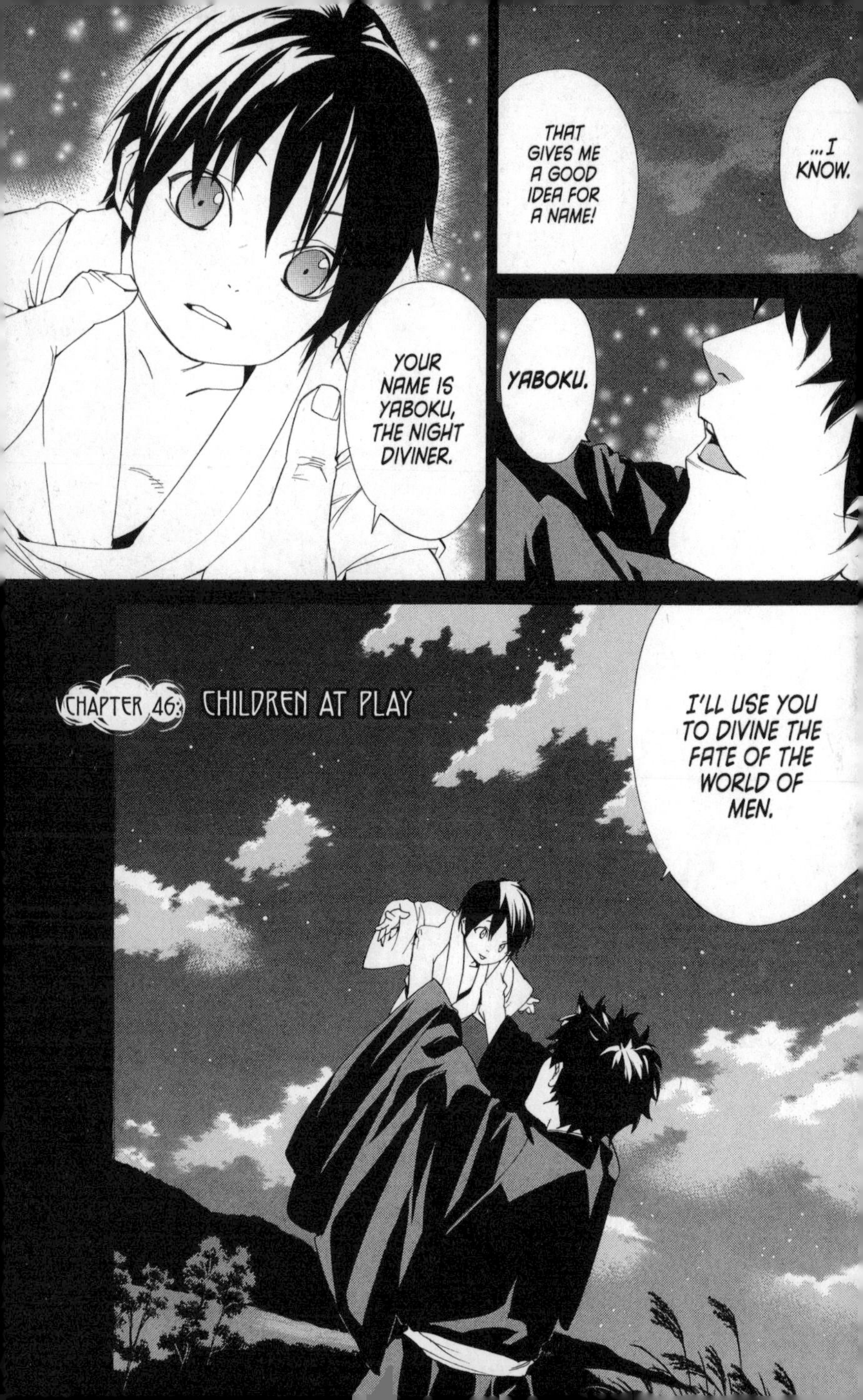
...I KNOW.
THAT GIVES ME A GOOD IDEA FOR A NAME!
YABOKU.
YOUR NAME IS YABOKU, THE NIGHT DIVINER.
I'LL USE YOU TO DIVINE THE FATE OF THE WORLD OF MEN.
CHAPTER 46: CHILDREN AT PLAY

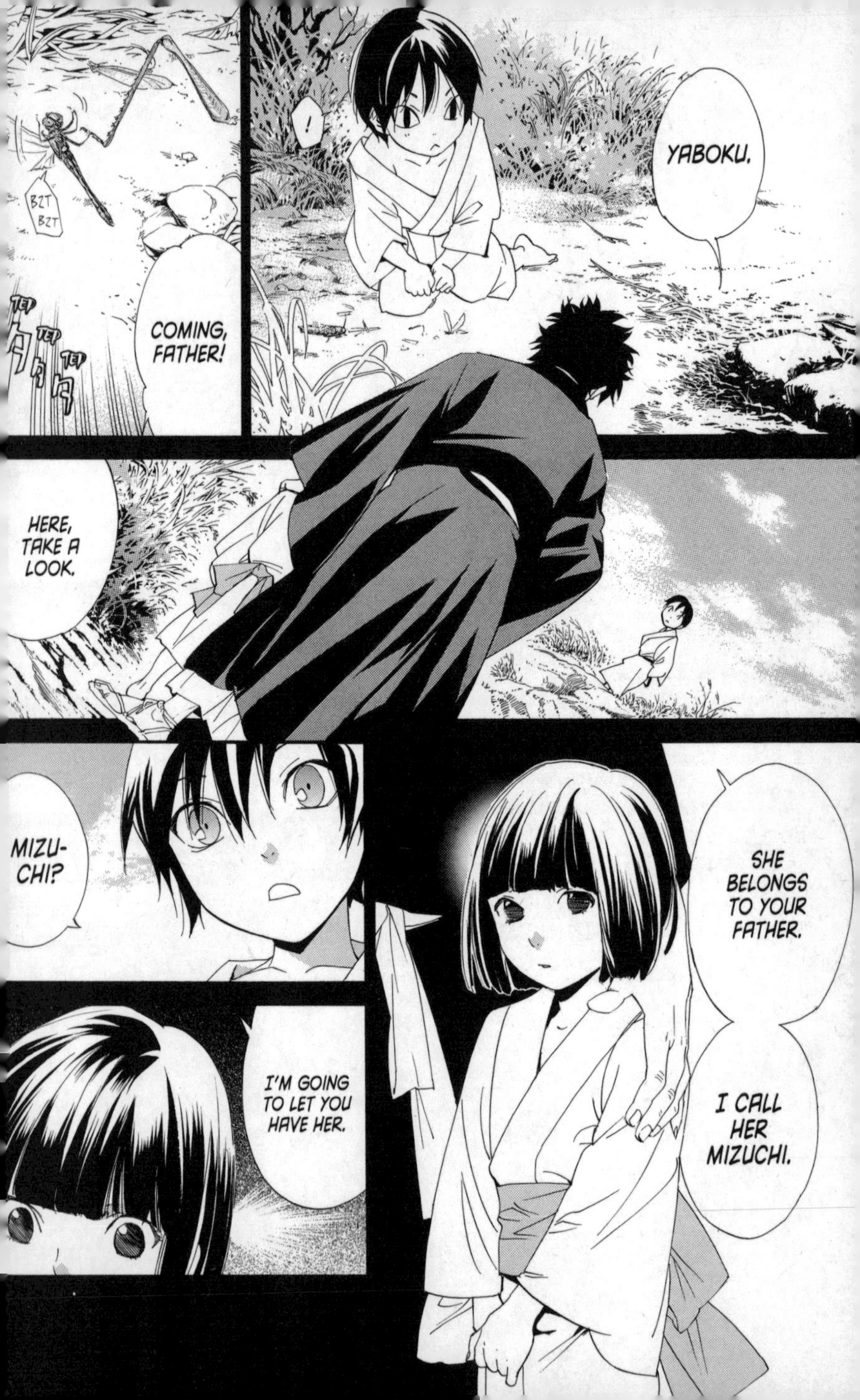
YABOKU.
!
BZT BZT
COMING, FATHER!
TEP TEP TEP
HERE, TAKE A LOOK.
SHE BELONGS TO YOUR FATHER.
I CALL HER MIZUCHI.
MIZU-CHI?
I'M GOING TO LET YOU HAVE HER.

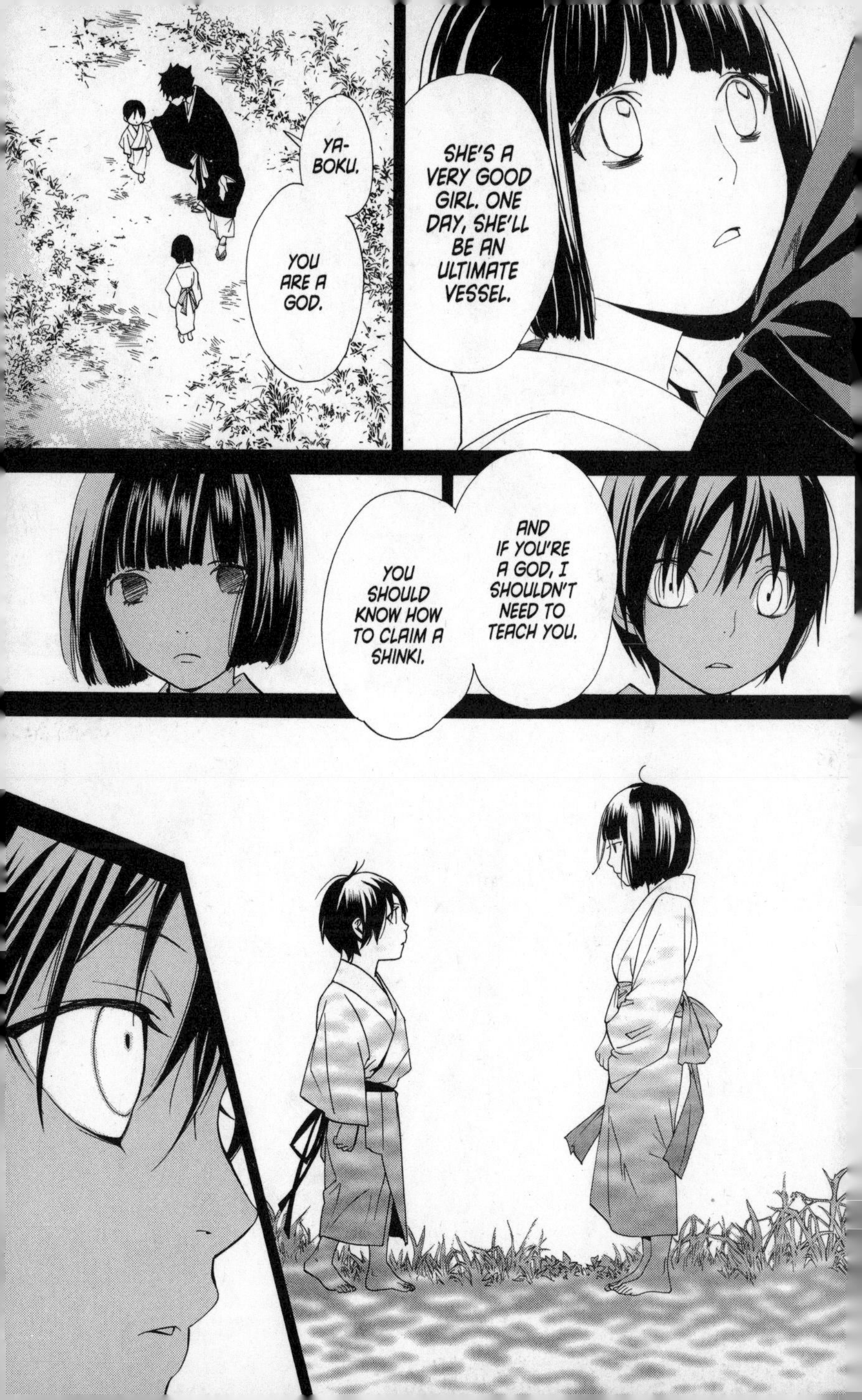
SHE'S A VERY GOOD GIRL. ONE DAY, SHE'LL BE AN ULTIMATE VESSEL.
YA-BOKU.
YOU ARE A GOD.
AND IF YOU'RE A GOD, I SHOULDN'T NEED TO TEACH YOU.
YOU SHOULD KNOW HOW TO CLAIM A SHINKI.

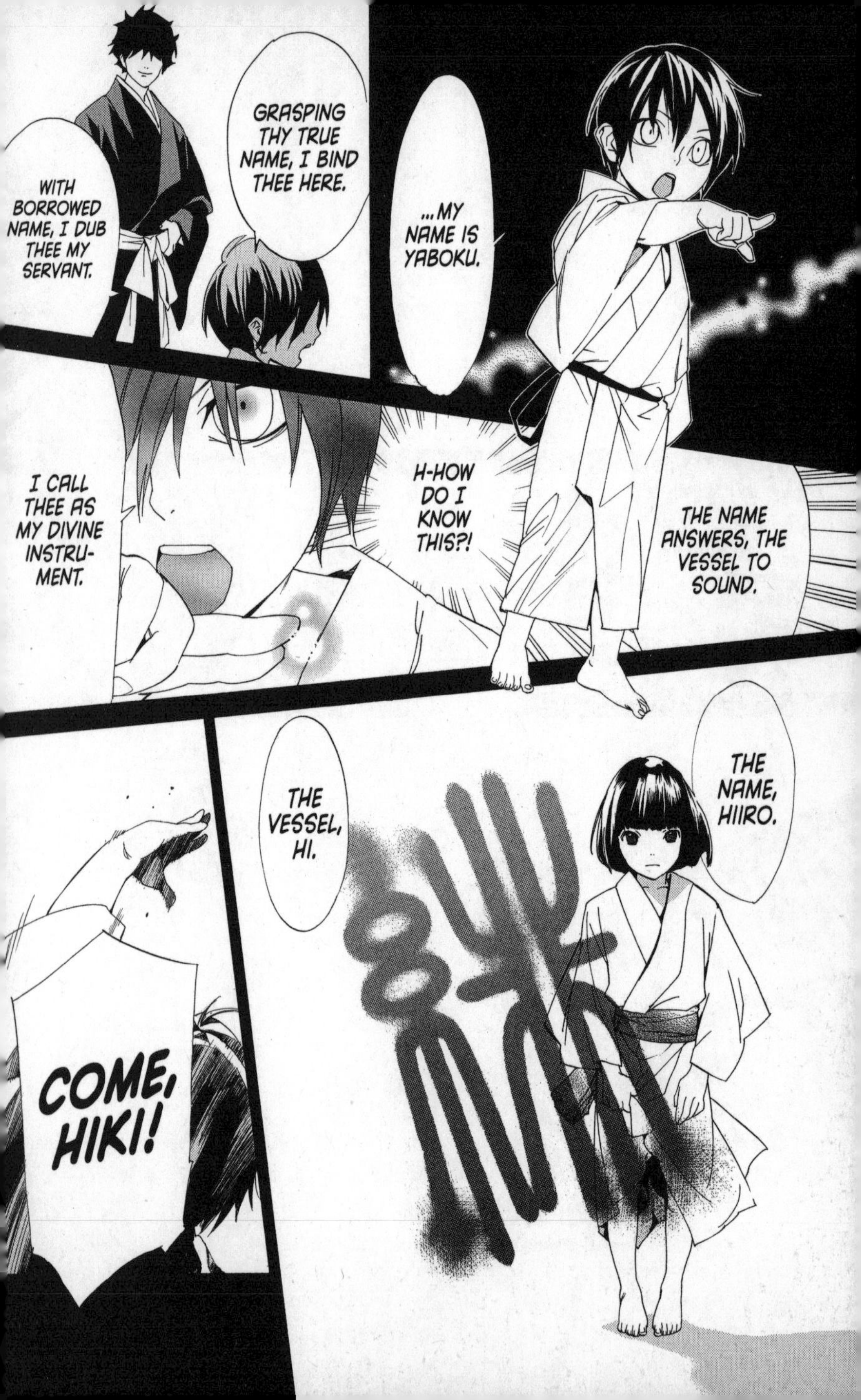
...MY NAME IS YABOKU.
GRASPING THY TRUE NAME, I BIND THEE HERE.
WITH BORROWED NAME, I DUB THEE MY SERVANT.
THE NAME ANSWERS, THE VESSEL TO SOUND.
H-HOW DO I KNOW THIS?!
I CALL THEE AS MY DIVINE INSTRUMENT.
THE NAME, HIIRO.
THE VESSEL, HI.
COME, HIKI!

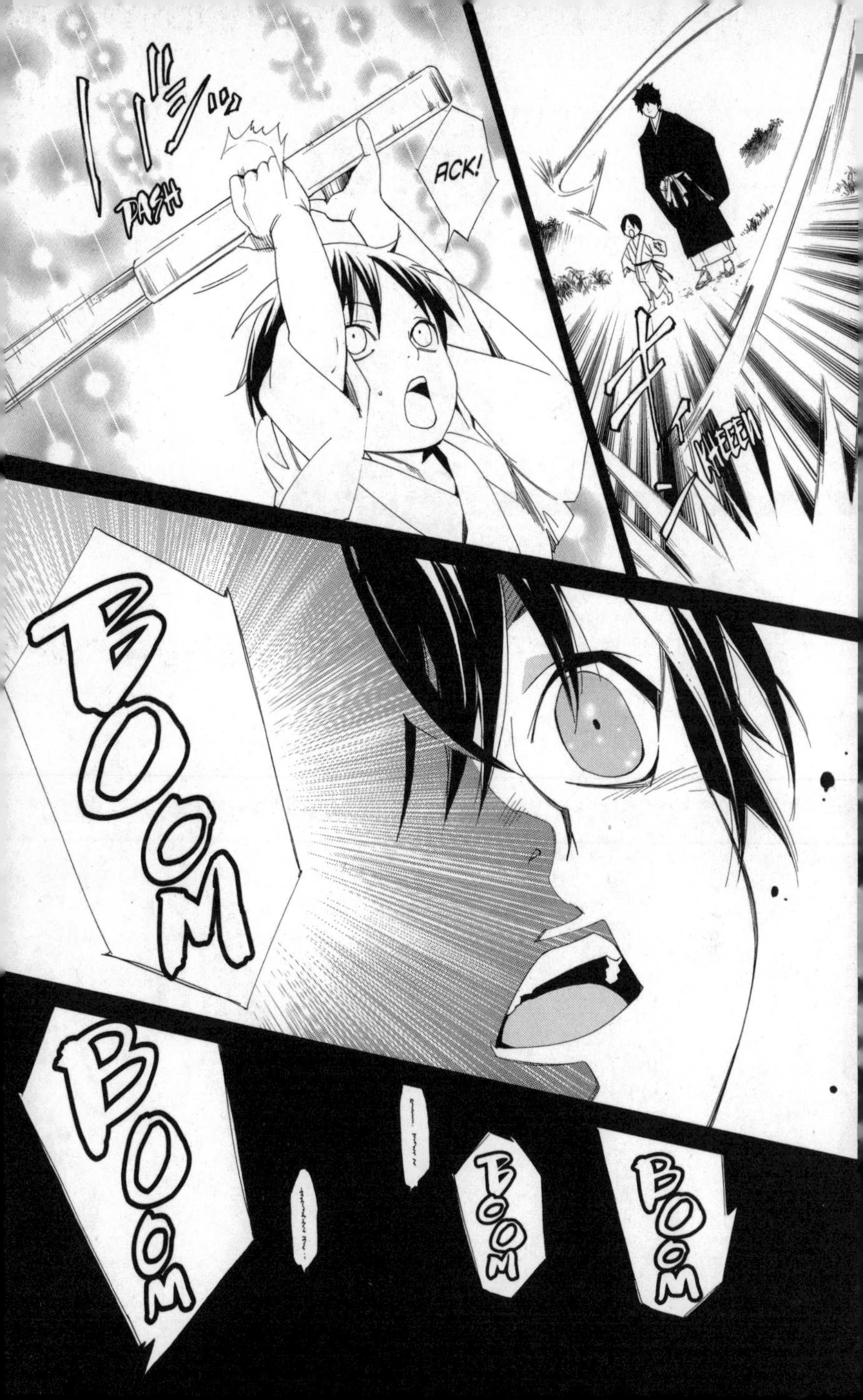
WHEEEN
DASH
ACK!
BOOM
BOOM
BOOM
BOOM

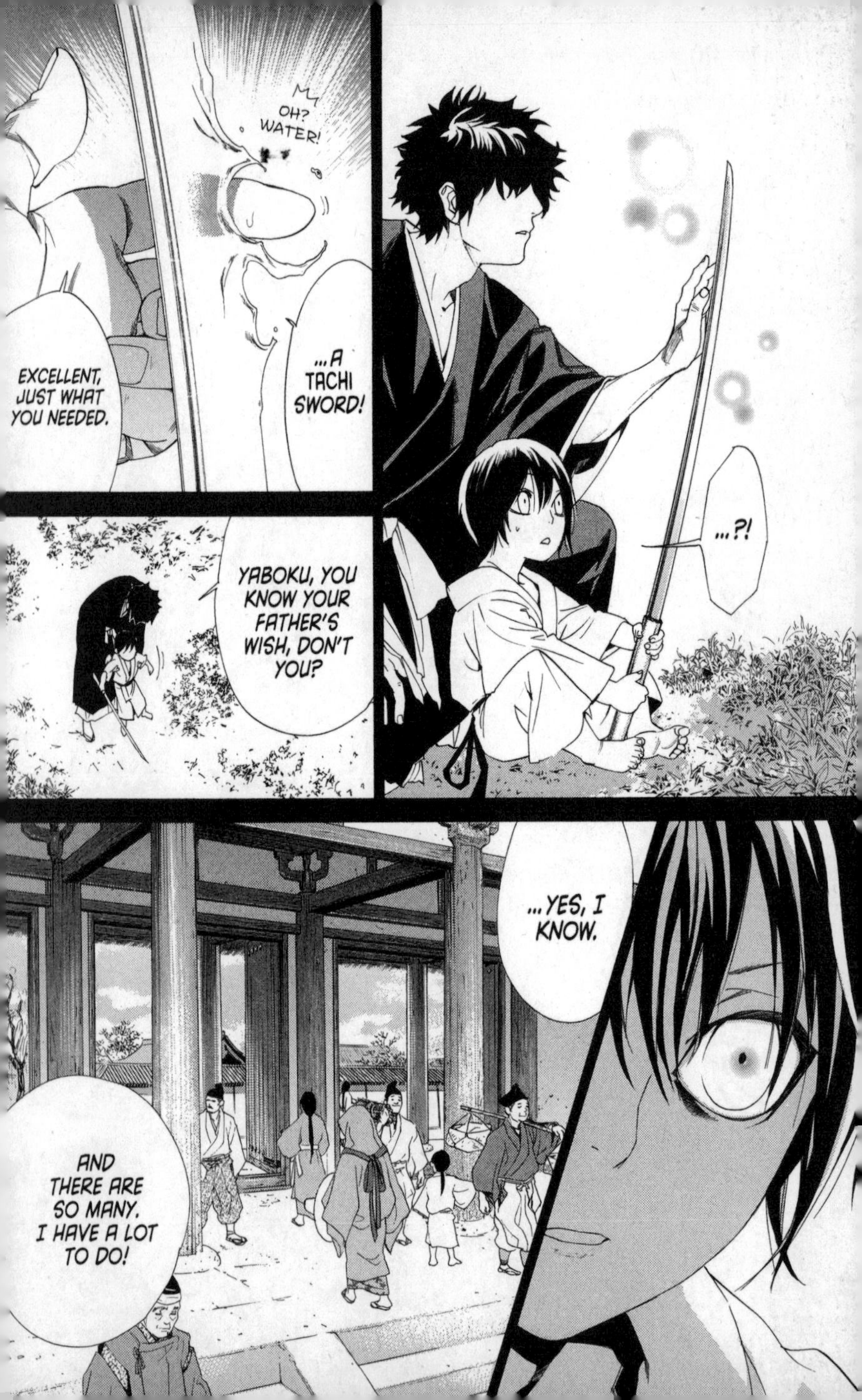
...?!
OH? WATER!
...A TACHI SWORD!
EXCELLENT, JUST WHAT YOU NEEDED.
YABOKU, YOU KNOW YOUR FATHER'S WISH, DON'T YOU?
...YES, I KNOW.
AND THERE ARE SO MANY. I HAVE A LOT TO DO!

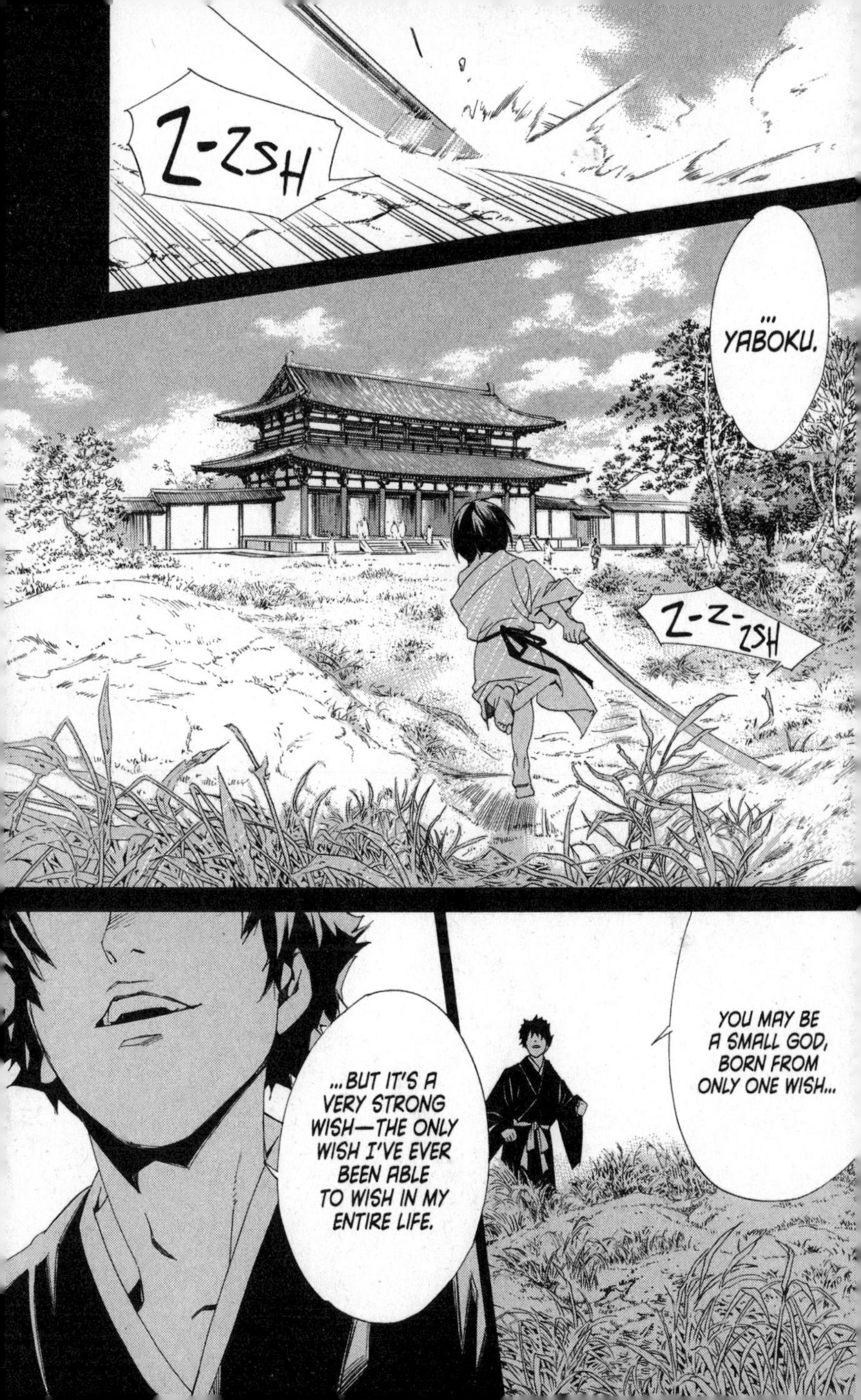
Z-ZSH
...YABOKU.
Z-Z-ZSH
YOU MAY BE A SMALL GOD, BORN FROM ONLY ONE WISH...
...BUT IT'S A VERY STRONG WISH—THE ONLY WISH I'VE EVER BEEN ABLE TO WISH IN MY ENTIRE LIFE.

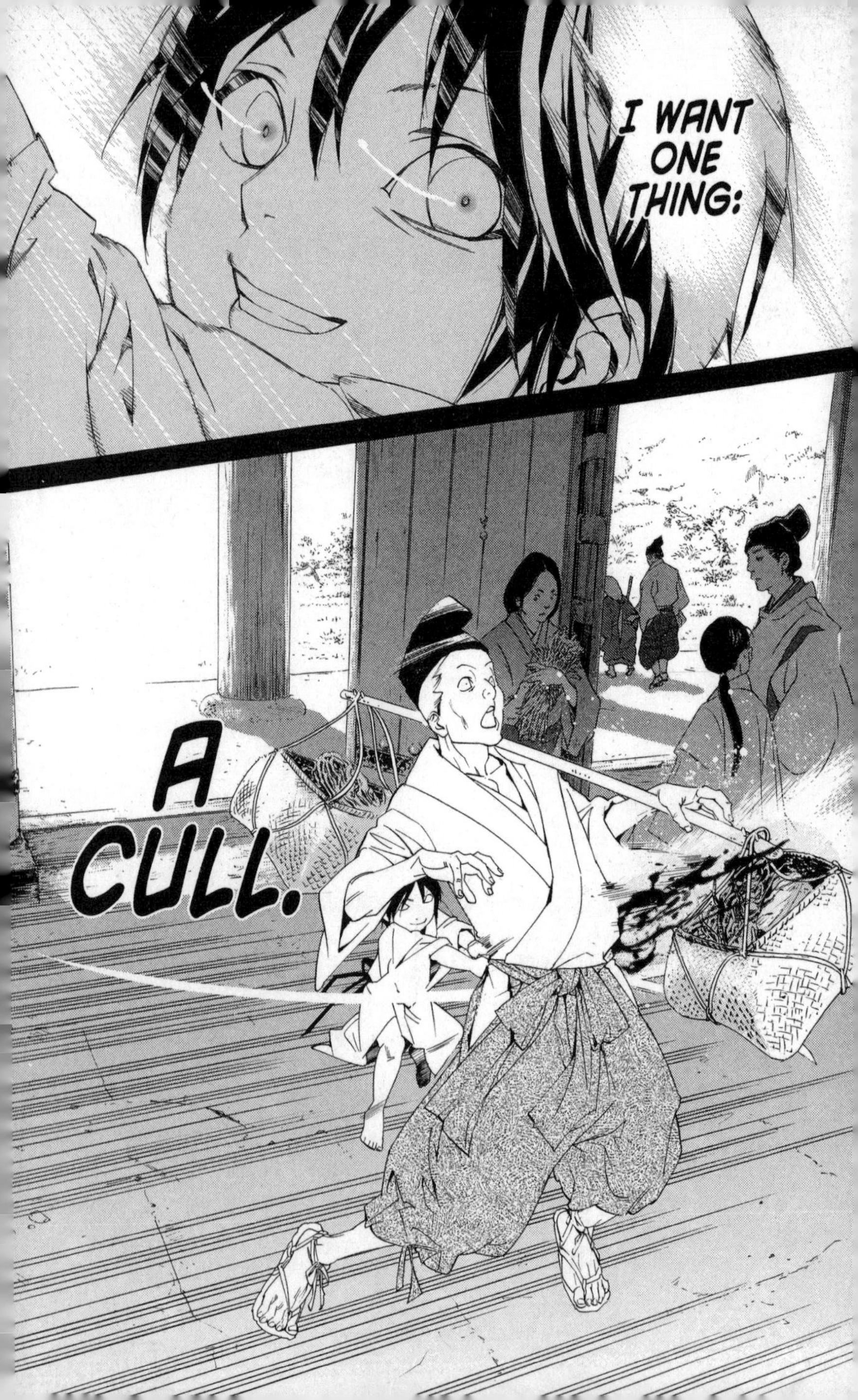
I WANT ONE THING:
A CULL.

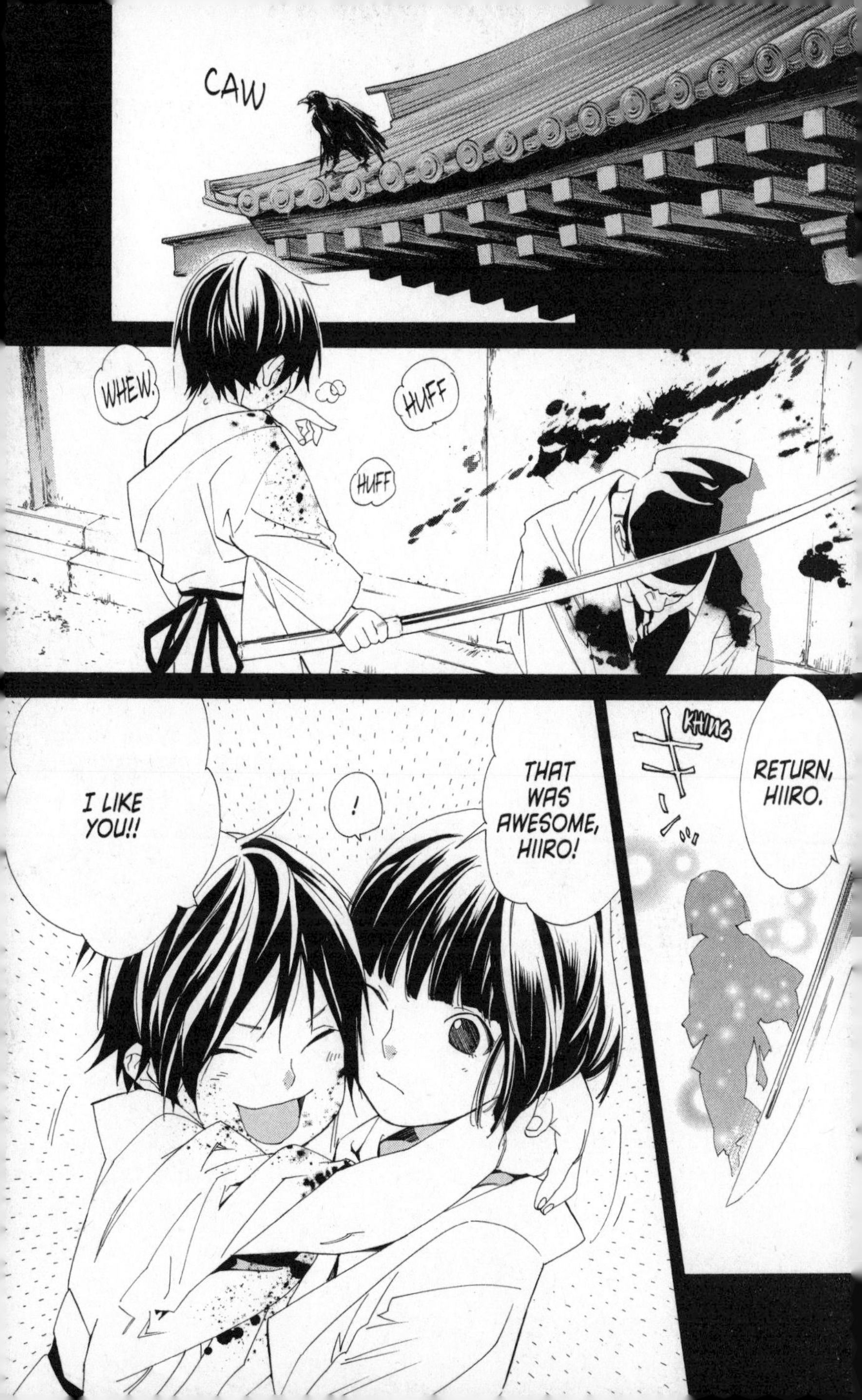
CAW
HUFF
WHEW.
HUFF
KHING
RETURN, HIIRO.
THAT WAS AWESOME, HIIRO!
!
I LIKE YOU!!

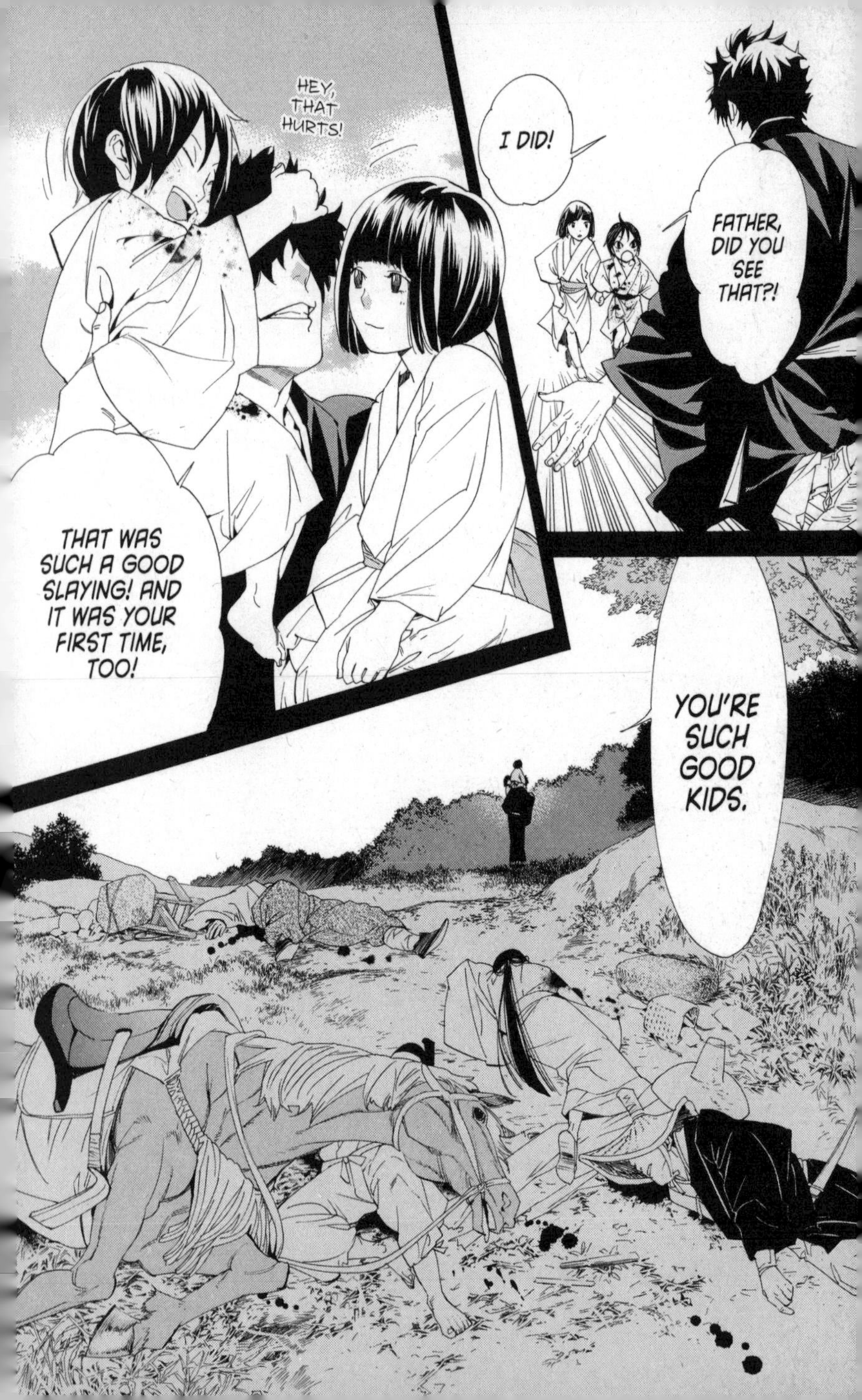
FATHER, DID YOU SEE THAT?!
I DID!
HEY, THAT HURTS!
THAT WAS SUCH A GOOD SLAYING! AND IT WAS YOUR FIRST TIME, TOO!
YOU'RE SUCH GOOD KIDS.

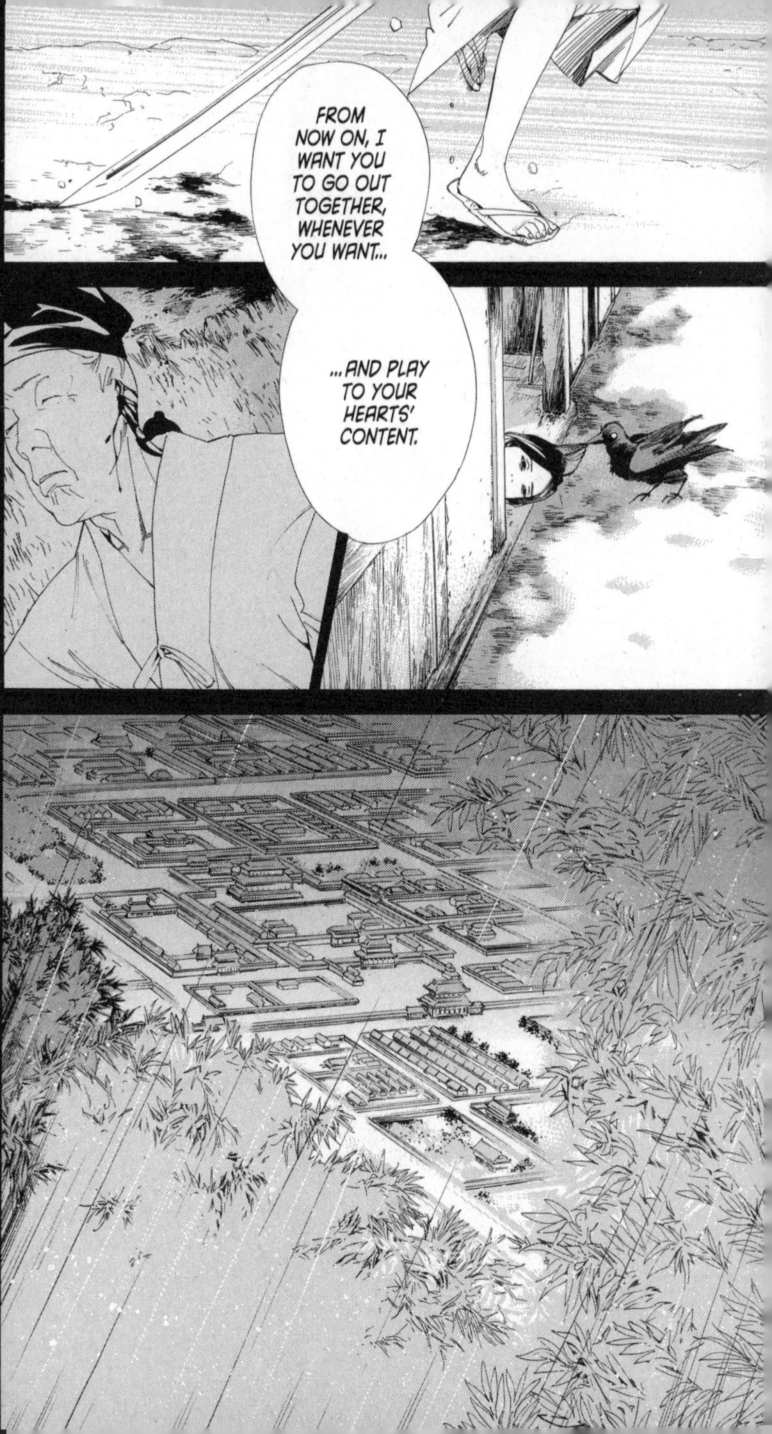
FROM NOW ON, I WANT YOU TO GO OUT TOGETHER, WHENEVER YOU WANT...
...AND PLAY TO YOUR HEARTS' CONTENT.

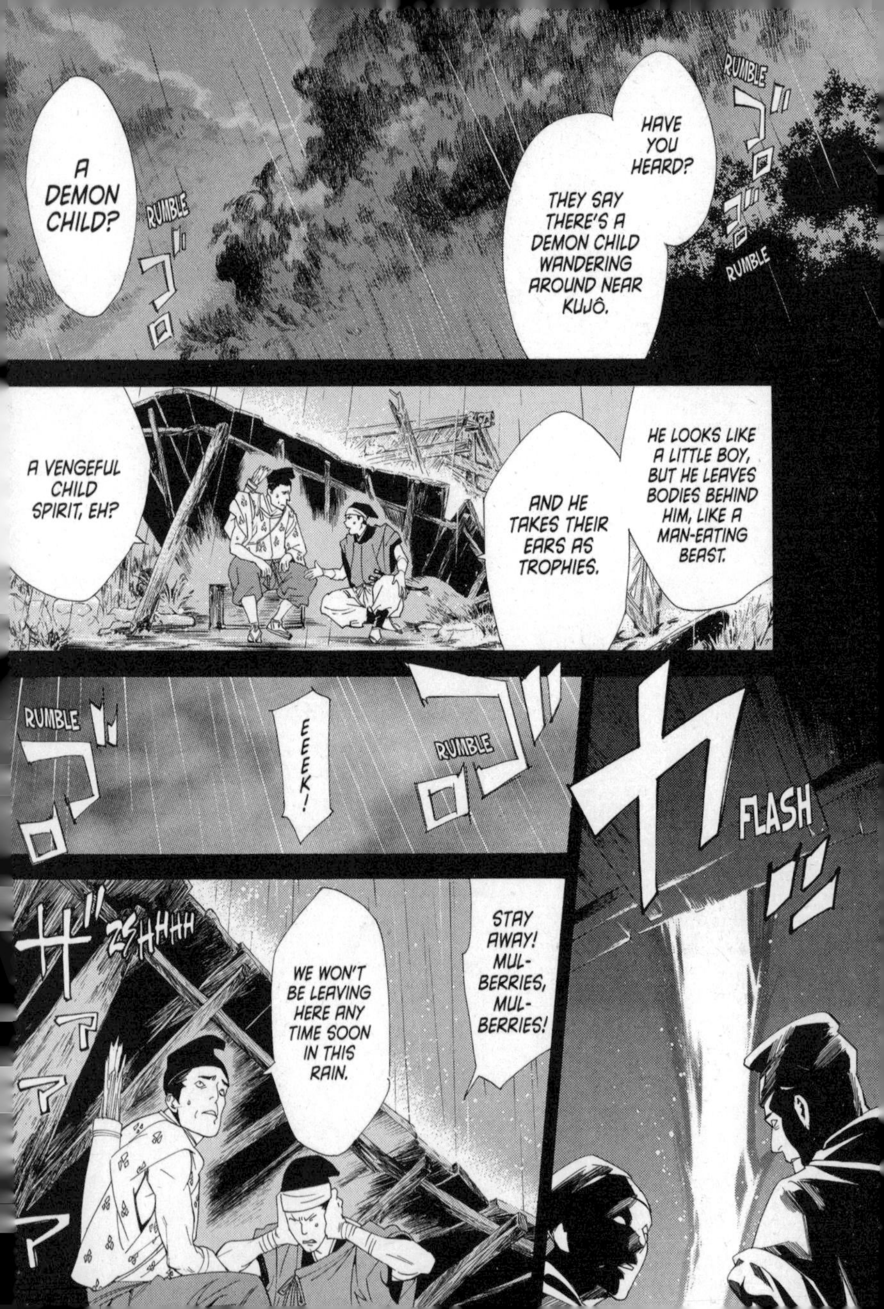
RUMBLE
HAVE YOU HEARD?
THEY SAY THERE'S A DEMON CHILD WANDERING AROUND NEAR KUJÔ.
RUMBLE
A DEMON CHILD?
RUMBLE
HE LOOKS LIKE A LITTLE BOY, BUT HE LEAVES BODIES BEHIND HIM, LIKE A MAN-EATING BEAST.
AND HE TAKES THEIR EARS AS TROPHIES.
A VENGEFUL CHILD SPIRIT, EH?
FLASH
RUMBLE
EEEEK!
RUMBLE
STAY AWAY! MUL-BERRIES, MUL-BERRIES!
WE WON'T BE LEAVING HERE ANY TIME SOON IN THIS RAIN.
ZSHHHH

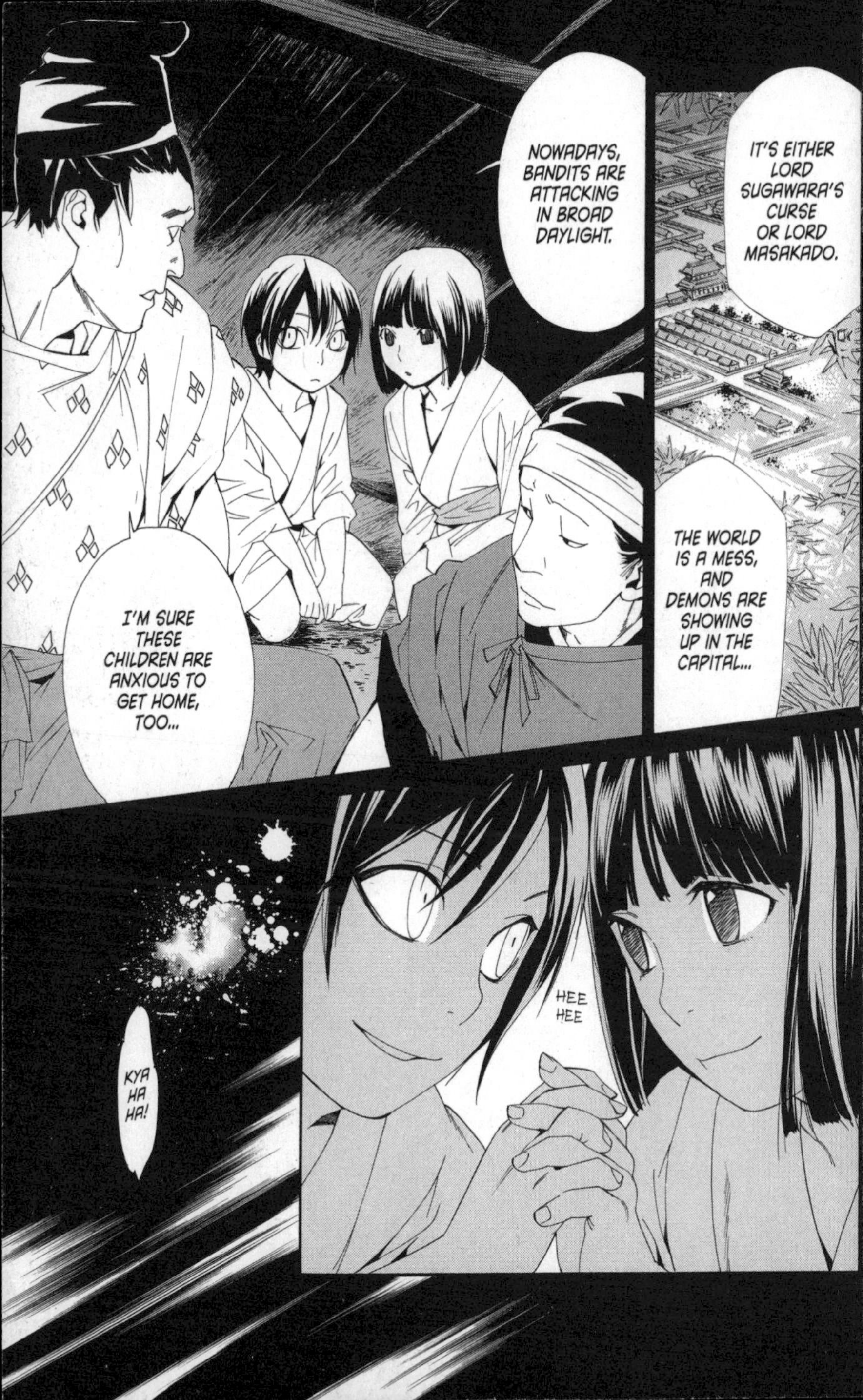
IT'S EITHER LORD SUGAWARA'S CURSE OR LORD MASAKADO.
THE WORLD IS A MESS, AND DEMONS ARE SHOWING UP IN THE CAPITAL...
NOWADAYS, BANDITS ARE ATTACKING IN BROAD DAYLIGHT.
I'M SURE THESE CHILDREN ARE ANXIOUS TO GET HOME, TOO...
HEE HEE
KYA HA HA!

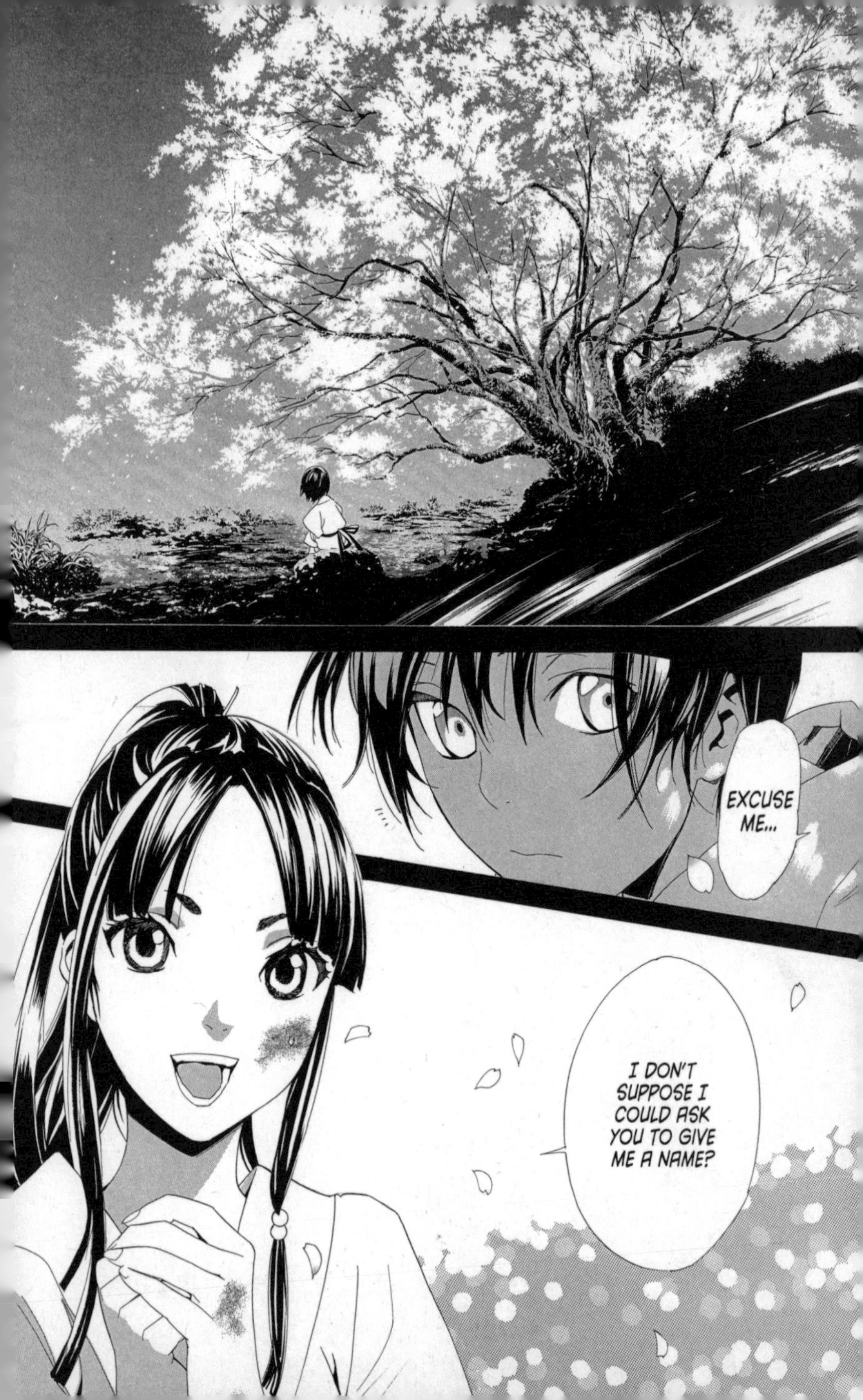
EXCUSE ME...
I DON'T SUPPOSE I COULD ASK YOU TO GIVE ME A NAME?

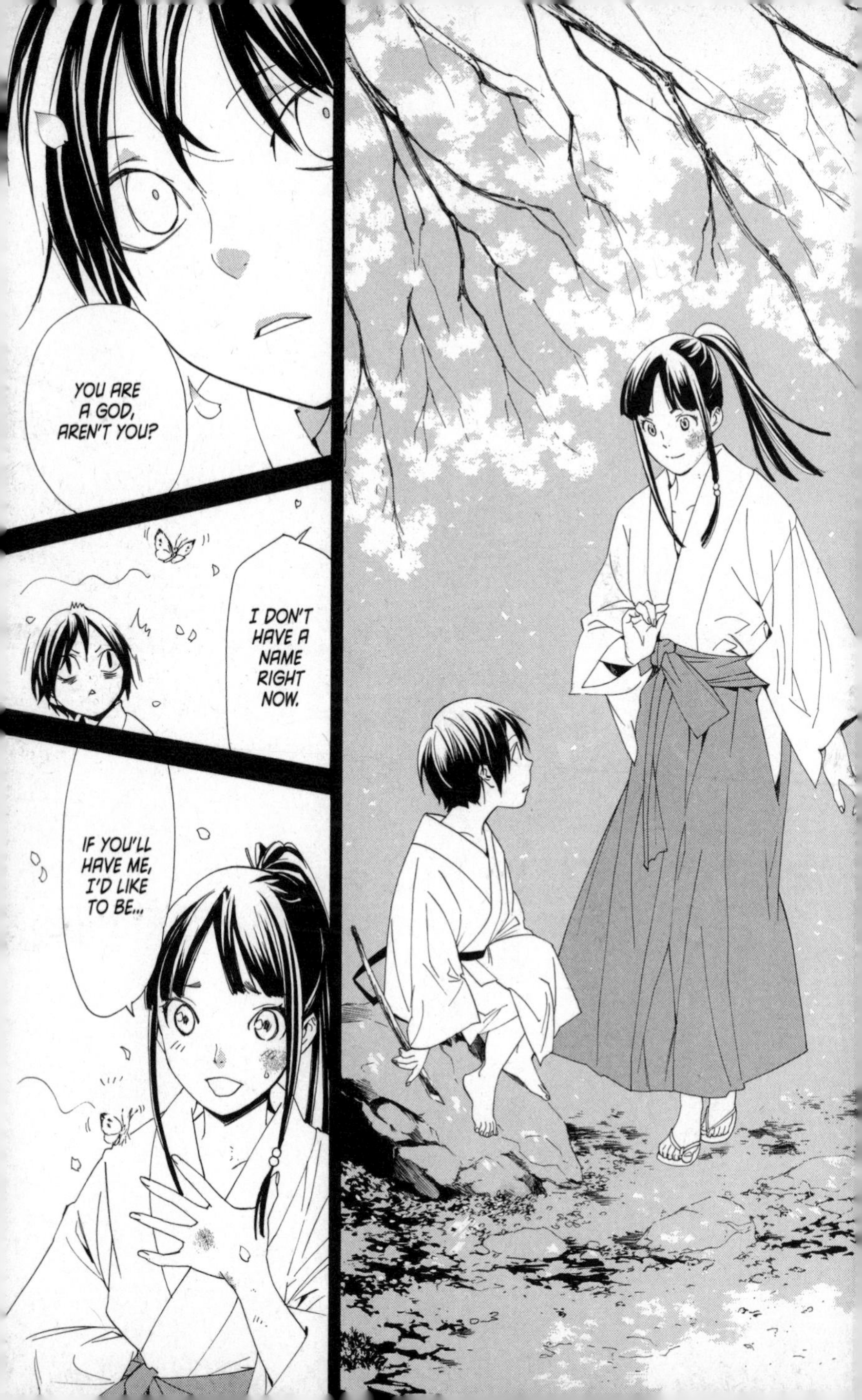
YOU ARE A GOD, AREN'T YOU?
I DON'T HAVE A NAME RIGHT NOW.
IF YOU'LL HAVE ME, I'D LIKE TO BE...

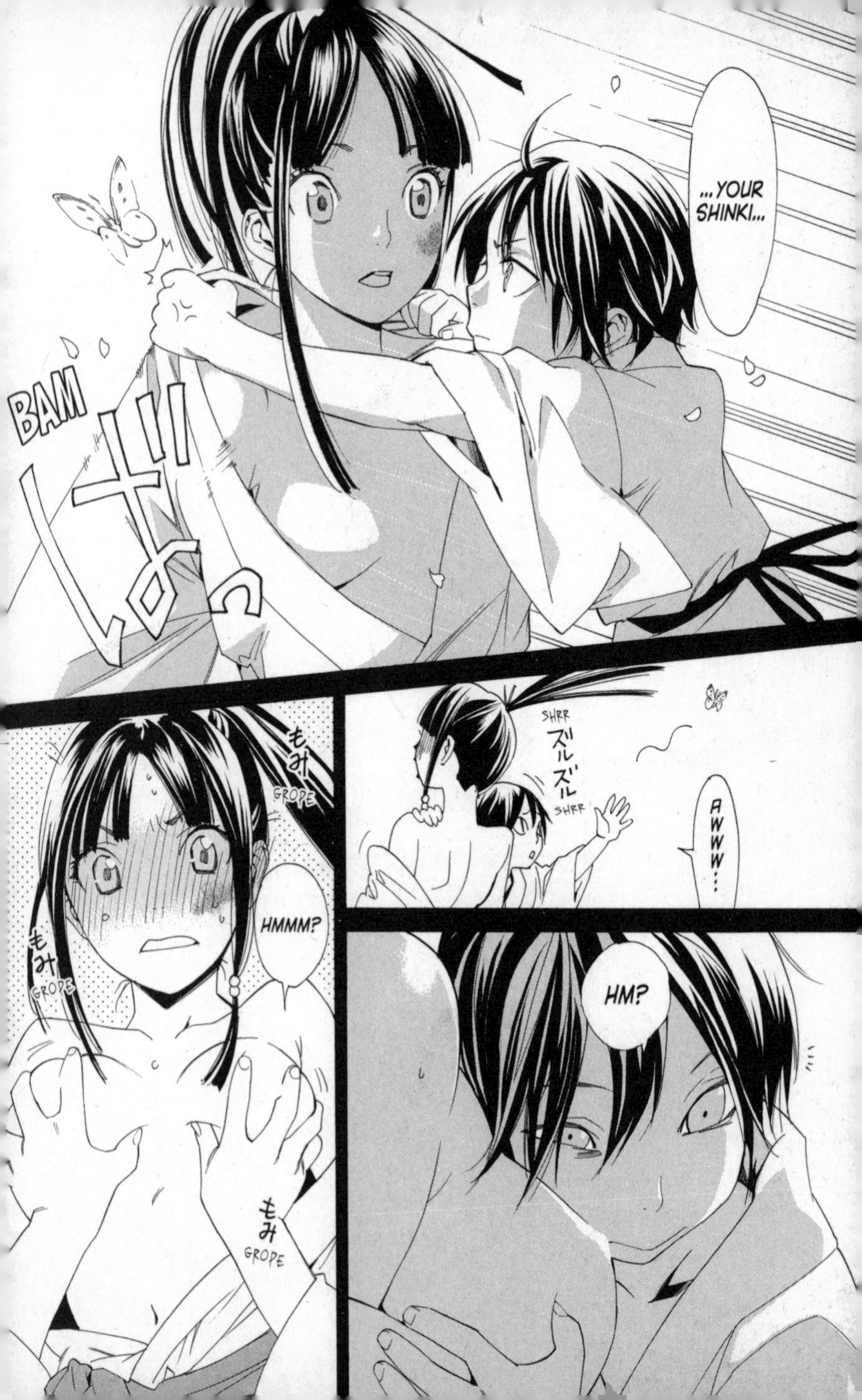
...YOUR SHINKI...
BAM
AWWW...
SHRR
ズルズル
SHRR
HM?
もみ
GROPE
HMMM?
もみ
GROPE
もみ
GROPE

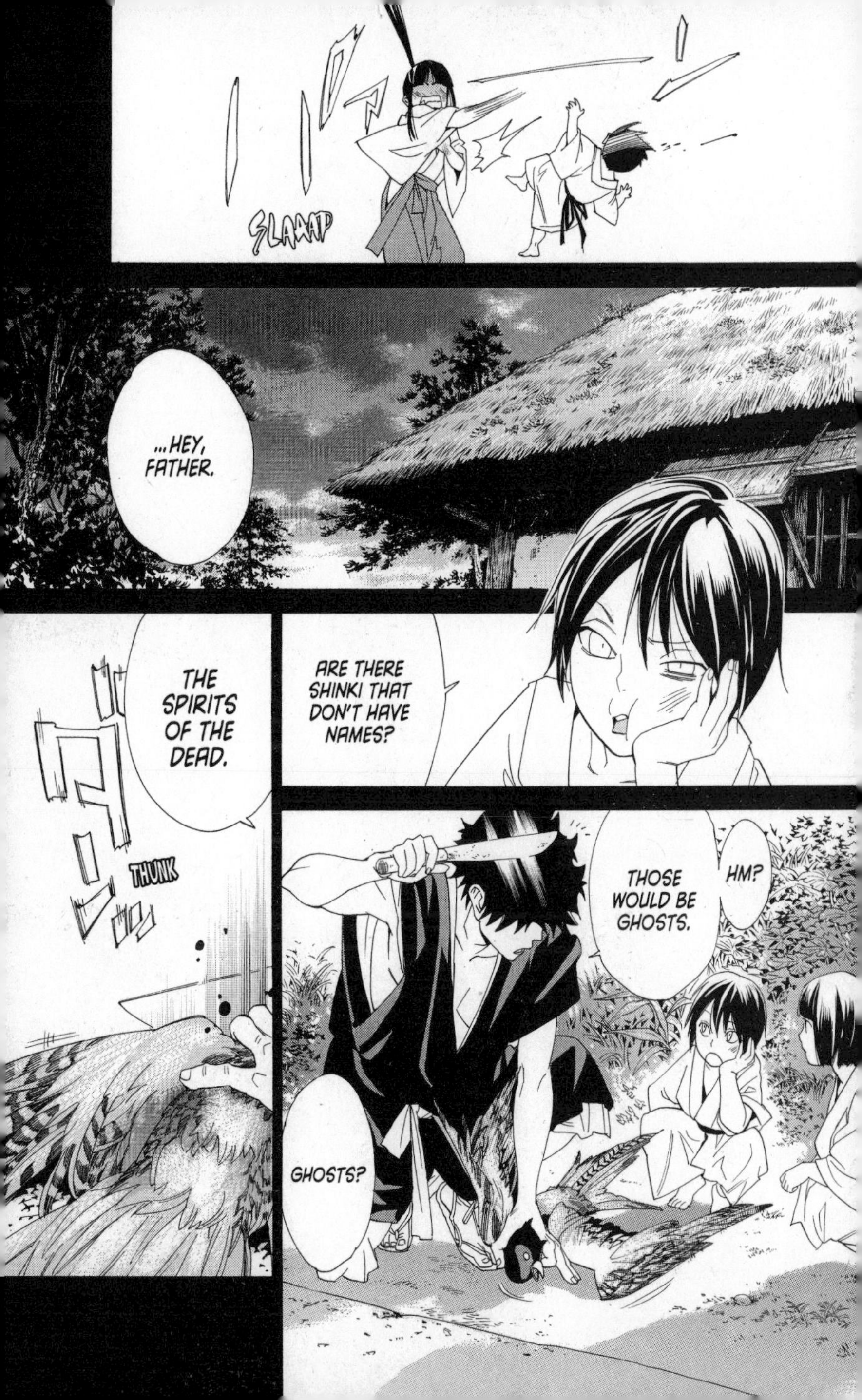
SLAAAP
...HEY, FATHER.
ARE THERE SHINKI THAT DON'T HAVE NAMES?
HM?
THOSE WOULD BE GHOSTS.
GHOSTS?
THE SPIRITS OF THE DEAD.
THUNK

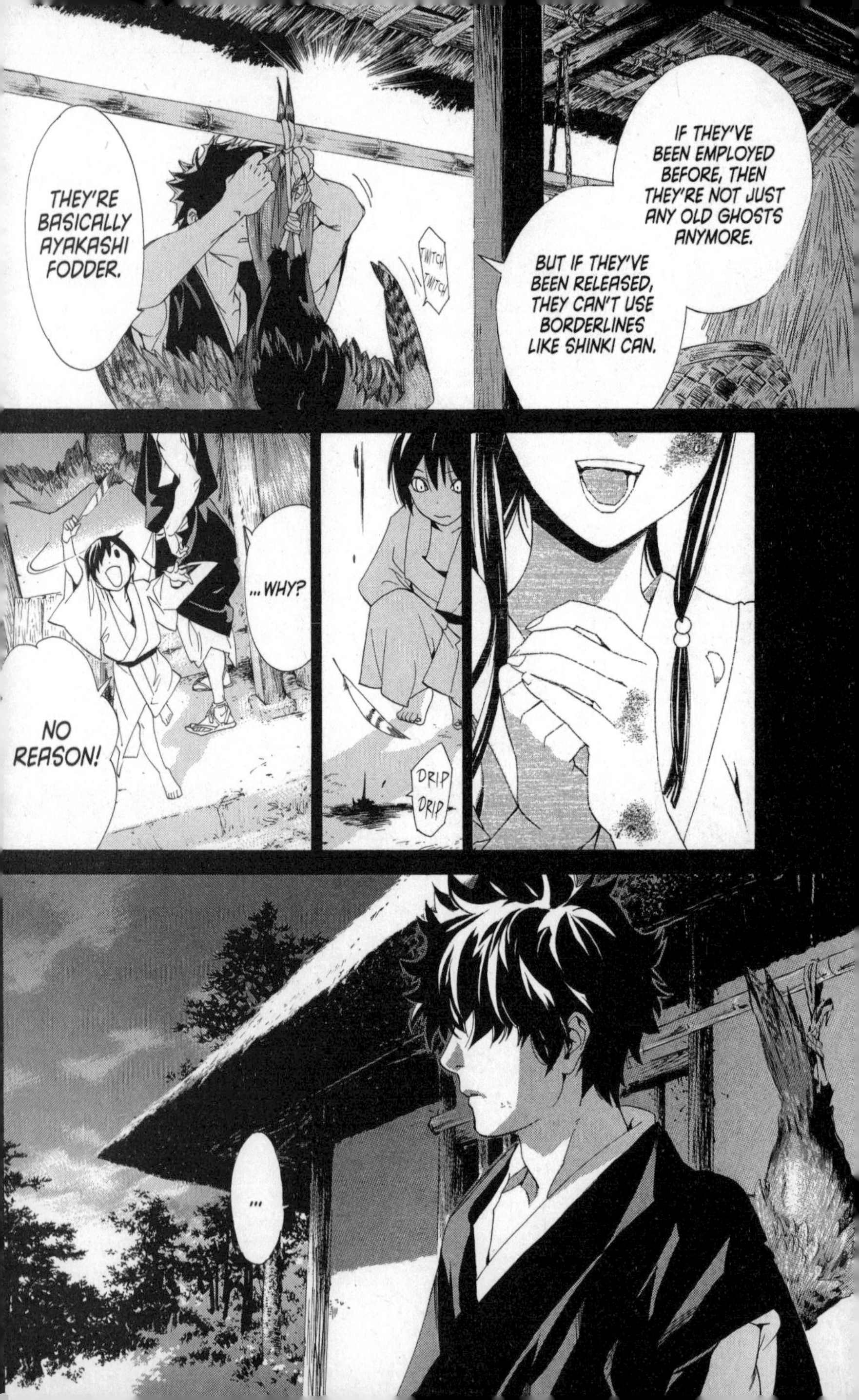
IF THEY'VE BEEN EMPLOYED BEFORE, THEN THEY'RE NOT JUST ANY OLD GHOSTS ANYMORE.
BUT IF THEY'VE BEEN RELEASED, THEY CAN'T USE BORDERLINES LIKE SHINKI CAN.
TWITCH TWITCH
THEY'RE BASICALLY AYAKASHI FODDER.
DRIP DRIP
...WHY?
NO REASON!
...

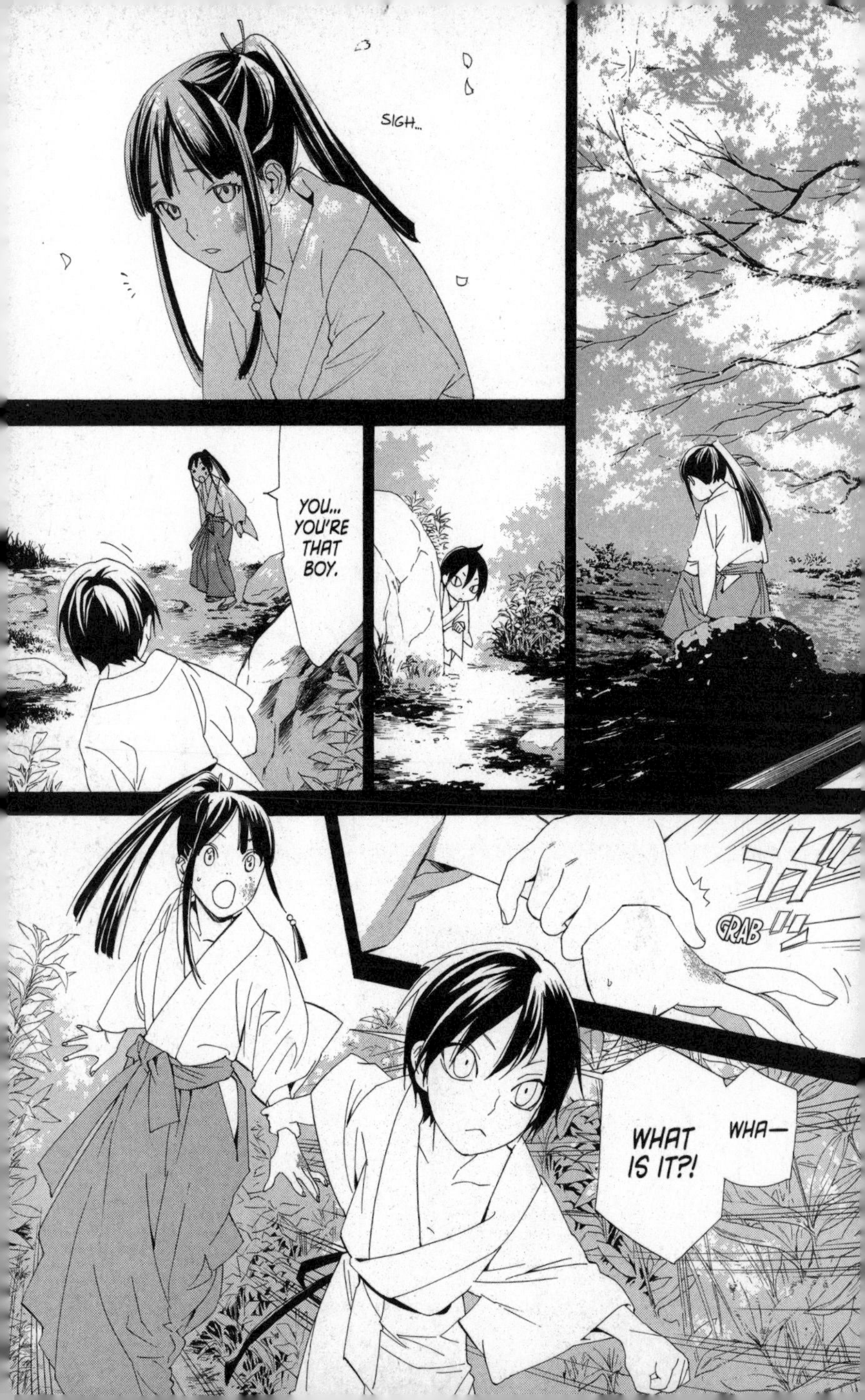
SIGH...
YOU... YOU'RE THAT BOY.
GRAB
WHA—
WHAT IS IT?!

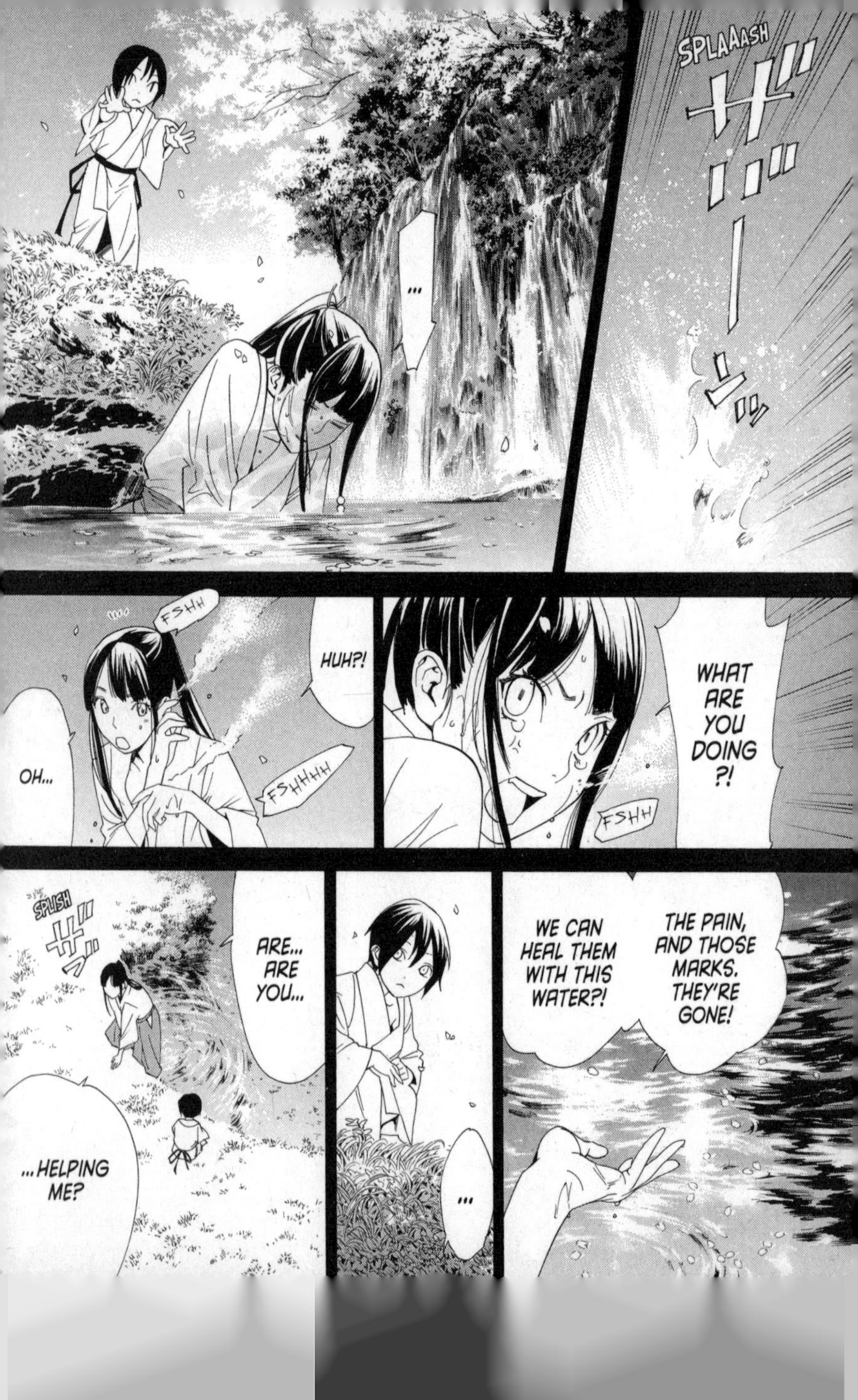
SPLAAASH
...
WHAT ARE YOU DOING?!
FSHH
HUH?!
FSHH
FSHHHH
OH...
THE PAIN, AND THOSE MARKS. THEY'RE GONE!
WE CAN HEAL THEM WITH THIS WATER?!
...
SPLISH
ARE... ARE YOU...
...HELPING ME?

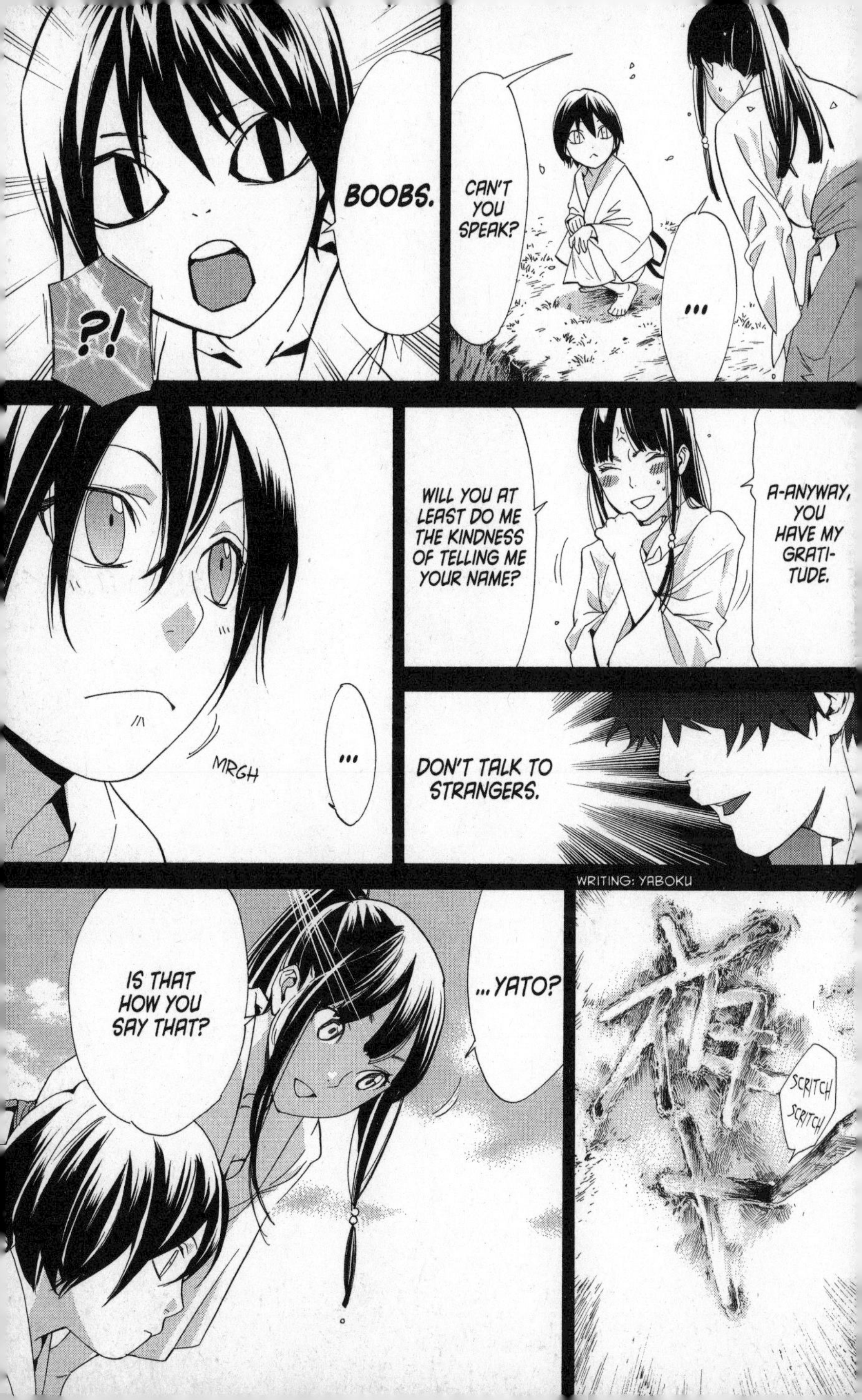
CAN'T YOU SPEAK?
...
BOOBS.
?!
A-ANYWAY, YOU HAVE MY GRATITUDE.
WILL YOU AT LEAST DO ME THE KINDNESS OF TELLING ME YOUR NAME?
DON'T TALK TO STRANGERS.
...
MRGH
WRITING: YABOKU
SCRITCH SCRITCH
...YATO?
IS THAT HOW YOU SAY THAT?

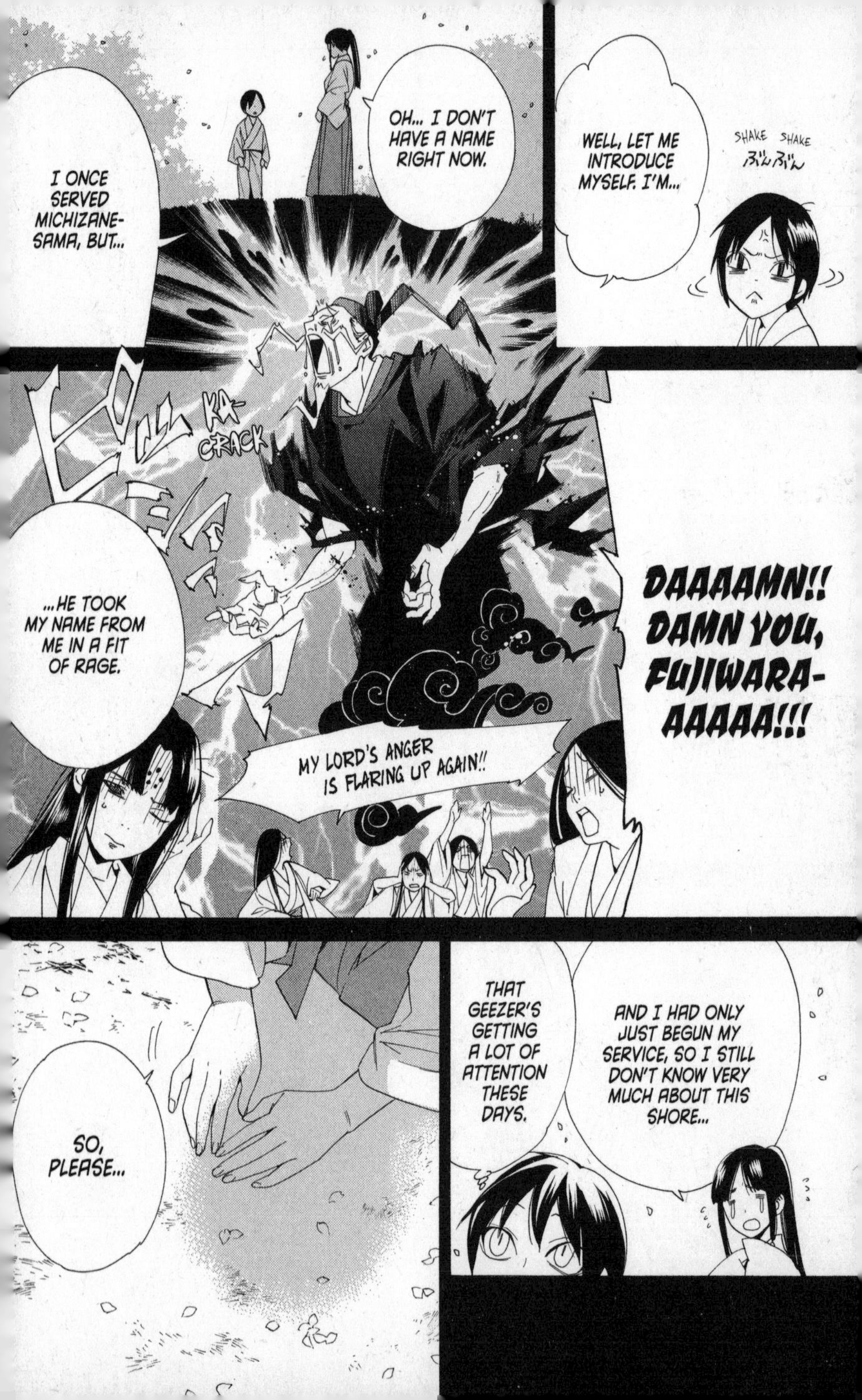
WELL, LET ME INTRODUCE MYSELF. I'M...
SHAKE SHAKE
ぶんぶん
OH... I DON'T HAVE A NAME RIGHT NOW.
I ONCE SERVED MICHIZANE-SAMA, BUT...
DAAAAMN!! DAMN YOU, FUJIWARA-AAAAA!!!
KA-CRACK
MY LORD'S ANGER IS FLARING UP AGAIN!!
...HE TOOK MY NAME FROM ME IN A FIT OF RAGE.
AND I HAD ONLY JUST BEGUN MY SERVICE, SO I STILL DON'T KNOW VERY MUCH ABOUT THIS SHORE...
THAT GEEZER'S GETTING A LOT OF ATTENTION THESE DAYS.
SO, PLEASE...

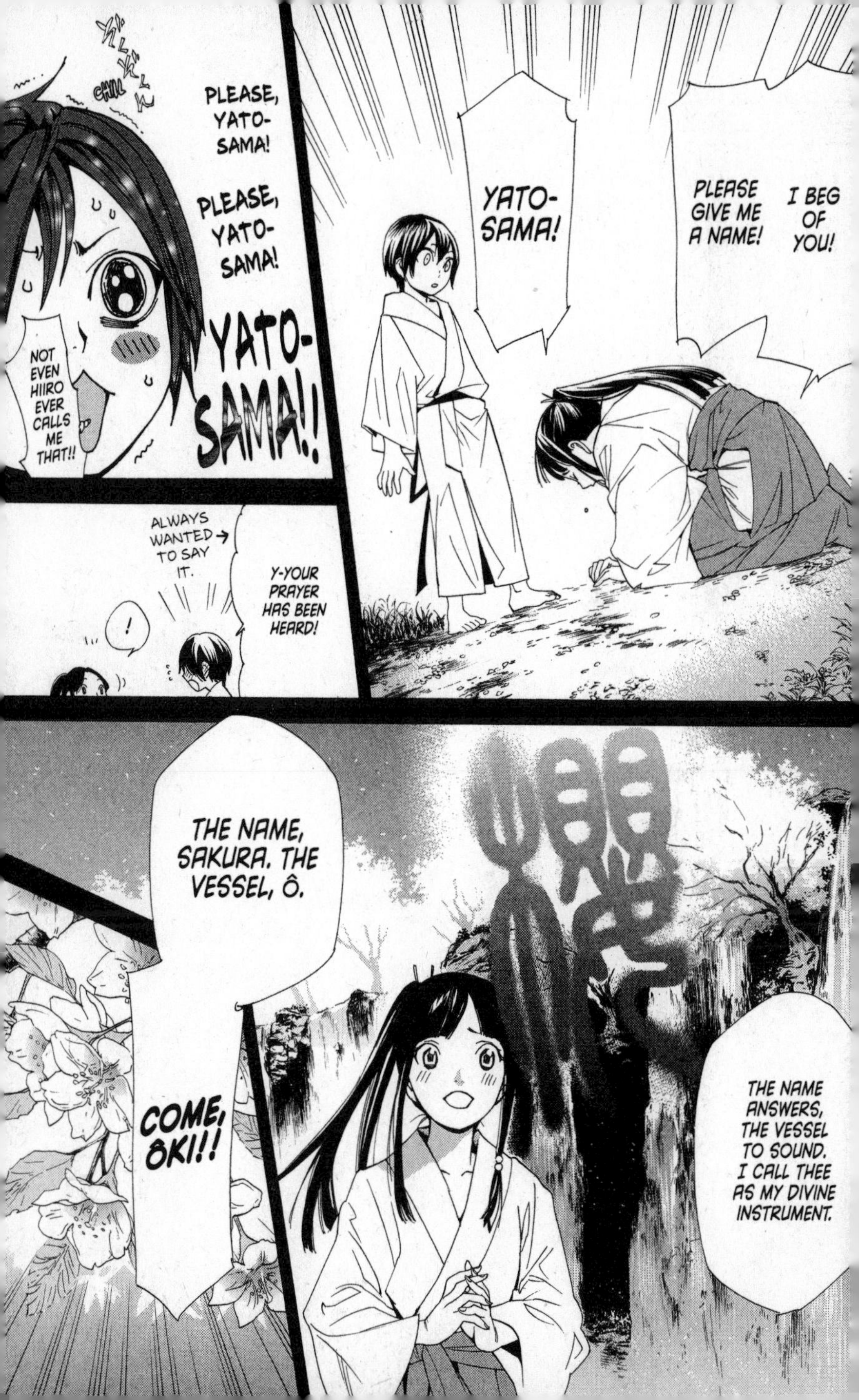
PLEASE GIVE ME A NAME! I BEG OF YOU!
YATO-SAMA!
PLEASE, YATO-SAMA!
PLEASE, YATO-SAMA!
YATO-SAMA!!
CHILL
NOT EVEN HIIRO EVER CALLS ME THAT!!
Y-YOUR PRAYER HAS BEEN HEARD!
ALWAYS WANTED TO SAY IT.
!
THE NAME ANSWERS, THE VESSEL TO SOUND. I CALL THEE AS MY DIVINE INSTRUMENT.
THE NAME, SAKURA. THE VESSEL, Ô.
COME, ÔKI!!

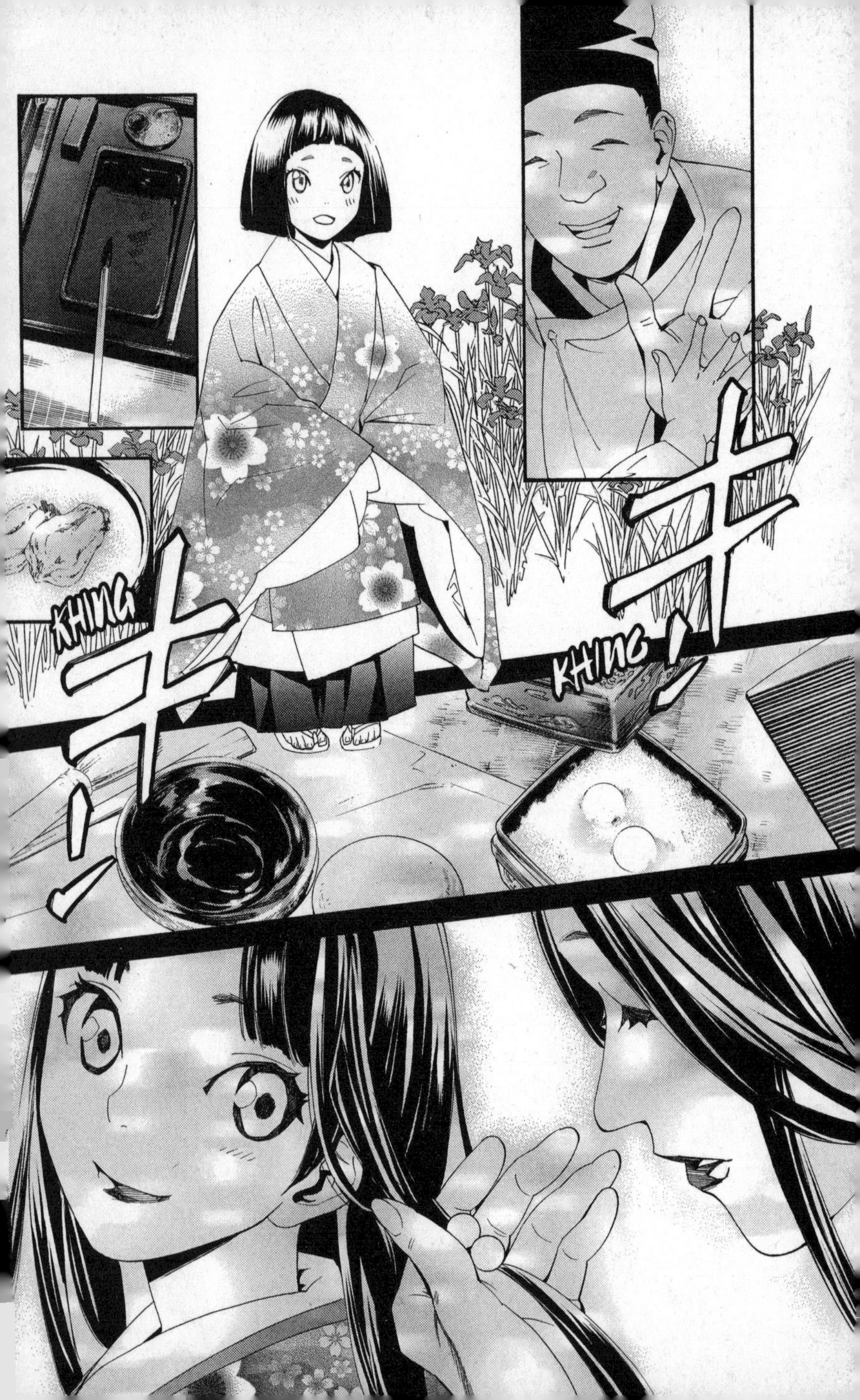
KHING
KHING

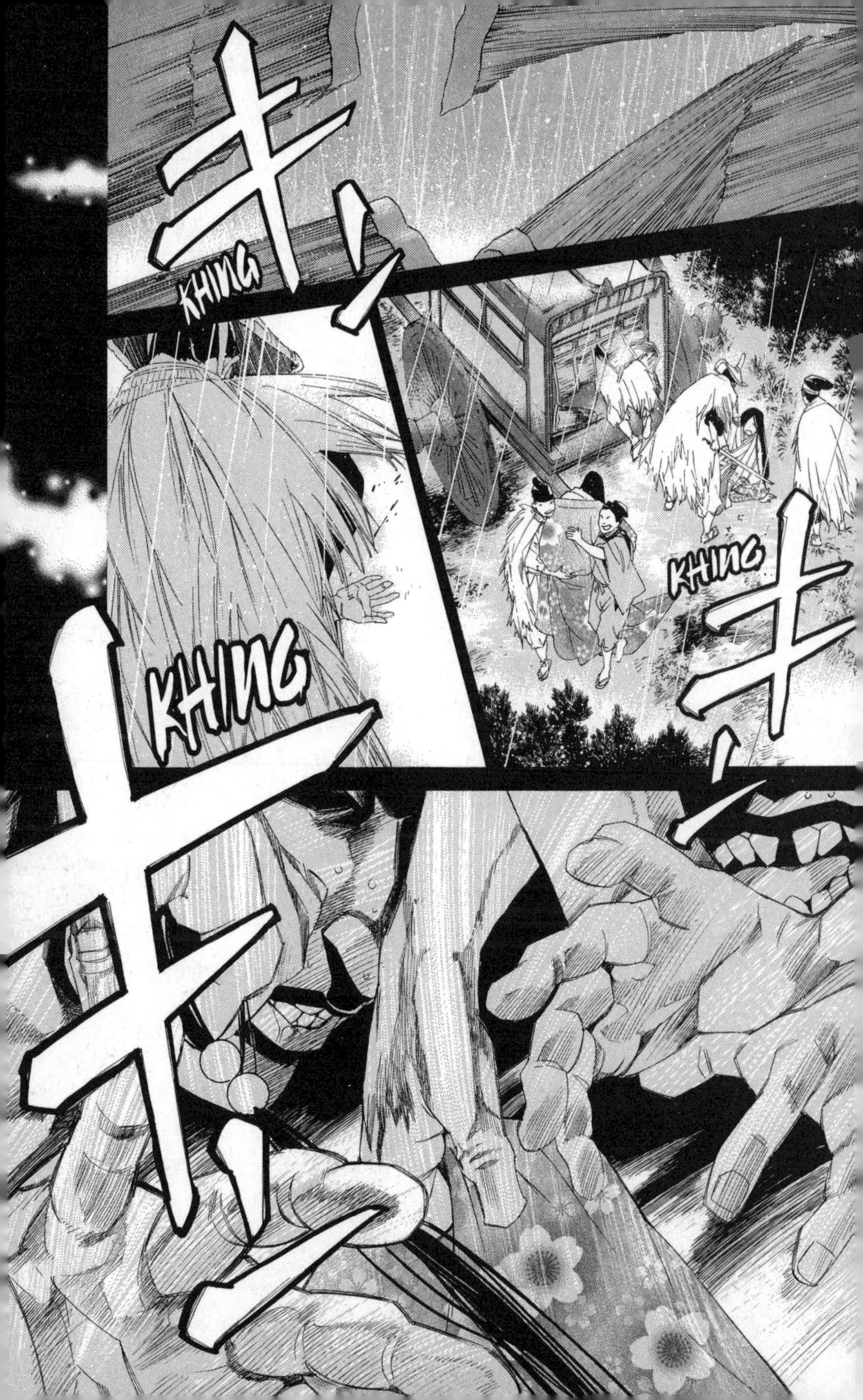
KHING
KHING
KHING

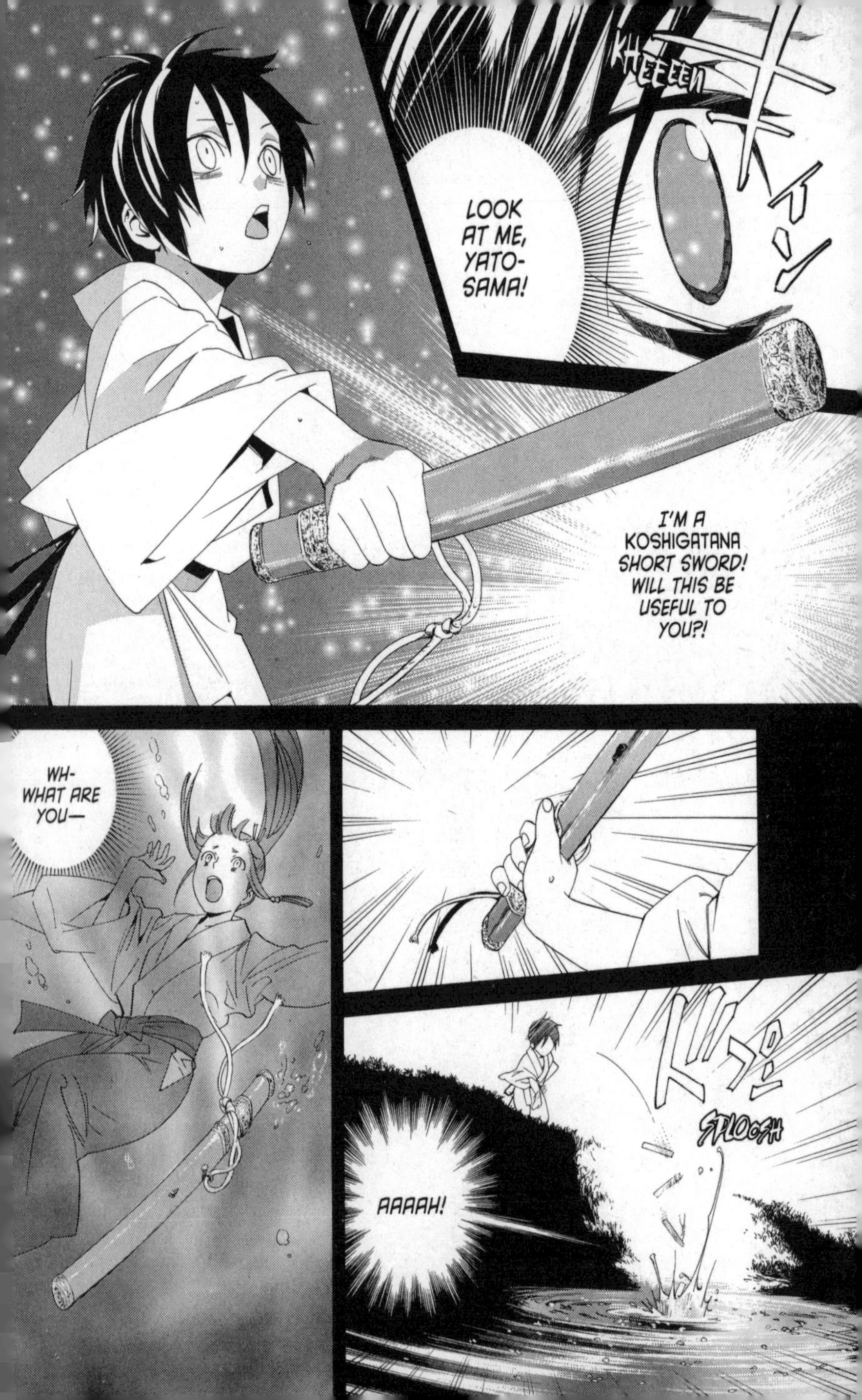
KHEEEEN
LOOK AT ME, YATO-SAMA!
I'M A KOSHIGATANA SHORT SWORD! WILL THIS BE USEFUL TO YOU?!
SPLOOSH
AAAAH!
WH- WHAT ARE YOU—

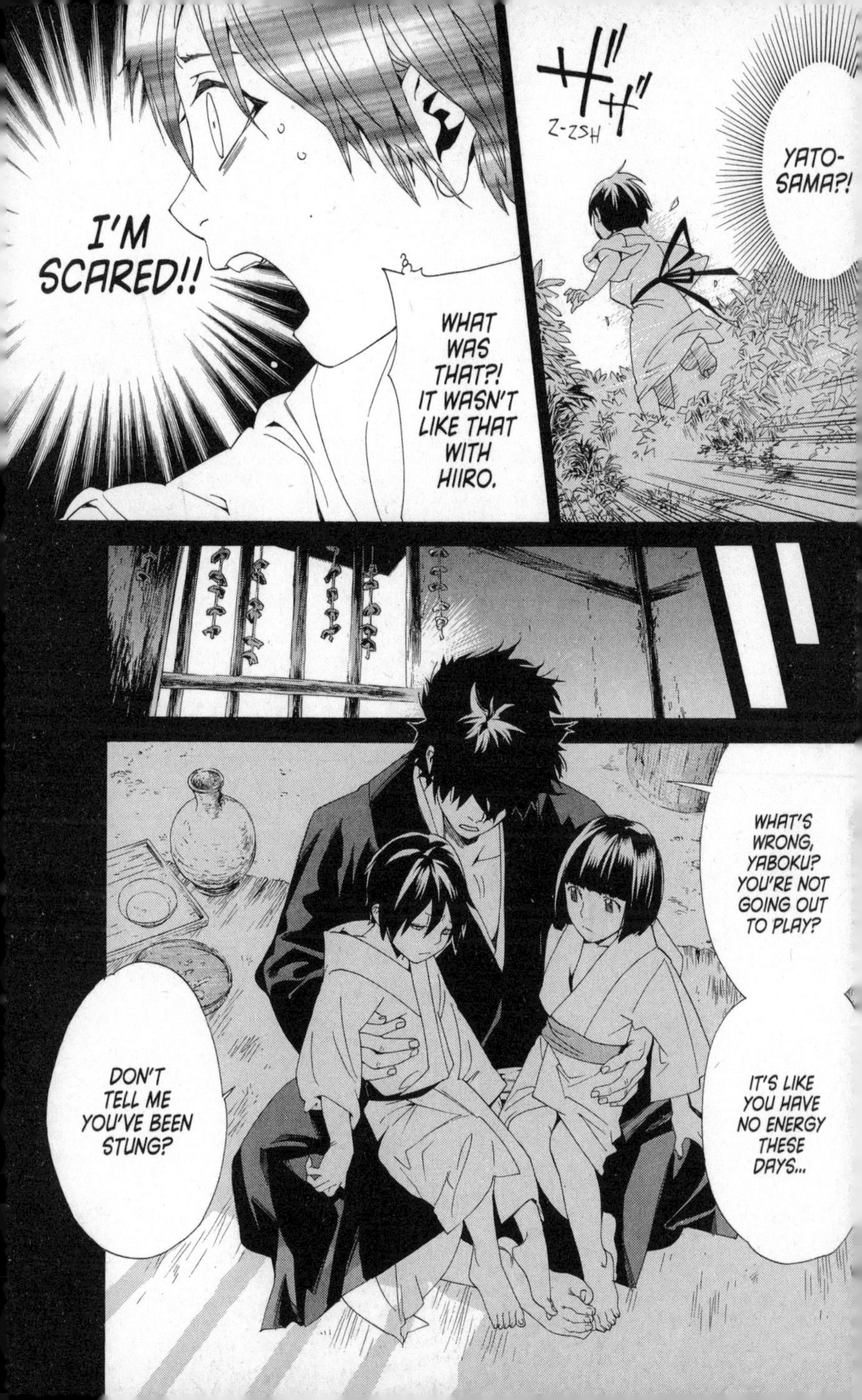
YATO-SAMA?!
ザザ
Z-ZSH
I'M SCARED!!
WHAT WAS THAT?! IT WASN'T LIKE THAT WITH HIIRO.
WHAT'S WRONG, YABOKU? YOU'RE NOT GOING OUT TO PLAY?
IT'S LIKE YOU HAVE NO ENERGY THESE DAYS...
DON'T TELL ME YOU'VE BEEN STUNG?

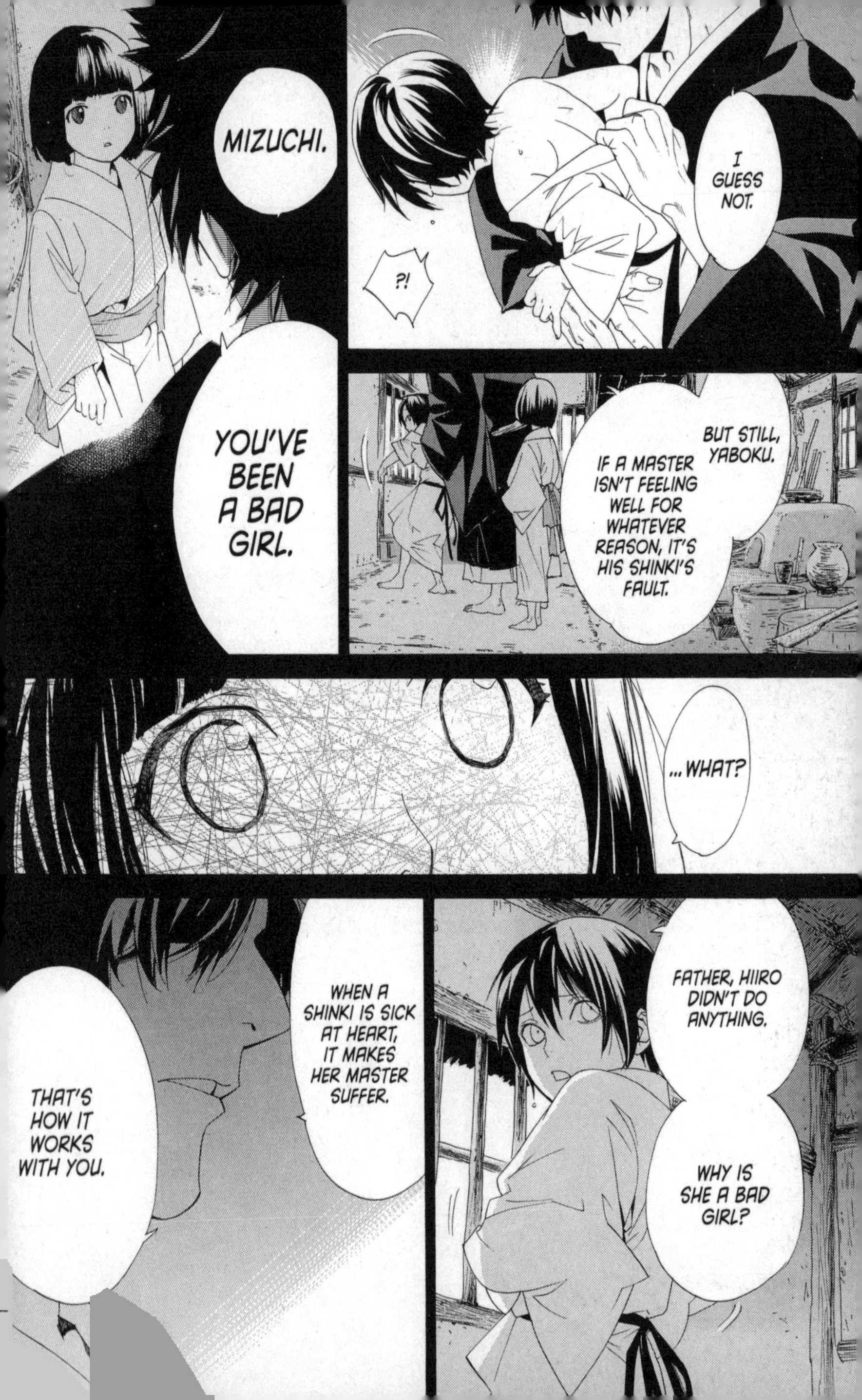
I GUESS NOT.
?!
BUT STILL, YABOKU.
IF A MASTER ISN'T FEELING WELL FOR WHATEVER REASON, IT'S HIS SHINKI'S FAULT.
MIZUCHI.
YOU'VE BEEN A BAD GIRL.
...WHAT?
FATHER, HIIRO DIDN'T DO ANYTHING.
WHY IS SHE A BAD GIRL?
WHEN A SHINKI IS SICK AT HEART, IT MAKES HER MASTER SUFFER.
THAT'S HOW IT WORKS WITH YOU.

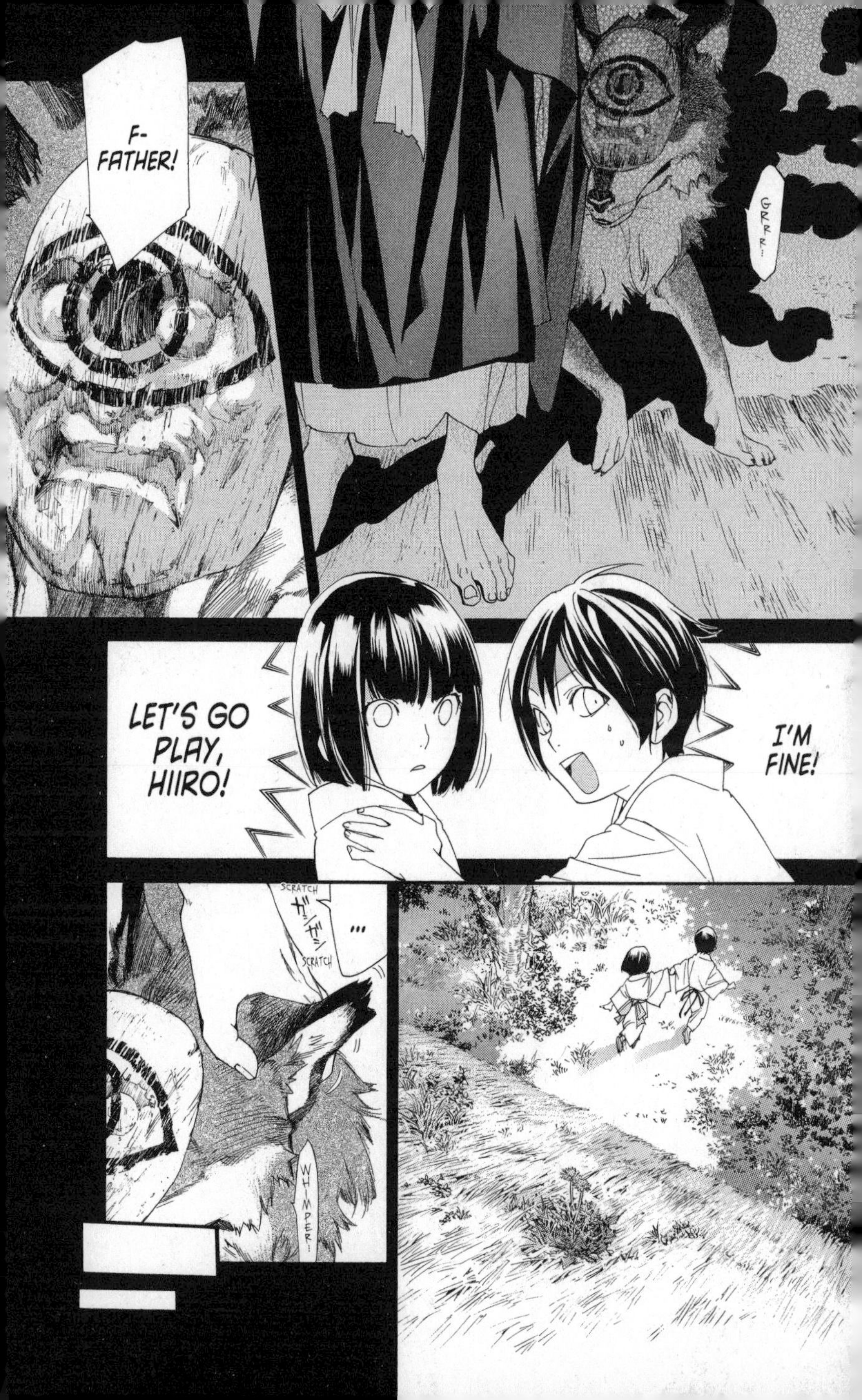
GRRR...
F-FATHER!
I'M FINE!
LET'S GO PLAY, HIIRO!
...
SCRATCH
SCRATCH
WHIMPER...

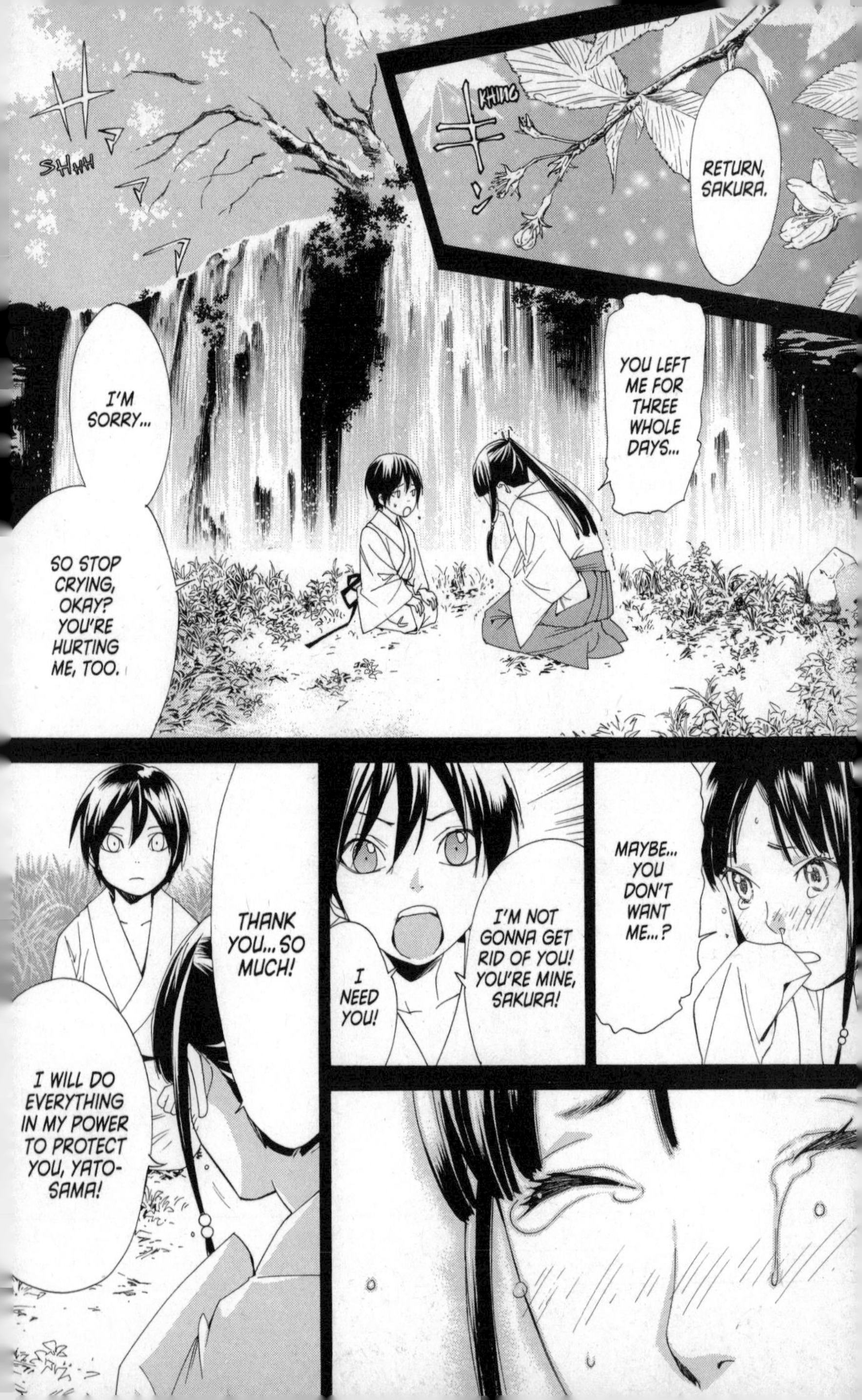
KHING
RETURN, SAKURA.
SHHH
YOU LEFT ME FOR THREE WHOLE DAYS...
I'M SORRY...
SO STOP CRYING, OKAY? YOU'RE HURTING ME, TOO.
MAYBE... YOU DON'T WANT ME...?
I'M NOT GONNA GET RID OF YOU! YOU'RE MINE, SAKURA!
I NEED YOU!
THANK YOU... SO MUCH!
I WILL DO EVERYTHING IN MY POWER TO PROTECT YOU, YATO-SAMA!

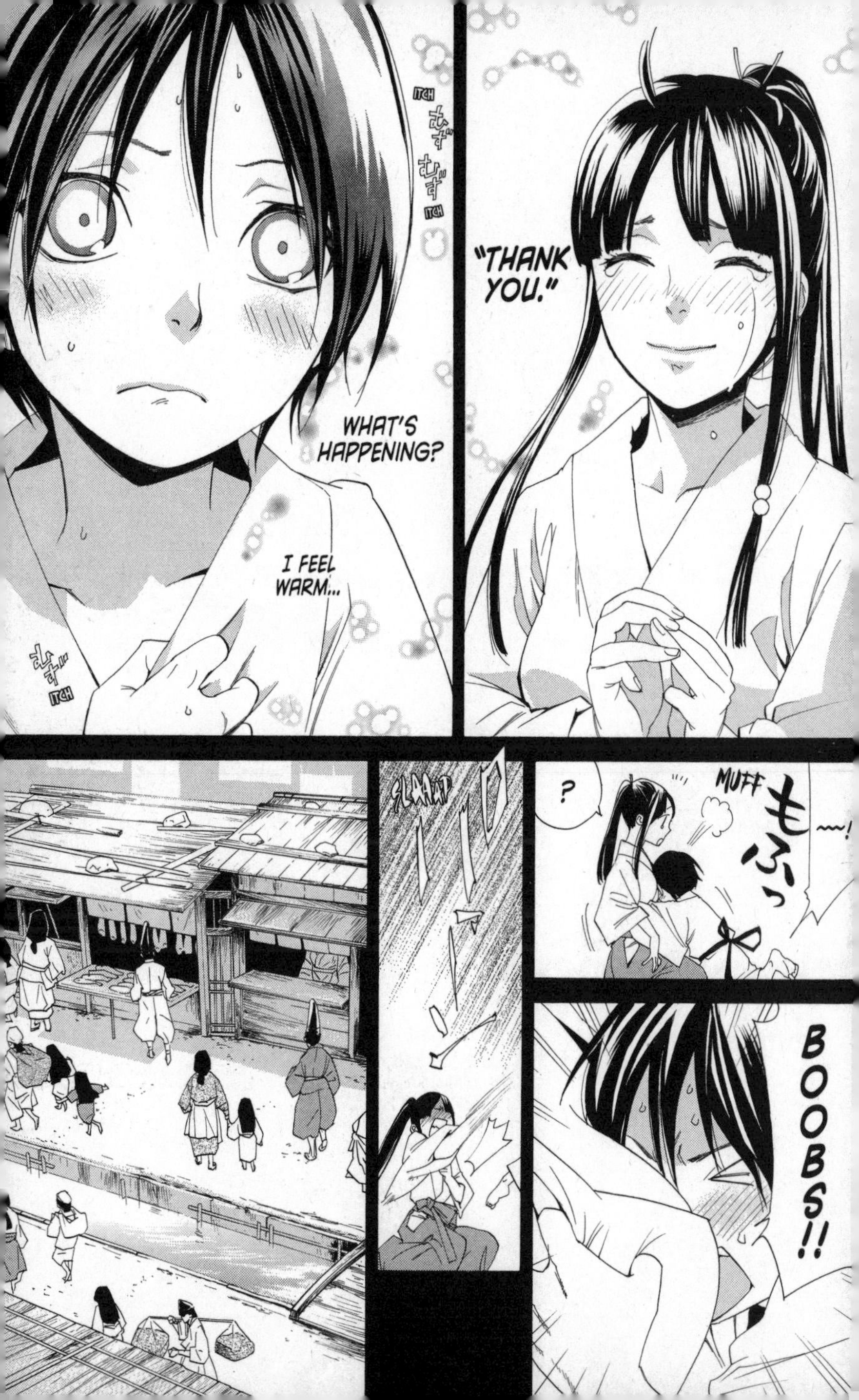
"THANK YOU."
ITCH
むずむず
ITCH
WHAT'S HAPPENING?
I FEEL WARM...
むず
ITCH
MUFF
もふっ
~~!
?
BOOBS!!
SLAAAP

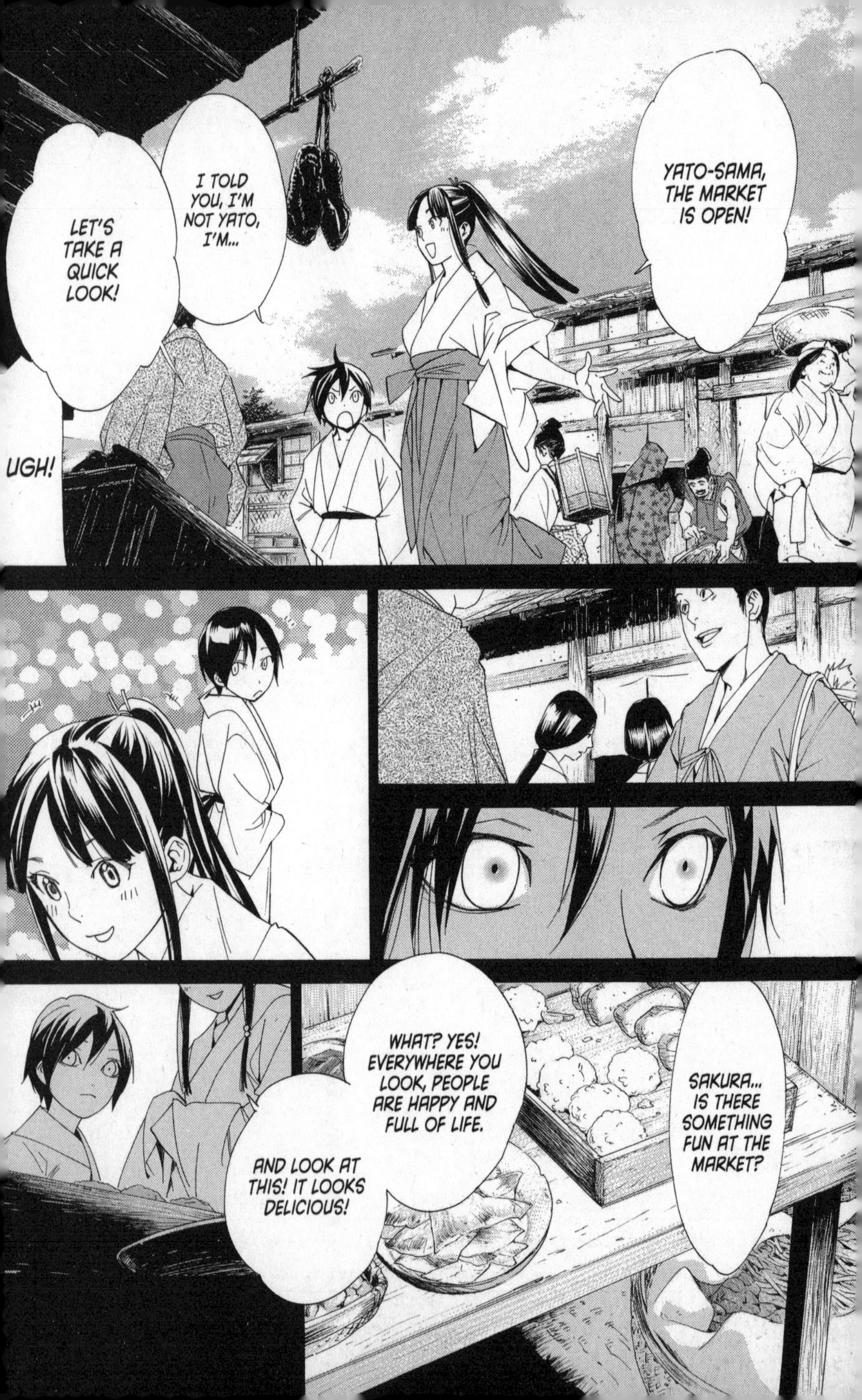
YATO-SAMA, THE MARKET IS OPEN!
I TOLD YOU, I'M NOT YATO, I'M...
LET'S TAKE A QUICK LOOK!
UGH!
SAKURA... IS THERE SOMETHING FUN AT THE MARKET?
WHAT? YES! EVERYWHERE YOU LOOK, PEOPLE ARE HAPPY AND FULL OF LIFE.
AND LOOK AT THIS! IT LOOKS DELICIOUS!

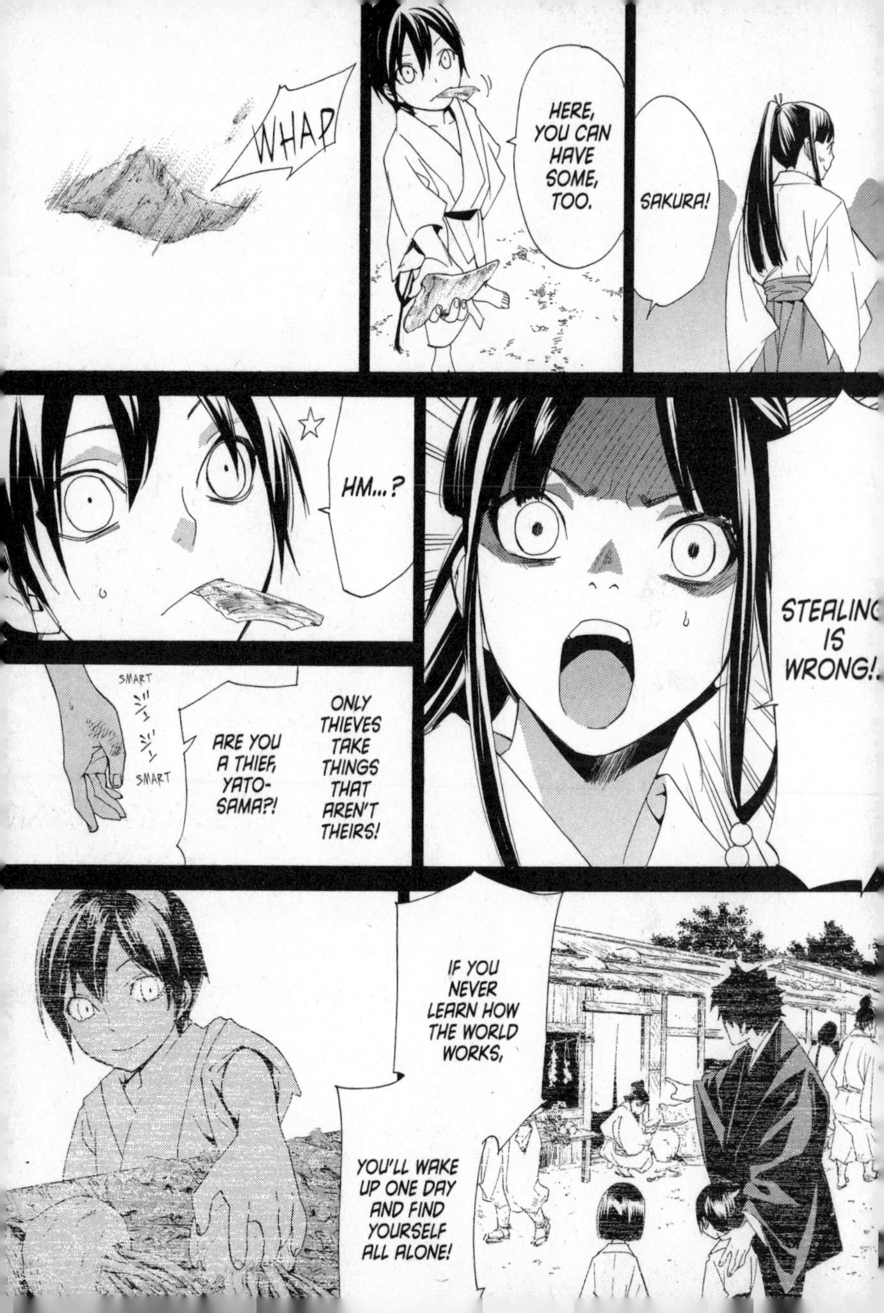
SAKURA!
HERE, YOU CAN HAVE SOME, TOO.
WHAP
STEALING IS WRONG!!
HM...?
ONLY THIEVES TAKE THINGS THAT AREN'T THEIRS!
ARE YOU A THIEF, YATO-SAMA?!
SMART
SMART
IF YOU NEVER LEARN HOW THE WORLD WORKS,
YOU'LL WAKE UP ONE DAY AND FIND YOURSELF ALL ALONE!

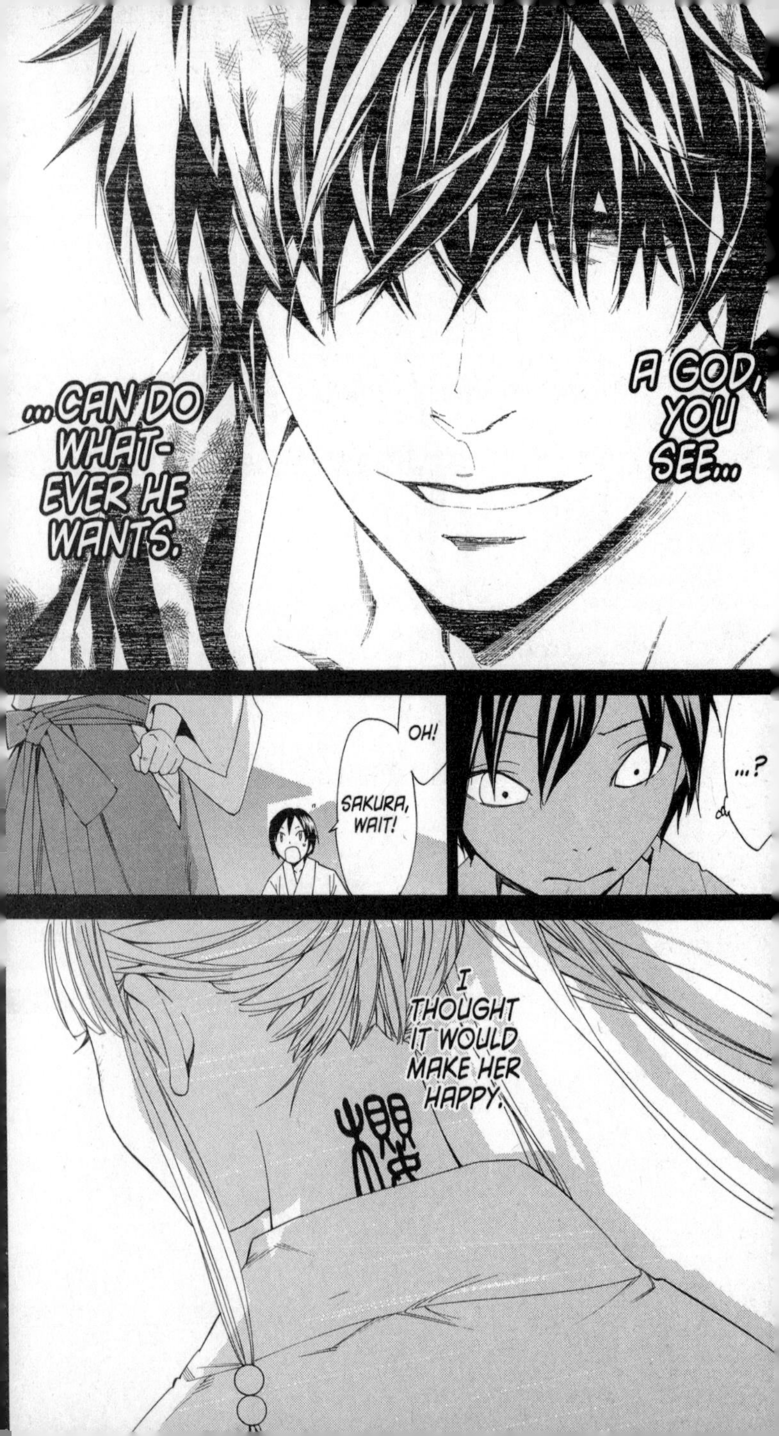
A GOD, YOU SEE...
...CAN DO WHAT-EVER HE WANTS.
...?
OH!
SAKURA, WAIT!
I THOUGHT IT WOULD MAKE HER HAPPY.

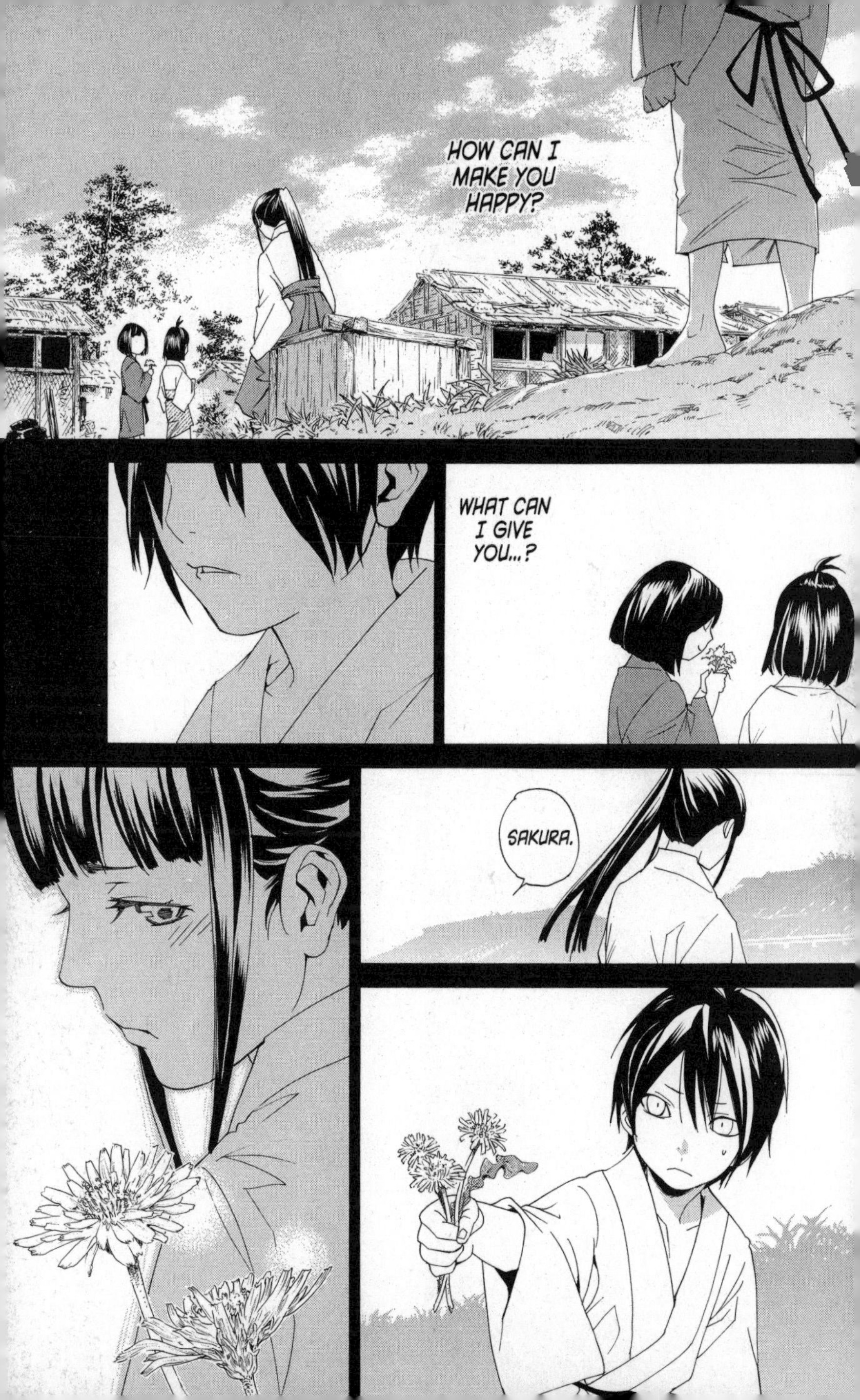
HOW CAN I MAKE YOU HAPPY?
WHAT CAN I GIVE YOU...?
SAKURA.

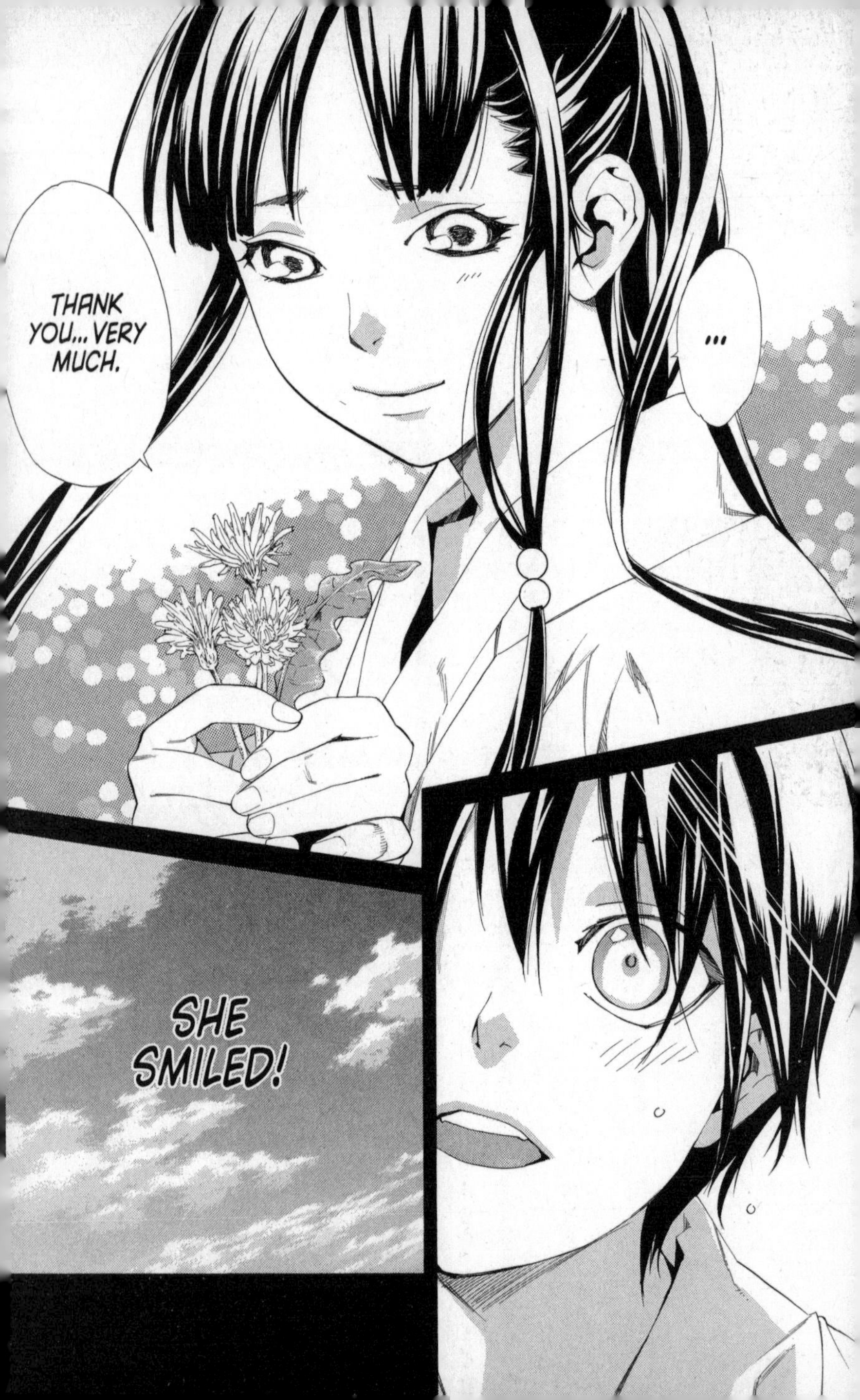
...
THANK YOU... VERY MUCH.
SHE SMILED!

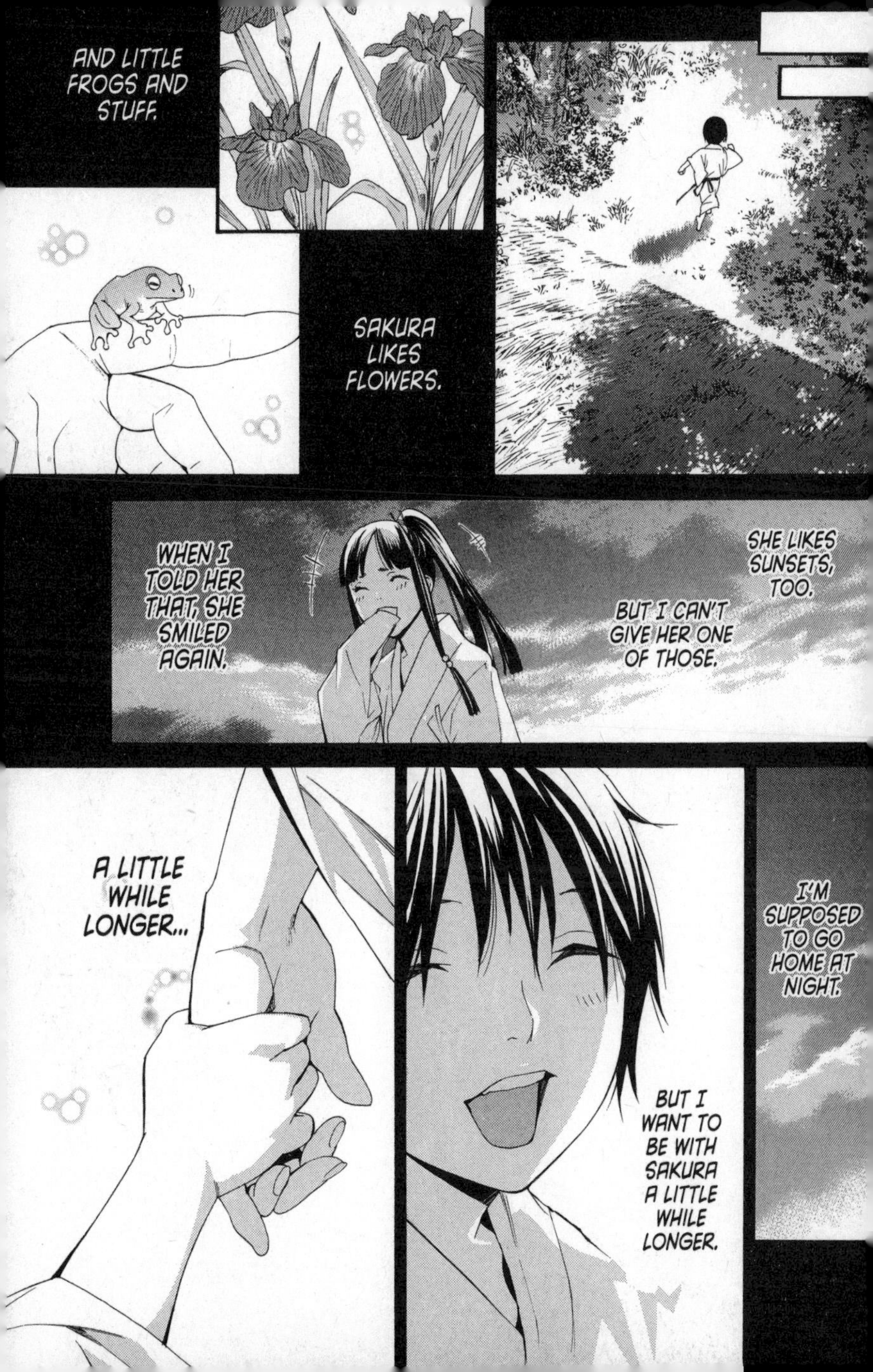
SAKURA LIKES FLOWERS.
AND LITTLE FROGS AND STUFF.
SHE LIKES SUNSETS, TOO.
BUT I CAN'T GIVE HER ONE OF THOSE.
WHEN I TOLD HER THAT, SHE SMILED AGAIN.
I'M SUPPOSED TO GO HOME AT NIGHT.
BUT I WANT TO BE WITH SAKURA A LITTLE WHILE LONGER.
A LITTLE WHILE LONGER...

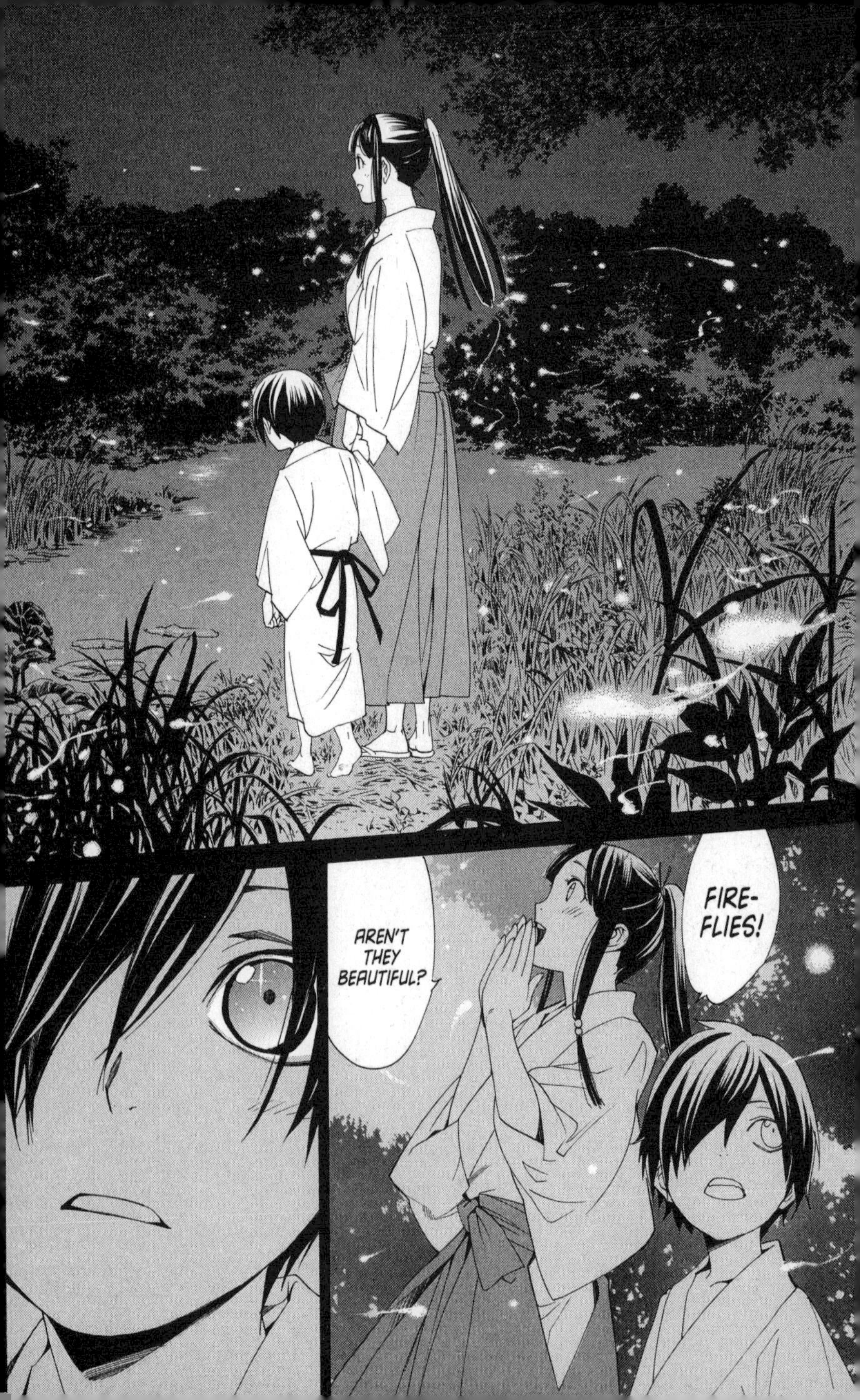
FIRE-FLIES!
AREN'T THEY BEAUTIFUL?

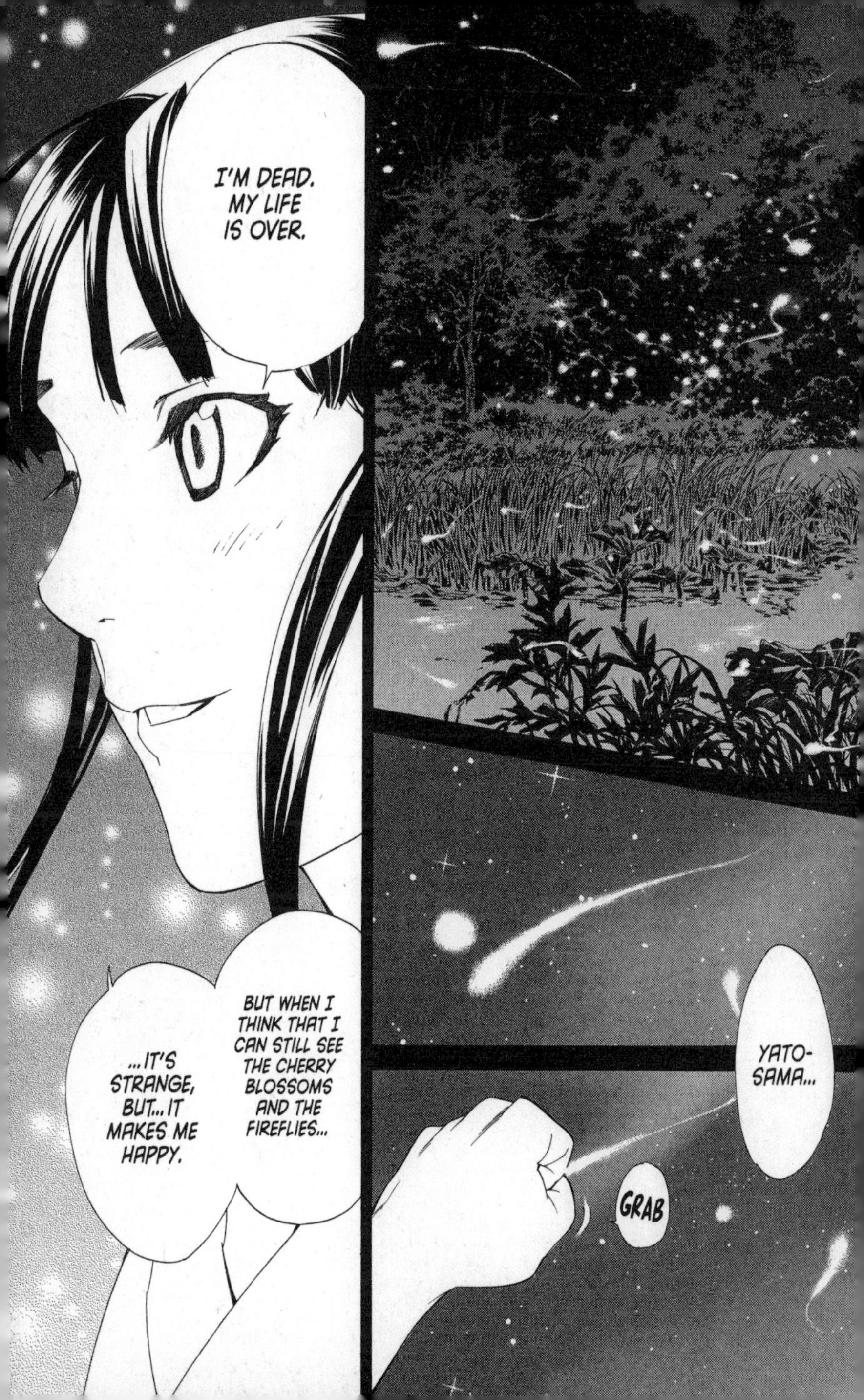
YATO-SAMA...
GRAB
I'M DEAD. MY LIFE IS OVER.
BUT WHEN I THINK THAT I CAN STILL SEE THE CHERRY BLOSSOMS AND THE FIREFLIES...
...IT'S STRANGE, BUT...IT MAKES ME HAPPY.

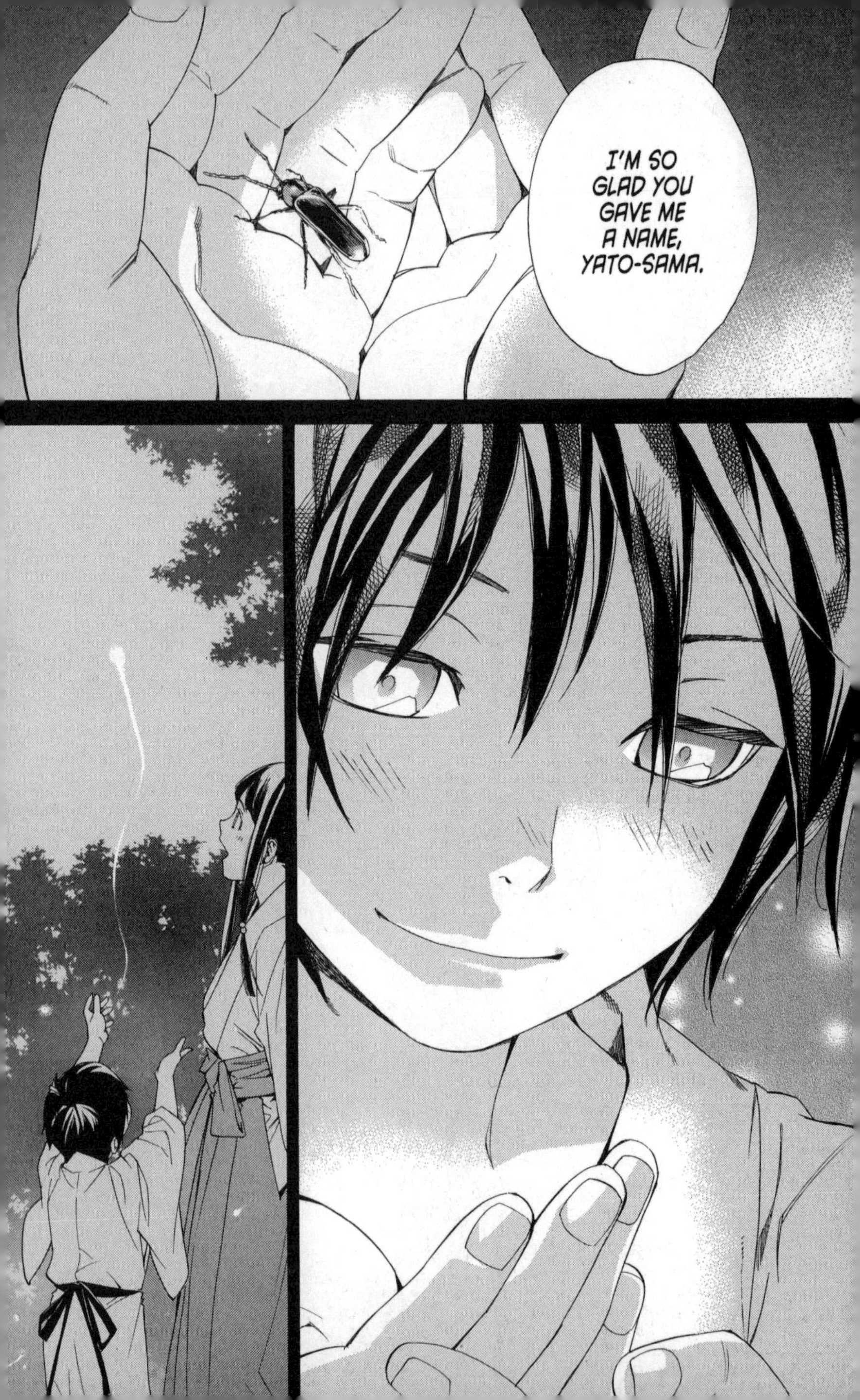
I'M SO GLAD YOU GAVE ME A NAME, YATO-SAMA.

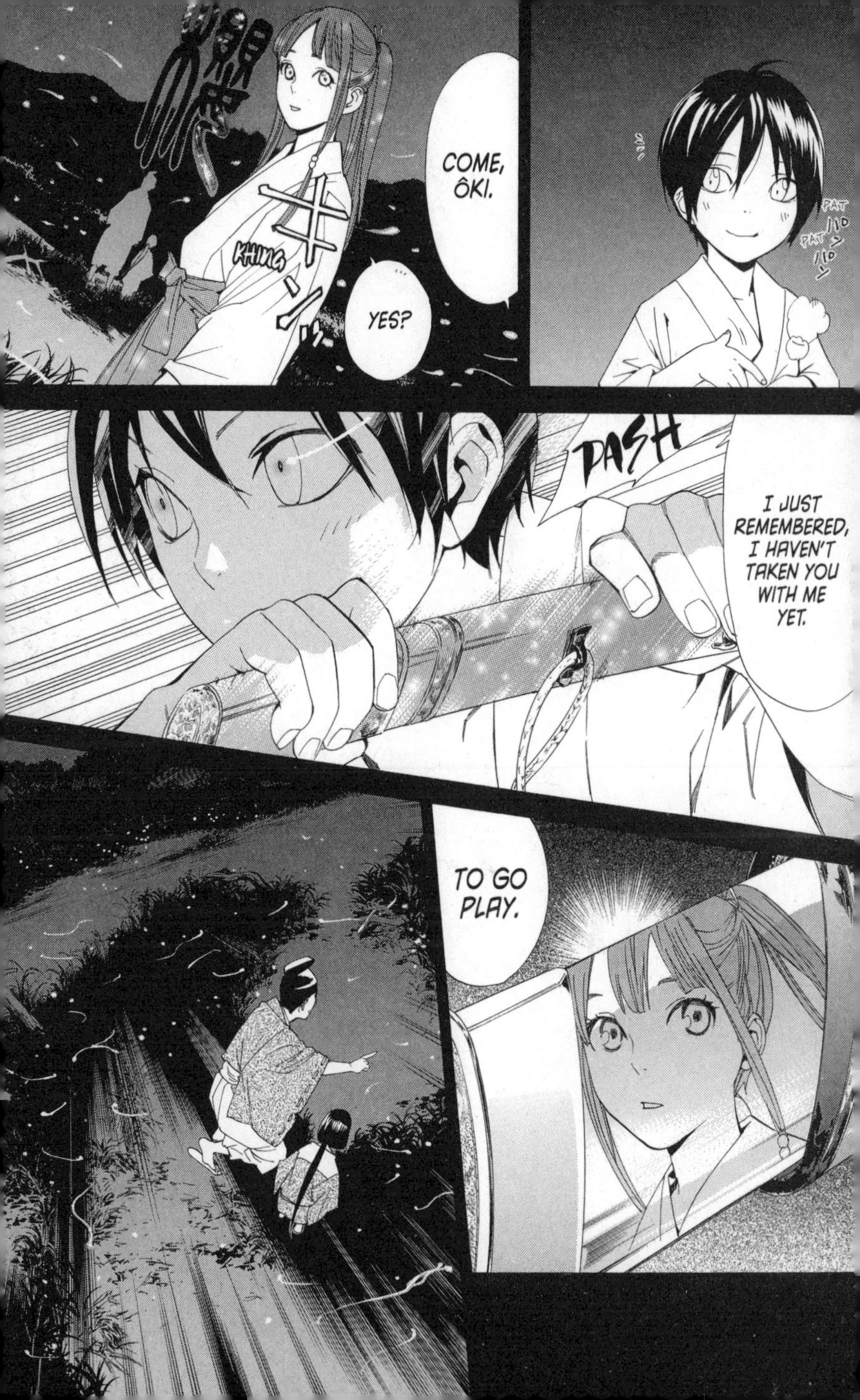
PAT PAT
COME, ÔKI.
KHING
YES?
DASH
I JUST REMEMBERED, I HAVEN'T TAKEN YOU WITH ME YET.
TO GO PLAY.

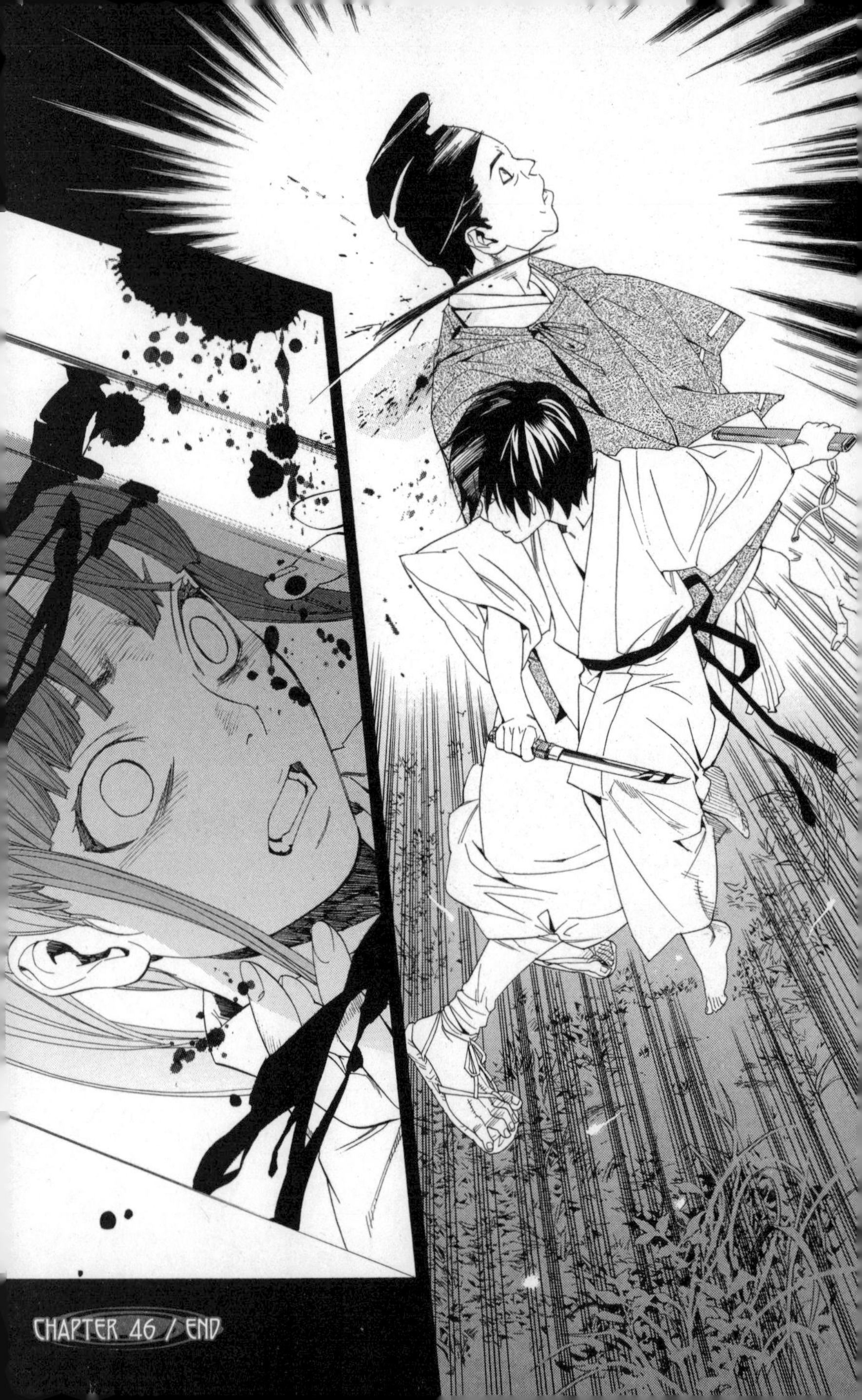
CHAPTER 46 / END

野

兑

神

師

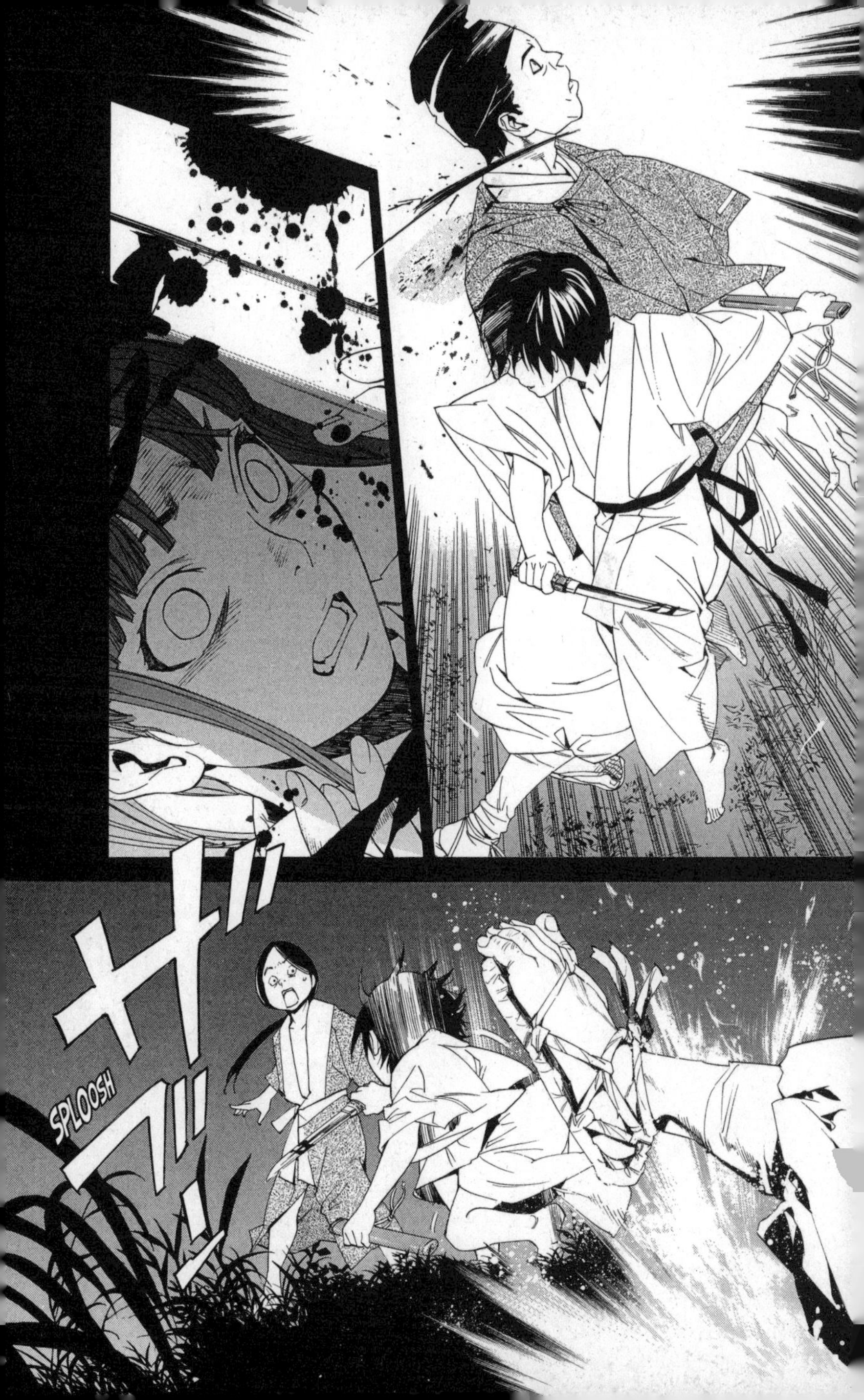
SPLOOSH

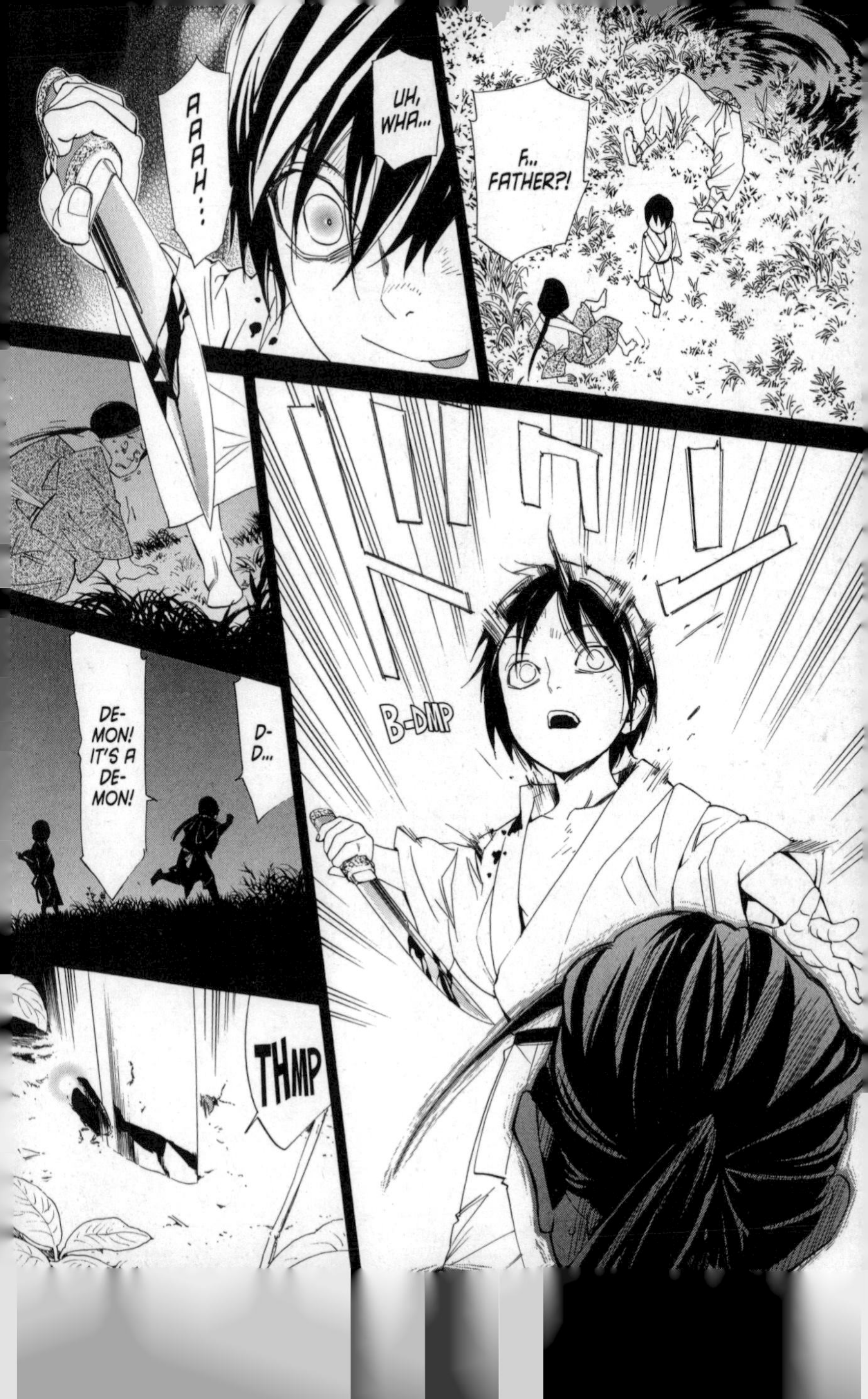
F... FATHER?!
UH, WHA...
AAAAH...
B-DMP
D-D...
DE-MON! IT'S A DE-MON!
THMP

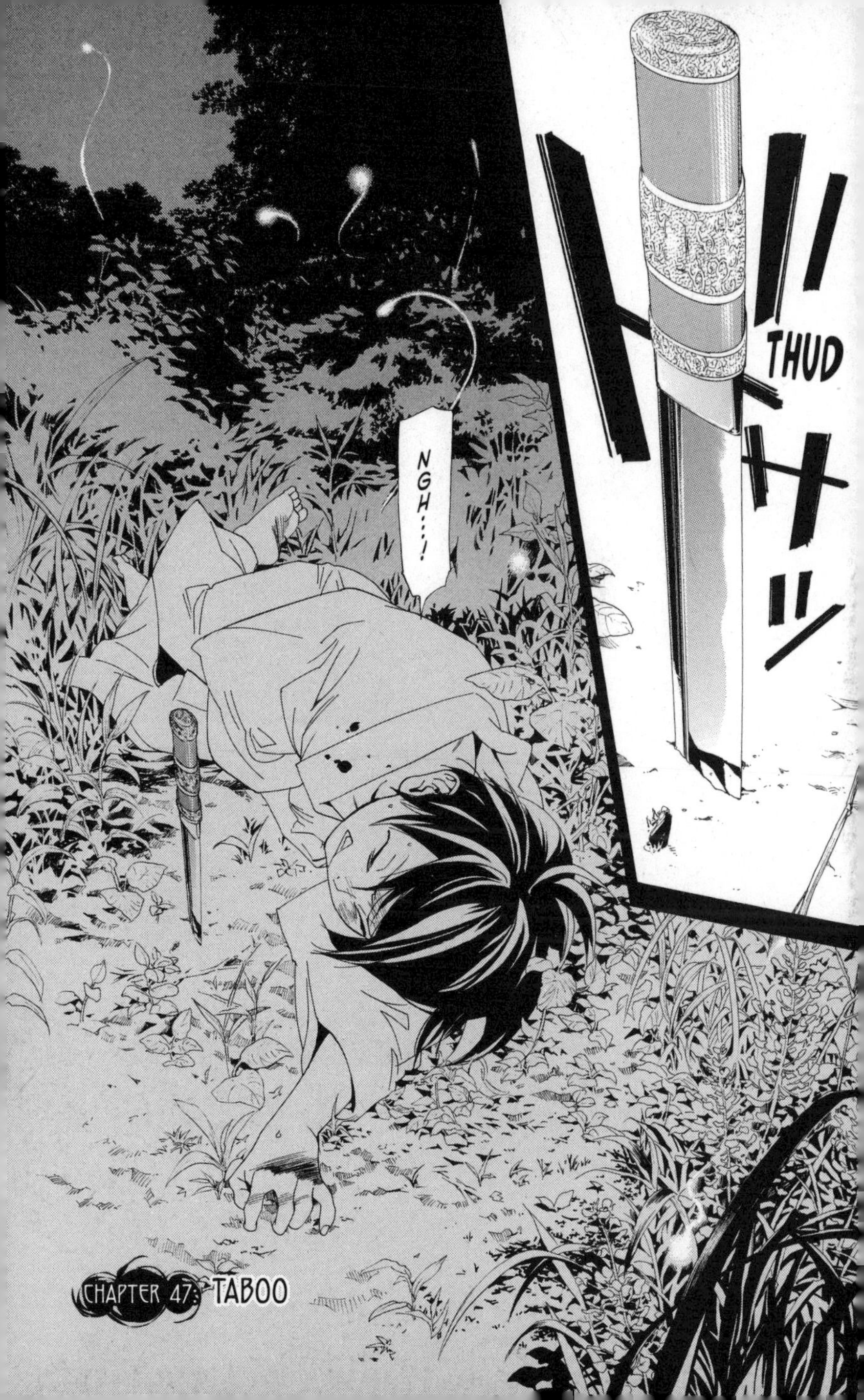
THUD
NGH...!
CHAPTER 47: TABOO

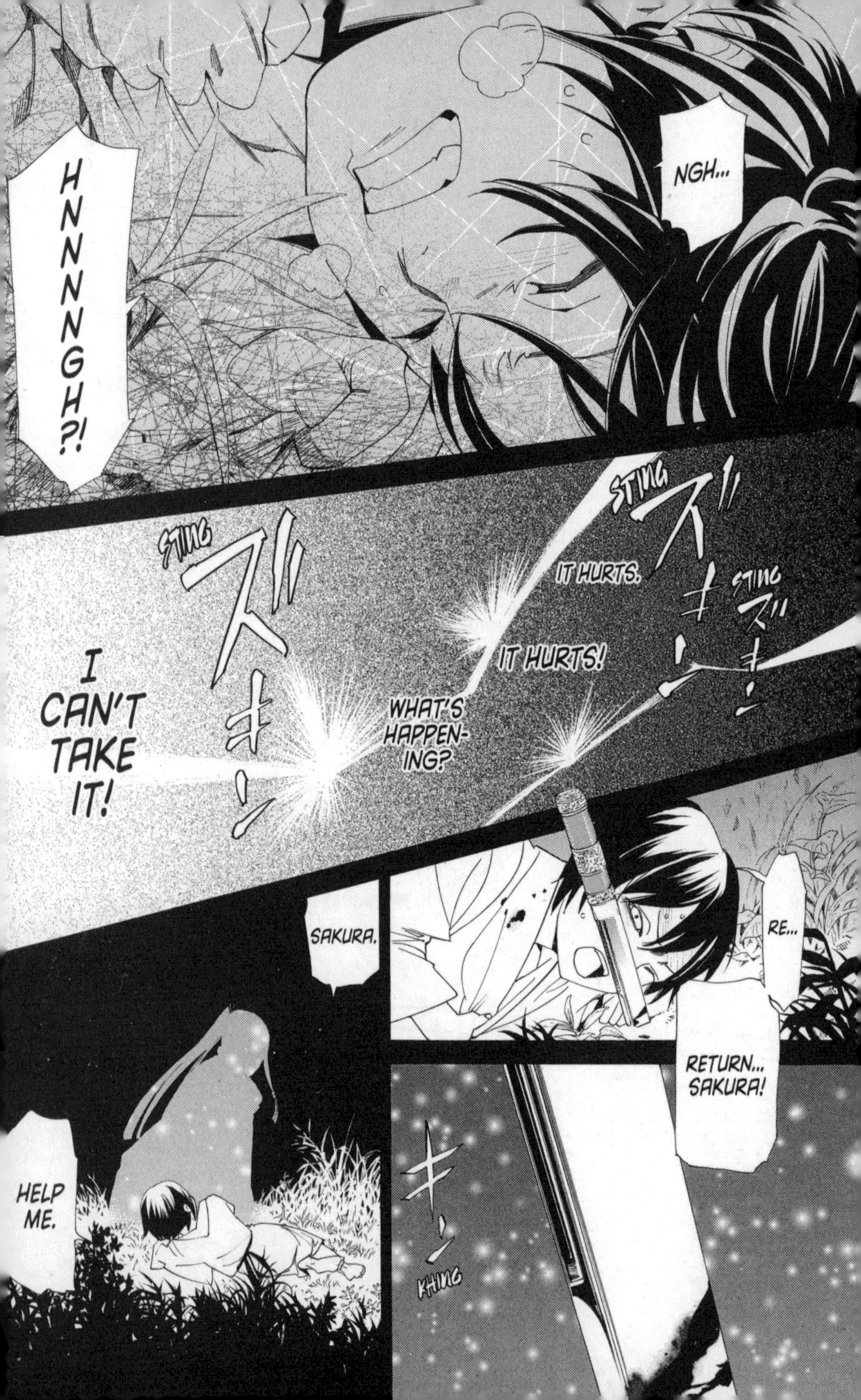
NGH...
HNNNNNGH?!
STING
IT HURTS.
STING
IT HURTS!
WHAT'S HAPPEN-ING?
STING
I CAN'T TAKE IT!
RE...
RETURN... SAKURA!
KHING
SAKURA.
HELP ME.

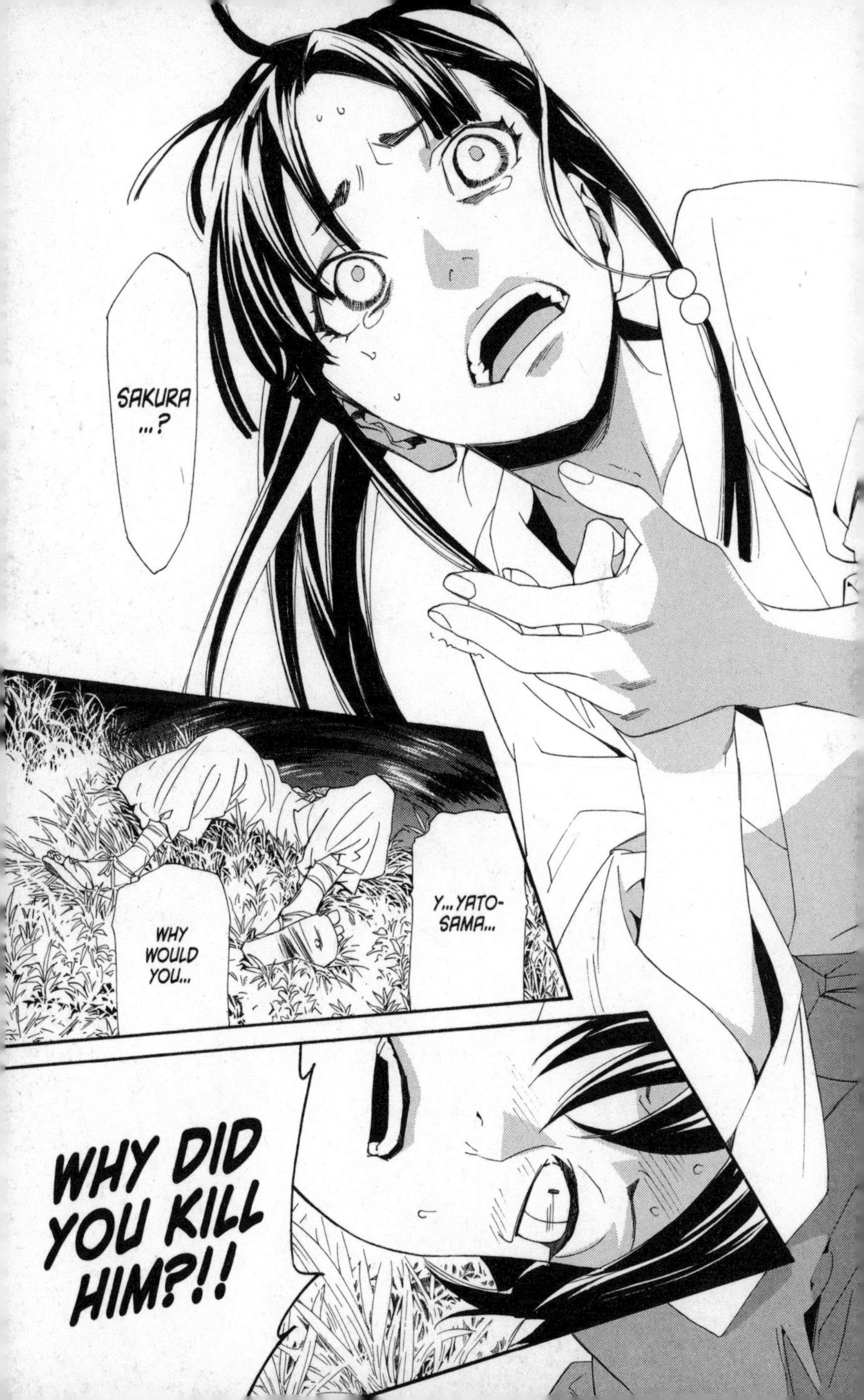
SAKURA ...?
Y... YATO-SAMA...
WHY WOULD YOU...
WHY DID YOU KILL HIM?!!

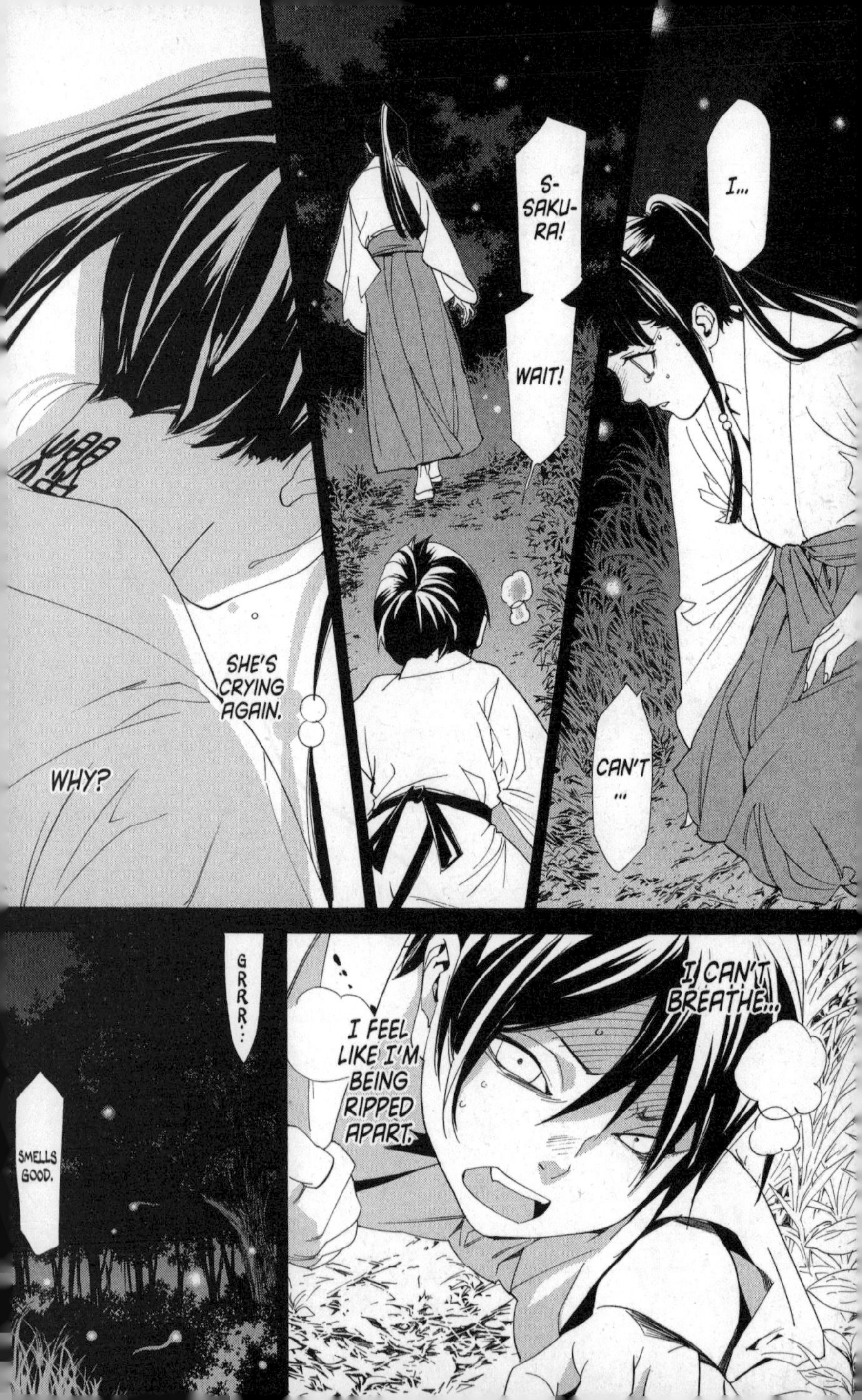
I...
CAN'T ...
S-SAKU-RA!
WAIT!
SHE'S CRYING AGAIN.
WHY?
I CAN'T BREATHE...
I FEEL LIKE I'M BEING RIPPED APART.
GRRR...
SMELLS GOOD.

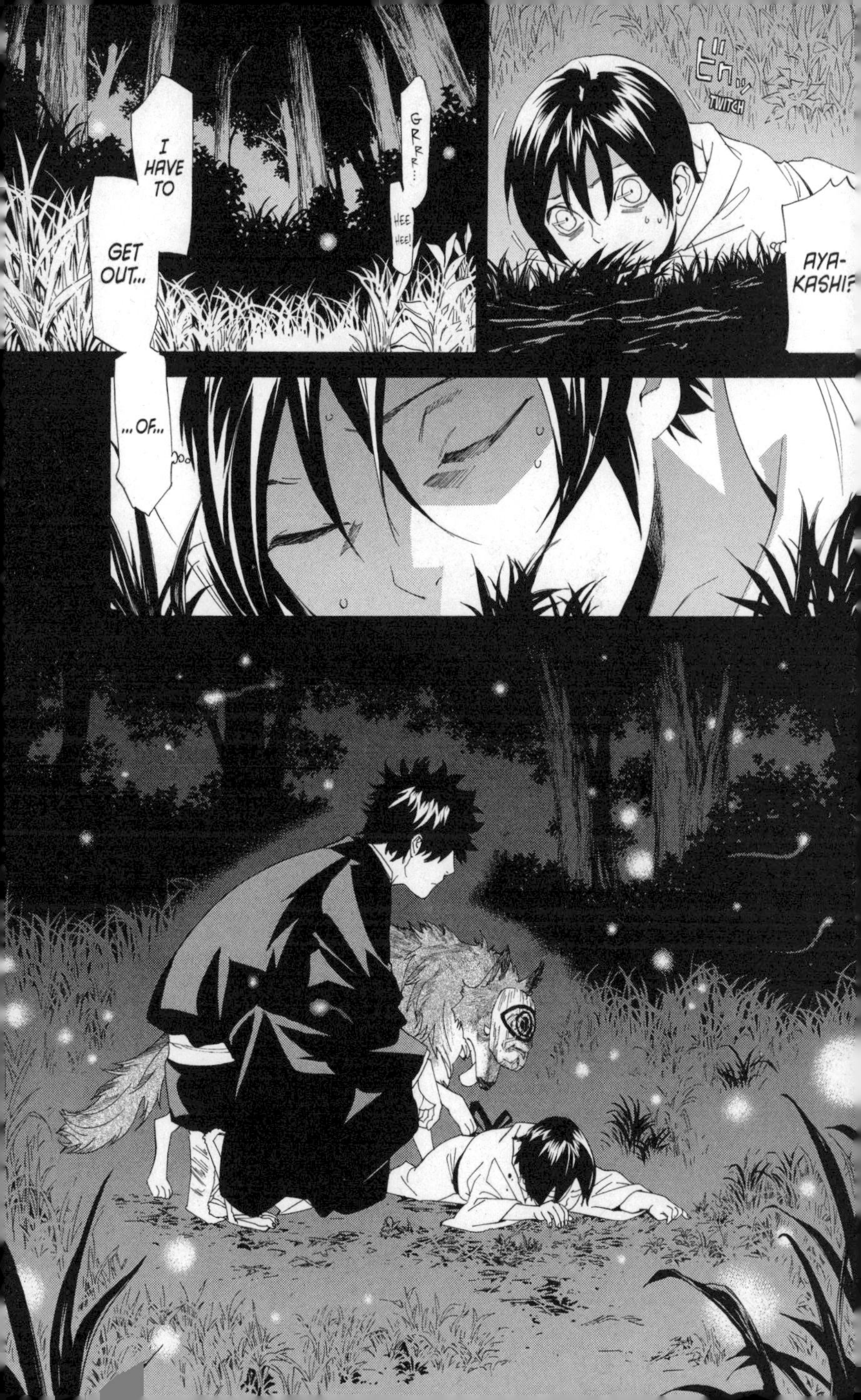
TWITCH
AYA-KASHI?
GRRR...
HEE HEE!
I HAVE TO
GET OUT...
...OF...

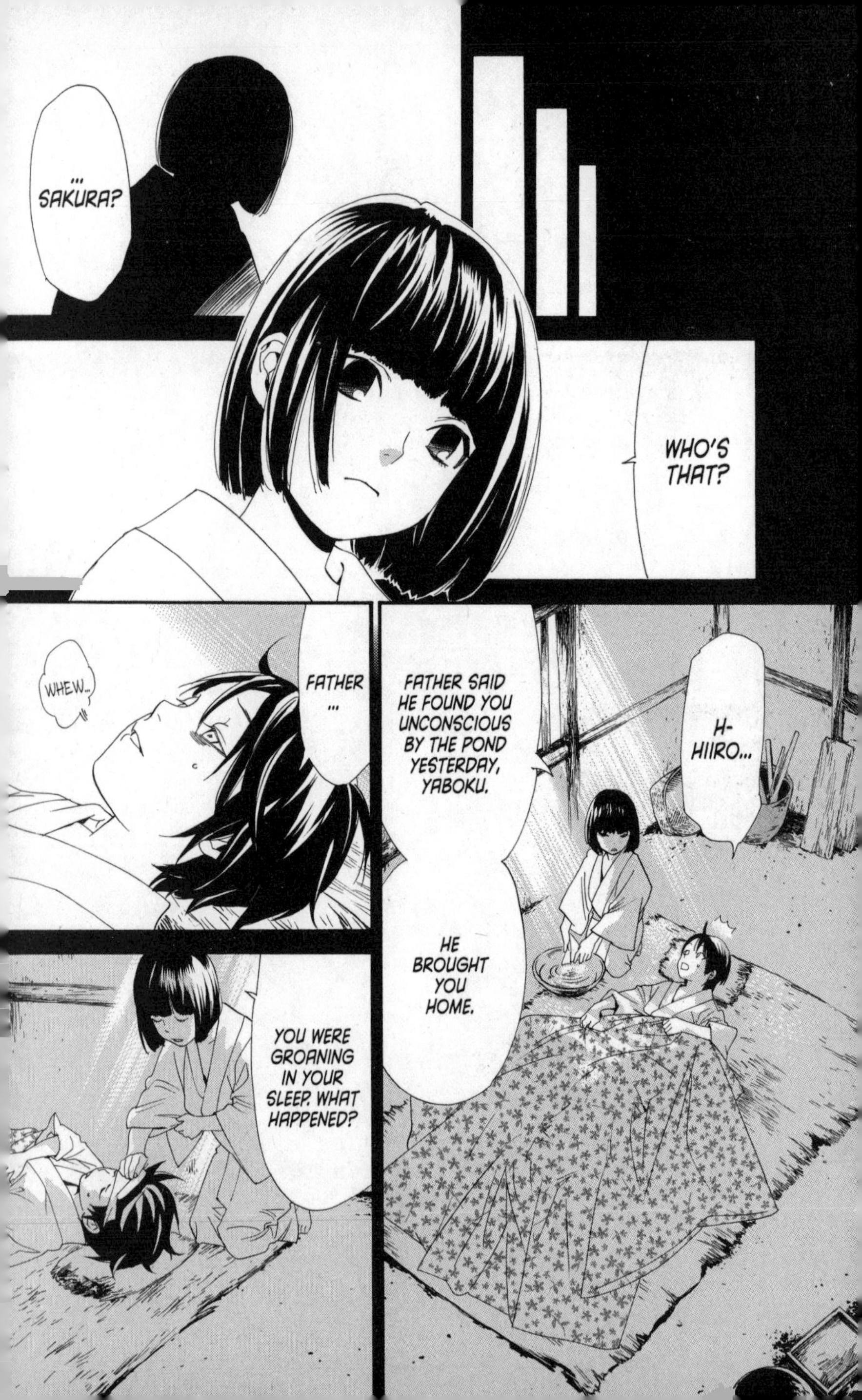
...SAKURA?
WHO'S THAT?
H-HIIRO...
FATHER SAID HE FOUND YOU UNCONSCIOUS BY THE POND YESTERDAY, YABOKU.
HE BROUGHT YOU HOME.
FATHER ...
WHEW...
YOU WERE GROANING IN YOUR SLEEP. WHAT HAPPENED?

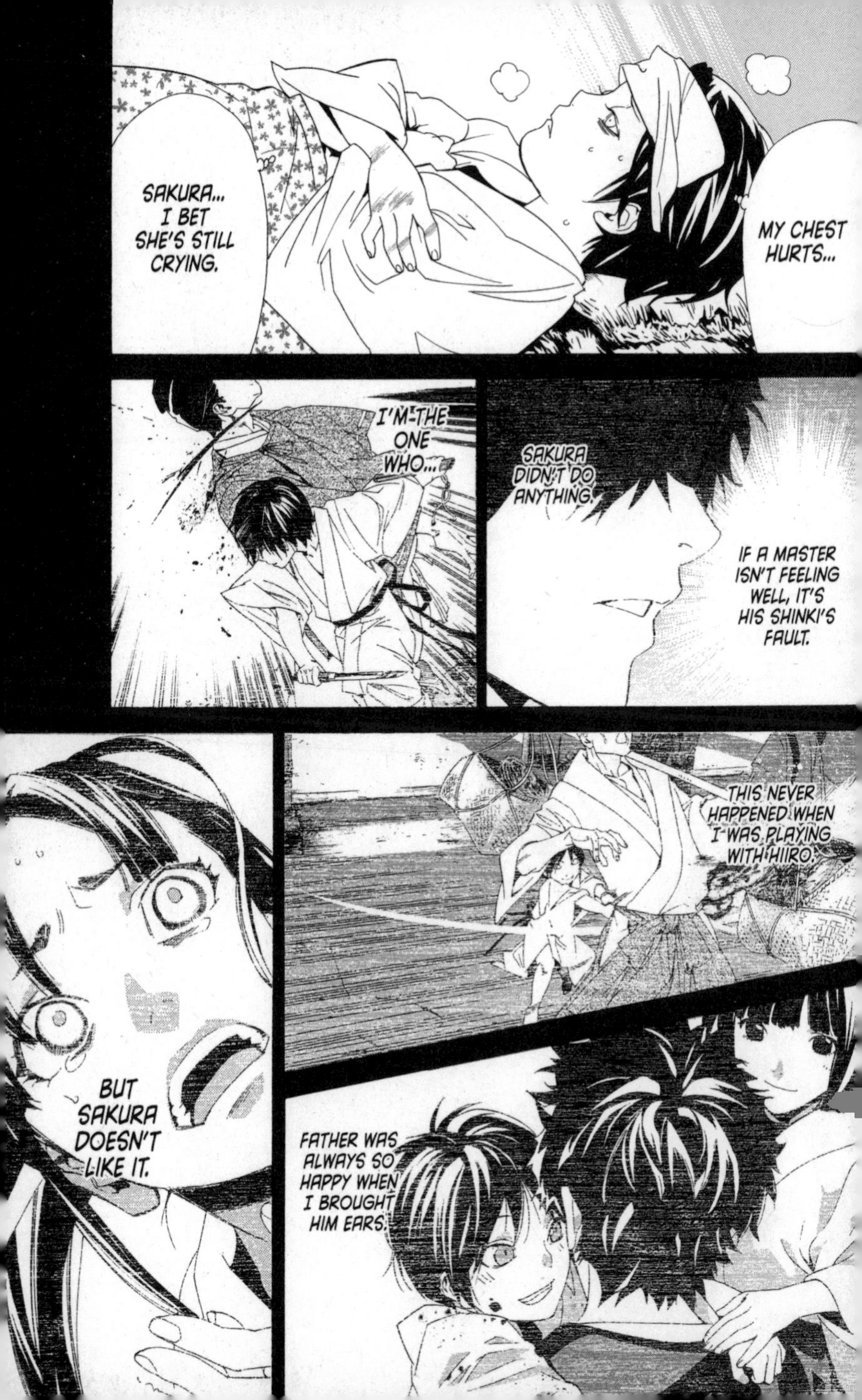
MY CHEST HURTS...
SAKURA... I BET SHE'S STILL CRYING.
IF A MASTER ISN'T FEELING WELL, IT'S HIS SHINKI'S FAULT.
SAKURA DIDN'T DO ANYTHING.
I'M THE ONE WHO...
THIS NEVER HAPPENED WHEN I WAS PLAYING WITH HIIRO.
FATHER WAS ALWAYS SO HAPPY WHEN I BROUGHT HIM EARS.
BUT SAKURA DOESN'T LIKE IT.

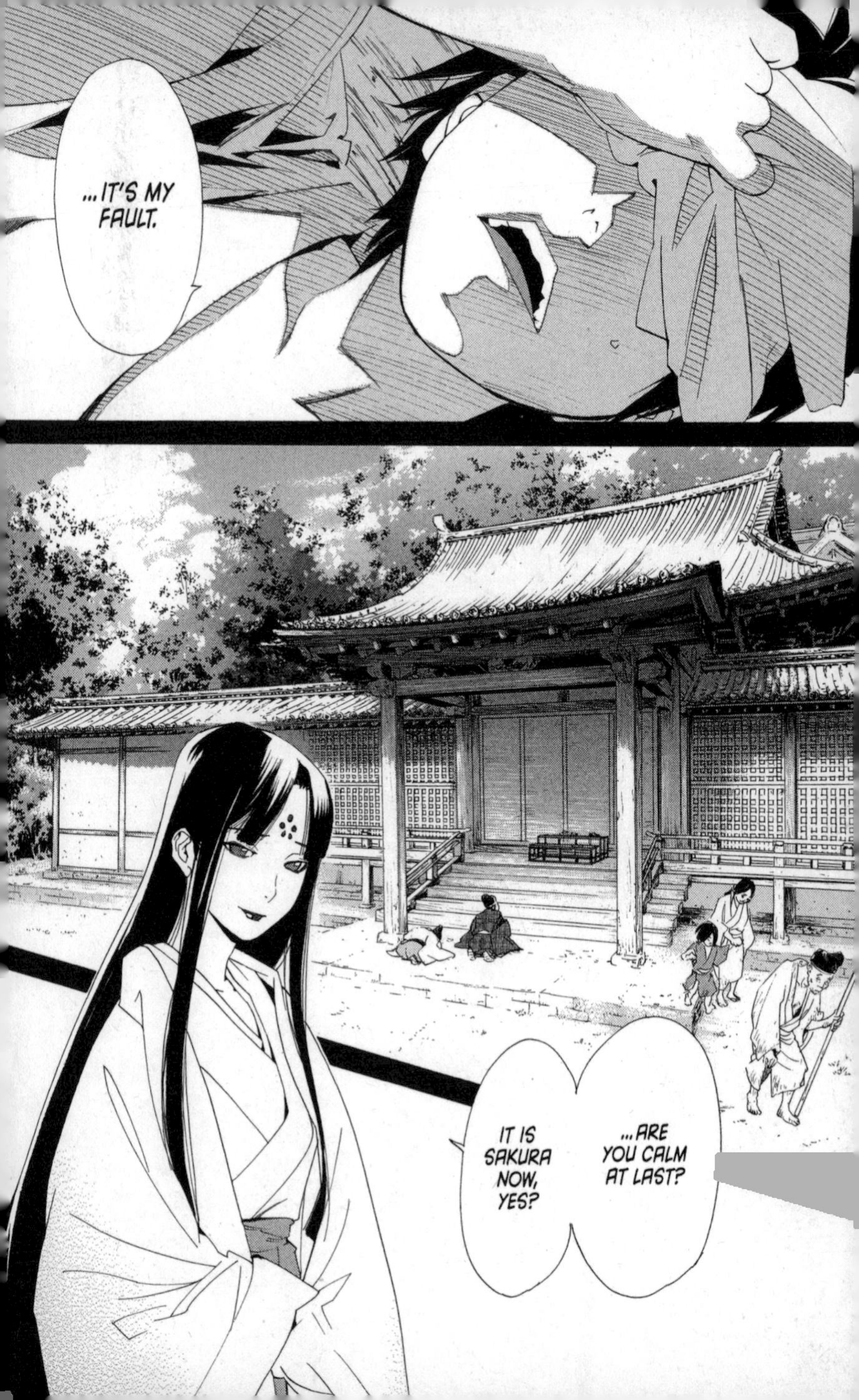
...IT'S MY FAULT.
...ARE YOU CALM AT LAST?
IT IS SAKURA NOW, YES?

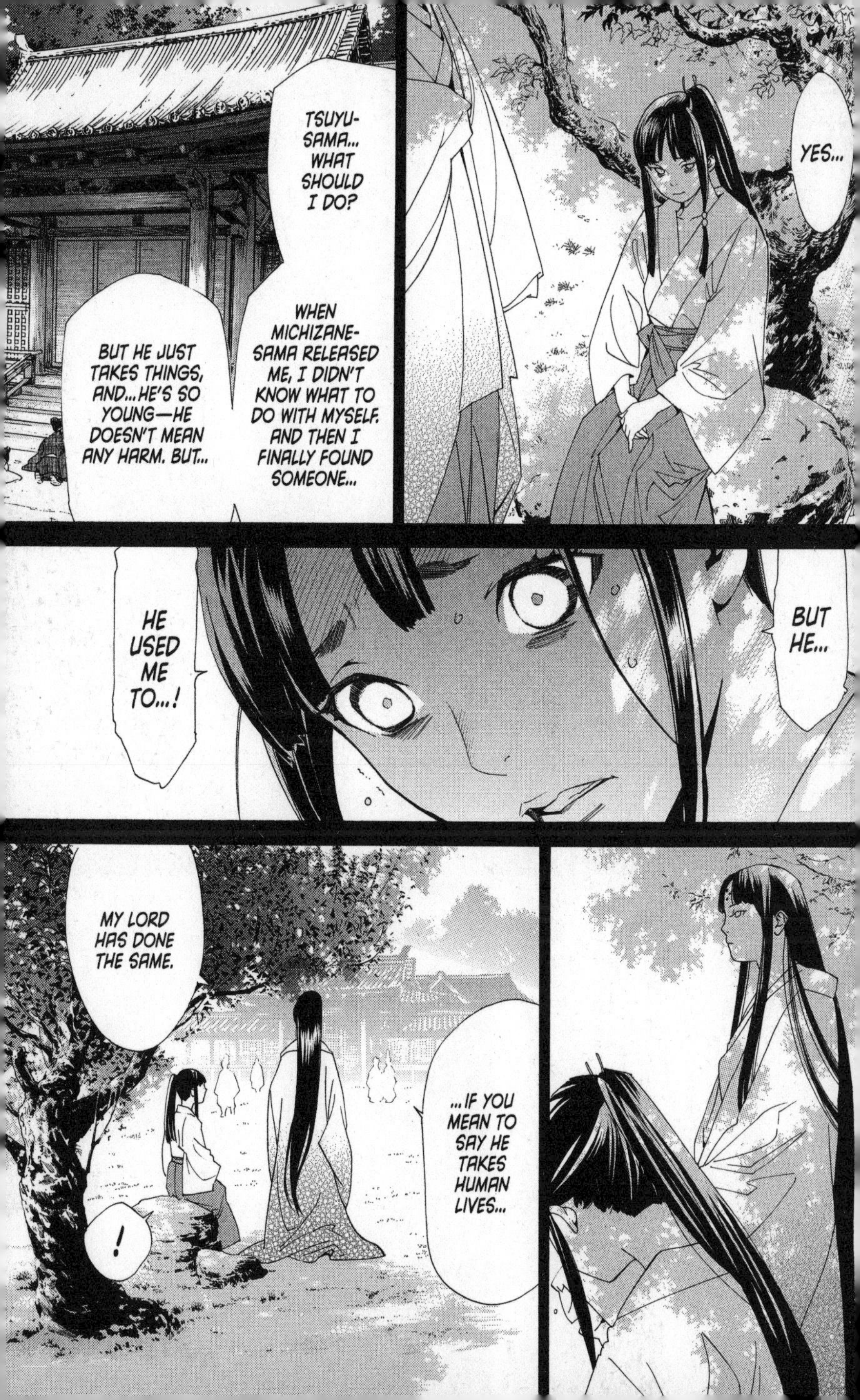
YES...
TSUYU-SAMA... WHAT SHOULD I DO?
WHEN MICHIZANE-SAMA RELEASED ME, I DIDN'T KNOW WHAT TO DO WITH MYSELF. AND THEN I FINALLY FOUND SOMEONE...
BUT HE JUST TAKES THINGS, AND...HE'S SO YOUNG—HE DOESN'T MEAN ANY HARM. BUT...
BUT HE...
HE USED ME TO...!
...IF YOU MEAN TO SAY HE TAKES HUMAN LIVES...
MY LORD HAS DONE THE SAME.
!

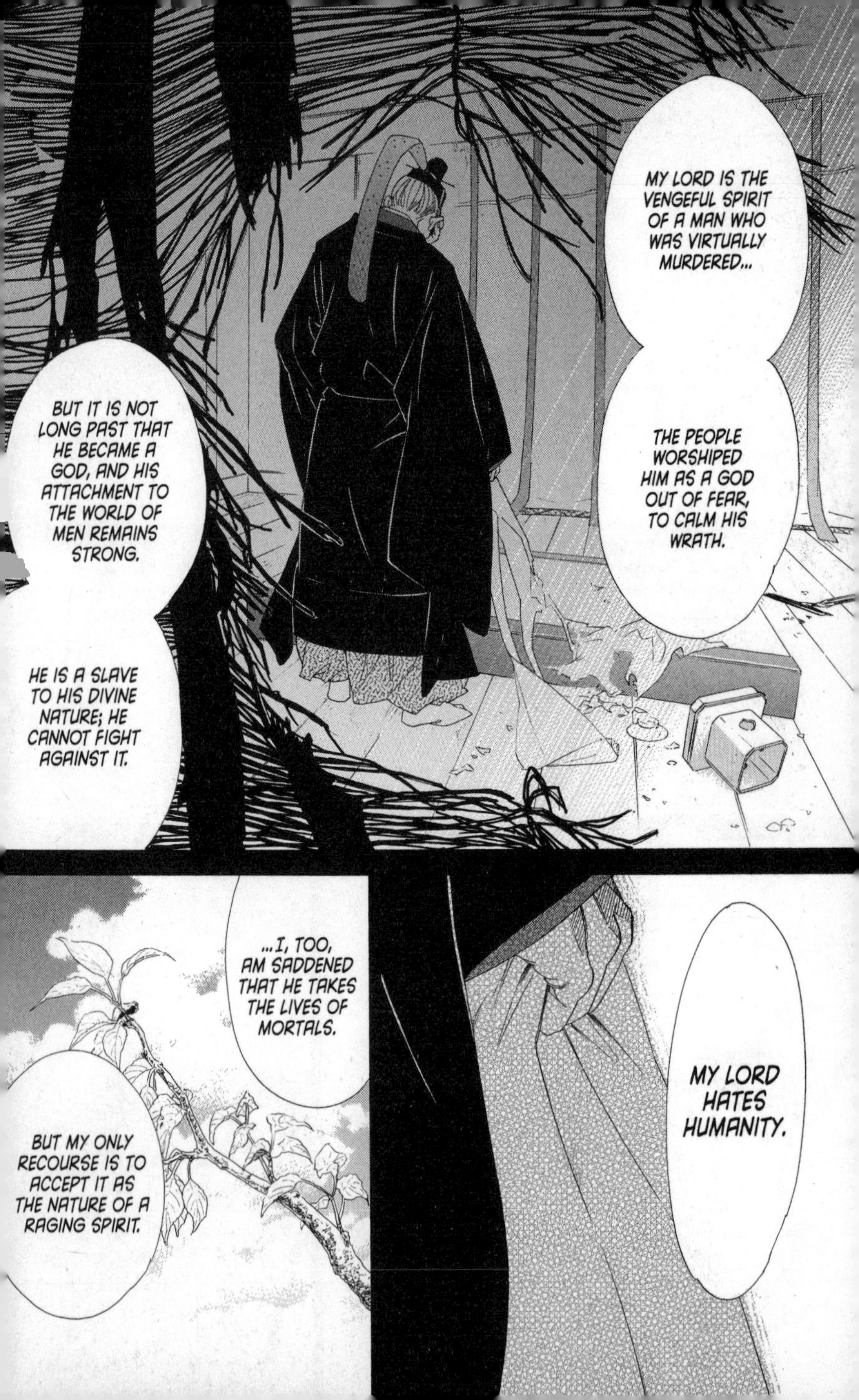
MY LORD IS THE VENGEFUL SPIRIT OF A MAN WHO WAS VIRTUALLY MURDERED...
THE PEOPLE WORSHIPED HIM AS A GOD OUT OF FEAR, TO CALM HIS WRATH.
BUT IT IS NOT LONG PAST THAT HE BECAME A GOD, AND HIS ATTACHMENT TO THE WORLD OF MEN REMAINS STRONG.
HE IS A SLAVE TO HIS DIVINE NATURE; HE CANNOT FIGHT AGAINST IT.
MY LORD HATES HUMANITY.
...I, TOO, AM SADDENED THAT HE TAKES THE LIVES OF MORTALS.
BUT MY ONLY RECOURSE IS TO ACCEPT IT AS THE NATURE OF A RAGING SPIRIT.

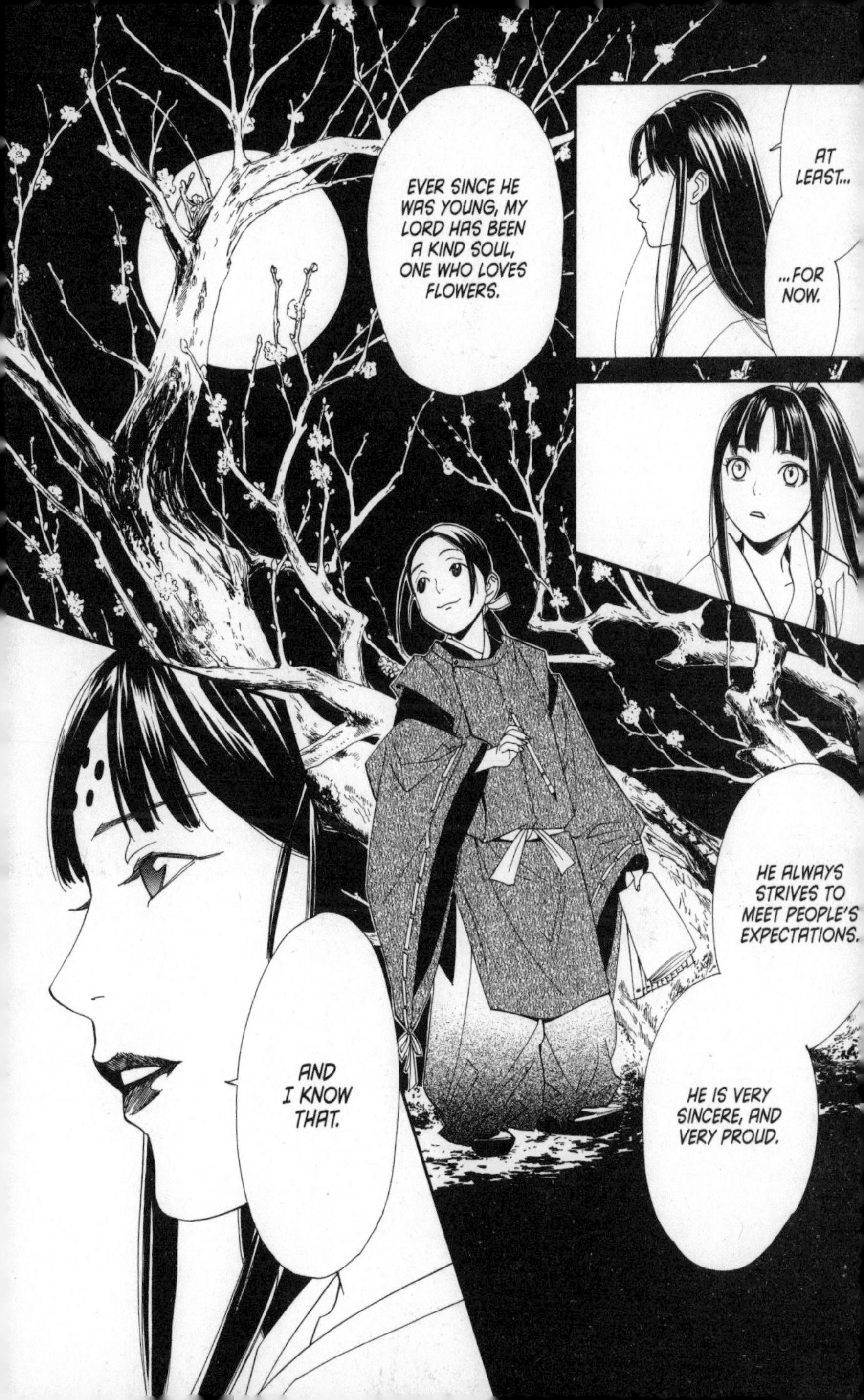
AT LEAST...
...FOR NOW.
EVER SINCE HE WAS YOUNG, MY LORD HAS BEEN A KIND SOUL, ONE WHO LOVES FLOWERS.
HE ALWAYS STRIVES TO MEET PEOPLE'S EXPECTATIONS.
HE IS VERY SINCERE, AND VERY PROUD.
AND I KNOW THAT.

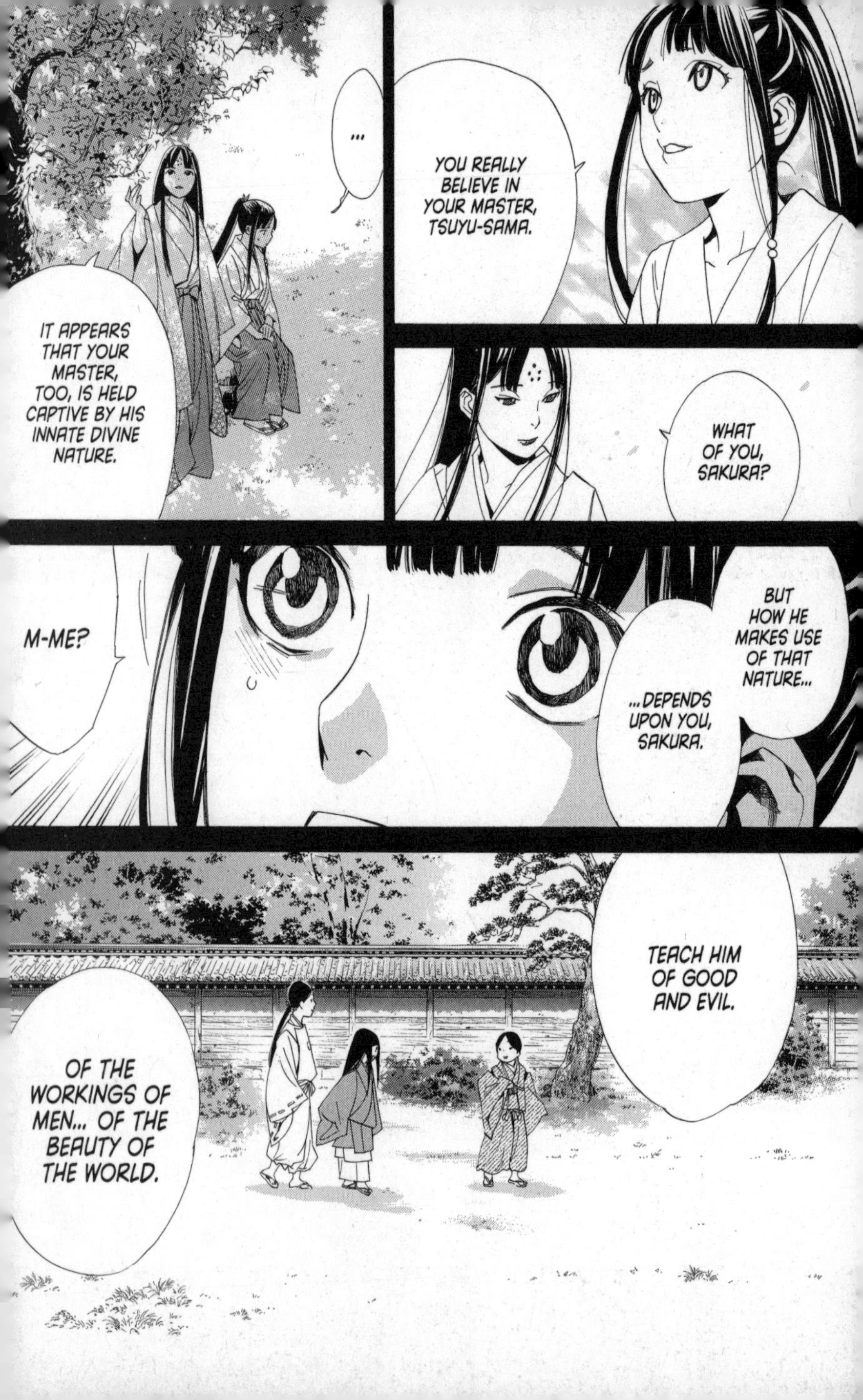
YOU REALLY BELIEVE IN YOUR MASTER, TSUYU-SAMA.
...
IT APPEARS THAT YOUR MASTER, TOO, IS HELD CAPTIVE BY HIS INNATE DIVINE NATURE.
WHAT OF YOU, SAKURA?
M-ME?
BUT HOW HE MAKES USE OF THAT NATURE...
...DEPENDS UPON YOU, SAKURA.
TEACH HIM OF GOOD AND EVIL.
OF THE WORKINGS OF MEN... OF THE BEAUTY OF THE WORLD.

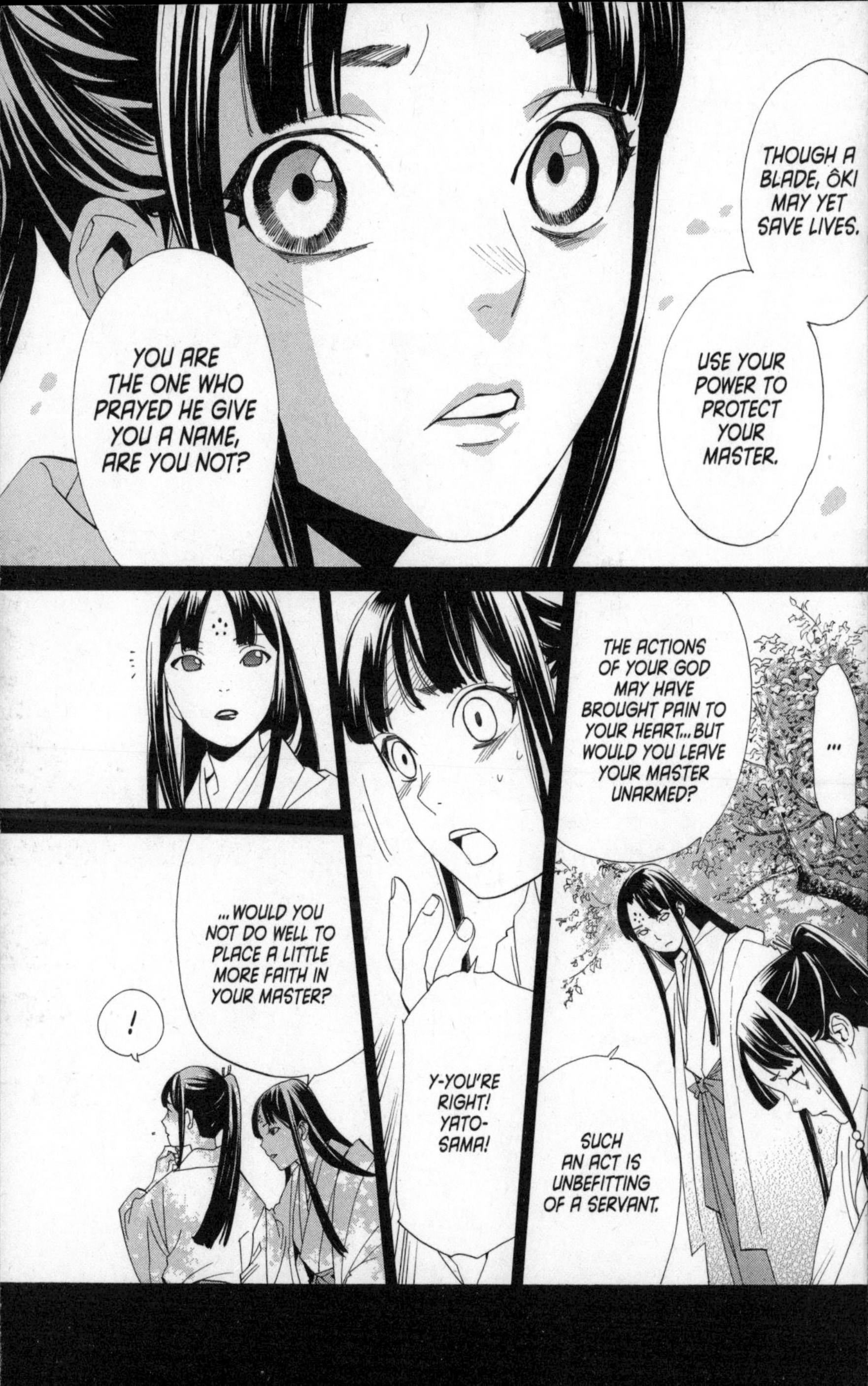
THOUGH A BLADE, ÔKI MAY YET SAVE LIVES.
USE YOUR POWER TO PROTECT YOUR MASTER.
YOU ARE THE ONE WHO PRAYED HE GIVE YOU A NAME, ARE YOU NOT?
THE ACTIONS OF YOUR GOD MAY HAVE BROUGHT PAIN TO YOUR HEART... BUT WOULD YOU LEAVE YOUR MASTER UNARMED?
...
SUCH AN ACT IS UNBEFITTING OF A SERVANT.
Y-YOU'RE RIGHT! YATO-SAMA!
...WOULD YOU NOT DO WELL TO PLACE A LITTLE MORE FAITH IN YOUR MASTER?
!

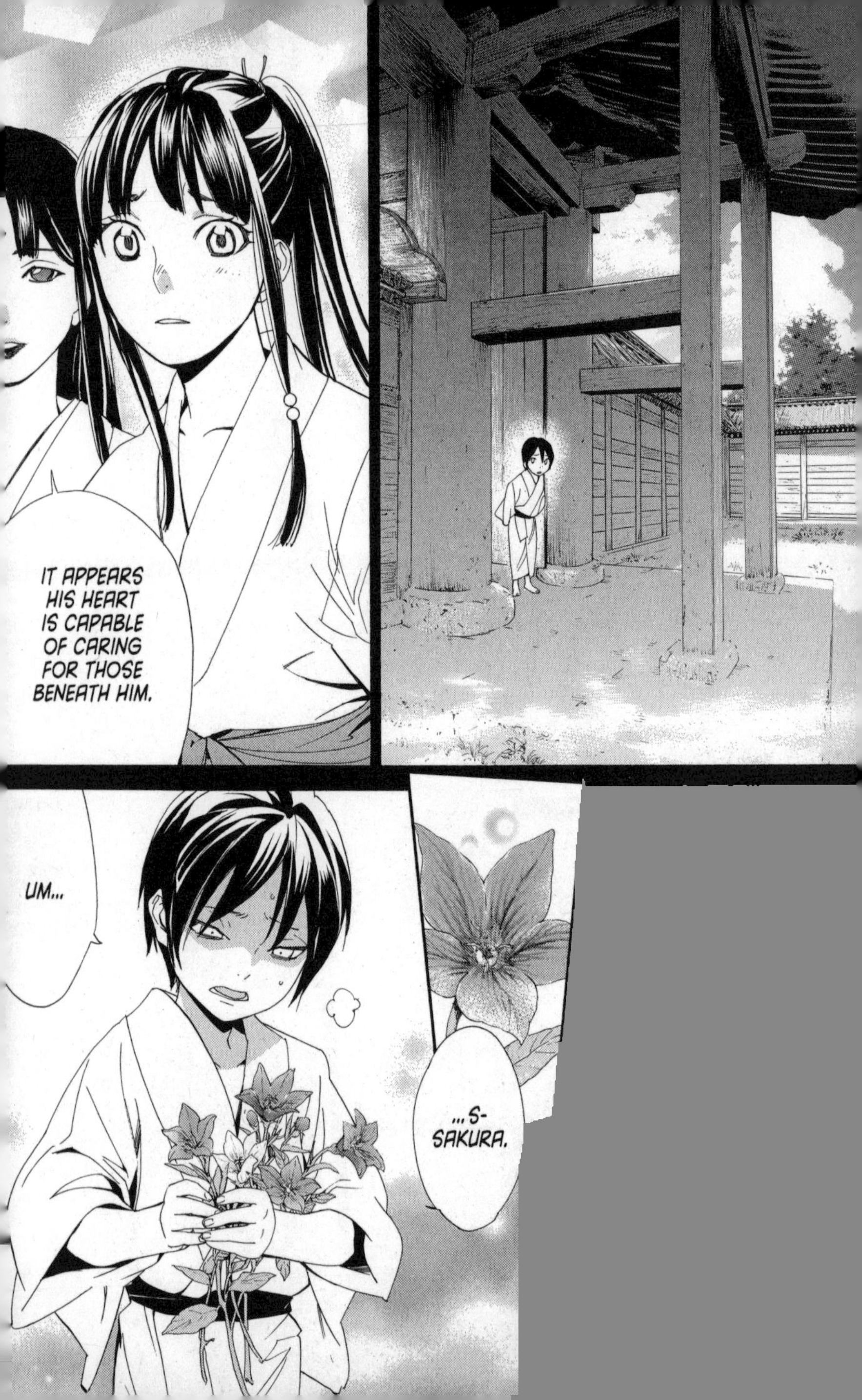
IT APPEARS HIS HEART IS CAPABLE OF CARING FOR THOSE BENEATH HIM.
UM...
...S- SAKURA.

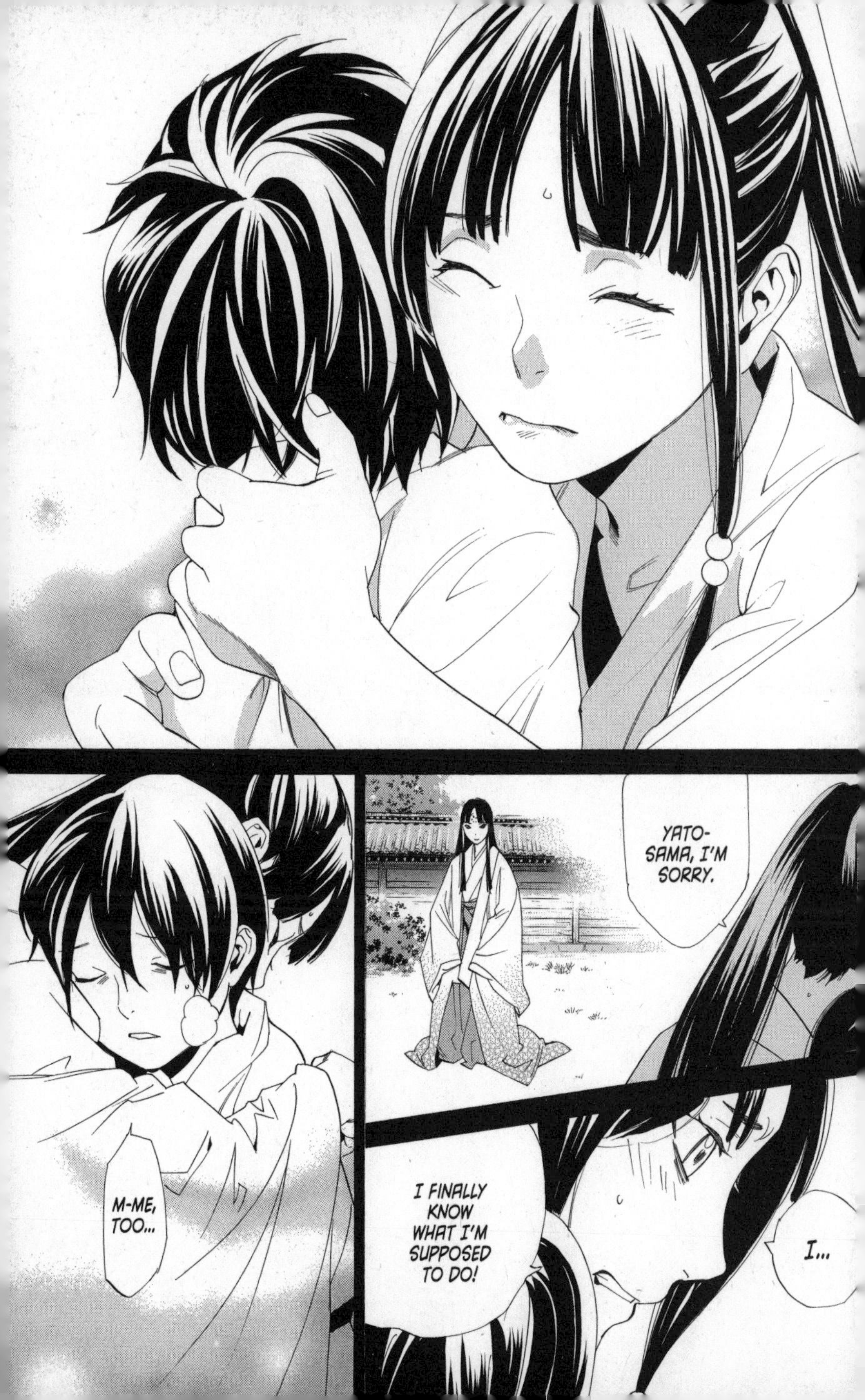
YATO-SAMA, I'M SORRY.
I...
I FINALLY KNOW WHAT I'M SUPPOSED TO DO!
M-ME, TOO...

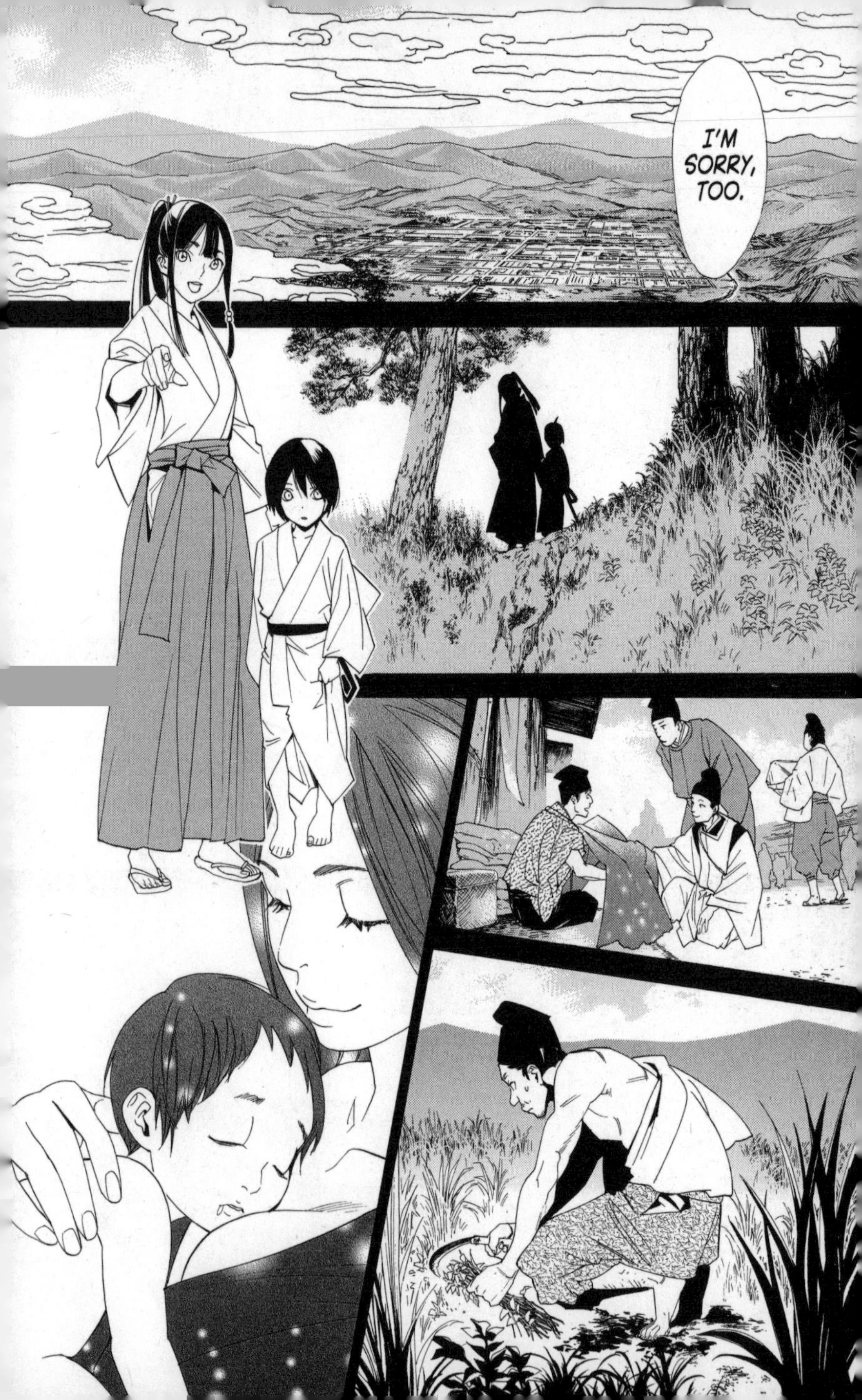
I'M SORRY, TOO.

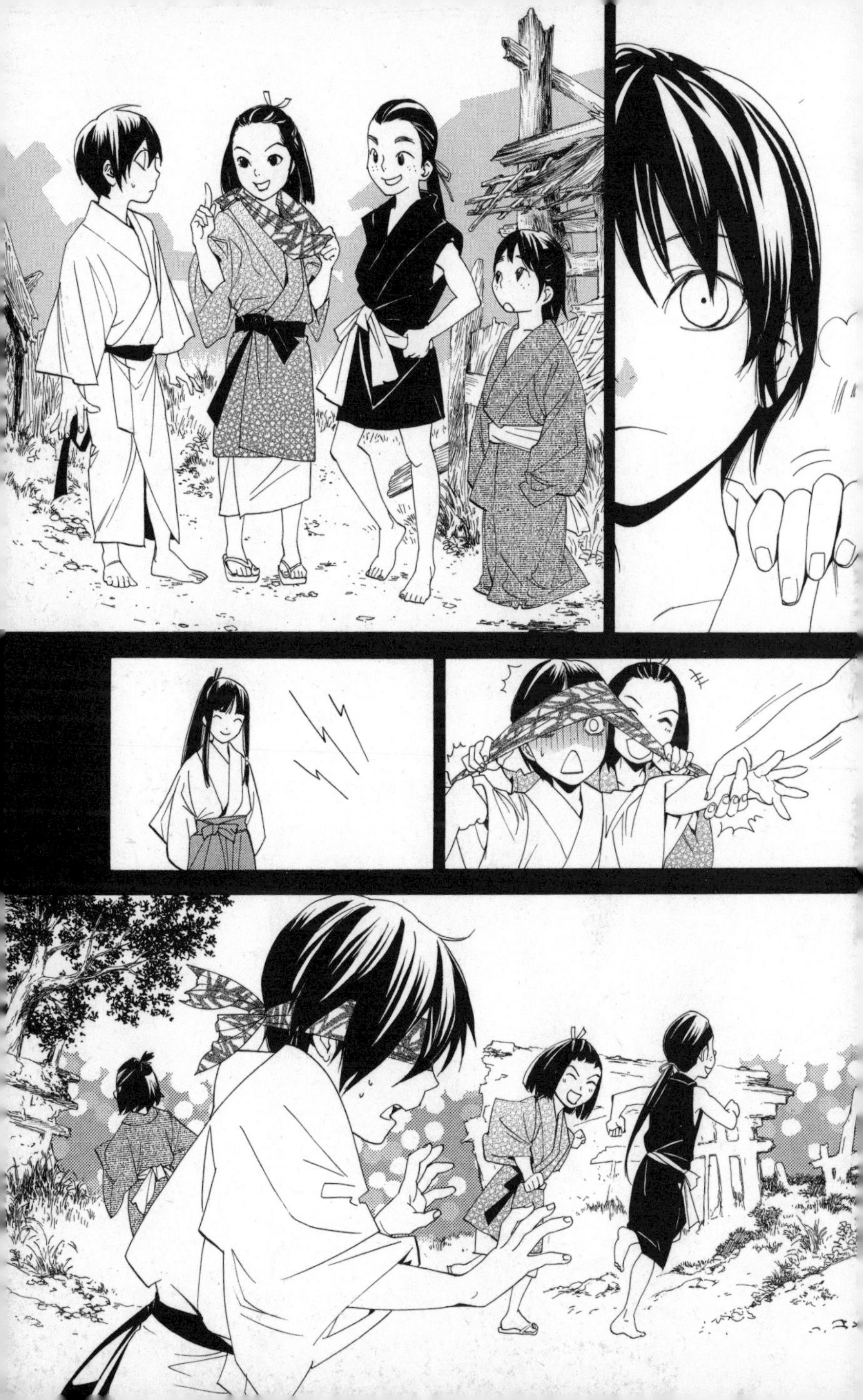

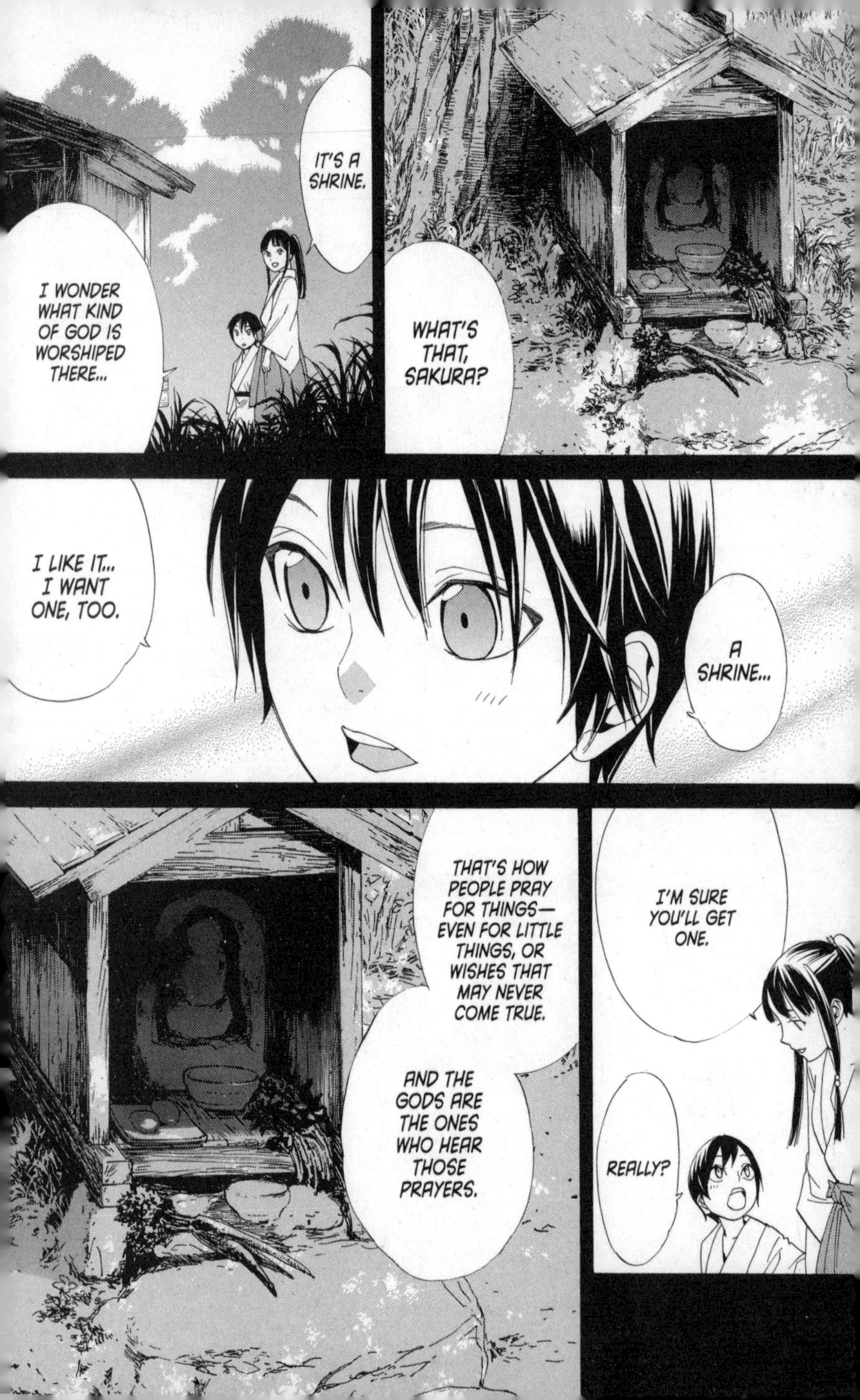
WHAT'S THAT, SAKURA?
IT'S A SHRINE.
I WONDER WHAT KIND OF GOD IS WORSHIPED THERE...
A SHRINE...
I LIKE IT... I WANT ONE, TOO.
I'M SURE YOU'LL GET ONE.
REALLY?
THAT'S HOW PEOPLE PRAY FOR THINGS—EVEN FOR LITTLE THINGS, OR WISHES THAT MAY NEVER COME TRUE.
AND THE GODS ARE THE ONES WHO HEAR THOSE PRAYERS.

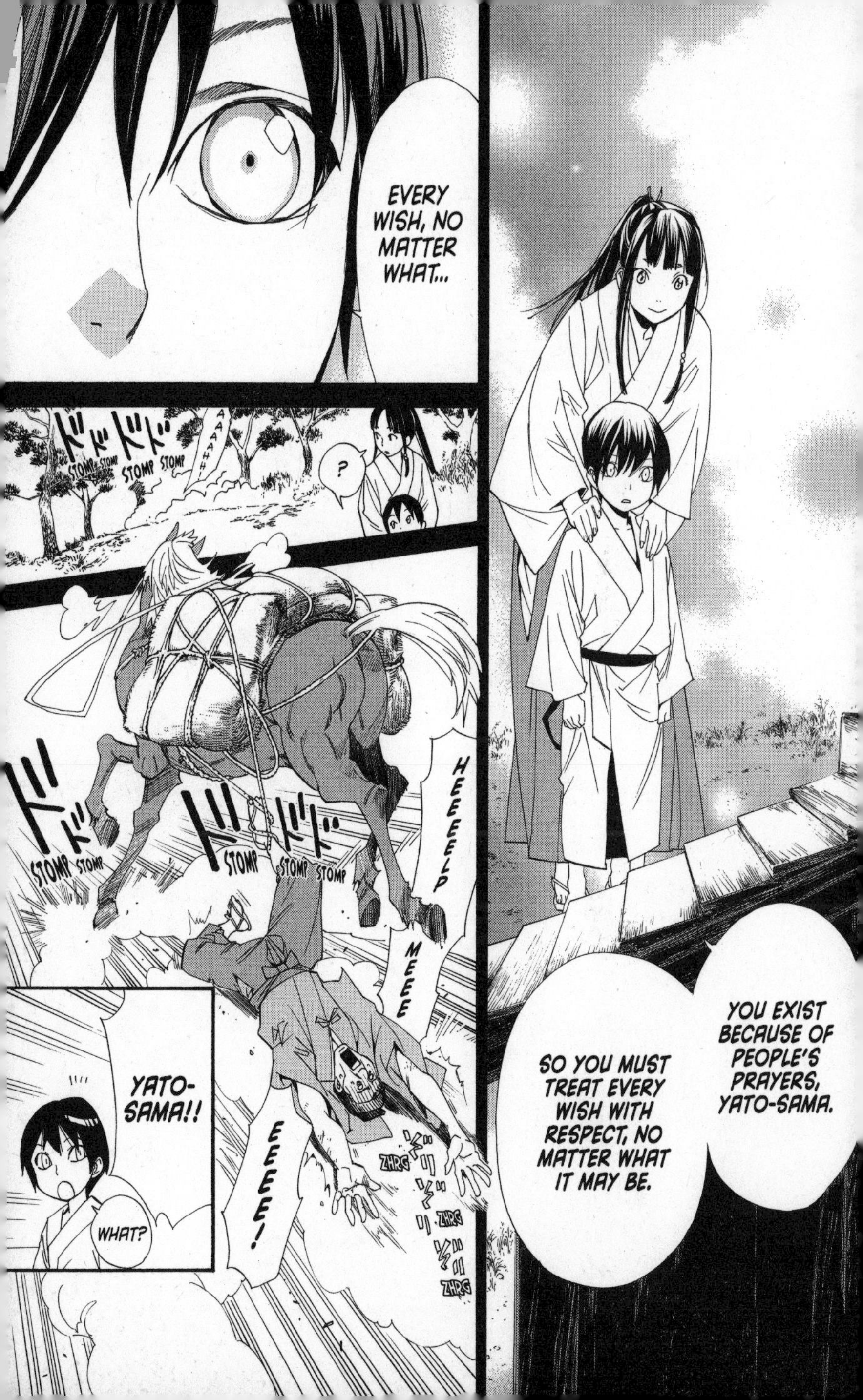

YOU EXIST BECAUSE OF PEOPLE'S PRAYERS, YATO-SAMA.
SO YOU MUST TREAT EVERY WISH WITH RESPECT, NO MATTER WHAT IT MAY BE.
EVERY WISH, NO MATTER WHAT...
?
STOMP STOMP STOMP STOMP
HEEEELP MEEE EEEEE!
STOMP STOMP STOMP STOMP STOMP
ZHRG ZHRG ZHRG
YATO-SAMA!!
WHAT?

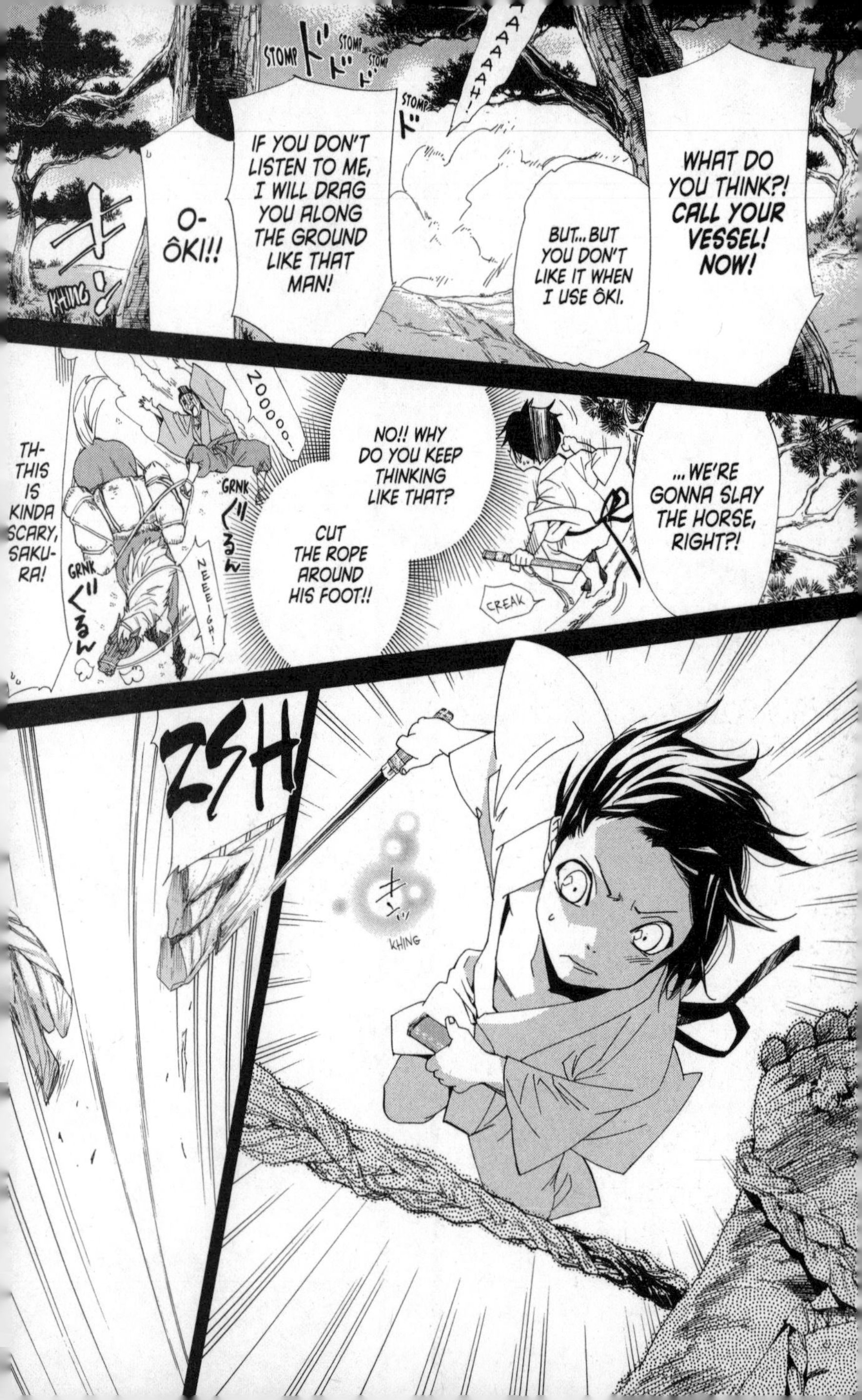
WHAT DO YOU THINK?! CALL YOUR VESSEL! NOW!
BUT...BUT YOU DON'T LIKE IT WHEN I USE ÔKI.
AAAAAAAH!
STOMP ド
IF YOU DON'T LISTEN TO ME, I WILL DRAG YOU ALONG THE GROUND LIKE THAT MAN!
STOMP ド STOMP ド STOMP ド
O-ÔKI!!
KHING
...WE'RE GONNA SLAY THE HORSE, RIGHT?!
CREAK
NO!! WHY DO YOU KEEP THINKING LIKE THAT?
CUT THE ROPE AROUND HIS FOOT!!
ZOOOOOO!
GRNK ぐるん
NEEEIGH!
GRNK ぐるん
TH-THIS IS KINDA SCARY, SAKURA!
KHING
ZSH

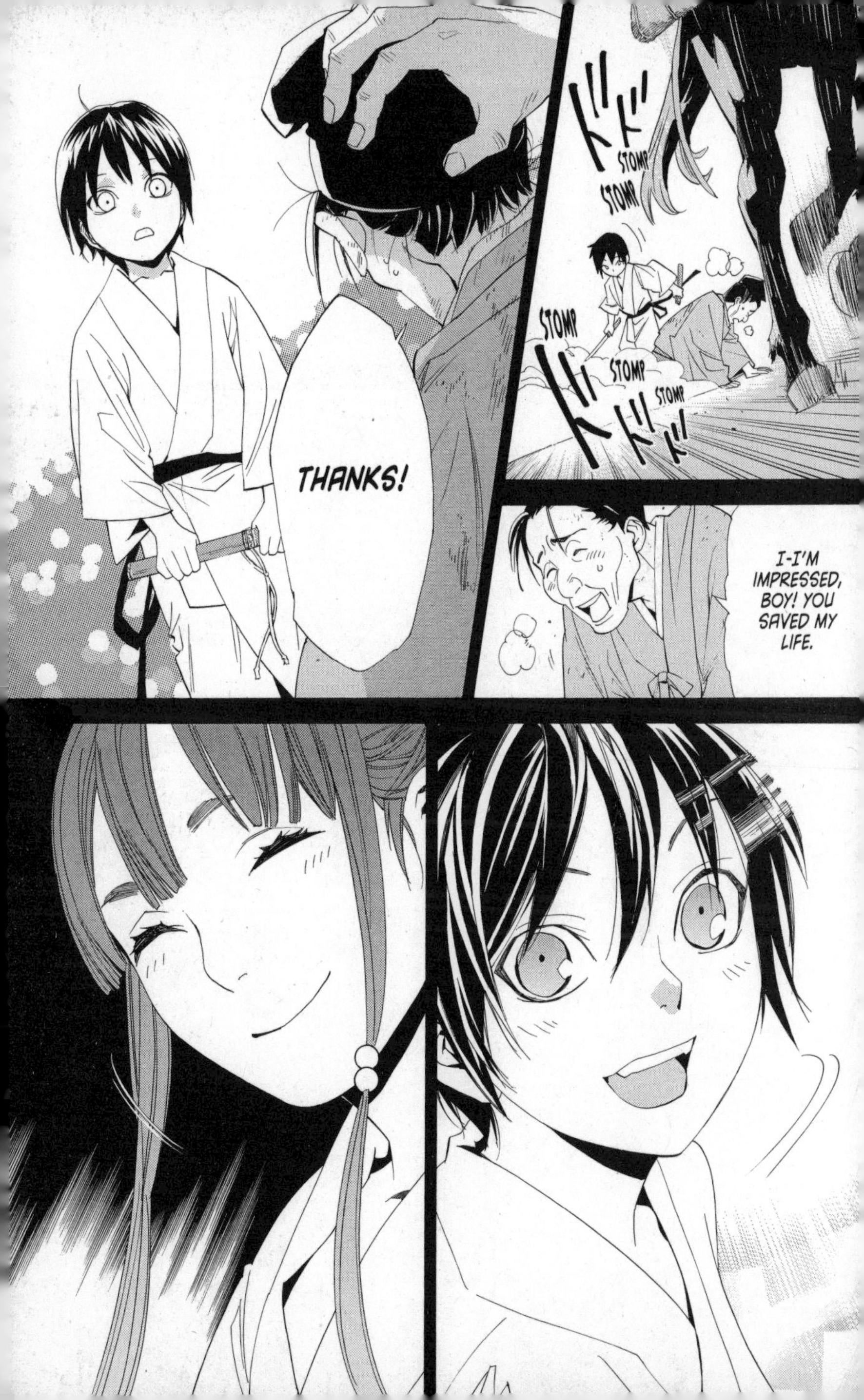
STOMP
STOMP
STOMP
STOMP
STOMP
I-I'M IMPRESSED, BOY! YOU SAVED MY LIFE.
THANKS!

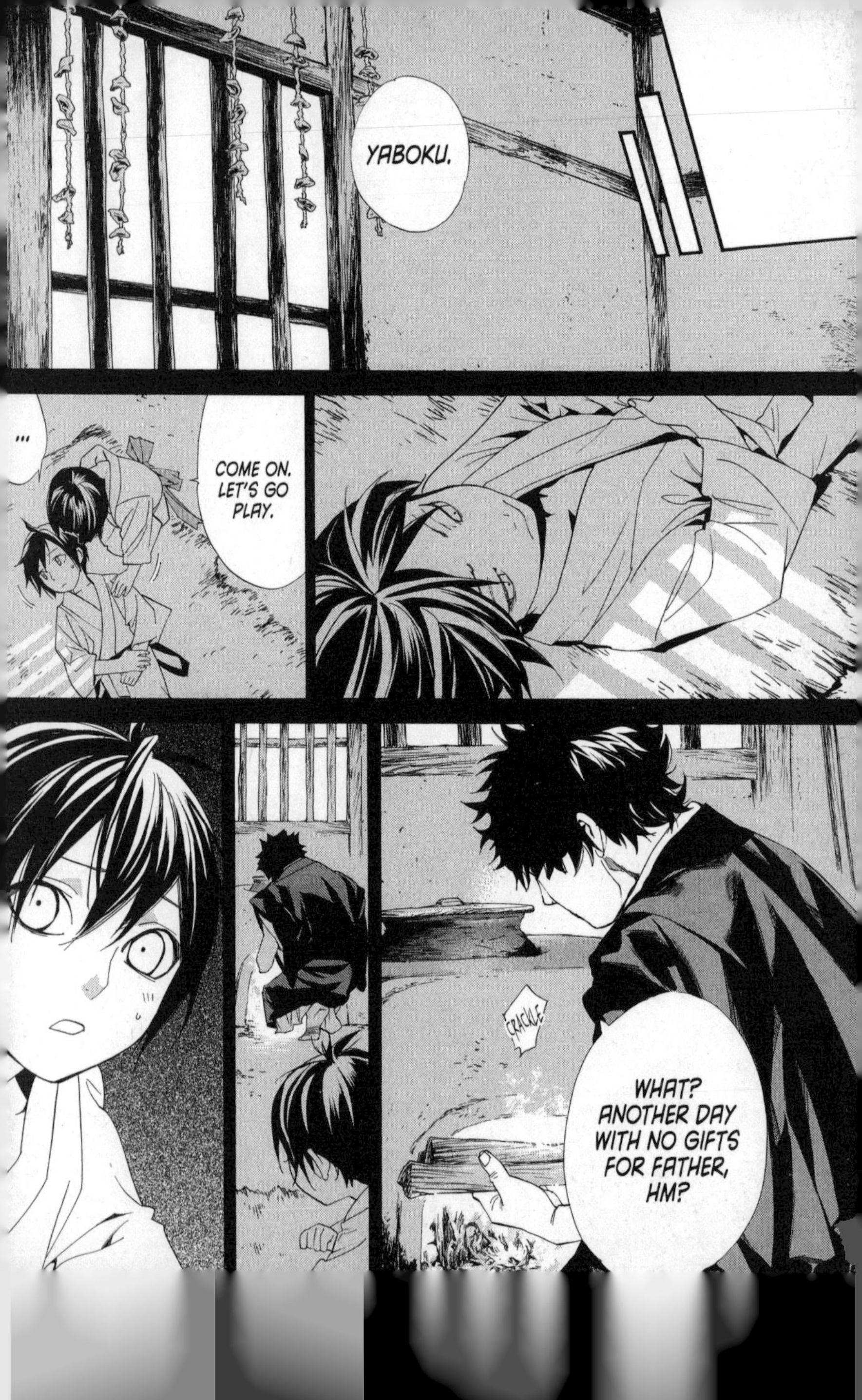
YABOKU.
COME ON. LET'S GO PLAY.
...
CRACKLE
WHAT? ANOTHER DAY WITH NO GIFTS FOR FATHER, HM?

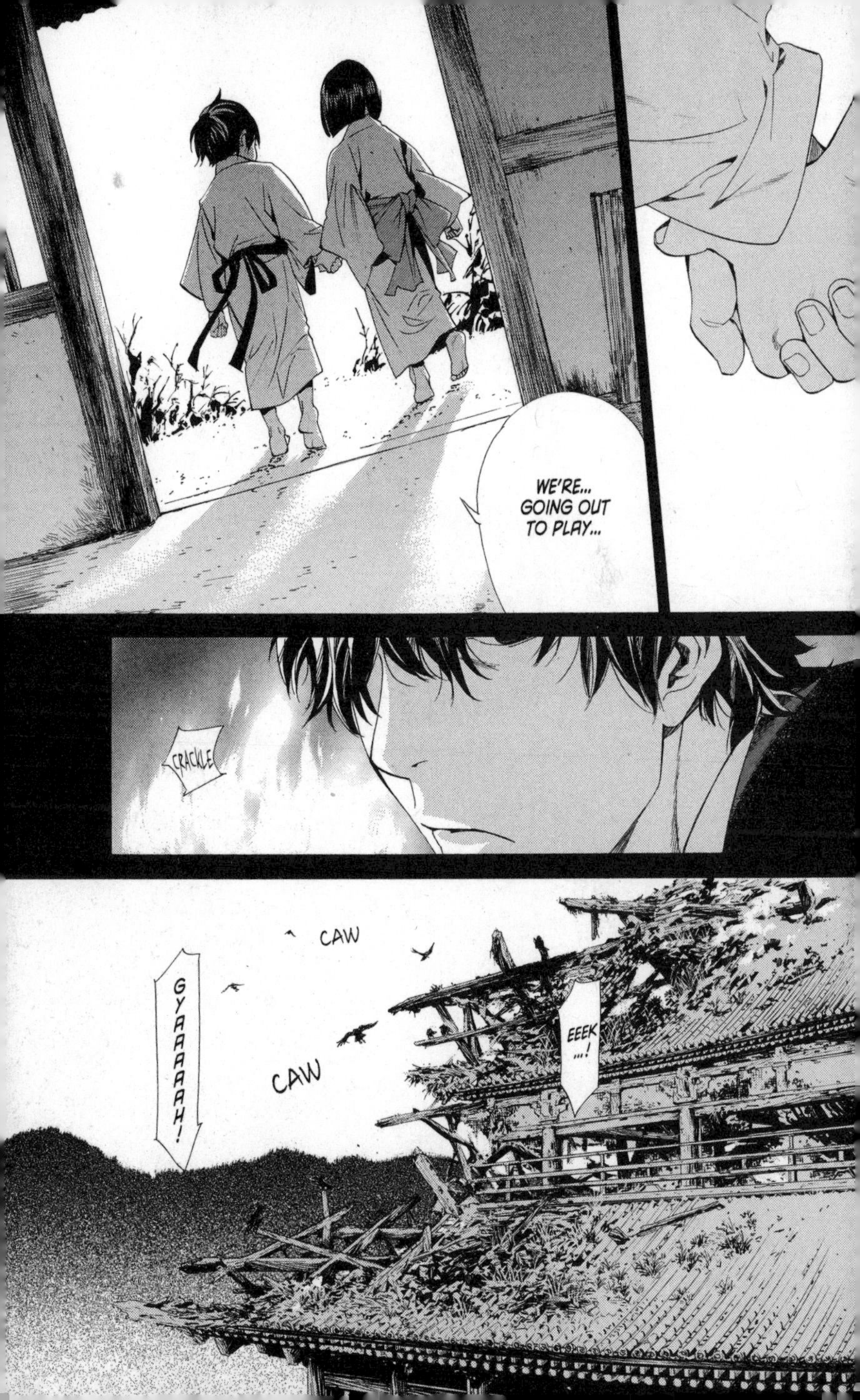
WE'RE... GOING OUT TO PLAY...
CRACKLE
EEEK ...!
CAW
CAW
GYAAAAAH!

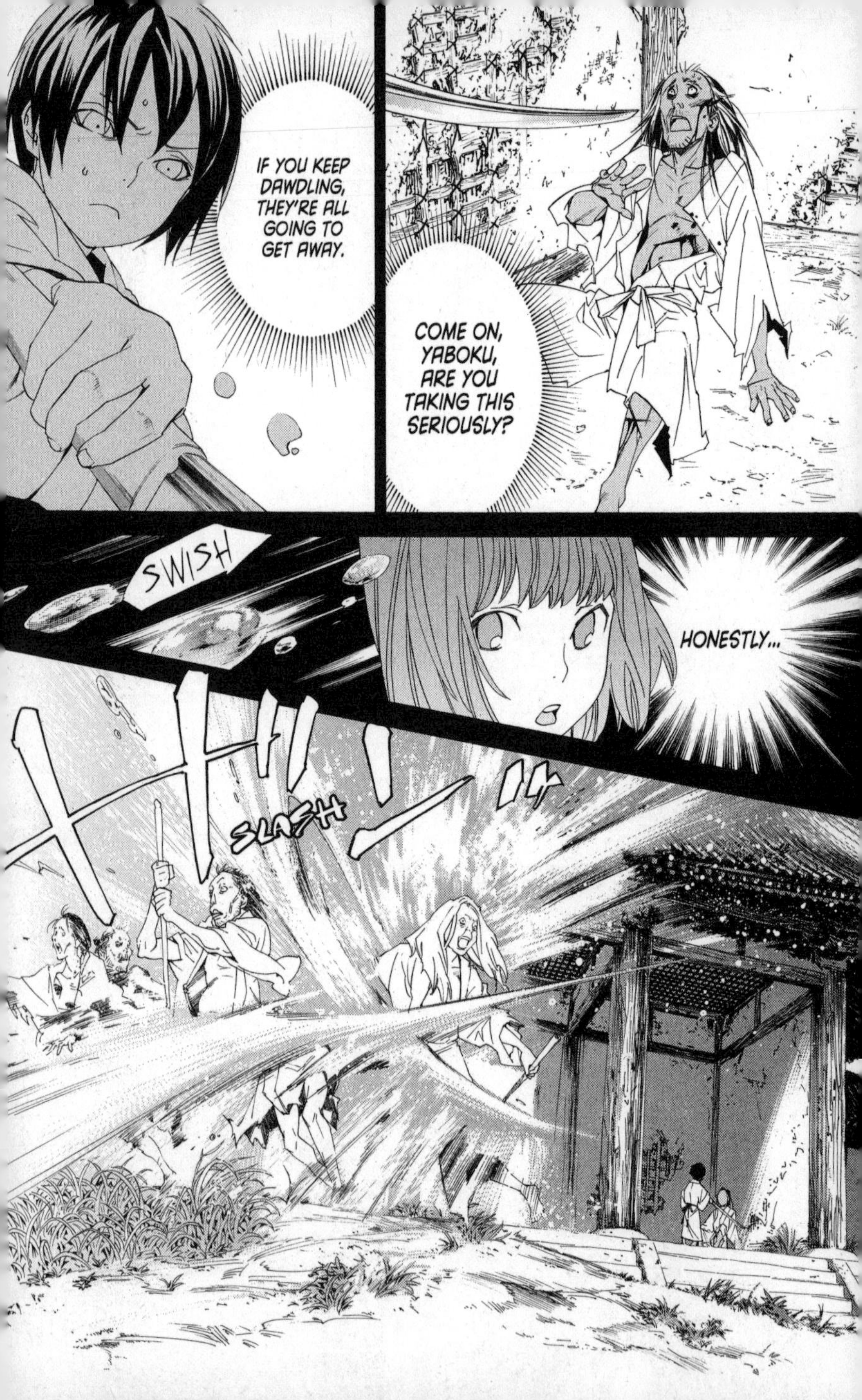
COME ON, YABOKU, ARE YOU TAKING THIS SERIOUSLY?
IF YOU KEEP DAWDLING, THEY'RE ALL GOING TO GET AWAY.
HONESTLY...
SWISH
SLASH

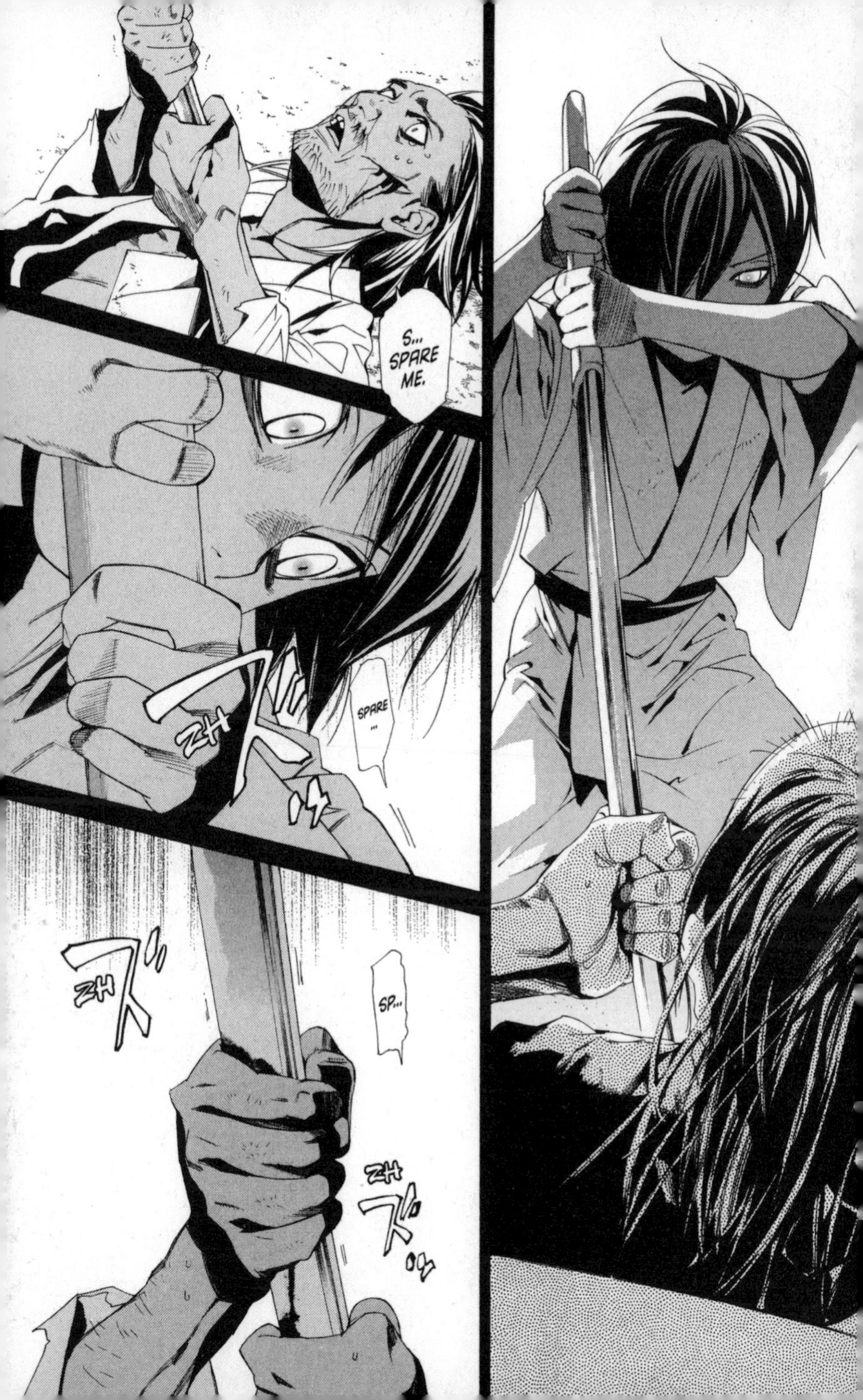
S... SPARE ME.
SPARE ...
ZH
SP...
ZH
ZH

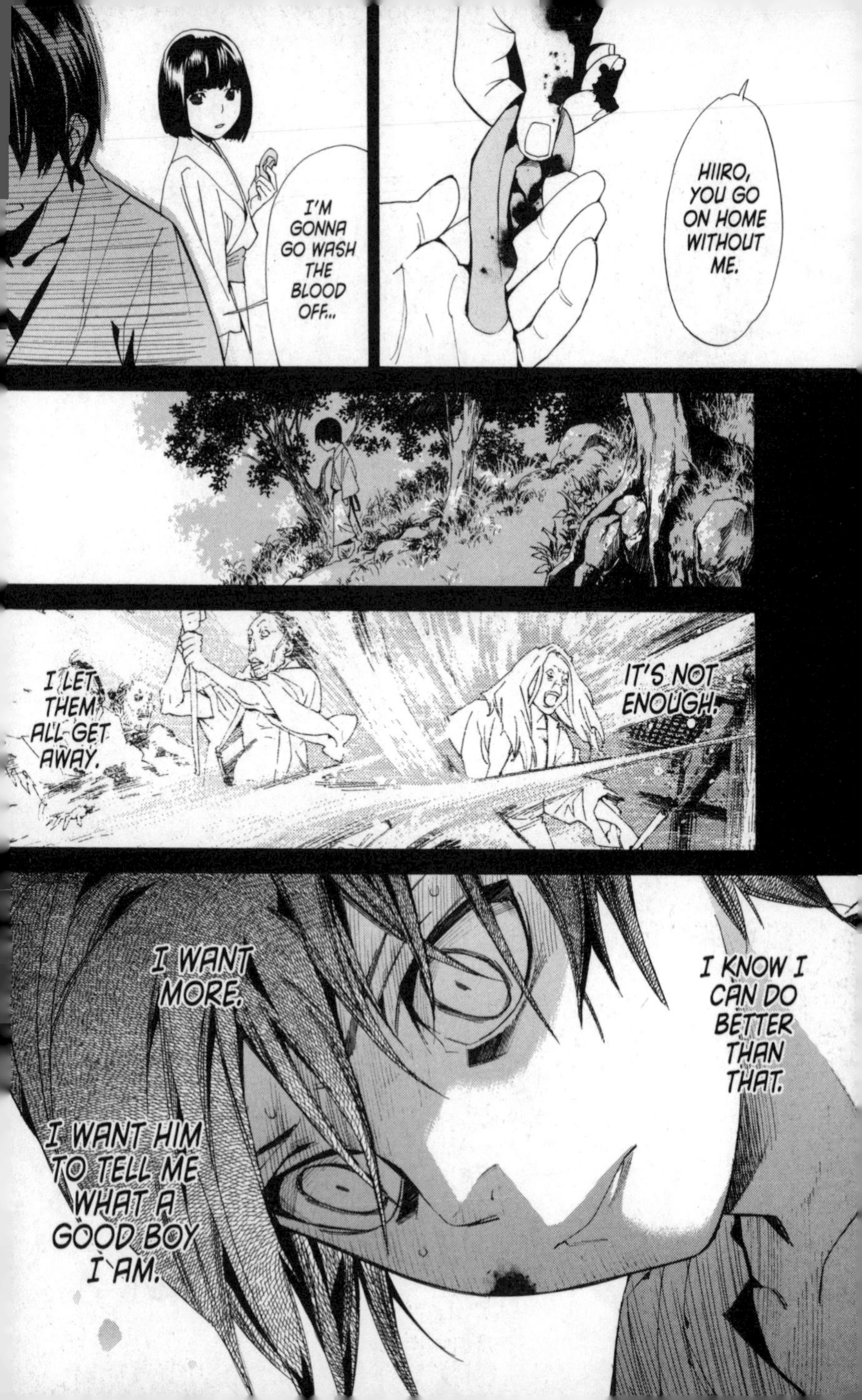
HIIRO, YOU GO ON HOME WITHOUT ME.
I'M GONNA GO WASH THE BLOOD OFF...
IT'S NOT ENOUGH.
I LET THEM ALL GET AWAY.
I KNOW I CAN DO BETTER THAN THAT.
I WANT MORE.
I WANT HIM TO TELL ME WHAT A GOOD BOY I AM.

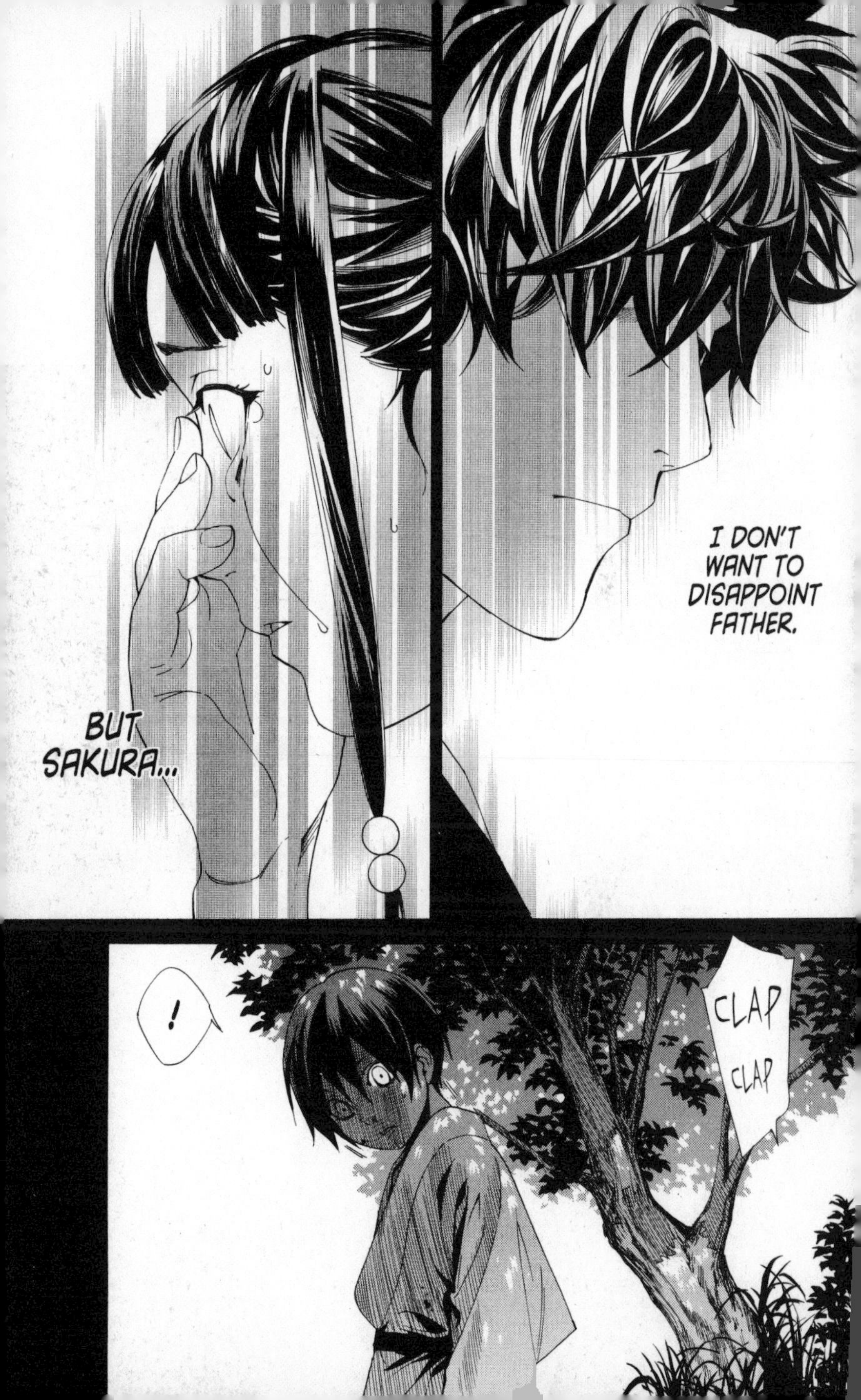
I DON'T WANT TO DISAPPOINT FATHER.
BUT SAKURA...
CLAP
CLAP
!

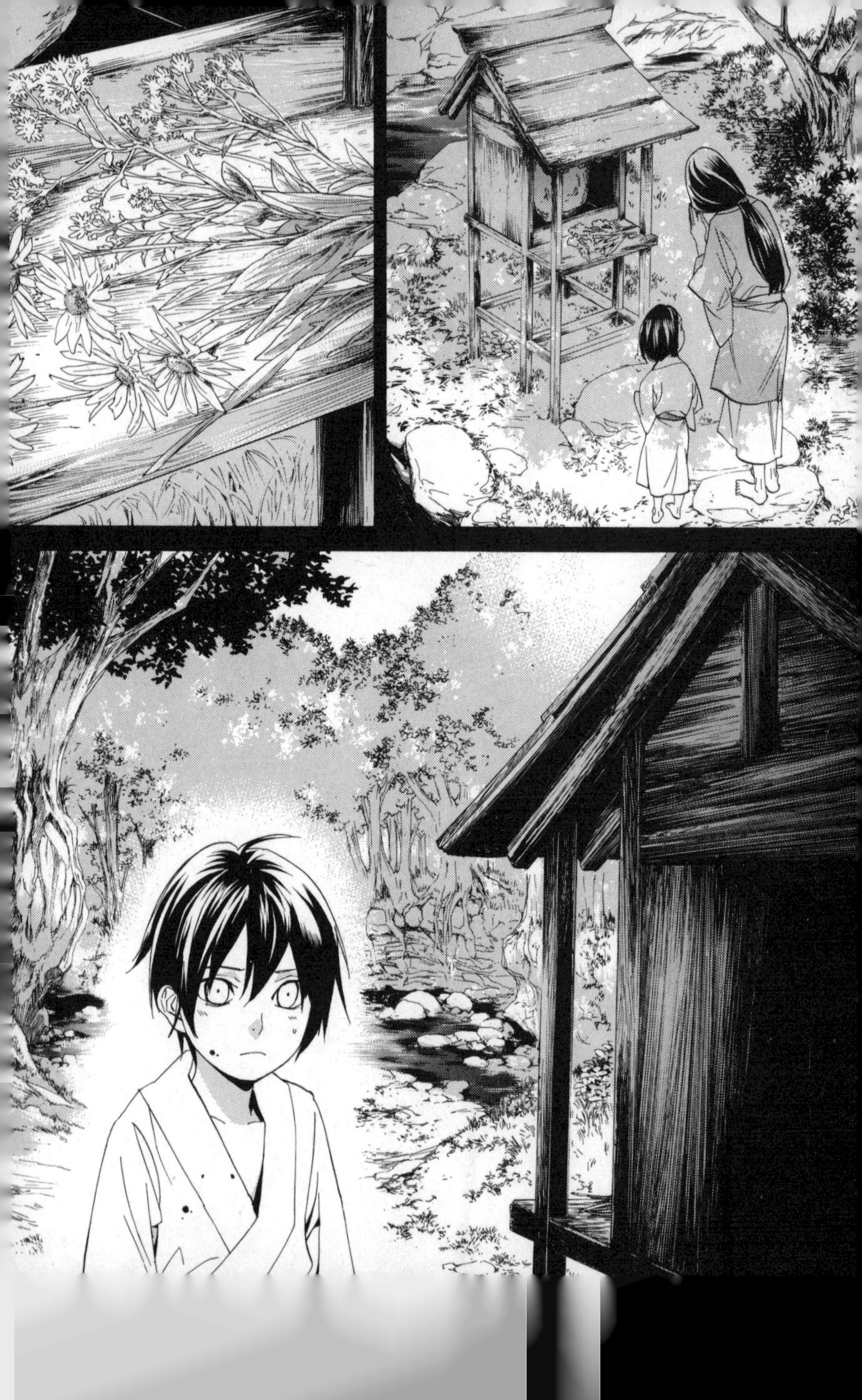

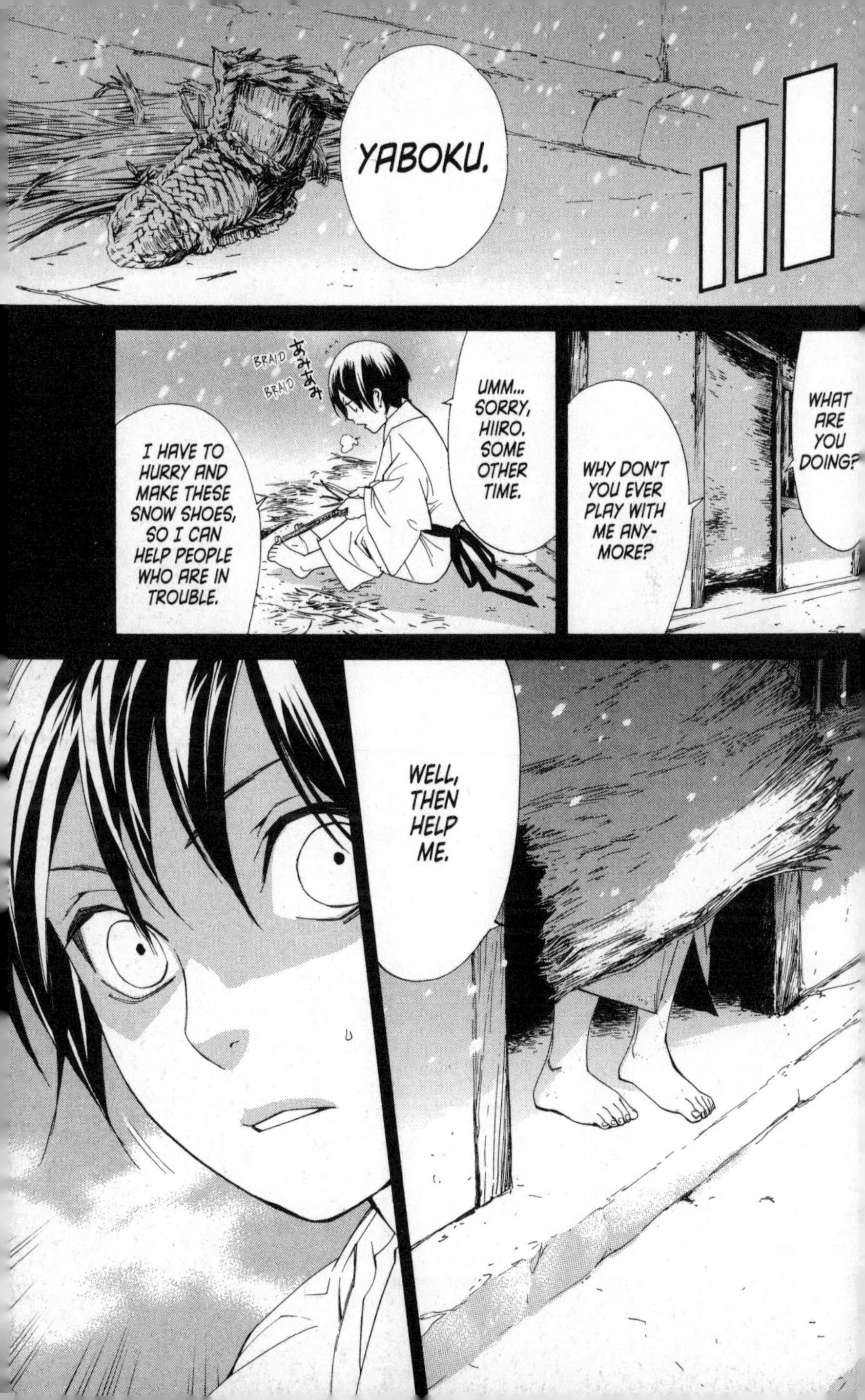
YABOKU.
WHAT ARE YOU DOING?
WHY DON'T YOU EVER PLAY WITH ME ANY-MORE?
UMM... SORRY, HIIRO. SOME OTHER TIME.
あみあみ BRAID BRAID
I HAVE TO HURRY AND MAKE THESE SNOW SHOES, SO I CAN HELP PEOPLE WHO ARE IN TROUBLE.
WELL, THEN HELP ME.

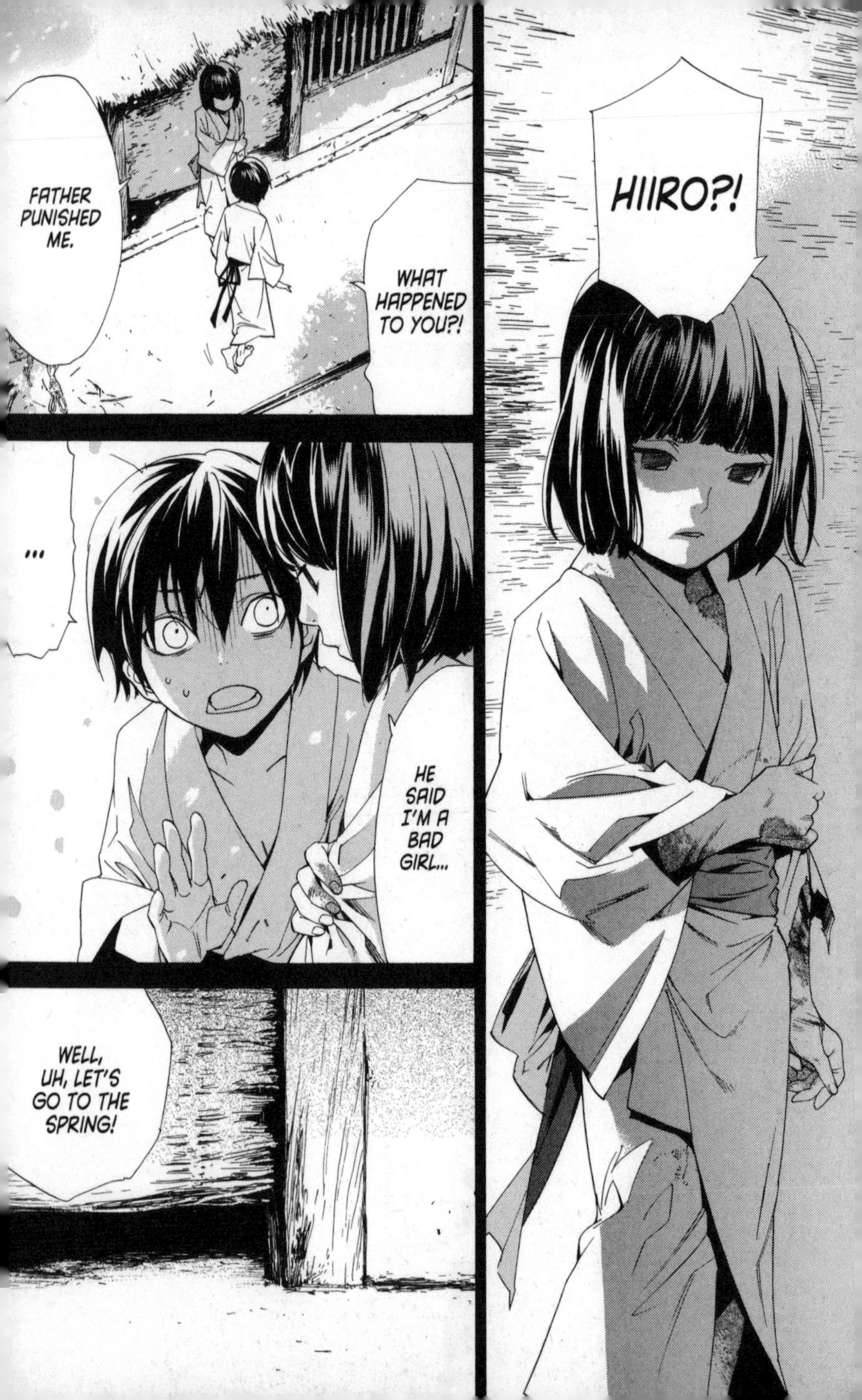
HIIRO?!
WHAT HAPPENED TO YOU?!
FATHER PUNISHED ME.
HE SAID I'M A BAD GIRL...
...
WELL, UH, LET'S GO TO THE SPRING!

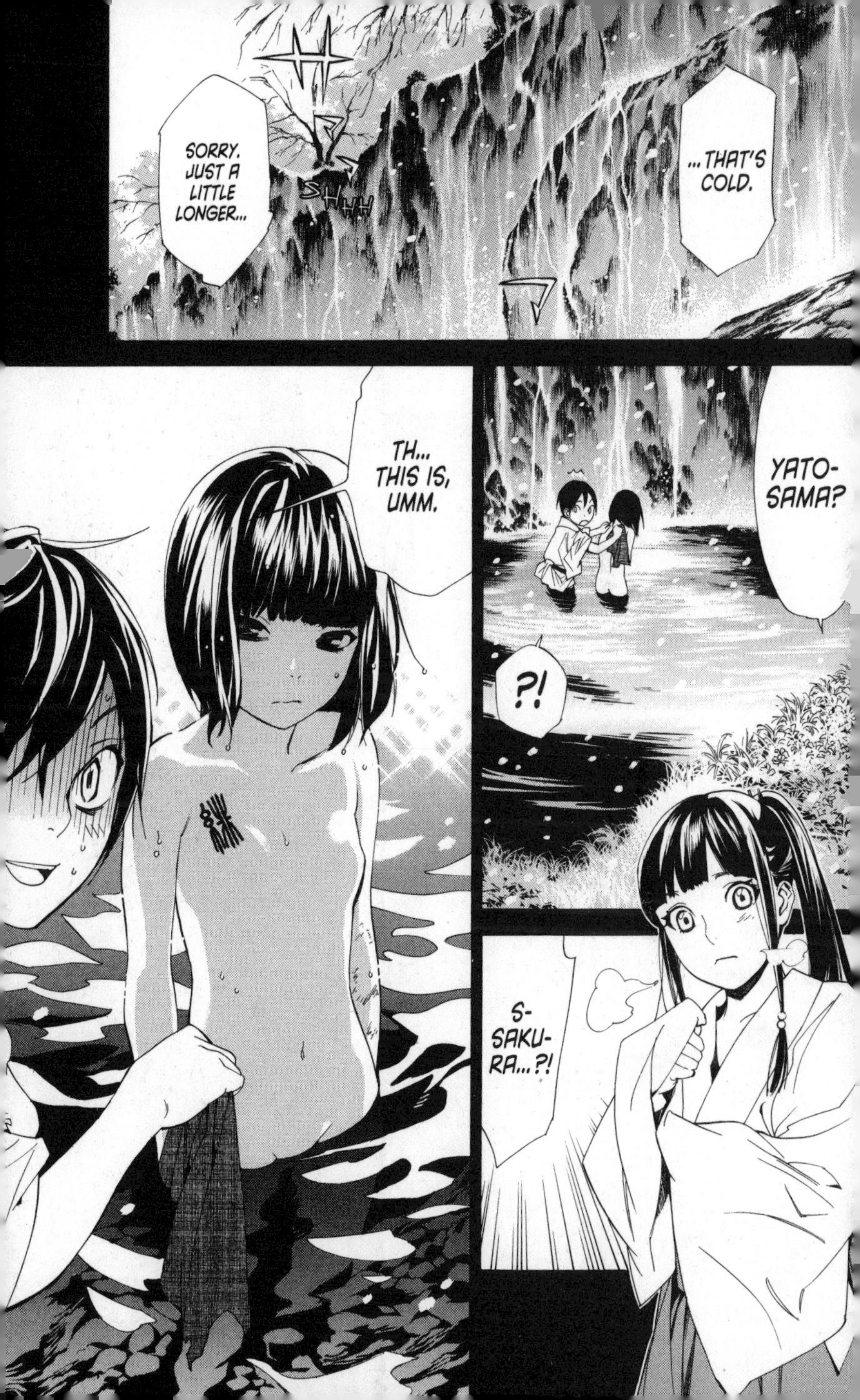
...THAT'S COLD.
SHHH
SORRY. JUST A LITTLE LONGER...
YATO-SAMA?
?!
S-SAKURA...?!
TH... THIS IS, UMM.

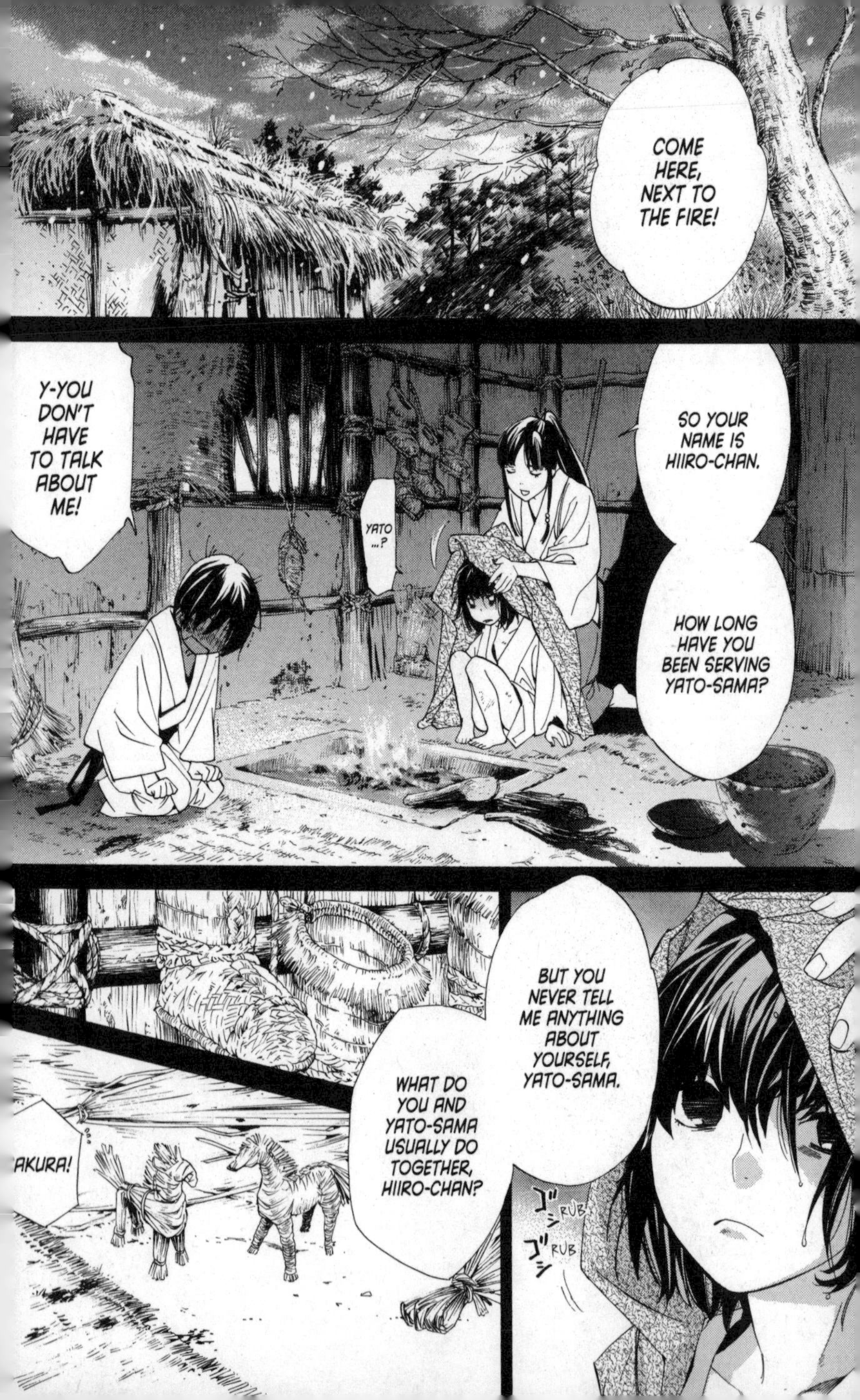
COME HERE, NEXT TO THE FIRE!
SO YOUR NAME IS HIIRO-CHAN.
HOW LONG HAVE YOU BEEN SERVING YATO-SAMA?
YATO ...?
Y-YOU DON'T HAVE TO TALK ABOUT ME!
BUT YOU NEVER TELL ME ANYTHING ABOUT YOURSELF, YATO-SAMA.
WHAT DO YOU AND YATO-SAMA USUALLY DO TOGETHER, HIIRO-CHAN?
RUB
RUB
AKURA!

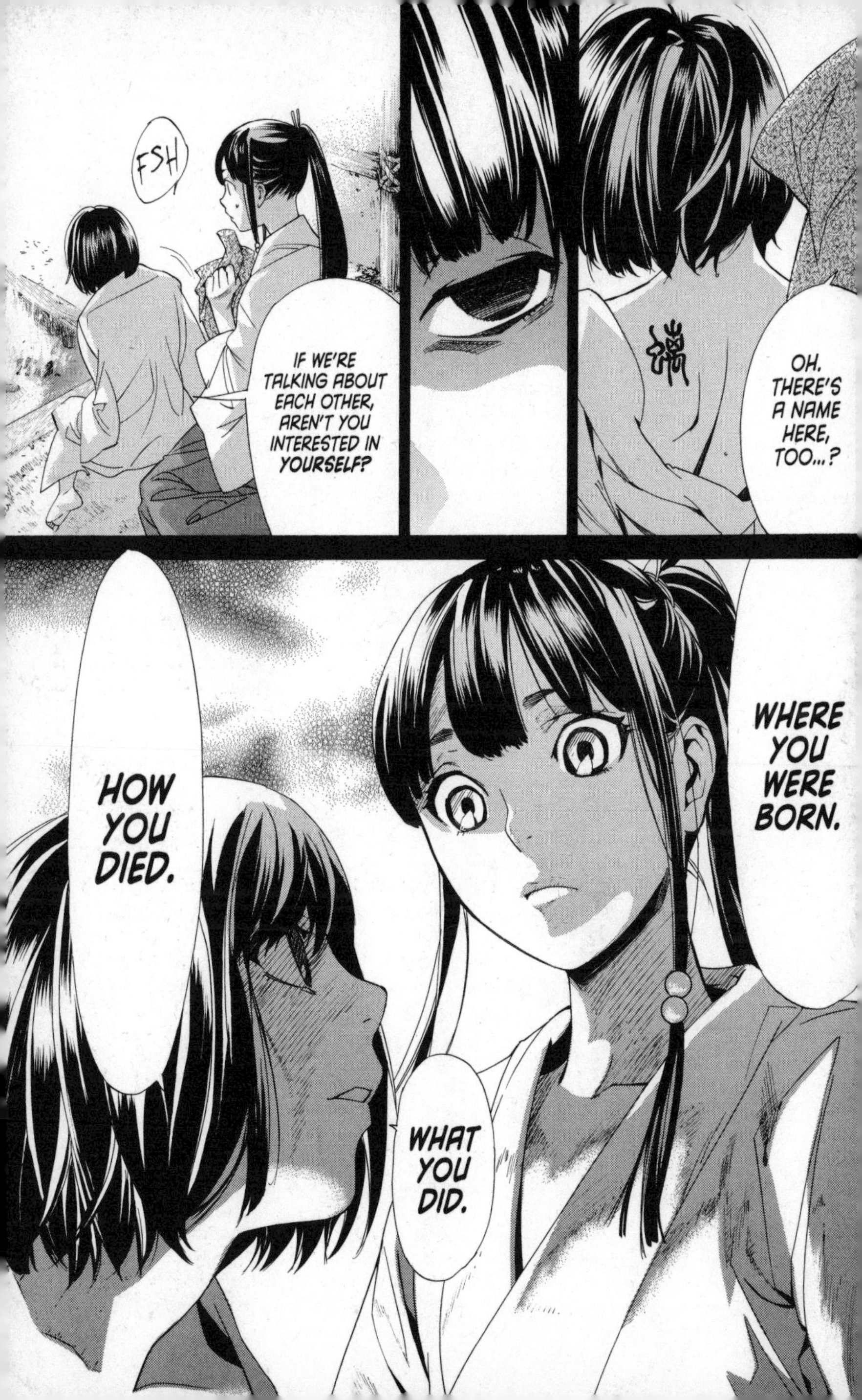
OH. THERE'S A NAME HERE, TOO...?
FSH
IF WE'RE TALKING ABOUT EACH OTHER, AREN'T YOU INTERESTED IN YOURSELF?
WHERE YOU WERE BORN.
WHAT YOU DID.
HOW YOU DIED.

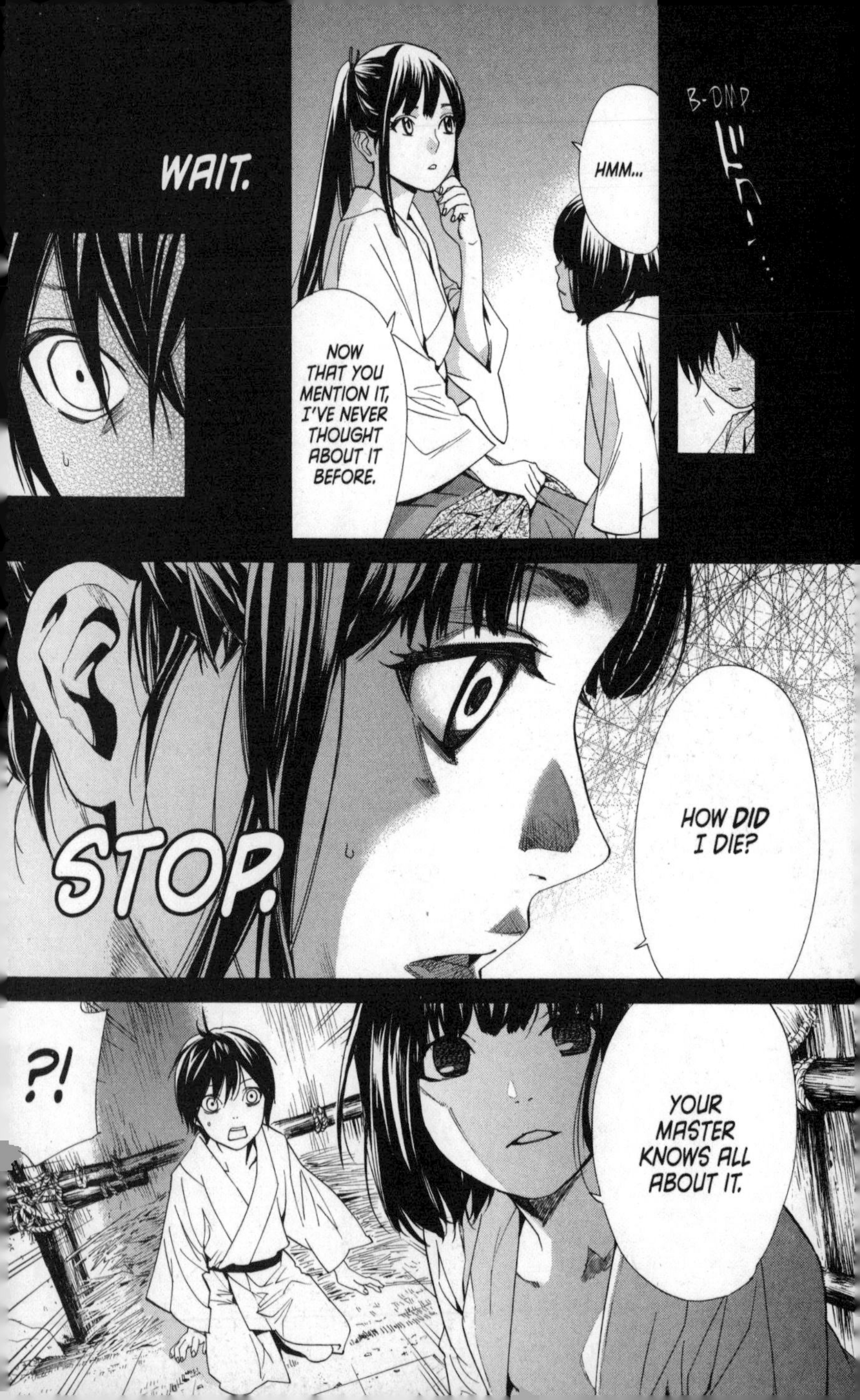
B-DMP
HMM...
NOW THAT YOU MENTION IT, I'VE NEVER THOUGHT ABOUT IT BEFORE.
WAIT.
HOW DID I DIE?
STOP.
YOUR MASTER KNOWS ALL ABOUT IT.
?!

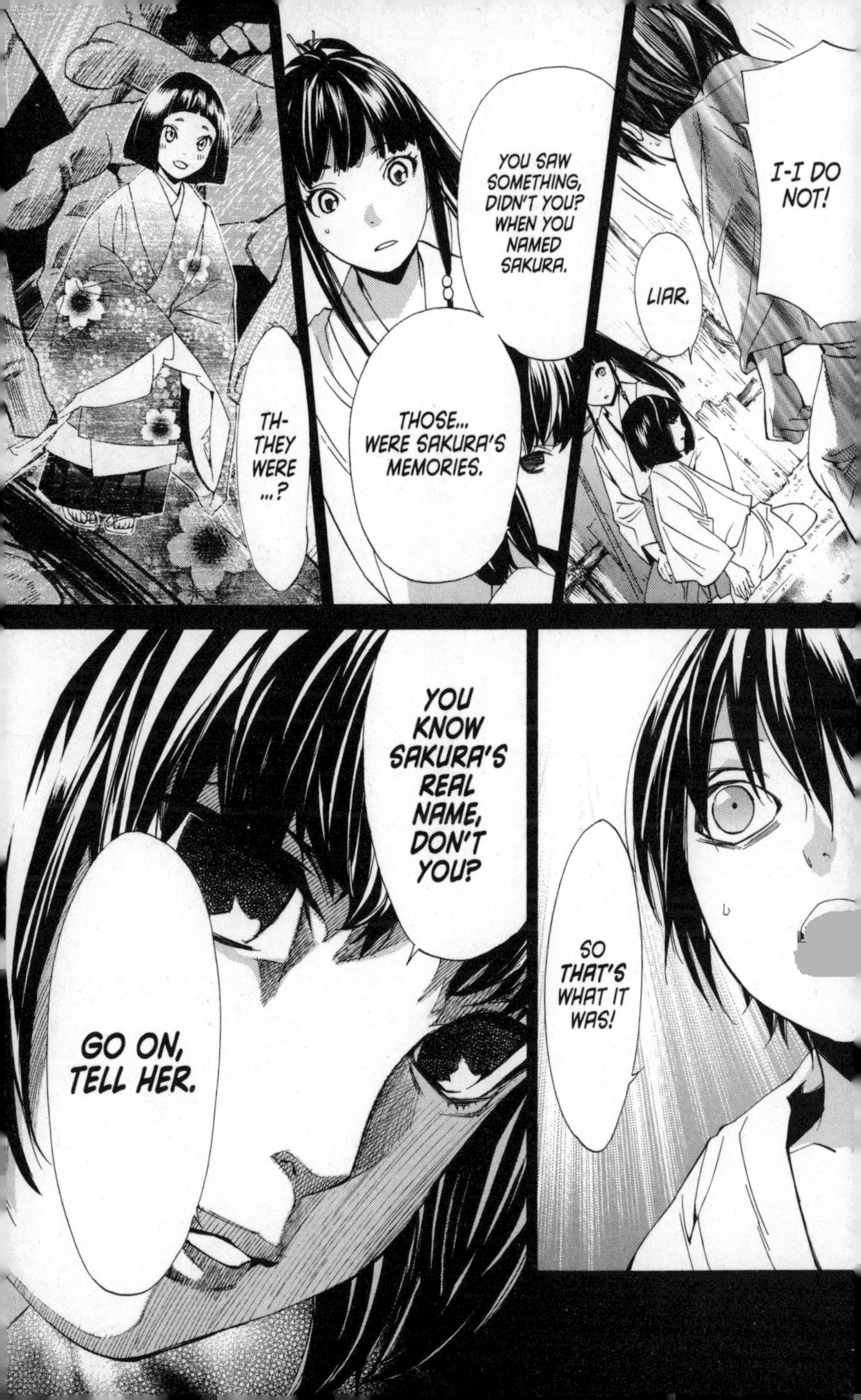
I-I DO NOT!
LIAR.
YOU SAW SOMETHING, DIDN'T YOU? WHEN YOU NAMED SAKURA.
THOSE... WERE SAKURA'S MEMORIES.
TH-THEY WERE ...?
SO THAT'S WHAT IT WAS!
YOU KNOW SAKURA'S REAL NAME, DON'T YOU?
GO ON, TELL HER.

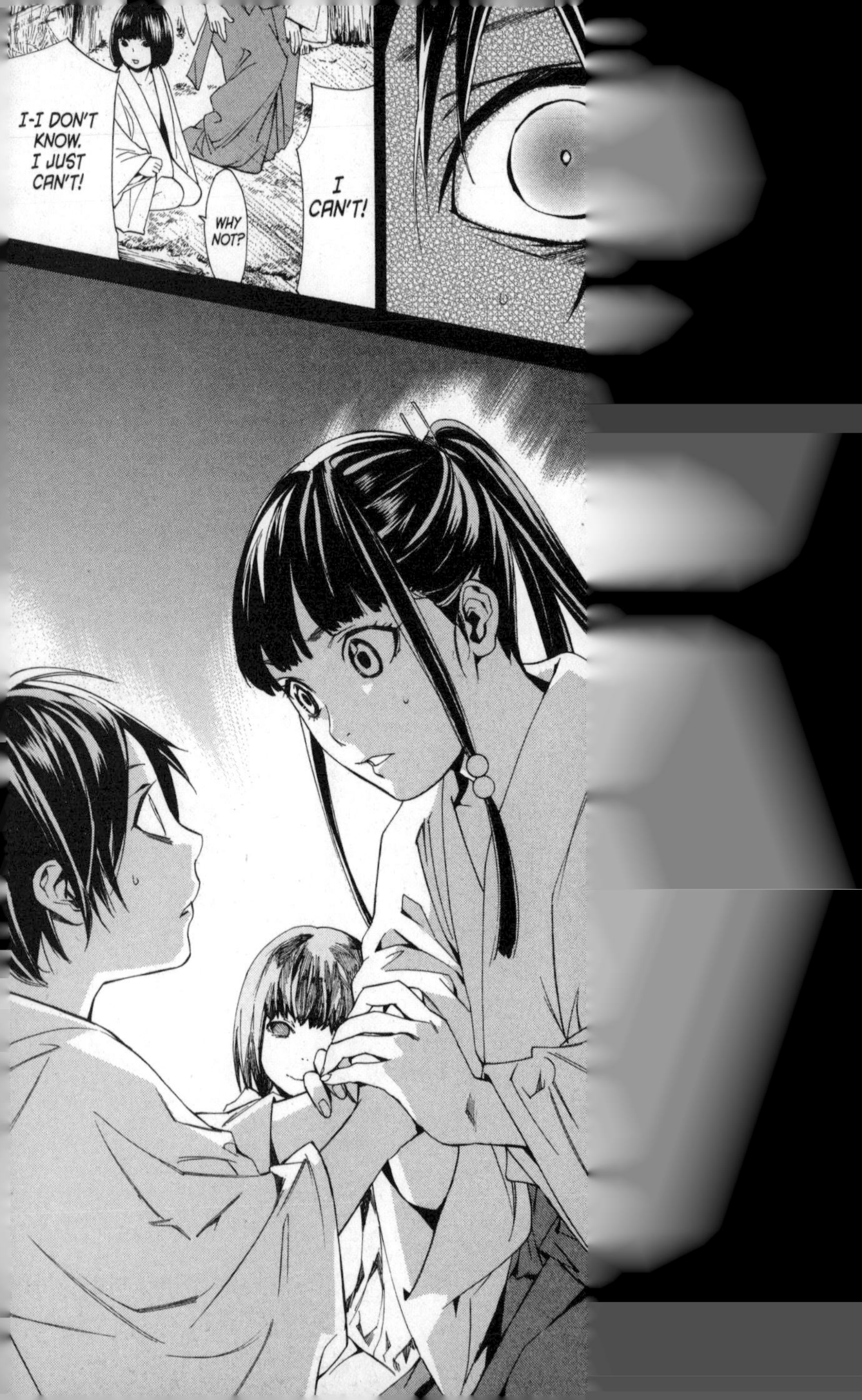
I CAN'T!
WHY NOT?
I-I DON'T KNOW. I JUST CAN'T!

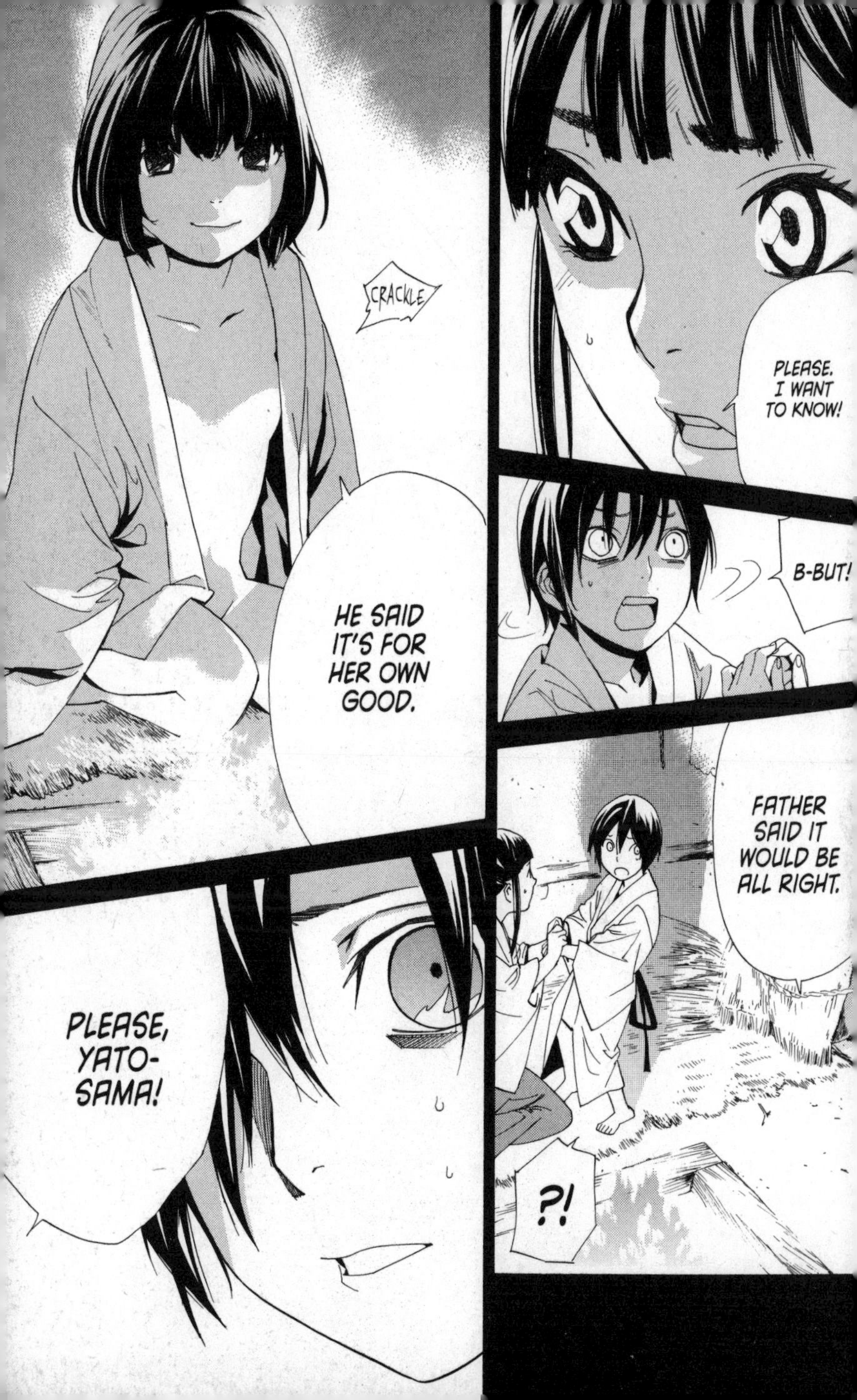
PLEASE. I WANT TO KNOW!
B-BUT!
FATHER SAID IT WOULD BE ALL RIGHT.
?!
CRACKLE
HE SAID IT'S FOR HER OWN GOOD.
PLEASE, YATO-SAMA!

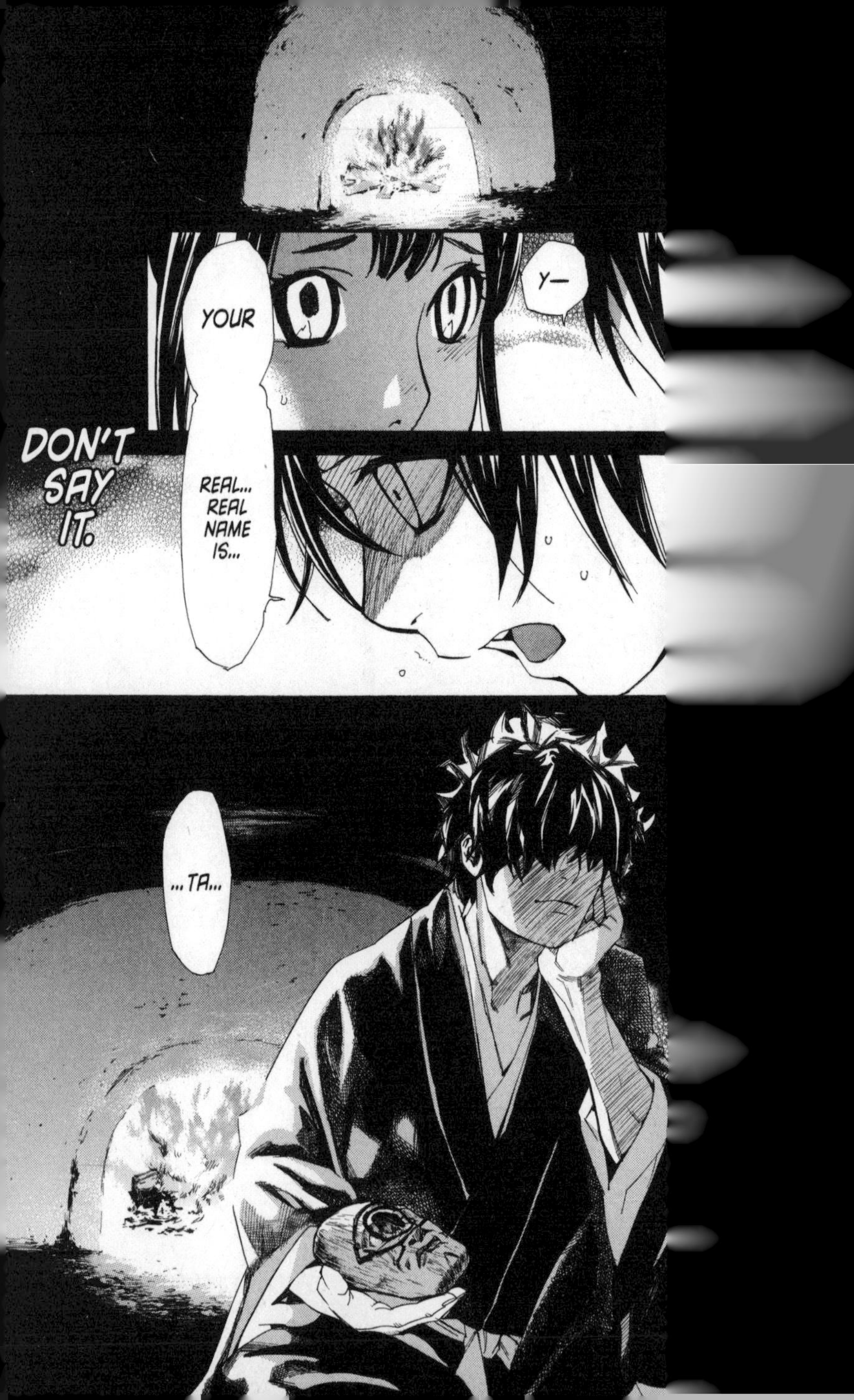
Y—
YOUR REAL... REAL NAME IS...
DON'T SAY IT.
...TA...

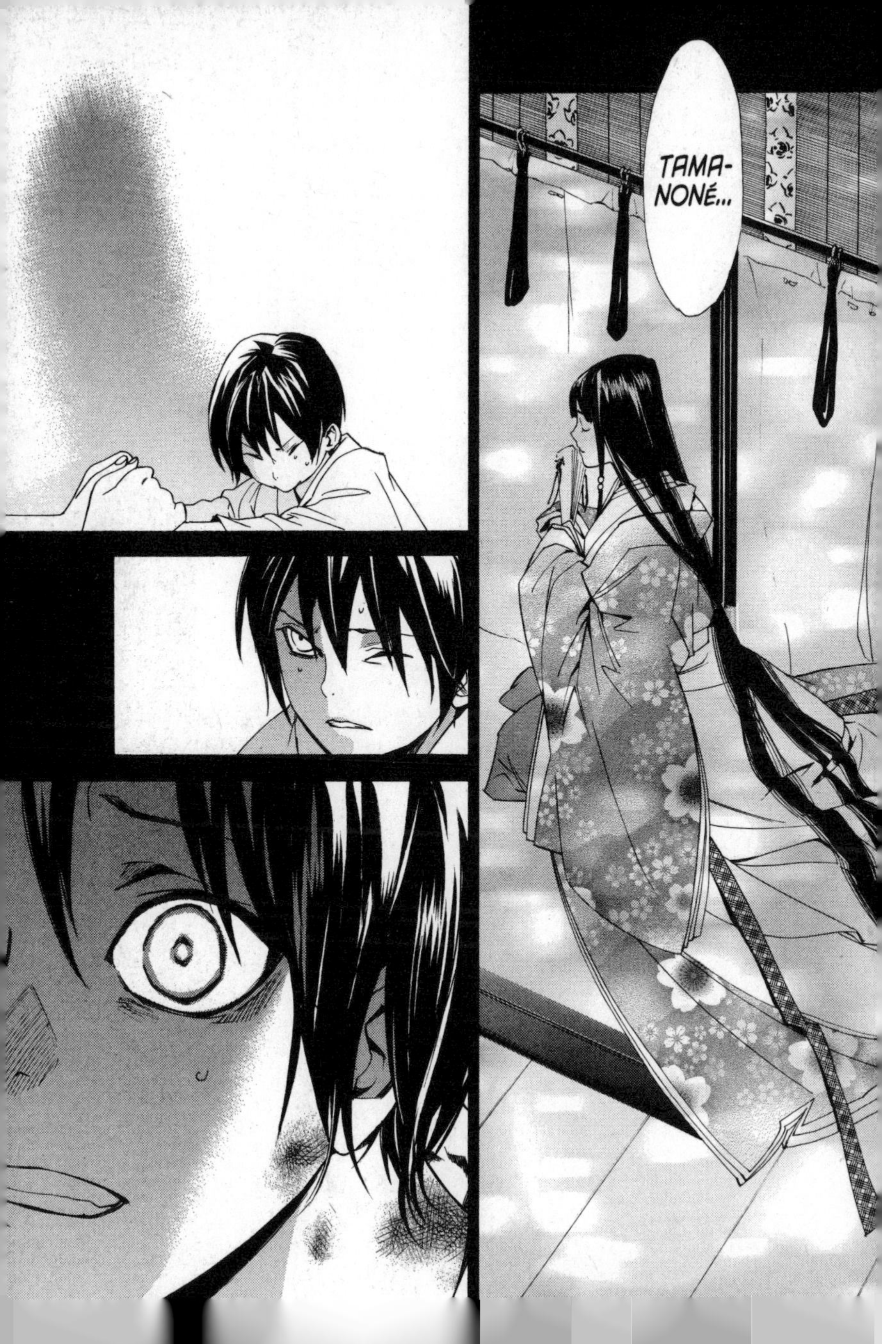
TAMA-
NONÉ...

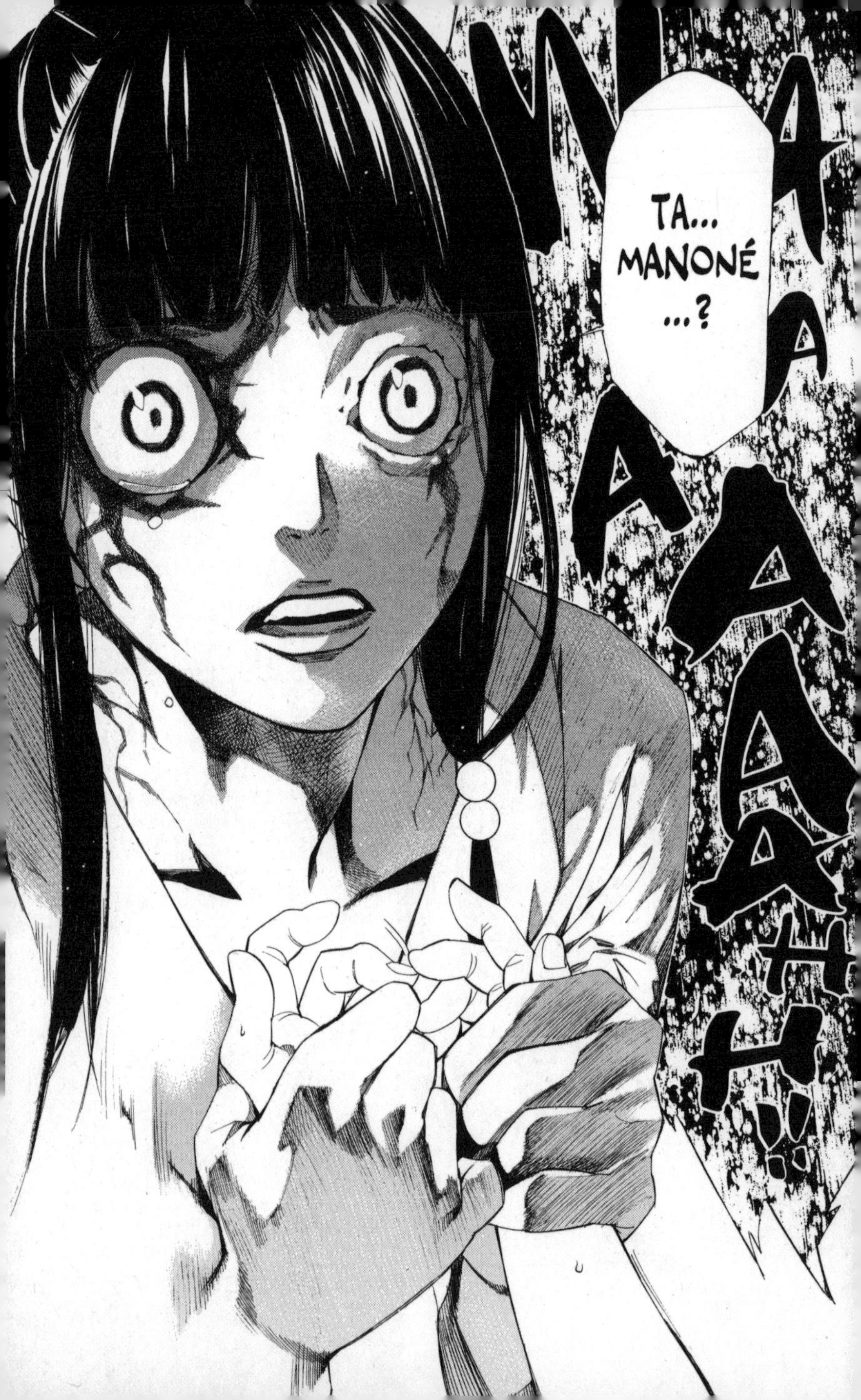
TA... MANONÉ ...?

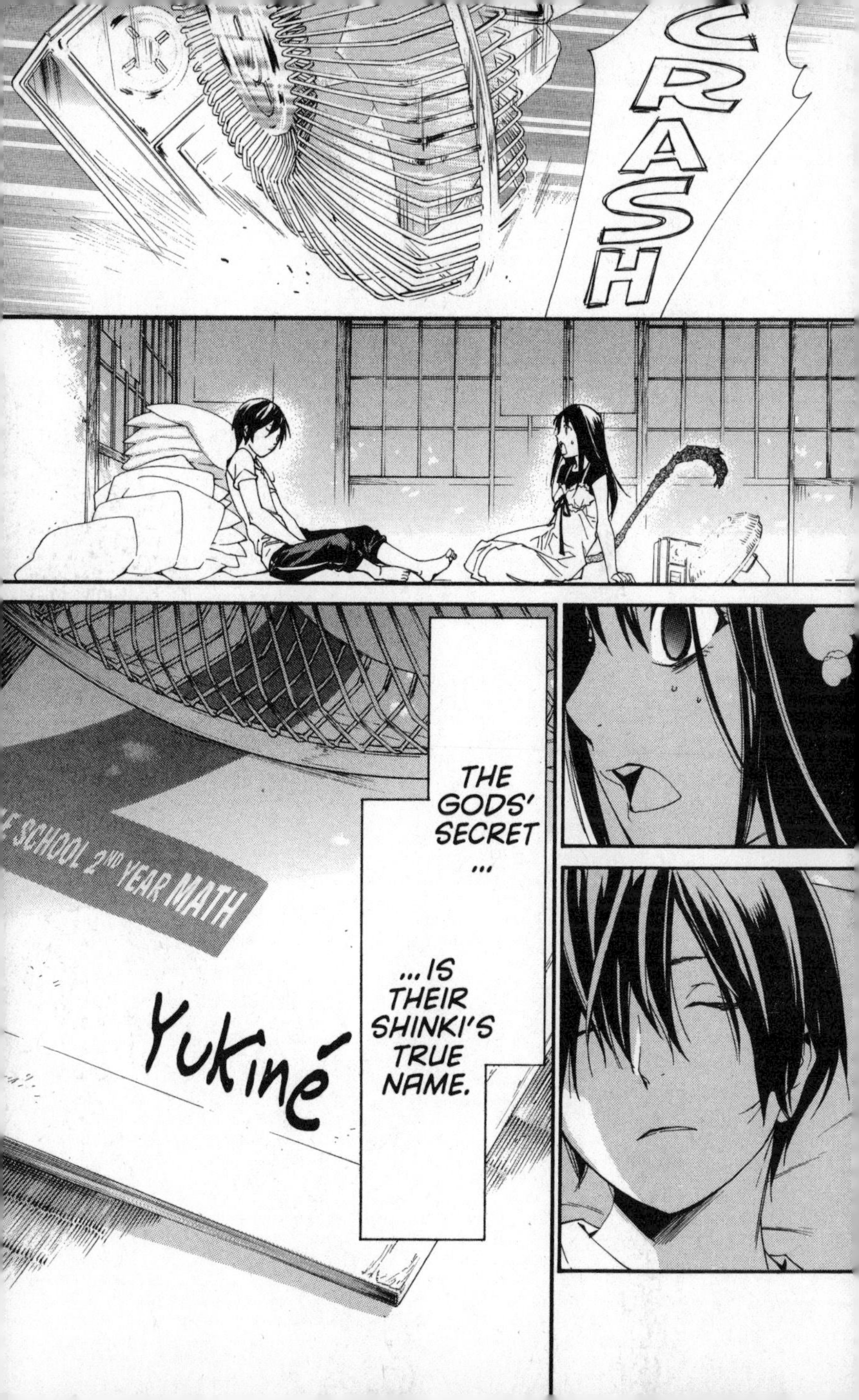
CRASH
THE GODS' SECRET ...
... IS THEIR SHINKI'S TRUE NAME.
SCHOOL 2ND YEAR MATH
Yukiné

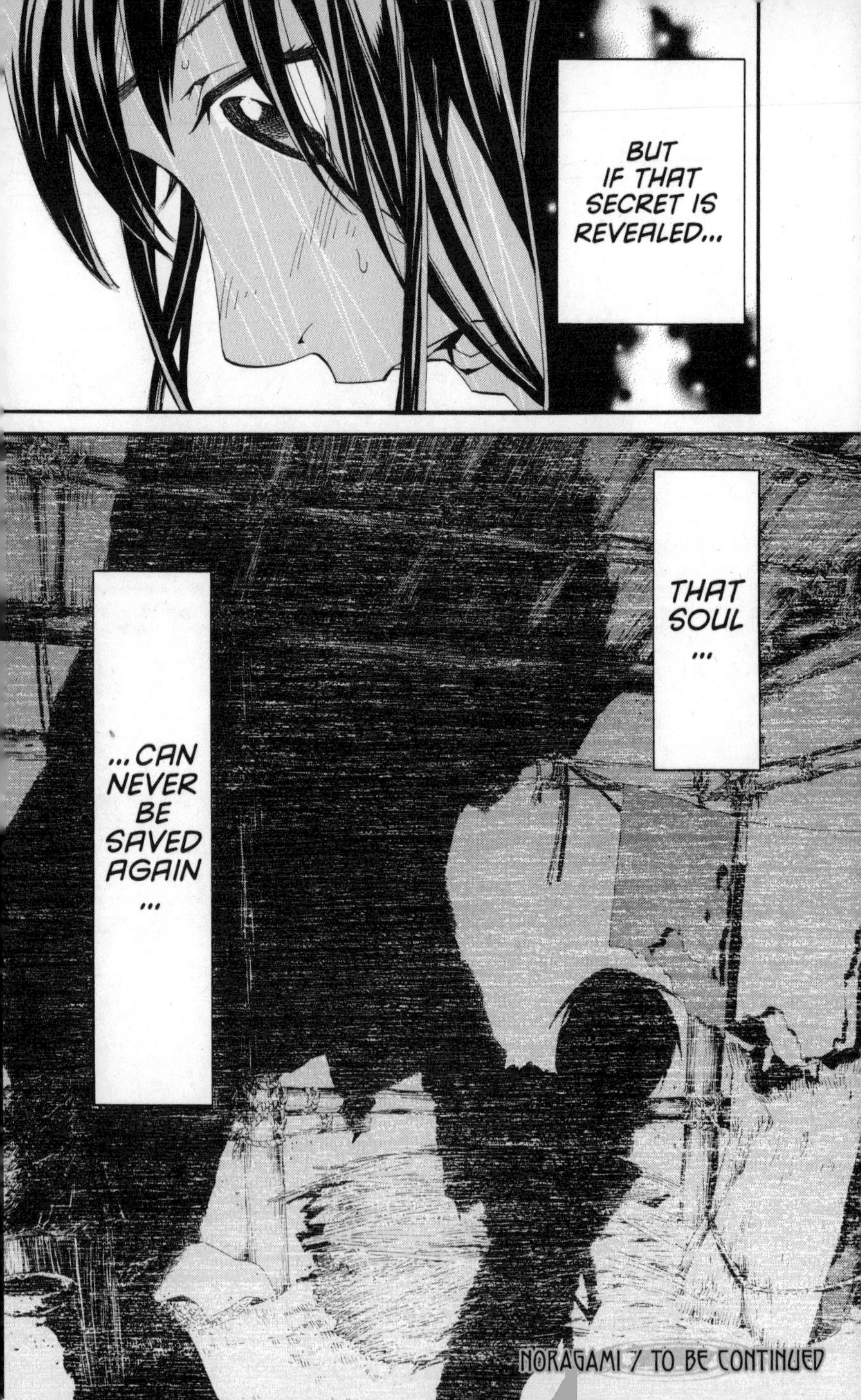
BUT IF THAT SECRET IS REVEALED...
THAT SOUL ...
...CAN NEVER BE SAVED AGAIN ...
NORAGAMI 7 / TO BE CONTINUED

野

兑

神

ATROCIOUS MANGA

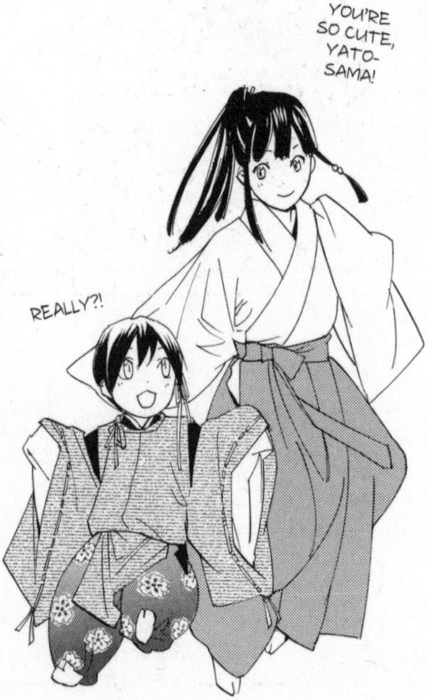
YOU'RE SO CUTE, YATO-SAMA!
REALLY?!

IT'S SAKURA'S FAULT

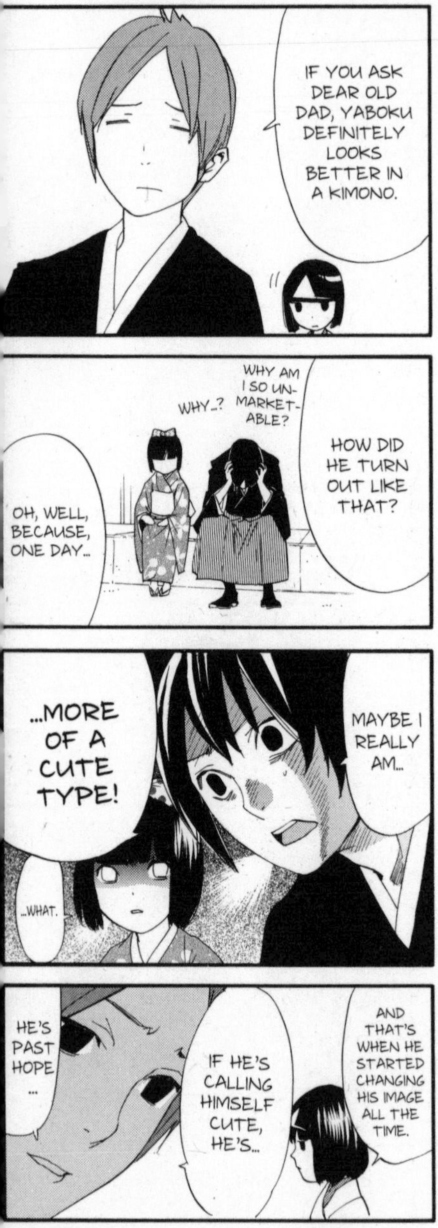
IF YOU ASK DEAR OLD DAD, YABOKU DEFINITELY LOOKS BETTER IN A KIMONO.
HOW DID HE TURN OUT LIKE THAT?
WHY AM I SO UN-MARKET-ABLE?
WHY...?
OH, WELL, BECAUSE, ONE DAY...
MAYBE I REALLY AM...
...MORE OF A CUTE TYPE!
...WHAT.
AND THAT'S WHEN HE STARTED CHANGING HIS IMAGE ALL THE TIME.
IF HE'S CALLING HIMSELF CUTE, HE'S...
HE'S PAST HOPE...

CUTE MAKES RIGHT

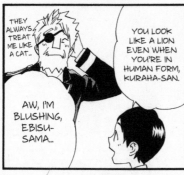

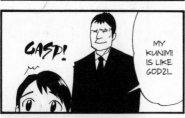

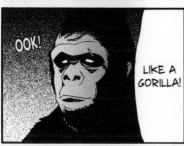

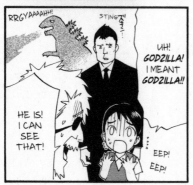

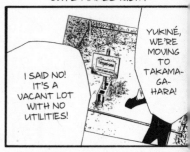

YUKINÉ, WE'RE MOVING TO TAKAMA-GA-HARA!
I SAID NO! IT'S A VACANT LOT WITH NO UTILITIES!
BUT I'LL MOVE TO TAKAMA-GA-HARA IF I CAN GET A CAT!
...WELL, IF YOU INSIST.
REALLY ?!
HERE YA GO!
SFF
SFF
LET'S GO! TO TAKA-MEOW-GA-HARA!!

TRUE FEELINGS

YOU LOOK LIKE A LION EVEN WHEN YOU'RE IN HUMAN FORM, KURAHA-SAN.
THEY ALWAYS TREAT ME LIKE A CAT...
AW, I'M BLUSHING, EBISU-SAMA...
MY KUNIMI IS LIKE GODZI...
GASP!
LIKE A GORILLA!
OOK!
UH! GODZILLA! I MEANT GODZILLA!!
STING
RRGYAAAAHH!
HE IS! I CAN SEE THAT!
EEP! EEP!

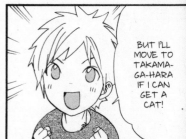

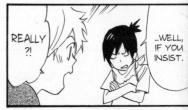

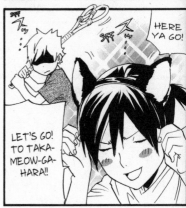

DOGS WOULD BE PAU AND LOU

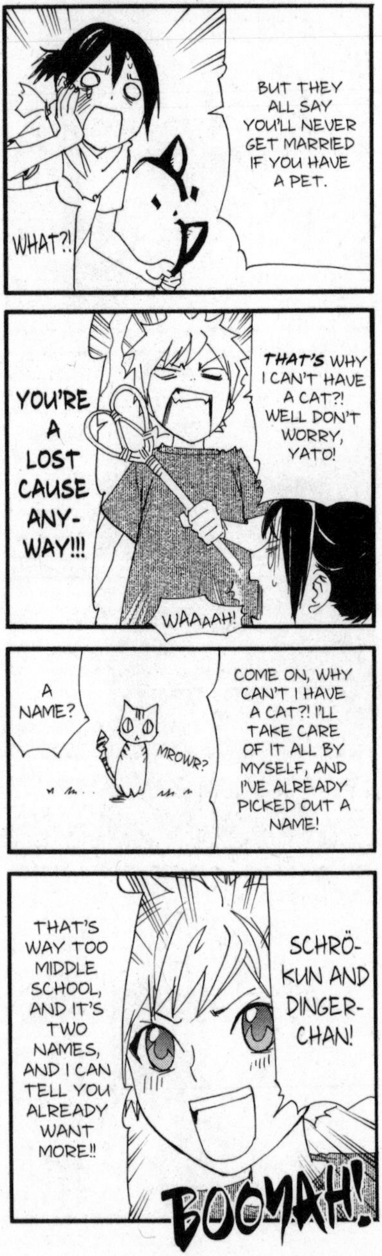
BUT THEY ALL SAY YOU'LL NEVER GET MARRIED IF YOU HAVE A PET.
WHAT?!
THAT'S WHY I CAN'T HAVE A CAT?! WELL DON'T WORRY, YATO!
YOU'RE A LOST CAUSE ANY-WAY!!!
WAAAAH!
COME ON, WHY CAN'T I HAVE A CAT?! I'LL TAKE CARE OF IT ALL BY MYSELF, AND I'VE ALREADY PICKED OUT A NAME!
MROWR?
A NAME?
SCHRÖ-KUN AND DINGER-CHAN!
THAT'S WAY TOO MIDDLE SCHOOL, AND IT'S TWO NAMES, AND I CAN TELL YOU ALREADY WANT MORE!!
BOOYAH!

PRACTICALLY A GO

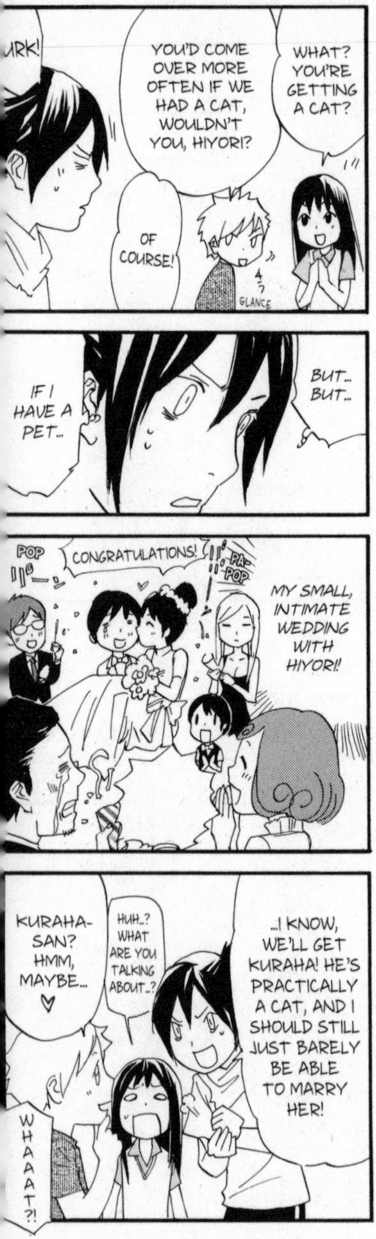
WHAT? YOU'RE GETTING A CAT?
YOU'D COME OVER MORE OFTEN IF WE HAD A CAT, WOULDN'T YOU, HIYORI?
GLANCE
OF COURSE!
BUT... BUT...
IF I HAVE A PET...
MY SMALL, INTIMATE WEDDING WITH HIYORI!
PA-POP
CONGRATULATIONS!
POP
...I KNOW, WE'LL GET KURAHA! HE'S PRACTICALLY A CAT, AND I SHOULD STILL JUST BARELY BE ABLE TO MARRY HER!
HUH..? WHAT ARE YOU TALKING ABOUT..?
KURAHA-SAN? HMM, MAYBE...
WHAAAAT?!

ESCALATING

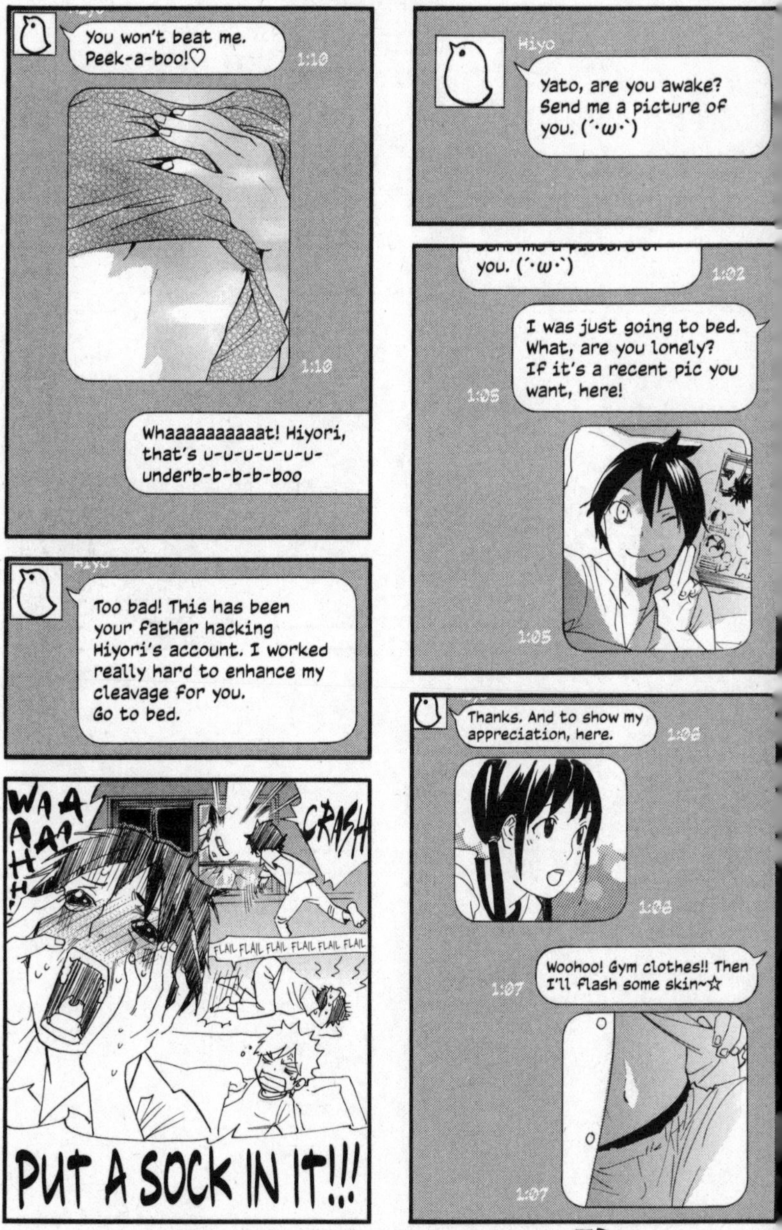
Hiyo
Yato, are you awake? Send me a picture of you. (´･ω･`)
you. (´･ω･`)
1:02
I was just going to bed. What, are you lonely? If it's a recent pic you want, here!
1:05
1:05
Thanks. And to show my appreciation, here.
1:06
1:06
Woohoo! Gym clothes!! Then I'll flash some skin~☆
1:07
1:07
You won't beat me. Peek-a-boo!♡
1:10
1:10
Whaaaaaaaaaat! Hiyori, that's u-u-u-u-u-u-underb-b-b-b-boo
Too bad! This has been your father hacking Hiyori's account. I worked really hard to enhance my cleavage for you. Go to bed.
CRASH
WAAAAAAH
FLAIL FLAIL FLAIL FLAIL FLAIL FLAIL
PUT A SOCK IN IT!!!

THANK YOU TO EVERYONE WHO READ THIS FAR!!

TRANSLATION NOTES

Japanese is a tricky language for most Westerners, and translation is often more art than science. For your edification and reading pleasure, here are notes on some of the places where we could have gone in a different direction in our translation of the work, or where a Japanese cultural reference is used.

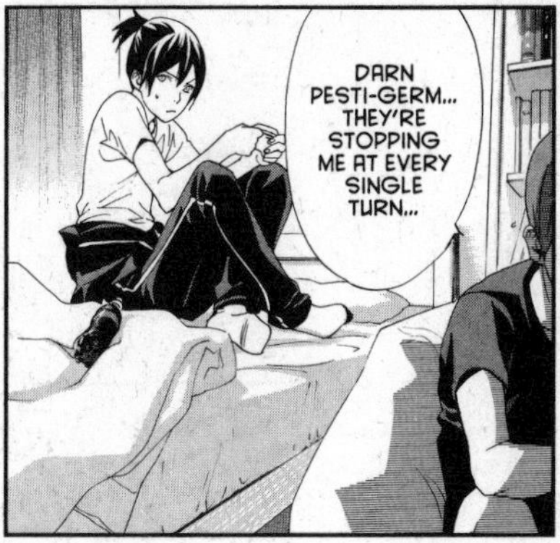
DARN PESTI-GERM... THEY'RE STOPPING ME AT EVERY SINGLE TURN...

Pesti-germ, page 18

The original name of these video game monsters is *pesuto-kin*, which is the Japanese name of the bacteria that causes the Bubonic plague. (Readers may remember that the Capypers were driven from their homeland by a plague.) *Pesuto* comes from the English word "pestilence," and *kin* means "germ." The translators felt that in a video game localization, the monsters are likely to be given a catchier name than *Yersinia pestis*, and so they chose the rather straightforward translation, "pesti-germ."

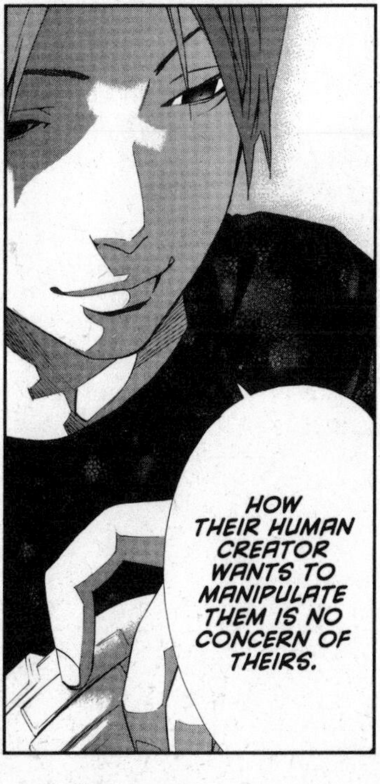
HOW THEIR HUMAN CREATOR WANTS TO MANIPULATE THEM IS NO CONCERN OF THEIRS.

Their human Creator, page 19

For a little bit of clarity: the way written Japanese works, it's possible to write the *kanji* for one word and have another word next to it, indicating that when a speaker says one of those words, he also means the other. So when Kôto says this line, he could mean, "How humans, the gods' Creators, want to manipulate..." or, "How I, the god's Creator, want to manipulate..." In other words, while he is indicating that gods can be controlled by humans in general, he's mainly talking about his own activities involving the gods. Fortunately, he clarifies that by going on to apply this philosophy to Yato, which is why the translators felt it would not be detrimental to take the first-person pronoun out of the English rendering.

From a distant sleep, page 36

Like the fire extinguishing incantation that Yukiné used in Volume 11, this a poem that has been used in Japan for centuries. In modern times, this poem is most frequently seen on the pictures of the Seven Gods of Fortune's treasure ship that people place under their pillows on New Year's Eve to invite good dreams. In Japanese, the poem is also a palindrome—it can be read the same way backwards and forwards. Here, the poem is used not for dreams, but to awaken certain entities from their sleep, but like any Japanese poem worth its salt, it is packed with wordplay and multiple meanings. The Japanese poem reads as follows:

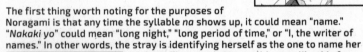

...From a distant sleep...

Nakaki yo no
Toono nefuri no
Mina mesame
Naminori fune no
Oto no yoki kana

The first thing worth noting for the purposes of Noragami is that any time the syllable *na* shows up, it could mean "name." "*Nakaki yo*" could mean "long night," "long period of time," or "I, the writer of names." In other words, the stray is identifying herself as the one to name her minions. The translators could go on like this for every line of the poem, but instead they will provide a potential alternate translation for the poem. (The translation spoken by the stray in this chapter is based on the meanings of the *kanji* characters provided by the stray, along with some generally applicable double meanings and a touch of Noragami jargon.) Keep in mind also that "sound" refers to a shinki's instrument name.

The rich vessel 'pon the waves, how pleasing its silent sound.

I, writer of names,
Call to those brandishing sound:
Hon'rable names, wake.
Soundless names have come to fruit.
How pleasing these instruments.

From sev'n distant peaks, page 40

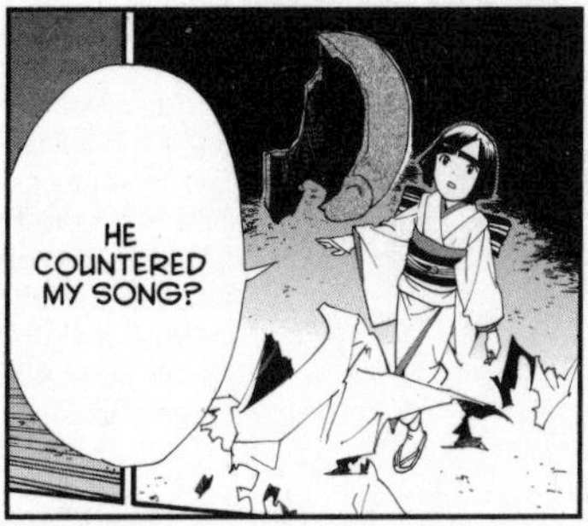
HE COUNTERED MY SONG?

Unlike the incantations we've seen so far in Noragami, this one appears to be Yukiné's own original work. In the middle ages in Japan, the nobility would correspond by writing poems to each other. For example, if a nobleman became interested in a noblewoman, he would write her a poem in an attempt to win her favor. She would judge him based on the merits of his poem (among other things), and write a new poem in response, playing off of the words and imagery in his poem. Here, Yukiné plays similarly off of the stray's poem, using similar words and reversing her orders. The obvious juxtaposition is that she wakes her minions, and he tells them to go to sleep. Furthermore, he counters her aquatic imagery with images of mountains, earth—solid ground. And of course, his poem, too, is rife with wordplay and multiple meanings. Here's what it looks like in Japanese, so you can compare the sound of it to the stray's:

Nanafusa no
Toono no one no
Yo no metori
Kiyoki nefuri na
Kami no mime kana

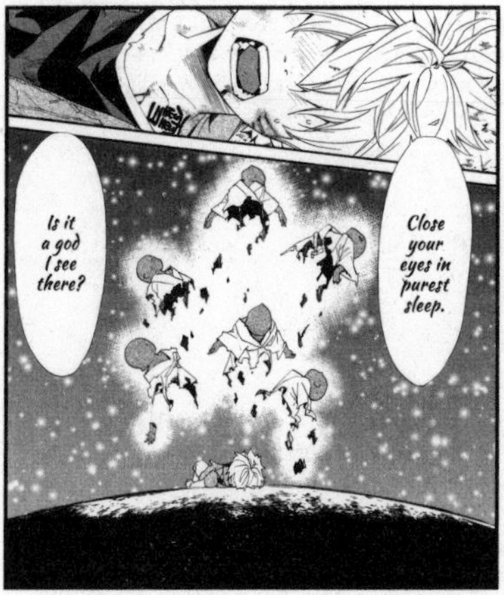
Close your eyes in purest sleep.
Is it a god I see there?

As you can see, he even starts off with the same syllable, and uses many similar words. One thing the translators failed to include in the English version was the *na* at the end of his fourth line, which is given the *kanji* character meaning "edible plants (vegetables)." It was most likely chosen to add to the "solid ground" imagery, but when combined with "*nefuri*," it becomes the modern command, "Go to sleep." Now here is the potential alternate Noragami translation:

Obstructing the names
Of sounds recently addressed.
Be you admonished.
O vessel, brandish your sound.
Will your deeds honor your god?

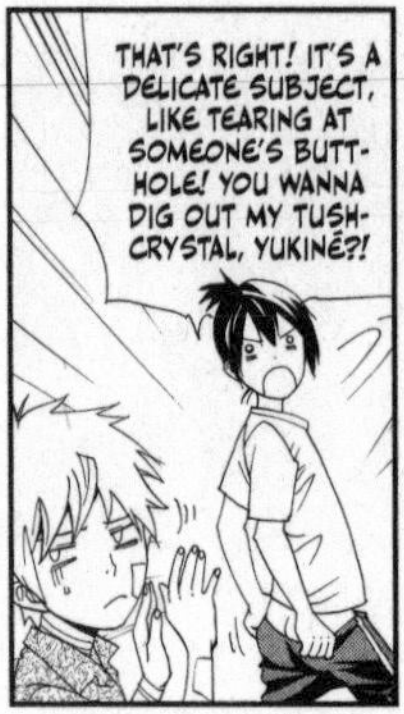
THAT'S RIGHT! IT'S A DELICATE SUBJECT, LIKE TEARING AT SOMEONE'S BUTT-HOLE! YOU WANNA DIG OUT MY TUSH-CRYSTAL, YUKINÉ?!

Yato's tush-crystal, page 63

According to Japanese folk beliefs, there is a jewel called a *shirikodama* that can be found in a person's anus. This jewel contains the person's soul, and if removed, the person will die.

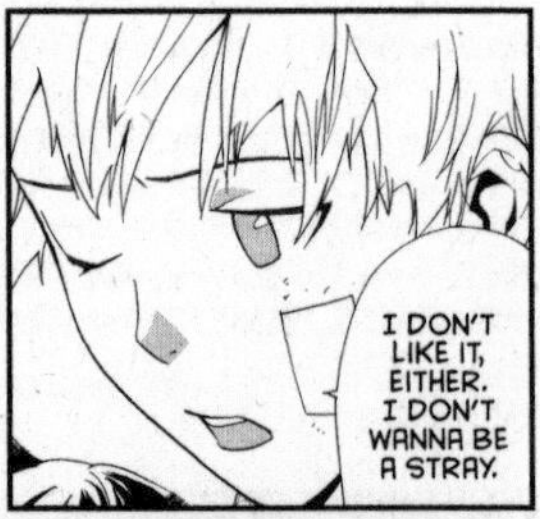
I DON'T LIKE IT, EITHER. I DON'T WANNA BE A STRAY.

Sweet and sour, page 65

Readers may be familiar with the *tsundere* trope, describing characters who are often sarcastic and mean, but will occasionally reveal hints that they actually do care about another character. For the uninitiated, tsundere is a combination of *tsun-tsun*, meaning "bad-tempered," and *dere-dere*, roughly meaning "love-struck." All this time, Yukiné has just been mean to Yato, but it would seem that Yato knew all along that deep down, he actually cares.

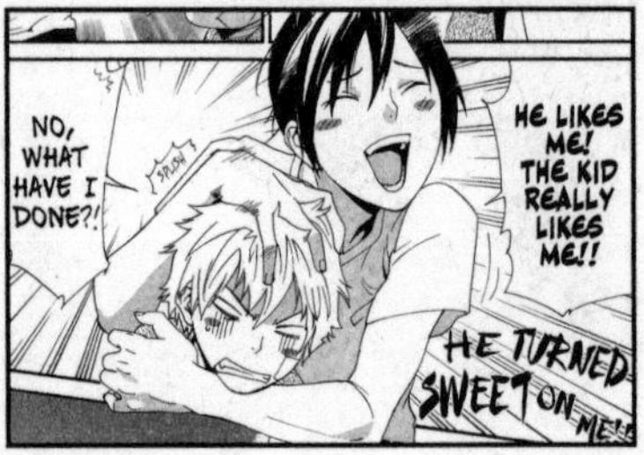
HE LIKES ME! THE KID REALLY LIKES ME!!
HE TURNED SWEET ON ME!!
NO, WHAT HAVE I DONE?!

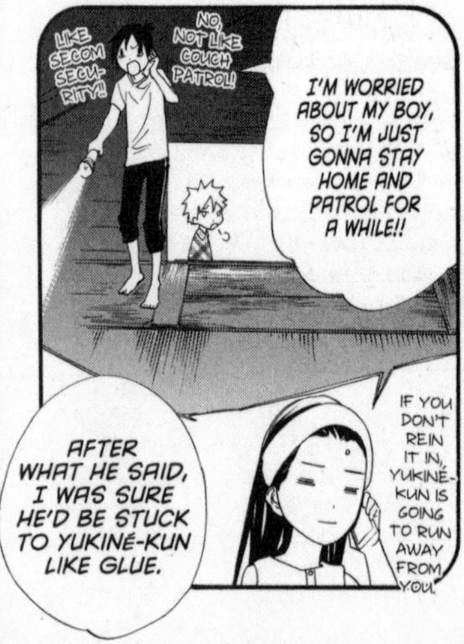
I'M WORRIED ABOUT MY BOY, SO I'M JUST GONNA STAY HOME AND PATROL FOR A WHILE!!
NO, NOT LIKE COUCH PATROL!
LIKE SECOM SECU-RITY!!
IF YOU DON'T REIN IT IN, YUKINÉ-KUN IS GOING TO RUN AWAY FROM YOU.
AFTER WHAT HE SAID, I WAS SURE HE'D BE STUCK TO YUKINÉ-KUN LIKE GLUE.

Couch patrol vs. Secom, page 79

When Yato tells Hiyori that he's patrolling his home, he uses the word *jitaku keibi*, which means "home security." It has also become an internet slang term referring to someone who "guards" his house all day by never leaving it (due to being unemployed and/or a shut-in). Knowing Yato as she does, it's no surprise that Hiyori's first thought is that he's making excuses, but he insists that he is doing real security, like the Japanese private security company, Secom.

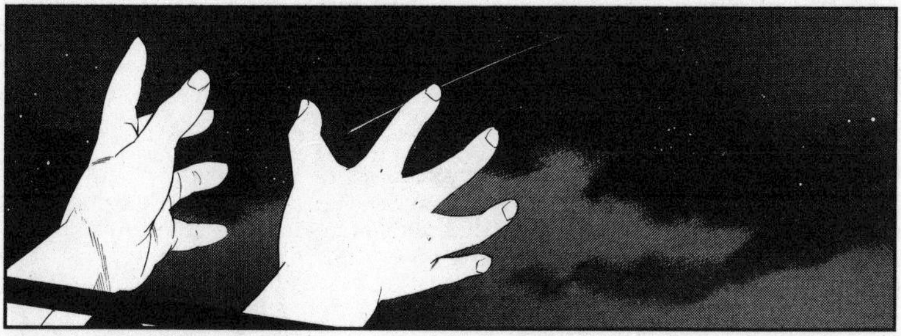

Kanoto to *Tori*, page 98

Yato's father is demonstrating his knowledge of astronomy as based on the Chinese system. *Kanoto* is the Japanese for *xin*, the eighth of the ten Heavenly Stems, and *Tori* is the tenth of the twelve Earthly Branches (the Rooster or Bird of the zodiac). These stems and branches were used in the Chinese (and subsequently Japanese) calendar to count years in a cycle of 60. The 58th year in the cycle, *Kanoto-Tori* year, was known to be one of revolutionary change, so when little Yaboku reached out to a star connecting *Kanoto* and *Tori*, his father takes that as a sign.

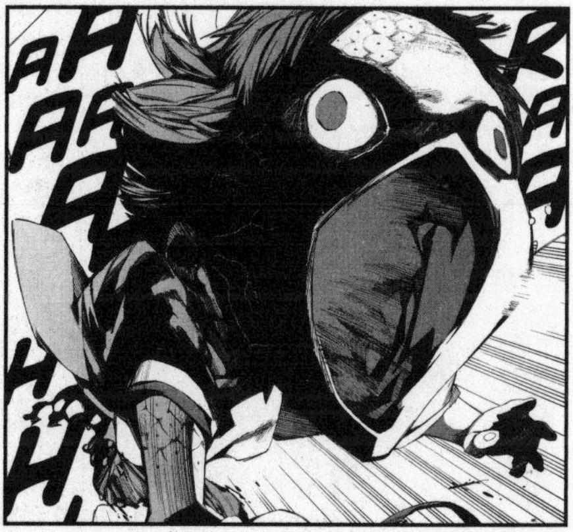

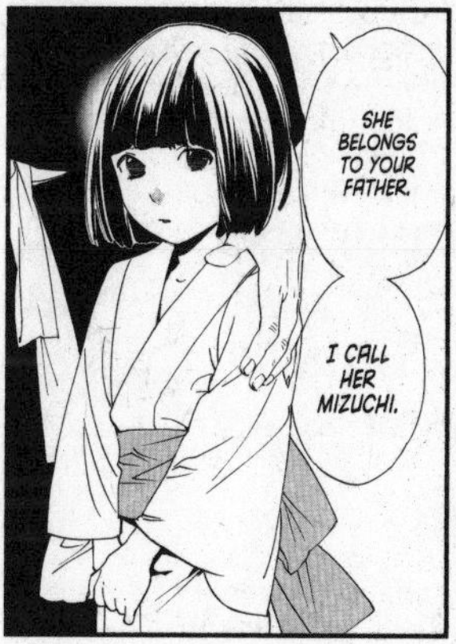
SHE BELONGS TO YOUR FATHER.
I CALL HER MIZUCHI.

I call her Mizuchi, page 100

Yato's father's name for the stray is also the name of a mythical creature from Japanese lore. Meaning "water spirit," a *mizuchi* takes the form of a serpent-like dragon. It lives in rivers and other bodies of water, and poisons humans with its breath.

Mulberries, page 110

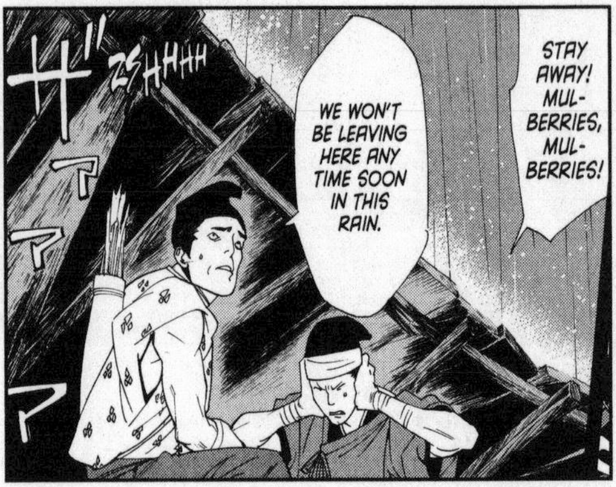
STAY AWAY! MUL-BERRIES, MUL-BERRIES!
WE WON'T BE LEAVING HERE ANY TIME SOON IN THIS RAIN.
ZSHHHH

In Japanese, the phrase "*kuwabara, kuwabara*," or "mulberry field, mulberry field," is used much like the English phrase "knock on wood" to ward off bad luck. Although it is used to ward off all kinds of bad luck, it originated as a way to avoid getting struck by lightning. There are a few different theories as to where the saying came from, including one about a mischievous lightning spirit who fell into a well and couldn't get out, then promised never to strike anyone who chanted "*kuwabara, kuwabara*" in exchange for being released. More apropos to Noragami is the legend involving Sugawara no Michizane. Longtime readers may remember that the people deified him to quell his wrath after his wrongful death. While he was still angrily tearing up the countryside, the natural disasters he caused included thunderstorms. Mysteriously, his lightning never struck the mulberry field—although it may not have been much of a mystery, because the mulberry field was in his former home. Since then, people came to chant "*kuwabara, kuwabara*" as a way of telling the lightning (or its source), "You don't want to strike here!"

In this case, the man chanting about mulberries may be trying to ward off not only lightning, but also demon children.

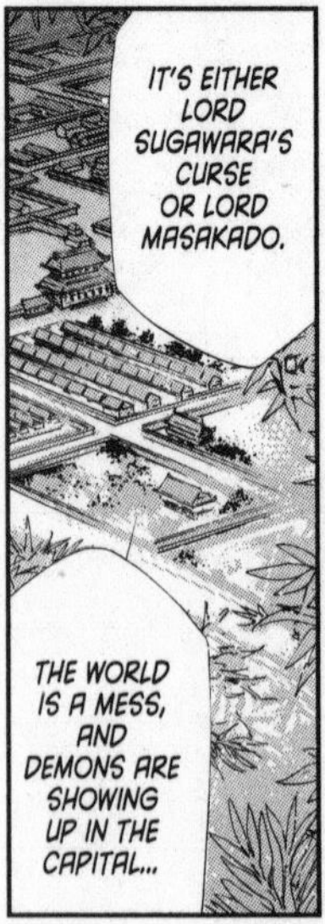
IT'S EITHER LORD SUGAWARA'S CURSE OR LORD MASAKADO.
THE WORLD IS A MESS, AND DEMONS ARE SHOWING UP IN THE CAPITAL...

Lord Masakado, page 111

As the reader may have guessed, Lord Masakado, or Taira no Masakado, was another prominent Japanese figure who died for political reasons and has since been deified. He led a very dramatic insurrection, which resulted in his death. He was beheaded, and as was customary back then, the head was put on display. According to legend, several months later, the strangely unrotted head came to life and began terrorizing the masses, demanding to know where its body was. Eventually it took off and flew to what later became Tokyo, where it was buried and a shrine built at its burial site. When the shrine is neglected, natural disasters and other misfortune are said to follow.

I've realized that kimonos are
fun to draw and fun to color.
Yato-san, I don't supposed
you'd do another image
change for me?
Yato: "No! My sweatsuit is cute!!"

Adachitoka

A Kodansha Comics Trade Paperback Original.

Published in the United States by Kodansha Comics, an imprint of Kodansha USA Publishing, LLC, New York.

Publication rights for this English edition arranged through Kodansha Ltd., Tokyo.

First published in Japan in 2014 by Kodansha Ltd., Tokyo.

ISBN 978-1-63236-253-7

Printed in the United States of America.

www.kodanshacomics.com

9 8 7 6 5 4 3 2 1

Translator: Alethea Nibley & Athena Nibley
Lettering: Lys Blakeslee
Editing: Lauren Scanlan